Children Remembered

Children Remembered

Responses to Untimely Death in the Past

ROBERT WOODS

LIVERPOOL UNIVERSITY PRESS

First published 2006 by
Liverpool University Press
4 Cambridge Street
Liverpool
L69 7ZU

British Library Cataloguing-in-Publication Data
A British Library CIP Record is available

ISBN 1-84631-021-0 cased
ISBN-13 978-1–84631-021-8 cased

Typeset in Garamond Premier by Koinonia, Bury
Printed and bound in the European Union by MPG Books Ltd, Bodmin

For our children

Contents

List of Tables   ix
List of Figures   x
List of Illustrations   xi

1   Introduction: 'the lines of life'   1

2   *Après la mort des enfants*   7
    Ariès, parental indifference and *l'histoire de la mort*   7
    Vovelle and *la longue durée*   24
    Representing mentalities   29

3   Mortality, Childcare and Mourning   33
    The risk of dying at an early age   35
    Childcare in France and England   55
    Mourning practices   57

4   Children in Pictures and Monuments   61
    Historians, pictures and the deceased   61
    The changing representation of children, and what it signifies   67
    Funeral memorials to departed children and their mothers   88
    Pictorial ambiguities?   93

5   Emotions and Literature   95
    Grief and other emotions   96
    Reception and contextual literary history   101
    Autobiographical writing   104
    Selection   118

6   Poems, Mainly of Child Loss   131

7   The Vocabulary of Grief   169
    Emotion lexicons   170
    How language changed   175
    Relationships   179
    Death without grief   200

8 Parallel Histories: Experience and Expression   209

Acknowledgements   217
Notes on the Sixty-Nine Poems   219
Notes   231
Select Bibliography   270
Index   281

List of Tables

2.1	The principal publications of Philippe Ariès	9
2.2	The birth history of Maria Branwell Brontë from 1812 to 1821	22
2.3	Michel Vovelle's three-levels model	25
3.1	Selected early-age mortality measures for France	40
3.2	Selected early-age mortality measures for England (and Wales)	46
3.3	Maternal mortality rates for England (and Wales)	50
4.1	Example pictures of children and families from the sixteenth to the nineteenth centuries arranged in chronological order	68
4.2	The birth history of Barbara Gamage, Lady Barbara Sidney, Countess of Leicester, from 1584	74
4.3	The birth history of Lady Margaret Legh	90
4.4	Styles of American gravestones	92
5.1	The birth history of Grace Wallington from 1621 to 1632	106
5.2	The birth history of Jane Josselin from 1640 to 1663	107
5.3	The birth history of Anne Shakespeare	116
5.4	Some characteristics of the sixty-nine poems	128
7.1	Emotion keywords	172
7.2	Grief and mourning keywords	173
7.3	Full content analysis of Anne Bradstreet's four poems to her grandchildren: Elizabeth (E), Anne (A) and Simon (S), and her daughter-in-law Mercy (M)	174
7.4	Ten word-groups	176
7.5	Authors and subjects of the selected poems	180
7.6	The birth history of John Milton from 1645 to 1658	191
7.7	The birth history of Mary Wordsworth from 1802 to 1810	197
7.8	The birth history of Percy Bysshe Shelley from 1812 to 1822	199
7.9	The birth history of Ann Donne from 1602 to 1617	203
8.1	Summary of early-age deaths among the ten birth histories	210

List of Figures

2.1   Une courbe du deuil (mourning curve) after Philippe Ariès   12
2.2   Vovelle's representation of secularisation using evidence from wills for
      eighteenth-century Provence, France   30
3.1   Framework to illustrate the likely proportion of all deaths occurring to
      children aged less than 10 years in populations with 0 and 1 per cent
      per year growth rates, organised by life expectancy at birth in years ($e(0)$)   34
3.2   Infant and childhood mortality trends for France, 1806–2001   36
3.3   Cumulative infant and childhood mortality trends for France, 1806–2001   37
3.4   Timepath for France, 1806–2001, showing the decline of early-age
      mortality (0–9) and the rise of life expectancy at birth ($e(0)$) plotted
      on the framework provided by figure 3.1   38
3.5   Infant and childhood mortality trends for France, 1680s to 1851   42
3.6   Infant mortality variations in France, 1806–10 ($q(0)$ per 1000)   44
3.7   Infant and childhood mortality trends for England (and Wales),
      1580s to 2001   48
3.8   Maternal mortality rate (MMR) and stillbirth rate (SBR) estimates for
      England (and Wales), 1551 to 2001   52
3.9   Variations in stillbirth (SBR) and infant mortality rates (IMR), historical
      northern European and other international comparisons   54
5.1   'Grief work' models   98
5.2   Linguistic and reception theory models   102
7.1   Word-group occurrence patterns   178
7.2   Occurrence of the words 'death' and 'grief' in Shakespeare's plays   206
8.1   A triangular model: demography, grief and mourning   214
8.2   Experience and expression compared: early-age mortality and word
      occurrence patterns   215

List of Illustrations

A   *A little girl*, 1520s, Jan Gossaert (also known as Mabuse) (*c*.1478–1532), National Gallery, London

B   *William Brooke, 10th Lord Cobham and his family*, 1567, Unknown British artist (Master of the Countess of Warwick), Longleat House, Warminster, Wiltshire (Marquis of Bath)

Ci   *Mary Rogers, Lady Harington*, 1592, Marcus Gheeraerts the Younger (*c*.1561–1636), Tate Britain, London

Cii   *Portrait of an unknown lady*, *c*.1595, Marcus Gheeraerts the Younger (*c*.1561–1636), Tate Britain, London

D   *Barbara Gamage and her six children*, 1596, Marcus Gheeraerts the Younger (*c*.1561–1636), Penshurst Place, Tonbridge, Kent (Viscount De L'Isle)

E   *The Cholmondeley ladies*, 1600–10, Unknown British artist, Tate Britain, London

F   *Sir Thomas Aston at the deathbed of his wife*, 1635, John Souch (1594–*c*.1645), Manchester City Art Galleries

G   *The Saltonstall family*, *c*.1637, David Des Granges (1611–*c*.1675), Tate Britain, London

H   *The Streatfield family*, *c*.1640, William Dobson (1611–46), Yale Center for British Art, New Haven

I   *Elizabeth Clarke Freake and baby Mary*, 1671–1674, Unknown American artist, Gift of Mr and Mrs Albert W. Rice, Worcester Art Museum, Massachusetts

J   *The James family*, 1751, Arthur Devis (1712–87), Tate Britain, London

K   *The painter's daughters chasing a butterfly*, *c*.1756, Thomas Gainsborough (1727–88), National Gallery, London

L   *A visit to the child at nurse*, *c*.1788, George Morland (1763–1804), Fitzwilliam Museum, Cambridge

M   *Penelope Boothby*, 1788, Sir Joshua Reynolds (1723–92), Ashmolean Museum, Oxford (Private collection)

N   *Monument to Penelope Boothby*, 1793, Thomas Banks (1735–1805),
Ashbourne church, Derbyshire

O   *Five children of the Budd family*, c.1818, Unknown American artist,
Gift of Edgar William and Bernice Chrysler Garbisch, National
Gallery of Art, Washington DC

P   *Roulin's baby*, 1888, Vincent van Gogh (1853–90), Chester Dale
Collection, National Gallery of Art, Washington DC

Q   *Child with a dove*, 1901, Pablo Picasso (1881–1973), National Gallery,
London

Ri   *Lady Margaret Legh*, 1600, Marcus Gheeraerts the Younger (c.1561–1636),
Private collection   91

Rii   *Monument to Lady Margaret Legh*, after 1605, Perhaps associated with
Maximilian Colt, Fulham church, London   91

I

Introduction: 'the lines of life'

How did adults, and especially parents, respond to the early deaths of children? Was the bond of emotional attachment between parents and offspring as close in the past as it is said to be today? How was that attachment expressed? What influence did the demographic environment in which people lived, especially the risk of dying, have on attitudes and behaviour when survival chances were largely beyond human control? How, for how long and with what intensity were dead children mourned? Were children's short lives commemorated, and was their loss grieved over? These are important and intriguing questions, which have attracted considerable scholarly attention over the years. They still challenge because they have not been answered in ways that can be accepted as entirely satisfactory. There are three reasons for this: our expectations are poorly articulated, and theory lets us down; the empirical evidence that might be used to help clarify matters is fragmentary and open to a variety of interpretations; and the questions are broad, and demand multi-disciplinary approaches in an age that admires specialisation and focused enquiry. Answering these questions might have wider implications for social policy, and certainly for political ideology. For example, there has been a long-running debate, principally among psychologists, about whether human emotions are physiologically determined or socially constructed. Similarly, family historians have characterised parents as either 'loving' or 'indifferent' in the past. Thus, parents are by nature always loving and caring as part of an evolutionary strategy or parents are selectively indifferent according to the social, political and cultural circumstances that condition their behaviour.[1] Of course, neither is likely to be the full story.

This short introductory chapter merely sets the scene. It raises the questions, makes the case for their importance, suggests how they might be resolved, and sketches the approach that will be adopted in the chapters that follow. It also introduces the principal characters and some of their conflicting opinions on appropriate lines to take. The story is part of demographic history. It tells of the way in which children were regarded by adults and, in particular, the ways in which parents responded to their untimely deaths. In so doing it engages with Philippe Ariès's controversial 'parental indifference hypothesis' as well as the wider approach to death and dying in the past developed mainly by French historians, including Michel Vovelle, Pierre Chaunu and Daniel Roche. Vovelle's 'three-levels model', which combines demographic rates, mourning practices and discourses on death in literature, is adopted as a framework for further discussion. In terms of empirical evidence, three conspicuously long-term series are created. The first, corresponding to level 1 in Vovelle's model, uses early-age mortality rates for France and England to establish general trends in survival chances during several centuries. It also covers the risks to mothers in childbirth. This is traditional, quantitative, historical demography directed towards the description of average experience of risk. The second series uses portraits of children from the sixteenth to the nineteenth centuries as a device to reflect upon, and thereby recover, the feelings of parents for their offspring. Here the series is discontinuous and the task of interpreting the pictures is highly problematical. The third series relates to Vovelle's level 3 and again it is discontinuous, being made up of 69 poems, mostly elegies, written in English between the 1570s and the 1990s. These poems are used as 'sample texts' to explore the ways in which responses to child deaths were expressed, the vocabulary of grief that was used, and how language changed. Whether and how the expression of feelings through images and texts can be said to reflect demographic experience provides the study's principal challenge. Not surprisingly, the conclusions, and thus the answers to the initial questions, are far from straightforward. They depend upon the resolution of several methodological problems, including procedures for combining the three parallel series so that they provide one consistent account.

Few demographic historians have passed this way. They have preferred to focus on the causes of demographic change rather than its possible consequences and to deal exclusively with quantitative data. However, Peter Laslett's characteristically challenging essay entitled 'The wrong way through the telescope: a note on literary evidence in sociology and in historical sociology' (1976) is an important exception.[2] Laslett begins by defining 'literary evidence' in its broadest sense to include letters, diaries and autobiographies, as well as poetry and novels; but he then separates off 'high literature', the 'universally famous literary texts', in order to establish whether such texts can be used as sources of accurate historical information. In order to use this form of evidence Laslett argues that the historian must have a set of interconnected theories, theories that (1) cover the author's 'purpose in creating the particular work, and ... its relationship with the interests, attitudes, expectations and outlook of the society, class, group or sect' to which the author and the author's expected readership belong; (2) deal with the relationship between the conscious and deliberate, and the unconscious in the work of an artist; (3) consider how the work has been influenced by the 'social setting and personality of the writer'; (4) provide 'a theory of the relationships between "truths" of disparate kinds, poetic truths and historical truths especially'.[3] Laslett does not elaborate on these theories himself, but he does provide some interesting illustrations, particularly on the ways in which literary evidence can be used to illuminate the author's 'material environment'. Samuel Richardson's novel *Pamela* (1740–41) describes the rags to riches rise of Pamela the servant girl, and Robert Burns's poem 'The cottar's Saturday night' (1786) tells how a farm servant called Jenny gave money to support her parents. How typical were Pamela and

Jenny? It is Laslett's contention that we may only answer this and other like questions by using other forms of evidence, by what he calls 'corroborative comparison'. And in order to illustrate this point he develops a further example. Laslett asks whether English Restoration comedy (1660s to 1720s), which was notoriously licentious, reflected the sexual behaviour of society during the late seventeenth century. His answer is that we cannot tell. We should not draw conclusions until there is corroboration. In this case Laslett uses the bastardy ratio derived from the percentage of all baptisms marked illegitimate in the registers of 98 English parishes. The curve describing the ratio 'reveals real movement of illegitimacy over time, and implies a general phenomenon throughout the country and over the whole society'.[4] The bastardy ratio shows that illegitimacy was substantially lower in the late seventeenth than either the late sixteenth or late eighteenth centuries. This is a salutary example in several senses. First, Laslett's faith in the ability of quantitative data to provide the basis for a 'systematic investigation of behaviour' has proved to be misplaced. As we will see in Chapter 3, such curves, series and ratios do provide a valuable insight on certain aspects of behaviour, the lines of life and death, but their simplicity and apparent precision can give them a spuriously objective quality. They do not offer 'true facts'. Secondly, what we might ask of literary (or pictorial) evidence should go beyond the facts of behaviour. Literature is for the emotions, for feelings, often drawn from the imagination, yet with a grounding in personal experience, as well as the society and culture of the day. Evidence from plays and ratios can be joined, as long as one doesn't ask too much.

At about the same time, but on the other side of Cambridge, J. H. Plumb was inventing 'The new world of children in eighteenth-century England' (1975).[5] Plumb argued that adults had an 'autocratic, indeed ferocious' attitude towards children in the seventeenth century; they were 'constrained' and 'subservient'. At the end of the seventeenth century and certainly during the eighteenth, a 'perceptible new attitude' was obvious.

> Not all fathers and mothers were converted so easily from tyranny to benevolence, but, by the 1740s, a new attitude to children was spreading steadily among the middle and upper classes. This gentle and more sensitive approach to children was but a part of a wider change in social attitudes; a part of that belief that nature was inherently good, not evil, and what evil there was derived from man and his institutions; an attitude which was also reflected among a growing élite in a greater sensitivity towards women, slaves and animals.[6]

It is not entirely clear why adult attitudes changed so comprehensively, but the influence of John Locke (1632–1704), the philosopher and educational reformer, is emphasised. Plumb makes further speculations concerning expense: 'Children, in a sense, had become luxury objects upon which their mothers and fathers were willing to spend larger and larger sums of money, not only for their education, but also for their entertainment and amusement'.[7] And about how children were displayed: 'portraits of individual children are far more common in the eighteenth century than in the seventeenth, again arguing both for a change in fashionable attitudes, and also, may be, for a greater emotional investment in children by parents'.[8] Plumb was a self-declared 'conventional historian' who possessed the happy knack of combining interesting assertion with detailed, often anecdotal, examples. He also displayed great faith in eighteenth-century England as an age and place of improvement; children, women, slaves and animals all benefited, apparently.

Laslett and Plumb, their approaches to evidence and the history of children, still raise important points for debate. The one was interested in the long term and how change could be represented, with the application of social science theories and research methods to the study of that historical change, with breaking old moulds and seeing a lost world for what it was. The other was an historian of a period and a class, a biographer, who stayed close to the detail of event and experience, the empirical: how many children's books were printed, who made the rocking horses? Not surprisingly, this study falls closer to Laslett. Its concern is with long-term change, with varieties of evidence, with social science history, but it runs the risk of missing the single illuminating episode; of helping the reader think they know a particular individual better, a Jenny or a Pamela, and that they understand her motives and actions, the way she felt.

Before we turn to an outline of the chapters that follow, their content and the approaches they take, it may be useful to provide some markers on the current orthodoxies. Where, for example, does the history of the family now stand? In this we are greatly assisted by Steven Ozment's recent survey, *Ancestors: The Loving Family in Old Europe* (2001).[9] Ozment sets out the old model of the premodern family, constructed by scholars in the 1960s and 1970s, and the pre-conditions for change to the new domestic arrangement during the eighteenth and nineteenth centuries, with the 'new family' being confirmed in the twentieth. In the premodern form the psychological costs of a set of living arrangements 'vulnerable to the tyranny of man and nature' were so great that members of this 'impersonal' household were unable to 'establish bonds of deep affection or relationships of true equality'. For the European family to progress from premodern to modern, four 'defining conditions and features' needed to be met: separation of home and workplace; removal of servants and workers from the household giving a special prominence to the parent–child unit known as the nuclear family; withdrawal of the family from public into private life; and the sharing of power and decision-making between spouses.[10] However, Ozment is rather cautious about what the new model of family relationships should be, claiming that as far as the modern form is concerned, it is too difficult to generalise. What he does do is focus on continuities rather than transformations, and stresses the fluid nature of domestic living arrangements, since 'A family is not a standard product of some universal social mix, but an organisation of discrete individuals interacting with one another'.[11] The emphasis on continuity nonetheless encourages Ozment to the following generalisations.

If there were a turning point in parent–child relations, when the treatment of children appears to have improved, many today would see it occurring in the four centuries between 1100 and 1500.

Three developments are associated with the betterment of children: the growing affluence of cities; the increasing success of the Church's moral teaching; and the revival of classical educational models stressing patience and persuasion in child rearing.

In late medieval and Renaissance Europe, stillborn children were named, lamented, buried, and counted by their parents in family genealogies along with their surviving siblings.[12]

These are contentious observations that require far closer scrutiny and much more evidence than appears to be currently available to make them entirely acceptable. It is still not clear whether it is helpful to persist with the 'modernisation paradigm', to characterise a 'premodern family' and think of it being 'modernised' at some point in time, 1100–1500 or the seventeenth century or the 1740s or 1800, for example, just as it may not be appropriate to talk about Europe, 'old' or 'new', as though it was some undifferentiated whole as far as attitudes and behaviour were concerned. We know only too well that early modern Europe was made up of many different demographic regimes. Ozment has criticised an old model, questioned the propriety of generalisations and definitions, and set up some new 'straw children'.

In the chapters that follow we shall concentrate not on the history of the family as such, although this will always be in the background, but specifically on how demographic experience influenced parent–child relations. Chapter 2 takes us back to the work of Philippe Ariès and his 'parental indifference hypothesis', but it also considers the wider historiography of death and dying created by a group of mainly French historians associated with the *Annales* school. It discusses the way in which Ariès went about his work, what influenced his thinking, and why others have adopted his ideas about childhood and death. The chapter concludes with a review of Michel Vovelle's 'three-levels model' and the way he tackled the problem of measuring changes in attitudes and beliefs. Chapter 3 focuses on Vovelle's level 1. It offers a reconstruction of the pattern and long-term trends in early-age mortality in France and England. It also provides brief outlines of childcare and mourning practices in the two societies. The following chapters are concerned with the consequences of those mortality experiences. Chapter 4 emphasises the visual, how children were depicted in portraits and whether such evidence can be used to reflect on aspects of parent–child relations over the centuries. The next chapter turns our attention to literary evidence. It asks about the value of such materials for the recovery of emotions, especially grief, in the past; it justifies the use and selection of 69 poems in English composed between the 1570s and the 1990s. These poems are reproduced in Chapter 6. Chapter 7 turns to their analysis in terms of the vocabulary of grief. Which words were chosen, and how does the changing pattern of their occurrence help us to trace the way in which emotion was felt and grief expressed? This penultimate chapter also considers the influence of relationships, how responses to the untimely deaths specifically of children differed between parents and non-parents, for instance. Reactions to adult deaths, some of which may also be regarded as premature, will only be considered in passing. Chapter 7 also addresses a problem first considered by Sigmund Freud: what follows if the bereaved do not grieve? Chapter 8 summarises and concludes. It draws together the series – numbers, pictures, words – and considers the implications for those initial questions. Why was Ariès wrong in such an interesting way? Can Vovelle's model help us to recover the history of emotions over the long term? How may evidence drawn from very different sources and demanding contrasting styles of interpretation be combined into a more convincing story? These are just some of the new questions it will ask.

2

Après la mort des enfants

Philippe Ariès (1914–84) has provided many highly original perspectives on the history of the family and on attitudes to death in the West. While he is remembered most for the latter, his contribution to the new history of childhood has proved remarkably influential in both France and the English-speaking world. For historical demographers there is a special interest in his 'parental indifference hypothesis' and the behavioural conditioning that low infant survival chances may have engendered in the past. The development and continuing popularity of such a hypothesis provides us with a useful device for the exploration of childcare and parent–child relations in general. Ariès will be our 'straw man'. But he worked in an intellectual climate that gave particular attention to different concepts of time, especially *la longue durée*, as well as to the distinctions between ideologies and *mentalités*. While his approach was always to view change in the long term, often over several centuries, and to explore what had previously been little-used sources (family portraits, funeral monuments, cemeteries), several other French historians proved themselves to be more adept in their discussions of wider philosophical and methodological issues. Michel Vovelle (1933–), in particular, has not only taken the discussion of *mentalités* further, but he has also offered one of the most influential quantitative analyses of the ways in which attitudes varied and changed during the long term. Vovelle's version of the 'three-levels model' will be introduced here as a way of broadening Ariès's parental indifference hypothesis and of providing some order for subsequent chapters. In at least one important respect Ariès and Vovelle are unlikely companions, coming as they do from different ends of the political spectrum, yet their insights on the histories of dying, death and mortality still demand attention. Their boldness challenges; their inventiveness stimulates, and their neglect surprises.[13]

Ariès, parental indifference and *l'histoire de la mort*

L'enfant et la vie familiale sous l'Ancien Régime (1960), translated as *Centuries of Childhood* (1962, 1973), contains Ariès's most sustained contributions to the history of the family and of childhood. Although much of the book is devoted to a discussion of developments in education during the medieval and early modern periods (Part 2: 'Scholastic life'), Parts 1 and 3 deal, respectively, with 'The idea of childhood' ('Le sentiment de l'enfance') and 'The family'. Chapter 2, 'The discovery of childhood' ('La découverte de l'enfance') summarises the argument. The following passages are taken from this part of *Centuries of Childhood*.[14]

> No one thought of keeping a picture of a child if that child had either lived to grow to manhood or had died in infancy. In the first case, childhood was simply an unimportant phase of which there was no need to keep any record; in the second case, that of the dead child, it was thought that the little thing which had disappeared so soon in life was not worthy of remembrance: there were far too many children whose survival was problematical. (p. 36)

> The general feeling was, and for a long time remained, that one had several children in order to keep just a few. (p. 36)

> People could not allow themselves to become too attached to something that was regarded as a probable loss. This is the reason for certain remarks which shock our present-day sensibility, such as Montaigne's observation: 'I have lost two or three children in their infancy, not without regret, but without great sorrow', or Molière's comment on Louison in *Le Malade imaginaire*: 'The little girl doesn't count.' (p. 37)

> This indifference was a direct and inevitable consequence of the demography of the period. It lasted until the nineteenth century in the depths of the country, in so far as it was compatible with Christianity, which respected the immortal soul in every child that had been baptized. (p. 37)

> This feeling of indifference towards a too fragile childhood is not really very far removed from the callousness of the Roman or Chinese societies which practised the exposure of newborn children. We can now understand the gulf that separates our concept of childhood from that which existed before the demographic revolution or its preceding stages. There is nothing about this callousness that should surprise us: it was only natural in the community conditions of the time. (p. 37)

> It was only in the eighteenth century, with the beginning of Malthusianism and the extension of contraceptive practices, that the idea of necessary wastage would disappear. (p. 38)

> Thus, although demographic conditions did not greatly change between the thirteenth and seventeenth centuries, and although child mortality remained at a very high level, a new sensibility granted these fragile, threatened creatures a characteristic which the world had hitherto failed to recognise in them: as if it were only then that the common conscience had discovered that the child's soul too was immortal. There can be no doubt that the importance accorded to the child's personality was linked with the growing influence of Christianity on life and manners.
> This interest shown in the child preceded by more than a century the change in demographic conditions that can be roughly dated from Jenner's great discovery [of cowpox as a vaccination against smallpox in the late eighteenth century]. (p. 41)

> It was in the seventeenth century that portraits of children on their own became numerous and commonplace. It was in the seventeenth century, too, that the family portrait, a much older genre, tended to plan itself round the child. (p. 45)

Table 2.1 **The principal publications of Philippe Ariès**

Les traditions sociales dans les pays de France (Paris: Les Éditions de la Nouvelle France, 1943)

Histoire des populations françaises et de leurs attitudes devant la vie depuis le XVIIIe siècle (Paris: Éditions Self, 1948; Éditions du Seuil, 1971)

Le temps d'histoire (Monaco: Éditions du Rocher, 1954; Paris: Éditions du Seuil, 1986)

L'enfant et la vie familiale sous l'Ancien Régime (Paris: Libraire Plon, 1960; Éditions du Seuil, 1973 [published in an abridged form, without illustrations, but with a new preface by Ariès]), translated by Robert Baldick as *Centuries of Childhood* [abridged edition without illustrations and footnotes] (New York: Vintage Books, 1962; London: Jonathan Cape, 1962; Penguin, 1973, 1979; Pimlico, 1996)

'La mort inversée. Le changement des attitudes devant la mort dans les sociétés occidentales', *Archives Européennes Sociologie* 8 (1967), pp. 169–95, translated and reprinted as 'The reversal of death: changes in attitudes toward death in Western societies', *American Quarterly* 26 (1974), pp. 536–60, and in David E. Stannard (ed.), *Death in America* (Philadelphia, PA: University of Pennsylvania Press, 1975), pp. 134–58

Essais sur l'histoire de la mort en Occident du Moyen Age à nos jours [includes twelve reprinted articles originally published 1966–75] (Paris: Éditions du Seuil, 1975), translated by Patricia Ranum as *Western Attitudes Toward Death: From the Middle Ages to the Present* [original four lectures delivered at Johns Hopkins University in 1973] (Baltimore, MD: Johns Hopkins University Press, 1974)

L'homme devant la mort (Paris: Éditions du Seuil, 1977, 1985 [two volumes]), translated by Helen Weaver as *The Hour of Our Death* (New York: Alfred A. Knopf, 1981; Oxford: Oxford University Press, 1981; London: Penguin, 1983)

Un historien du dimanche (Paris: Éditions du Seuil, 1980) [Autobiographical sketches]

Images de l'homme devant la mort (Paris: Éditions du Seuil, 1983), translated by Janet Lloyd as *Images of Man and Death* (Cambridge, MA: Harvard University Press, 1985)

Essais de mémoire, 1943–83 (Paris: Éditions du Seuil, 1993) [Reprinted papers]

Le présent quotidien, 1955–66 (Paris: Éditions du Seuil, 1997) [Articles from the weekly journal *La nation française*]

Under the direction of Philippe Ariès and Georges Duby, *Histoire de la vie privée* [five volumes] (Paris: Éditions du Seuil, 1985–87), especially *Histoire de la vie privée, tome III: De la Renaissance aux Lumières* (Paris: Éditions du Seuil, 1986), translated by Arthur Goldhammer as *A History of Private Life, Volume III: Passions of the Renaissance* (Cambridge, MA: Harvard University Press, 1989)

Ariès's parental indifference hypothesis may be restated, therefore, in a succinct form without doing an injustice to the original. Before the seventeenth century (and in certain residual populations thereafter) parents were largely indifferent (naturally callous) to the fate of their young children (infants) because emotional investment could not be justified when the chances of their early loss were so high. Although this aspect of parental behaviour was, in general, conditioned by high childhood mortality rates, a new sentimental attachment did develop even before the demographic revolution of the eighteenth century. This revolution involved the adoption of both contraceptive practices and the rejection of the belief that infantile wastage was inevitable.[15] Evidence confirming these relationships can be found in both verbal (essays of Montaigne, plays of Molière, letters etc.) and plastic (paintings, monuments etc.) forms.

There is no doubt that *L'enfant* has proved highly influential not only in France but also, after translation, among a wide international audience. We shall return to its impact and place in the history of ideas in due course, but first let us consider Ariès's other contributions to *l'histoire de la mort*.

Table 2.1 gives a list of Ariès's principal publications between the 1940s and the 1980s. Apart from *L'enfant* he is best known for *Essais sur l'histoire de la mort en Occident* (*Western Attitudes toward Death*, 1974), *L'homme devant la mort* (*The Hour of Our Death*, 1981) and *Images de l'homme devant la mort* (*Images of Man and Death*, 1985). However, many of the ideas developed in the last three books were first outlined in the paper originally published in 1967 which subsequently appeared in the mid-1970s as 'The reversal of death: changes in attitudes toward death in Western societies'. Here, and in the essays and books that followed, Ariès traced the history of changing attitudes to death and dying as they were manifest before and after the event.

As we have already seen, it is not easy to express in clear and simple terms the core of Ariès's argument since it is concerned with change over several centuries, with feelings, sentiments and certain forms of mass behaviour which became part of popular culture for a period and were then abandoned to be replaced by other forms. Some of the changes were so slow they were imperceptible, while others came in quickly, were adopted, had their day and were discarded as though they were mere fashions. One device employed by Ariès in 'The reversal of death' involves sketching *une courbe du deuil* (a mourning curve).

> If one were to draw a 'mourning curve', there would first be a peak stage of frank, violent spontaneity until somewhere around the thirteenth century, then a long phase of ritualization until the eighteenth century, and then in the nineteenth century a period of impassioned, self-indulgent grief, dramatic demonstration of funereal mythology.
>
> In the mid twentieth century the ancient necessity for mourning—more or less spontaneous, or enforced, depending on the century—has been succeeded by its prohibition.[16]

This mourning curve is clearly a schematic device; it is higher or lower in certain periods since mourning lacks precise magnitude. 'The reversal of death' is particularly concerned with the contrast between the nineteenth and the second half of the twentieth century. Death is now denied and grief must be hidden for 'death, that familiar friend, has disappeared from the language, its name has become taboo', whereas 'although it is true that during the Middle Ages, and later among the common people, death occupied no more of a prominent place than it does now, it was absent not because of a taboo, but because the extreme familiarity with death deadened its power'.[17] The nineteenth was the century in which the dead were glorified. It was the age of dramatic obsequies, of the cult of remembrance and of pilgrimages to graves collected together in new urban cemeteries, the great 'cities of the dead'. Beyond the outward display of grief in public mourning, Ariès also used the notion of a curve as a way of reflecting a number of other, perhaps more ambiguous, distinctions and contrasts. For example, mourning could be spontaneous or ritualised, left to professionals; the family of the dead could be expected to exclude themselves from social intercourse for a period; dying might be in public, among close relatives at least, or alone; with knowledge that death was coming and due preparations made (the 'good death') or with the dying kept in ignorance; women and children may be excluded as witnesses or as formal mourners. Through statements like these on its course and characteristics at significant points, the rough outlines of Ariès's mourning curve can be reconstructed.

Figure 2.1 provides an illustration. In the early medieval period (A) mourning was violent and spontaneous, but by the fourteenth century (B1) death had become an overwhelming preoccupation in literature and representational art. By the seventeenth century (B2) the family had taken over responsibility for the dying and the dead, yet mourning had also become ritualised with professional mourners (including children) in use, female relatives excluded, and families secluded. The Romantic era (C1) brought a new sensibility to death, as to nature, and a new impassioned, self-indulgent grief. By the end of the nineteenth century (C2) the dead were formally glorified and worshipped. Death was a popular obsession again. But in the late twentieth century (D) death, the dying and the dead were banished. Dying was lonely and denied, the dead were physically removed, grief took on a private introversion, and public mourning faded to one modest, brief scene.

In *Western Attitudes toward Death* Ariès gave further elaboration to these ideas, but he left the periodisation of the mourning curve largely intact. In period A the living and the dead were not separated; death was a ritual organised by the dying person himself; it was Christian, customary and public. By B1 death had become more personalised as 'one's own death'; it was 'the occasion when man was most able to reach an awareness of himself' since it was as an individual that he would be judged in the afterlife. This was reflected in, for instance, the personalisation of tomb inscriptions. After B2 death became dramatised, but now it was 'the death of the other person, whose loss and memory inspired in the nineteenth and twentieth

Figure 2.1 Une courbe du deuil (mourning curve) after Philippe Ariès

A frank, violent, spontaneous

B loss of sponteneity, professional mourners (including children), women excluded, family seclusion for shelter and perpetuation of rememberance

C dramatic obsequies, pilgrimages to graves, cult of rememberance (Romantic era), moral rather than physical seclusion of family, inclusion of women, glorification of dead and worship of their tombs, cult of dead and veneration of cemeteries

D prohibition of mourning, grief hidden from public, secret grief, unemotional self-control, fear of 'cracking', exclusion of grandchildren, loneliness of hospital death, cremation as means of escaping cult of the dead

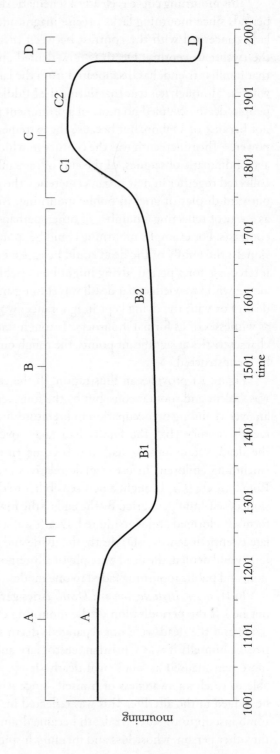

centuries the new cult of tombs and cemeteries and the romantic, rhetorical treat-ment of death'. The family grew stronger as the focus for feelings and affection at the same time that people became complaisant to the idea of death. At D we find, again, that death had become 'shameful and forbidden'. *The Hour of Our Death* adds relatively little by way of new ideas, although it does, as we shall see, make explicit certain methodological issues as well as providing more detailed discussions of both verbal and plastic sources.

It will probably be obvious by now that with very few exceptions Ariès's lengthy discussion of mourning and changing attitudes to death, spread over several papers and three major books, deals almost exclusively with the fate of adults. Certainly infants and children are mentioned as to their presence or absence (at the death or as mourners), but they are not the subjects. Nor is there discussion of parental loss as such. Only in *Images of Man and Death*, the album of iconography, do children appear, and then briefly.

> The deaths of children were the first deaths that could not be tolerated. Prior to the fifteenth century, children's tombs either did not exist or were very rare. In the seventeenth century, they were still rare and crude. But in the nineteenth century, the cemeteries were taken over by children. Parents evidently desired to represent their dead children in all kinds of attitudes in order to express their intense grief and their passionate desire to make their children survive in memory and in art, to exalt their children's innocence, charm and beauty.[18]

In order to construct a mourning curve specifically for children, and following figure 2.1, one would certainly need to emphasise the nineteenth century (C2) and the origins of mourning rituals for children in the seventeenth and eighteenth centu-ries (after B2). But before then, as *L'enfant* made clear, children were little mourned. Although Ariès did not discuss reactions to child death in the West during the late twentieth century, it would be consistent with his general approach to argue that the mourning curve for children at D should be higher and thus closer to the C2 position than it is shown for adults in figure 2.1. Since mortality in childhood is so low, grief for and mourning over their loss should be intense and persistent. This would mean that the mourning curve for children should differ most from that for adults during periods D and A, since the sentimental attachment of parents to their children was poorly developed and childhood largely undiscovered during the medieval period and, in general, prior to the seventeenth century.

Before we turn to a preliminary assessment of the parental indifference hypoth-esis it may prove useful to make a few brief observations on Ariès's method, the origins of at least some of his ideas and their early influence, especially via the work of family historians such as Lawrence Stone.

In his preface to *The Hour of Our Death* Ariès gives both an outline of his reasons for engaging in such a study and a short justification of his method.

> My original plan was modest. I had just finished a long study on the sense of family [*L'enfant*], in the course of which I had discovered that this sense which was said

to be very old and to be threatened by modern life, was, in fact, recent and was associated with a specific phase of modern life. I wondered whether this represented a general tendency, in the nineteenth and early twentieth centuries, to attribute remote origins to collective and mental phenomena that were really quite new. This would be tantamount to recognising, in an age of scientific progress, the capacity to create myths. (p. xiv)

Although there might be a few vestiges of them in our folklore, the funerary cults of antiquity had certainly disappeared. Christianity had disposed of the dead by abandoning them to the Church, where they were forgotten. It was not until the late eighteenth century that a new sensibility rejected the traditional indifference and that a piety was invented which became so popular and so widespread in the romantic era that it was believed to have existed from the beginning of time. (p. xv)

At the centre of Ariès's approach there is, therefore, an interest in time combined with the pace and perception of change, especially changing attitudes and feelings. Slow, imperceptible change over several generations and centuries or change between long periods of immobility are said to characterise man's attitude towards death, for example.[19] As for Ariès's own account of his method, he describes it as intuitive and subjective. It is the search for the 'collective unconscious'. 'The observer scans a chaotic mass of documents and tries to decipher, beyond the intentions of the writers or artists, the unconscious expression of the sensibility of the age.'[20] Of course these are élite materials, created by and for members of the powerful minority. How may their use be justified? 'In reality a theological idea, an artistic or literary theme, in short, anything that seems to be the product of an individual inspiration, can find form and style only if it is both very close to and slightly different from the general feeling of the age', because if it is too different, it is unlikely to be conceived by the author or to be appreciated by the élite, and if insufficiently different, it will go unnoticed, it will not 'pass the threshold of art'. Set against his intuitive-subjective use of élite materials to trace the 'collective unconscious', the sensibility of an age, Ariès places the quantitative analysis of homogeneous documentary series. Here he is thinking especially of Michel Vovelle's use of wills, but Pierre Chaunu's general discussion of *l'histoire sérielle* is also appropriate.[21]

Ariès was not an orthodox historian. Even by the conventions of French historical scholarship, his ideas were challenging, deliberately provocative even, and his sources widely drawn.[22] In the opening sentence of the introduction to *L'enfant* he described himself as a demographic historian.

Ce livre sur la famille d'Ancien Régime n'est pas l'oeuvre d'un spécialiste de cette époque, mais d'un historien démographe qui, frappé par les caractères originaux de la famille moderne, a senti la nécessité de remonter vers un passé plus lointain pour éprouver les limites de cette originalité.[23]

In his second book, *Histoire des populations Françaises et de leurs attitudes devant la vie depuis le XVIIIe siècle* (1948), and in an accompanying article in the journal

Population, Ariès established himself as a quantitative historian with a detailed analysis of regional population change, especially the causes and consequences of migration, during the nineteenth century. But the chapter entitled 'L'enfant dans la famille' contains some early references to now familiar themes, for example: 'Montaigne était incapable d'établir un compte exact de ses enfants, de toutes les couches de sa femme'; Jean-Jacques Rousseau on education, Frederic Le Play on the family; 'L'enfant, ignoré au XVIIe siècle, découvert au XVIIIe, devint bientôt tyrannique au XIXe'; 'La grande révolution démographique du XIXe siècle apparait liée à la modification d'un état de conscience: l'idée qu'on se fait de la famille et de l'enfant dans la famille'; and the transition between two family types – 'type fécond' and 'type malthusien' – in the former 'la personne de l'enfant est négligée. Seuls importent le patrimoine et sa main-d'oeuvre', and in the latter 'la fortune du ménage repose essentiellement sur l'enfant et son avenir'.[24] But Ariès was also influenced by a number of modern writers. In *L'homme et la mort dans l'histoire* (1951), for example, Edgar Morin drew the distinction between what he labelled 'la conscience humaine de la mort' and 'le risque de la mort', arguing that the latter must in some sense condition the former.[25] Johan Huizinga's *The Waning of the Middle Ages* (1924) also provided much stimulus, especially by its focus on 'The vision of death' and its simultaneous use of literature (poetry in particular) and art as sources of evidence.[26]

The influence of *L'enfant*, but especially *Centuries of Childhood*, has been considerable and lasting. Here are some examples of the use and persistence of the parental indifference hypothesis in particular. First, Lawrence Stone's *The Family, Sex and Marriage in England, 1500–1800* (1977) sets the seal on the indifference story.

Between upper-class parents and children, relations in the sixteenth century were also usually fairly remote. One reason for this was the very high infant and child mortality rates, which made it folly to invest too much emotional capital in such ephemeral beings. As a result, in the sixteenth and early seventeenth century very many fathers seem to have looked on their infant children with much the same degree of affection that men today bestow on domestic pets, like cats and dogs. Montaigne commented: 'I have lost two or three children in infancy, not without regret, but without great sorrow.' The phrase 'two or three' indicates a degree of indifference and casual unconcern that would be inconceivable today. (p. 105)[27]

In the seventeenth century there is no doubt whatever that 'restraint of emotional outpouring characterised infant departures as well as entries into the uncertain temporal scene', an observed psychological fact which stands in striking contrast with the evidence for the very late eighteenth and nineteenth centuries. There is no evidence, for example, of the purchase of mourning—not even an armband—on the death of very small children in the sixteenth, seventeenth and early eighteenth centuries, nor of parental attendance at the funeral. (pp. 105–6)[28]

At the height of the romantic period, the sufferings of parents at the death of a child reached an extreme intensity. (p. 249)

These numerous stories of extreme grief at the death of a child in the late eighteenth and the beginning of the nineteenth centuries mark a new phase in middle and upper-middle class responses to infant and child mortality. Among the classes sufficiently affluent to afford such luxuries, emotional anguish for the death of a baby was now both a social convention and a psychological reality, one which was later used to reinforce the profound religiosity of the mid-Victorian propertied classes. It is not merely that many more women were literate and were, therefore, putting their emotions on record. The nature and quality of those emotions were themselves changing. (p. 249)

The Family, Sex and Marriage has received considerable critical scrutiny, much of which has been ignored by those wishing to use the indifference hypothesis. It is also a study that is concerned explicitly with social classes and class relations, as the quotations reproduced above suggest. The élite, especially the English aristocracy, provide the documentary evidence, but the scope of generalisation is often widened to encompass society as a whole. However, on indifference, Stone himself warns his readers that 'It would be foolish to adopt a reductionist position that there is a simple and direct correlation between the level of mortality and the amount and degree of affect at any given moment in history'.[29]

Despite the success of *Centuries of Childhood*, it is Stone's account of the family that is often turned to, especially among popular historians. In Antonia Fraser's *The Weaker Vessel* (1984) we have the following.

> It has been suggested in recent years, notably by Lawrence Stone in *The Family, Sex and Marriage in England 1500–1800*, that the low expectation of infant life meant that people were as a whole less attracted to their children or at any rate during the child's first year of life, when its ability to survive the rigours of infant disease had not been established.[30]

In *Death, Burial and the Individual in Early Modern England* (1984), a study of funeral rites and rituals, Clare Gittings makes the following observation.

> The burial of little babies, however, occasioned rather less grief than is generally the case in modern Britain. Their parents were less attached to them, obviously in part because of the shortness of their life spans, but also by way of a deliberate policy. Since mortality in the first year of life was particularly high, the emotional suffering would have been too intense if a really firm bond were established between every child and its parents during the first precarious few months of its existence.[31]

Fourthly, there is Zelizer's influential *Pricing the Priceless Child* (1985) which focuses on the emergence of the economically worthless, but emotionally priceless child during the last century.

> Demographic theories ... contend that the new emotional value of children is best explained by falling birth and mortality rates in the twentieth century. Philippe Ariès and Lawrence Stone, in a landmark study of the English family, suggest that in periods of high mortality parents protect themselves against the emotional pain of a child's death by remaining affectively aloof. From this perspective it is 'folly to

invest too much emotional capital in such ephemeral beings.' (a) The decline in early mortality, therefore, can be seen as an independent variable that encouraged 'the deepening of emotional bonds between parents and children.'(b)[32]

Fifthly, in an otherwise highly critical essay on 'Lawrence Stone's family history' Mark Poster announces that 'Infant mortality was by today's standards very high in the early modern period. Approximately half of all live births never survived to age twenty. Most parents therefore experienced the death of their own children, probably more than once'; and 'Stone accepts, I think correctly, the tendency, during this period, toward emotional distance between parents and children'. Poster objects to Stone's explanation of the phenomenon rather than to his argument for its existence. For example, 'the specific explanation he [Stone] offers – that it is folly or unreasonable to love beings who might die and thereby cause grief – is decidedly gratuitous'.[33]

Our last example is the most recent and in some respects the most complicated. In *Medieval Children* (2001), Nicholas Orme is highly critical of the Ariès thesis concerning the late invention of childhood, arguing that 'adults regarded childhood as a distinct phase or phases of life, that parents treated children like children as well as like adults, that they did so with care and sympathy, and that children had cultural activities and possessions of their own'. But in answering the question 'how many children died?' he makes the following claim. In late Tudor England (1540–99), out of 1000 children born, 270 died during the first year of life, another 124 died aged one to four and a further 59 between ages five and nine years. This would mean that nearly 45 per cent of children died before reaching their tenth birthday; a truly phenomenal level of wastage which it would have been difficult to sustain in a large population. Fortunately, for England the more likely figure is closer to 21 per cent; less than a quarter died before reaching age ten. While rejecting Ariès's general thesis, Orme has still been willing to anticipate exceedingly high mortality at early ages.[34]

These examples, and there could be many more, clearly reflect the enduring significance of Ariès's parental indifference hypothesis (together with his approach to childhood and death) and the various ways it has been taken up, modified, advocated or attacked in whole or part. If not Ariès himself then Stone have been directly responsible for provoking discussion and much new research on the nature of childhood, the care of children, sentiments and emotional attachments, the pace and correct periodisation of social and cultural change, as well as the dangers of demographic reductionism. However, it would also be fair to say that it is through their role as providers of critical targets that most of their influence has accrued.

Ariès and his hypothesis have been the subject of many different kinds of criticism.[35] We shall focus on three broad categories at this stage: generality, impressionism and periodisation.

In geographical terms, we are dealing with the West and the attitudes of Westerners. One distinctive, yet far from homogeneous, cultural region is involved, initially comprising Christian Europe. There are no claims for non-Christian societies and little attempt to compare western Europe plus northern America with the remainder, although China and ancient Rome are mentioned. The parental indifference hypothesis is both regionally and culturally specified. Yet most supporting examples are drawn from Catholic France and, occasionally, Italy, Spain, England, New England and the United States. As Ariès explained, it is the broad sweep of slow-moving change that is of interest to him, not small geographical differences. It is also clear that Ariès is not concerned with popular culture; manners and sentiments are formed, expressed, controlled and changed by the social élite. They set the tone for practice in mourning as in child rearing. Why should the attitudes and behaviour of the French élite reflect those of the population of the West during the second millennium? Although the question is not asked by Ariès, there are good reasons to suppose that at the high level of abstraction with which we are concerned here, and certainly before the sixteenth-century Reformation, cultural practices were sufficiently homogeneous across Catholic Europe to encourage broad generalisation. After the Reformation and the tremendous expansion of European influence overseas there is more reason to be cautious, especially because that influence came particularly from Catholic Spain, not France, and Protestant England. However, it is also important to remember that *L'enfant* had a particularly strong French focus while *Essais sur l'histoire de la mort* made explicit its concern with the broader canvas of the West and Western attitudes in general.

As we have seen, Ariès was unapologetic about his intuitive, subjective, impressionistic approach; his selection from a very wide range of source materials rather than systematic, detailed analysis of just a single set (wills, family portraits or tomb monuments, for example). He also claimed that his method was more comprehensive, that in this area of historical discourse breadth was preferable to depth. The justification for this claim will depend to a considerable extent on Ariès's skill as a selector and interpreter, and on his mastery of eclecticism.

A couple of examples must suffice to illustrate the various difficulties. Montaigne and Molière are used in *L'enfant* while the novels and poetry of the Brontë sisters are engaged in *The Hour of Our Death*. The quotations reproduced from *Centuries of Childhood* on page 8 provide the first pair of examples. Ariès uses both Montaigne, in his *Essays*, and Molière in his last play, *Le malade imaginaire* (1673), to suggest parental indifference to either the deaths or the rites of young children. They are prime supporting examples for the hypothesis, coming as they do at the end of the sixteenth and seventeenth centuries, respectively. Yet neither is unambiguous. *Le malade imaginaire* is a rather inconsequential comedy of manners about marriage, family relations and the medical profession. There can be little justification for taking it as an expression of Molière's own true sentiments; indeed the most interesting feature of the play is the contrast between the imagined illness of its principal character and the real illness of the playwright. Molière died (probably from tuberculosis) shortly after the play's fourth performance on 21 February 1673. The facts of his life are these: he was born Jean-Baptiste Poquelin in January 1622; married

Armande Béjart (a woman twenty years his junior and the sister or daughter of his mistress, Madeleine) in 1662; his first son, Louis, was born and died in 1664; he was estranged from his wife between 1667 and 1671; and his second son was born and died in 1672.[36] Montaigne's *Essays* (a recognised influence on Molière) do, on the face of it, appear to offer instances of a father expressing callous indifference to the early deaths of his own children. One of the critical sentences written by Montaigne in his copy of the 1588 edition of *Essay* I.14 is:

> Et j'en ay perdu, mais en nourrice, deux ou trois, sinon sans regret, au moins sans fascherie.[37]

The word *la fâcherie* now has a particular meaning ('*Refroidissement ou rupture dans les relations de deux personnes que se sont fâchees l'une avec l'autre*'; *bouderie, brouille, désaccord* {falling out, sulking, quarrel, discord, disagreement}), but in the sixteenth century there were other, more subtle, possibilities (*incommodité, fatigue, malaise, affliction, tristesse, souffrance, douleur*).[38] This apparently straightforward instance brings us directly into contact with several of the most important issues associated with language, for example: meaning change, translation, author's intentions, reader's interpretation.[39] Close scrutiny of their context in the *Essays* indicates that Ariès's use of quotations from Montaigne as a prop for his parental indifference hypothesis cannot be justified. Montaigne may have been an enigmatic essayist, but he was a compassionate father to his one surviving daughter as well as a champion of children and childhood. Madame de Montaigne bore six daughters, five of whom died in infancy, *en nourrice*.[40]

The second pair of examples is taken from *The Hour of Our Death* and relate to the use by Ariès of *Jane Eyre: An Autobiography* and *Wuthering Heights*, the novels by, respectively, Charlotte and Emily Brontë, both first published in 1847.[41] From *Jane Eyre* Ariès takes the episode at Lowood Institution, during which Jane's friend Helen Burns dies, as an illustration for 'The age of the beautiful death'. The scene of Helen's death is remarkably calm and peaceful. Jane climbs onto Helen's crib, they lie there together warm and comfortable in each other's arms having a conversation about death.

> 'I am very happy, Jane; and when you hear that I am dead, you must be sure and not grieve: there is nothing to grieve about. We all must die one day, and the illness which is removing me is not painful; it is gentle and gradual: my mind is at rest. I leave no one to regret me much. [This is a real consolation, for if a death is painful here, it is not because it deprives us of the pleasures and riches of life, as in the Middle Ages, but because it separates us from those we love. *Ariès annotation*] I have only a father, and he is lately married, and will not miss me. By dying young, I shall escape great sufferings. I had not qualities or talents to make my way very well in the world: I should have been continually at fault.'[42]

Helen is completely confident: 'I believe; I have faith: I am going to God.' Heaven exists as a 'future state', where Jane will meet her again: 'You will come to the same region of happiness: be received by the same mighty, universal Parent, no doubt, dear Jane.' They say good-night; Jane sleeps and Helen dies.

This scene is rare among the Brontës, those wild spirits. This is almost a clandestine death, but not a solitary one. A great friendship has replaced the crowd of friends, relatives, and priests; the last words come from the heart.[43]

As for *Wuthering Heights*, Ariès uses it to illustrate a critical point in the history of attitudes towards death.

> For centuries these attitudes had remained almost fixed, only slightly disturbed by minor changes that did not alter their general stability. And suddenly, at the beginning of the nineteenth century, within one or two generations, there is a new sensibility that is different from everything that has preceded it. It is the first time in the course of this inquiry that we have seen opinions and attitudes change so quickly. Such a rapid transformation in a psychological field so durable, a history so gradual, is a remarkable phenomenon that requires some explanation. Emily Brontë's Wuthering Heights provides the missing transition.[44]

> It sits at the 'fragile boundary between two sensibilities': the demonic Gothic of the eighteenth century and the romantic nineteenth century during which passionate sentiments do not oppose conventional morality.
>
> Everything that in an earlier novel would have been erotic, macabre and diabolical becomes here passionate, moral, and funereal. The book is a symphony on the intertwined themes of love and death. In one episode we move imperceptibly from the macabre eroticism of the seventeenth and eighteenth centuries to the beautiful death of the nineteenth century.[45]

The episode referred to is the death in childbirth, and subsequent burial, of Catherine Linton (née Earnshaw) on 20 March 1784. The baby, a 'puny, seven months' child', was also named Catherine. The love and grief for the elder Catherine by Heathcliff, his desire to be physically with her in her grave, and his revenge on the Linton and Earnshaw families for their treatment of him as a foundling child dominate the second half of the novel.

Most critics would support Ariès's use of *Wuthering Heights* to reflect both the Gothic and the romantic, but there are several other points that require closer critical inspection, especially the matter of autobiography, the use of narrators, and the chronology of genealogy.

This is Ariès's brief sketch of the Brontës' family history.

> The mother dies, leaving six children. The eldest, Maria, takes the place of the mother, in spite of her youth; she is eight years old when Mrs Brontë dies. In 1824 she goes to school with her sister Elizabeth. She contracts tuberculosis and has to be sent home, where she dies immediately. Little Elizabeth follows her the same year to the grave. This first series of deaths does not prevent Mr Brontë from sending his other two daughters, Emily and Charlotte, to boarding school in 1825. They have to be sent home the following winter because of their health. Emily dies in 1848; her sister Anne follows her five months later.[46]

Table 2.2 illustrates Mrs Brontë's birth history more fully. It also gives what are believed to be the causes of death, tuberculosis in the main. It is usually claimed that Maria provides the inspiration for Helen Burns and for some of the manifestations of Catherine. Certainly the girls' boarding school to which the young sisters were sent became the much-vilified Lowood Institution. But it was some way from the cruel death camp portrayed, just as it was unlikely to have been the source of tuberculosis to which the family fell victim.[47] Despite its original subtitle, *Jane Eyre* was not, of course, an autobiography. This was a simple literary device, a means of engaging the reader (especially the reader's sympathy), and of establishing a clear, sequential structure. However, there were semi-autobiographical elements that may have included that interchange between Helen (Maria) and Jane (Charlotte) on the existence of heaven and the role of the universal Parent. *Wuthering Heights*, on the other hand, is unambiguously a novel, 'one of the most enigmatic of English novels' at that.[48] It has two narrators and a complex plot involving flashbacks, together with a series of marriages and intricate family relationships. Modern editions come with a genealogical table specifying the precise dates of births, marriages and deaths for thirteen characters over three generations between 1757 and 1803. In this sense at least the biographical detail is impressive; even Heathcliff's removal from the streets of Liverpool and introduction to the Earnshaw family can be dated (summer 1771). This is a work of intense, wild imagination; there is passion, but the loving care of romantic love is lacking. Fear, revenge, violence, tension, wind and spirits, self-destruction, little civility and no sensibility, death without love. *Wuthering Heights* is not a novel to be classified easily, to be placed neatly in the Victorian age, to be used in an historical argument.

The third broad category of criticism to be considered here is that of periodisation. Should we be convinced by Ariès's insistence (also Stone's) that the seventeenth century was the critical period during which childhood was discovered and attitudes towards infants changed? Are there other candidates? *Poor Monkey* (1957), Peter Coveney's study of the child in literature, argues that 'Until the last decades of the eighteenth century the child did not exist as an important and continuous theme in English literature'.[49] The appearance of the child coincided with the generation of William Blake and William Wordsworth, with the romantic revival and its associated changes in sensibility and thought. The child also became a vehicle for social commentary in the novels of Charles Dickens, a symbol of innocence and the life of the imagination, as an expression of nostalgia, insecurity, and possibly self-pity also.[50] Since *Centuries of Childhood* did not influence *Poor Monkey* it provides a particularly valuable insight, yet it also encounters the periodisation problem. For example, Coveney does not attempt to demonstrate an absence of interest in children prior to the 1790s, but Ariès has shown how a specialist literature specifically written for children developed in France from the 1690s.[51] We shall see whether Coveney is correct in his argument that new sensitivities towards children began to be expressed in the 1790s, sentiments which were enhanced during the 1840s, although this should not convince us of earlier literary indifference.

Table 2.2 The birth history of Maria Branwell Brontë from 1812 to 1821

Name	Born	Married	Died	Comments
Rev Patrick Brontë	17 April 1777	once	7 June 1861	
Maria Branwell	15 April 1783	29 December 1812	15 September 1821	cause of death: ovarian cancer
1 Maria	c 23 April 1814		6 May 1825	tuberculosis
2 Elizabeth	8 February 1815		15 June 1825	tuberculosis
3 Charlotte	21 April 1816	29 June 1854	31 March 1855	*m* Rev Arthur Bell Nichols, died in early pregnancy, tuberculosis
4 Patrick Branwell	26 June 1817		24 September 1848	tuberculosis
5 Emily Jane	30 July 1818		19 December 1848	tuberculosis
6 Anne	17 January 1820		28 May 1849	tuberculosis

Note: c baptised; *m* married; *b* buried

Source: Juliet Barker, *The Brontës* (London: Weidenfeld and Nicolson, 1994).

David Herlihy's remarkable, yet rather neglected, essay 'Medieval children' offers one of the most penetrating discussions of the periodisation problem.[52] His thesis is that both the social (the wealth and resources provided by society) and psychological (the attention children claimed and received) investments in children were growing substantially from approximately the eleventh and twelfth centuries, and that this continued through to the end of the Middle Ages and beyond.

> The medieval social investment in children thus seems to have grown from the twelfth century and to have passed through two phases: the first one, beginning from the twelfth century, largely involved a commitment, on the part of the urban communities, to the child's education and training; the second, from the late fourteenth century, reflected a concern for the child's survival and health under difficult hygienic conditions.[53]

These phases can be linked with the commercialisation of the European economy and the resultant need for a society with adequately trained adults and, from the late fourteenth century, the need to protect the very young from the heightened health risks brought on by the plague epidemics. Higher mortality risks foster improved childcare since in this account children are prized as their scarcity and human capital value rises. Herlihy may certainly be taken to task for his use of élite, urban, mainly Italian sources, but he also brings to this whole field of enquiry a refreshing realism.

> Historians would be well advised to avoid such categorical and dubious claims, that people in certain periods failed to distinguish children from adults, that childhood really did lie beyond the pale of collective consciousness. Attitudes toward children have certainly shifted, as has the willingness on the part of society to invest substantially in their welfare or education. But to describe these changes, we need terms more refined than metaphors of ignorance and discovery. I would propose that we seek to evaluate, and on occasion even to measure, the psychological and economic investment which families and societies in the past were willing to make in their children. However, we ought also to recognise that alternative and even competitive sets of child-related values can coexist in the same society, perhaps even in the same household. Different social groups and classes expect different things from their children; so do different epochs in accordance with the prevailing economic, social and demographic conditions. In examining the ways in which children were regarded and reared in the past, we should not expect either rigorous consistency across society or lineal progress over time.[54]

With Herlihy's advice in mind, let us turn to some preliminary evaluation of the parental indifference hypothesis and to Ariès's *l'histoire de la mort*. From what we have already seen it is clear that the hypothesis is both influential and controversial. Influential because many, knowingly or otherwise, have followed *L'enfant* in supposing that human behaviour must be demographically conditioned to at least some and perhaps a considerable, yet varying, extent. It is readily appreciated, especially in a society that condones abortion, that there are distinctive points between conception and the start of adulthood at which the existence of a separate being may be recognised so that it can be protected and cherished: conception itself, 'quickening', live birth, one year, seven years, these are all possibilities. What it is more difficult to appreciate, and here Ariès's critics find a ready target, is the mechanism by which demographic risk and sentiment are connected and how that relationship changed in the long term. The breadth of his canvas, his exploration of the mourning curve (figure 2.1), and the boldness of his approach to evidence will ensure Ariès's continuing legacy even if the detail, including that of the hypothesis, is rejected.

Vovelle and *la longue durée*

Michel Vovelle is probably best known in France as an historian of the Revolution, but his earlier contributions to *l'histoire de la mort*, to the debate over the distinction between ideologies and *les mentalités*, may offer us a way of exploring further the links between demographic risks and the expression of feelings for children as they changed during several centuries. But first, it is necessary to consider briefly how French historians in particular have dealt with *les temps* and employed *les trois niveaux* (the three levels or layers).

In the preface to his great work, *The Mediterranean and the Mediterranean World in the Age of Philip II* (1949), Fernand Braudel (1905–85) distinguished between three different ways of considering time.[55] At the base, the first level or layer, there is the 'almost changeless' *l'histoire immobile*, 'the history of man in relation to his surroundings'. This is geographical time. Above this 'unaltering history' comes 'the history of gentle rhythms, of groups and groupings', that is *la conjoncture* (situation or trend) which might also be called social time. On the third level comes *l'histoire événementielle*, the history of events, individual time. This is the history of 'short, sharp, nervous vibration'. Braudel's purpose here, and in his influential paper in *Annales: ESC* of 1958 ('History and the social sciences: the *longue durée*'), is to emphasise the importance of developing a history of the long term, of redirecting enquiries away from the single event, however momentous. It is, of course, this *longue durée* to which Ariès is referring and with which Marx was so adept. Braudel makes the point explicitly: 'Marx's genius, the secret of his long sway, lies in the fact that he was the first to construct true social models, on the basis of a historical *longue durée*'.[56] But Marx also sketched out a model of society in which the mode of production of material life (productive forces or technology) *conditions* social, political and intellectual life, and where social being *determines* consciousness (ideas, beliefs etc.).[57] Once again, there appear to be three levels (economic and material conditions influence social relations influence beliefs, consciousness). Although, unlike Braudel's, this is not a model that focuses on different forms of time; it is concerned with how the superstructure builds from the structure, how one level is influenced by another (lower) level. Marx generally favoured the notion of conditioning rather than determining, arguing that at least to some extent people make their own history, that their behaviour (ideas, beliefs) is not completely controlled by their material circumstances. This balance between structure and agency, as it is now known, continues to occupy a central position in history and the social sciences.

Vovelle's approach owes much to both Marx and Braudel. In 'Sur la mort' he outlined a new model, one framed by *la longue durée*, but also formed in three distinctive levels (table 2.3).[58]

Level 1, the base, represents biological death (suffered death) captured by the brutal facts of mortality which are inscribed in demographic statistics: *les courbes démographiques*. Vovelle assumed a society with a life expectancy at birth of between 20 and 30 years, one that 'allowed only half of any given generation, and sometimes fewer, to survive until the age of twenty'.[59] On the second level comes the experience of death, which involves all the procedures and rites that accompany the progression from final illness, through death itself, the grave and on to the afterlife. Here we engage with the 'formal exterior', with the rituals of death, the ceremonial rites of passage, funerals and mourning, the gestures and expressions of grief. At the top, on the third level, we find the collective discourses on death. These are organised discourses, compared with the largely unconscious and involuntary expressions of the second level, which have moved from the magical to the religious to the secular

Table 2.3 **Michel Vovelle's three-levels model**
(La mort dans la longue durée: les trois niveaux)

(3) *les discours sur la mort*	*l'histoire du discours collectif sur la mort, la sensibilité collectif* (formally organised: magic, religion, secular discourses, literary and media discourses)
(2) *la mort vécue*	*tout d'abord le réseau des gestes et des rites qui accompagnent le parcours de l'ultime maladie à l'agonie, au tombeau et à l'au-delà* (involuntary-unconscious: death rites, funerals, burial, mourning, gestures and expressions of grief)
(1) *la mort subie*	*c'est le fait brut de la mortalité, il s'inscrit dans les courbes démographiques* (life expectancy at birth of 20 to 30 years)

Examples of
(2) 'Cette sensibilité à la mort marque des avancées ou des reculs: à partir de quel moment la mort de l'enfant est-elle ressentie comme perte véritable, avant de devenir au cours du XIXe siècle la blessure essentielle, tout particulièrement douloureuse?'
(3) 'Enfin, on peut dire que l'époque contemporaine, à partir de la fin du XVIIIe siècle, est marquée par la prolifération du discours littéraire en liberté sur la mort.'

Source: based on Michel Vovelle, 'Sur la mort', in *Idéologies et mentalités* (Paris: Libraire François Maspero, 1982), pp. 103–05, (Paris: Gallimard, 1992), pp. 111–13.

over the centuries. The discussion of death and dying in literature appears at this level, along with its representation in the modern media. Although Vovelle does make a distinction between the unconscious and the conscious, the separation is not an exact one. If level 2 is occupied by the customs and conventions that surround dying (which may involve the physical expression of emotion, weeping for example), the third level is concerned with more considered responses (no less emotional) and may involve expressions of grief through the medium of verbal or plastic art (epitaphs or monuments). In English, and perhaps rather more loosely than Vovelle's original conception, we may think of these levels as representing: (1) the risks of dying (demography), (2) the social customs of death (mourning practice and grieving), and (3) the discussion of death and dying (grief in words).[60]

The remainder of 'On death' considers the history of death in more general terms, the sources of evidence that might be used, and the notion of the unconscious in human history. In this it also makes explicit its debt to Ariès's work.

> We can integrate the divisions proposed by Ariès into this primary global model without any contradiction. He traced the succession of medieval death, egoistic death (the death of the self emerging from the collective death of ancient times) to the death of the other, the romantic image of the loss of an irreplaceable individual followed by the death taboo of the twentieth century. Such directive trends are at once satisfactory and unsatisfactory. To reduce it to its essentials, Philippe Ariès's argument stresses the progressive individualisation of attitudes to death, a case which is hard to contradict, but which passes over more than one problem, particularly the problem of causes as modalities of what he defines as the collective unconscious.[61]

Vovelle also touches on some of the key problems to be faced in the use of his three-levels model. For example, in terms of *la longue durée* attitudes to death are not static. There are periods of 'convulsive history', of heightened levels of sensitivity towards death, some of which may be attributed to demographic factors. It is also the case that various different attitudes may co-exist at the same time; there may be social and geographical variations. Observing these differences will be affected by the availability of evidence, but in this regard there is a distinct 'history of silences' due partly to the obscurity of the anonymous masses and partly to the deliberate silences that may signify private grief. In terms of demographic evidence, Vovelle warns against over-mechanical correlation and reminds us of the presence of 'complex mediating factors'; while for literature and art he asks whether they give evidence of collective attitudes or simply reflect the personality of the author or artist. In all these points Vovelle directs us towards the central issue: how is it possible to reconstruct the changing history of mentalities?

It is on this question that we shall focus in the remainder of the chapter. First, we should look in a little more detail at *l'histoire des mentalités* in conjunction with *l'histoire de la mort* in the context set by *la longue durée*. Secondly, it will be helpful to tackle the related question of how in Vovelle's model the levels influence one another. If as in table 2.3 (1)→(2)→(3) (where → signifies 'determines' or 'conditions' or 'mediates' or 'influences' etc.), is it then possible to read (2) from (3), and (1) from (2)? This will lead us to the vexed question of representation, even measurement.

Historians, even French historians, agree that *l'histoire des mentalités* is a slippery concept to define. The medieval historian Jacques Le Goff's perspective is to think in terms of distinctive approaches to historical materials, ones which 'reveal those marginal or paroxysmal aspects of a society's attitudes and behaviour from which we can, indirectly, learn much about the common, central mentality of a period'.[62] In particular, such work often concentrates on irrational or abnormal behaviour (witchcraft, heresy), or themes at the margins of everyday existence (attitudes to death). This is also the line adopted by Ariès. His approach to definition involves a list of examples of work undertaken by up to three generations of scholars most recently on the family, sexuality and socialisation, but he also mentions in passing how demography can be used to reveal mentality: 'la démographie révèle les mentalités'.[63] According to Vovelle, 'The history of mentalities is the study of the mediations and dialectical relationship between the objective conditions of the life of men and the way they perceive them', that is 'the complex mediation between the real life of men and the image'.[64] Vovelle is especially interested in distinguishing between mentality and ideology. While there are several definitions of ideology, most recently the term has come to mean the ways in which ideas or representations may be used to maintain a particular social order. Political regimes develop a dominant ideology in order to maintain and reproduce themselves. By these means the real experiences of the people (poverty, powerlessness) may be disguised and their collective will moulded to submission or acquiescence. Ideology has a top-down connotation, therefore, while mentality suggests more a self-expression of popular culture.[65]

The most thorough analysis of the history of mentalities in English has come from Peter Burke. He identifies three distinctive features: (1) the emphasis on collective attitudes rather than individual ones, that is, beliefs shared by individuals; (2) the stress on 'unspoken or unconscious assumptions, on perception, on the workings/ of "practical reason", or "everyday thought" as well as on conscious thoughts or elaborated theories'; and (3) a concern with 'the structure of beliefs as well as their content, with categories, with metaphors and symbols, with how people think as well as what they think'.[66] Burke also identifies four distinct problems with the mentalities approach: the tendency to homogenise, to generalise too broadly about a particular society thereby ignoring individual variations; the need to conceptualise change in mentalities, since belief systems do alter over time, and thus how to avoid thinking of individuals as though they are in some way prisoners of the collective mentality; distinguishing the relation between beliefs and society from that between beliefs and other belief systems; finally, a tendency to make simple, even ethnocentric or present-time, judgments involving the distinction between, for example, primitive and civilised, traditional and modern, prelogical and logical.[67]

Does the history of death, and especially of death in childhood, offer ways of resolving or avoiding these problems? There are some possibilities, but also special difficulties. Certainly, death is an event that all must face and thus it would be reasonable for all societies at all times to develop some form of particular custom to mark the event, to allow the still living to react, to guide what should be done with the body, to establish rules for remembrance. Since children will not have achieved powerful positions, there can be little benefit in using their memory to glorify a regime through monuments to their lives and achievements. In this sense, the cynical manipulation of belief systems often associated with ideologies can be avoided. Mourning for children is politically innocent. In terms of Ariès's approach to the history of mourning, it is already possible to see how historical change over the long term can be incorporated in the study of mentalities without the need to make judgments on whether the response was adequate in any particular period. In addition, Vovelle's own three-levels model adds some new sophistication, admittedly by focusing only on attitudes to death, to the challenge of establishing links between society and beliefs. The temptation to describe mentalities in ways that emphasise homogeneity still remains to be avoided. But there is also the difficulty of distinguishing between mourning and grief. Both may be public or private, shown by an individual or by members of a group, but there is also a sense in which mourning involves certain ceremonial practices (the funeral, for instance) as well as signifying feelings of grief. Those feelings may be internalised and may not lead to the outward engagement in the rituals of mourning. When in his three-levels model Vovelle talks about grief and mourning, he appears to deal with them interchangeably. Yet although closely related, they are not the same. Ariès's mourning curve is intended to reflect outward, public display; although it might be used as an index of grief. Here we are especially concerned with the ways in which adults respond to the early deaths of children. Do they demonstrate their emotional attachment by expressing feelings of grief, and how, with what intensity, do they express those feelings? This means that we must continue to differentiate between mourning and grief even when, as is normal, they are combined.[68]

Although Ariès was apparently in no doubt that demography reveals mentality and, through his parental indifference hypothesis, that demography influences feelings, Vovelle's 'cellar to attic' model still leaves ill-defined how each level interacts with the others and whether, as in a house, it is possible to move easily between the floors, both up and down. At its crudest, the hypothesis states that parental indifference and childhood mortality are positively and significantly related. As the latter deteriorates it will cause the former to increase. In this sense demographic conditions determine (although neither exactly nor exclusively) a response (or lack of) in terms of behaviour (mourning, physical displays of grief). The three-levels model also has demographic conditions influence mourning, but now there is a separate layer that treats forms of discourse. Level 3 specifies conscious, considered expressions of grief while in level 2 the responses include involuntary, physical expressions of emotion and required behaviour. Here there is no specification of strength or direction of relationship, merely that a level will 'rest upon', 'be affected by' the circumstances that characterise the level immediately below. It is not that levels 2 and 1 cannot be related as Ariès stated, but that the arrangement in Vovelle's hands is far looser. The word 'shapes' (rather than the over-rigid 'determines' or 'conditions', or the vague 'influences') appears the most suitable for the level 1→2 relationship since it conveys the sense of a forming process, while 'reflects' will be used to express the relationship 2 → 3. Level 3 reflects 2 which is shaped by 1. By choosing different words we also indicate that the relationships may differ. Levels 3 and 2 can be regarded as offering different forms of expression for a common phenomenon (they interact and can be read in both directions). The biological facts of death will shape the customs of mourning, the expression of grief. These are the 'parallel histories' to be discussed in Chapter 8.

Representing mentalities

We are now in a position to state more clearly one of the principal objectives of this study: to use Vovelle's three-levels model as a framework not only for the examination of the parental indifference hypothesis, but also as a device for further exploration of the ways in which demographic circumstances affect patterns of social behaviour which are in their turn manifest in the forms of attitudes, beliefs, feelings and emotions in general. In order to achieve this objective it is obviously necessary to represent, if possible to measure, certain aspects of mentality. But how can this be done?

While Vovelle talks about *les courbes démographiques* (table 2.3) in his first level, and Ariès introduces us to *la courbe du deuil* (figure 2.1), it is still necessary to specify in more detail the particular demographic circumstances that should be measured, and how the mourning curve might be given greater precision. Beyond these two lies the problem of level 3 and the ways in which the various forms of discourse on mourning and grief can be analysed. There is little point assuming that these problems can be resolved easily, and even if this were possible we should still need to consider the matter of *shaping* and *reflection*, that is the relationships between levels 1 and 2, and 3 and 2. The French historians of mentality have certainly made considerable advances in tackling these issues, but they have tended to focus on individual levels – demography, ritual, discourse – rather than attempt some form of integration. Two exceptions, which we shall consider in more detail, are Vovelle's own work on piety in eighteenth-century Provence and Pierre Chaunu's efforts to explore the history of dying, death and mourning in Paris, also during the eighteenth century.

Piété baroque et déchristianisation en Provence au XVIIIe siècle (1973), Vovelle's doctoral thesis, gives a remarkable insight on the secularisation of Provençal society by analysing the contents of wills, specifically, the preamble to a will, which in the early eighteenth century usually requested, and provided for, masses to be said for the testator. These data allow for the construction of time-series, together with local, urban–rural, social class and gender comparisons. The summary results are illustrated

Figure 2.2 Vovelle's representation of secularisation using evidence from wills for eighteenth-century Provence, France

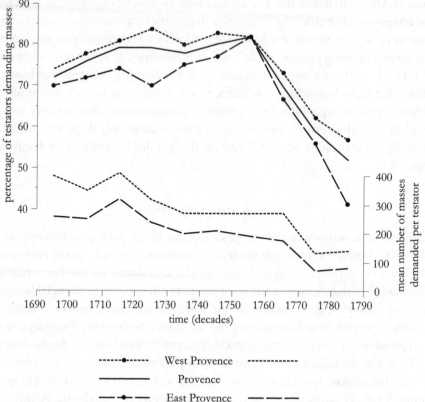

Source: redrawn from Michel Vovelle, *Piété baroque et déchristianisation en Provence au XVIIIe siècle* (Paris: Éditions Plon, 1973), graph II, p. 124.

in figure 2.2.[69] This shows the percentage of testators requesting masses as well as the average number of masses requested per testator. It also distinguishes between the eastern and western districts of Provence. In terms of the popularity of masses, there is little change before the 1750s but continuous reduction thereafter, indicating that secularisation was gathering momentum several decades before the Revolution. In his essay on 'The prerevolutionary sensibility' Vovelle also utilises time-series for adult male literacy, illegitimacy and criminality, each one of which conveys some element of social attitude and collective beliefs.[70] But what additional conclusions may be drawn? In fact, Vovelle leaves us with more questions than answers; for instance: 'Are mentalities and sensibilities only a reflection of culture and ideology?' The important point, however, is that there are, on level 2, certain manifestations of collective belief systems that lend themselves to simple, yet rather precise, quantitative representation. What is in more doubt is how those representations should be interpreted. Vovelle, for example, contrasts his emphasis on ideology (a class diffusion model in which the bourgeoisie are the innovators) with Ariès's insistence on a collective psychology that has its own semi-autonomous ebb and flow, quite independent of the economic and power relations within a society.[71]

La mort à Paris, XVIe, XVIIe et XVIIIe siècles (1978) summarises a major project directed by Pierre Chaunu.[72] The project's principal source of data was similar to that used for Provence, namely wills. The trend of increased secularisation predated that in Provence; in particular it was ahead of Marseilles (the Provençal leader) by ten to fifteen years, suggesting a continuous increase throughout the eighteenth century. Although this finding is interesting, and perhaps not unexpected, it is Chaunu's attempt to consider all three levels that demands our attention. Ultimately the project is frustrated, however, by problems at the first and third levels. Urban historical demography is a treacherous field in general, but the case of Paris proves especially intractable. While there are estimates of total population and summary counts of births, marriages and deaths, the ability to calculate mortality rates is limited. Further, the use of testamentary evidence supplied in wills proves resistant to all but the form of analysis adopted by Vovelle. Ultimately, 'l'assault récent du quantitatif au troisième niveau' fails to realise its early promise; the subtleties in individuals' testimonies defy easy summary.[73]

Beyond these two examples, Vovelle has offered other approaches to the third level; one is of special interest here. The second chapter of *Ideologies and Mentalities* discusses 'The relevance and ambiguity of literary evidence'.[74] Here Vovelle sketches the case for the historical study of literature and identifies two ways of developing the use of literary texts in the study of attitudes towards death. 'In the *longue durée*, which many see as the proper time scale for the history of mentalities, literature acts as a vehicle for images, clichés, memories and traditions – all the ceaselessly reworked and distorted products of the collective imagination.' Another part of the case is that literature not only registers the changes in collective sensibility, but like other forms of ideology it also helps to support particular belief systems. Literature, Vovelle suggests, can be used in the following ways: as 'elementary evidence' and as the 'deliberate discourse of death', which has tended to be dominated by religious literature. The former appears deceptively straightforward. The literary text can be taken as 'a simple reflection of contemporary social practice', but even here the challenge is 'to decode the latent meanings, from a much more complex discourse which is charged with ulterior motives'. Vovelle's case is a strong one in principle and potential but, as we shall see, there are many problems to be overcome.[75]

It is rather disappointing that Vovelle did not follow up his own suggestions. Although *Mourir autrefois* (1974) does employ a variety of texts in its illustration of collective attitudes to death, there is no attempt at a systematic analysis of a particular genre that could parallel his work on Provençal wills. Daniel Roche has demonstrated the importance of work on the 'deliberate discourse of death', however.[76] As part of a wider study of literacy, reading and the book, Roche has analysed the publication histories of 236 titles that appeared in France in the seventeenth and eighteenth centuries. These books dealt in whole or in part with the preparations for death. Roche is able to map the distribution of their place of publication and to construct time-series for their production. The broad picture, dominated as it is by Paris publications, reflects the decline in interest in the subject of preparation for death during the eighteenth century. It coincides with the trend of secularisation reflected in the Paris wills, while some of the provincial series match neatly with those constructed by Vovelle (figure 2.2). In combination, the quantitative analyses of publication histories and testaments have been shown to provide powerful descriptions of changing attitudes to death in France. But the problem remains of how literary sources may be used to establish serial history, since even in the case of Roche's study it is the existence of the book (date and place of publication together with a classification of its content) that matters rather than the subtle qualities of its text.

*　*　*

There are several important lessons to be learnt from this outline of the largely French history of death. First, it is clear that many methodological problems remain to be resolved satisfactorily. If Vovelle's three-levels model is to provide an analytical framework then far more attention will need to be given to the use of literary texts, or other sources, as means to recover and represent past mentalities, especially those associated with the emotions. This is attempted in Chapters 4, 5 and 7 which focus on the plastic (pictures and monuments) and literary (poems) as sources for level 3. Secondly, more will need to be done to chart the significant mortality variations which Vovelle and Ariès both tend to treat as given, accepting in a rather uncritical way what evidence their demographer colleagues provide. Demographic series appear the most secure, yet there are still significant problems of construction and comparison. The following chapter takes up this challenge. Thirdly, we still have the matter of *shaping* and *reflecting* to resolve; that is, of how the three levels inter-relate. This is the main subject for Chapter 8. Fourthly, *la longue durée* appears a particularly exacting master, but one that still promises much. It is only at this scale that we shall be able to discern real changes, and this is still our objective. Finally, there is the principal question of the parental indifference hypothesis itself, its sustainability and versatility, together with the applicability of the general mourning curve. Ariès's own analysis is far from secure, despite its imaginative insights and influential supporters. This is our recurring theme.

3

Mortality, Childcare and Mourning

> There is still a great deal of uncertainty about infant mortality rates at delivery or in
> the first few days postpartum. There is no question that mortality rates in the first
> year varied from 15 to 30 per cent, but much of that was certainly due to environ-
> mental circumstances – malnutrition, dysenteric and gastric diseases – rather than
> to obstetric malpractice. At any rate, the assumption that the stillborn rate in prein-
> dustrial Europe was higher than for industrial Europe should certainly not be taken
> for granted.[77]

These three sentences tell us everything, and nothing. They are largely correct, yet
they express our deep ignorance. Perhaps the best way to begin this discussion of the
risk of premature death in the past, to place it on as secure a footing as possible, is to
demonstrate the importance of the problem. The proportion of all deaths that would
have occurred to infants and children under 10 years of age is likely to have varied with
the general level of mortality. In a society with very high mortality (life expectancy
at birth less than 30 years), one should expect upwards of 40 per cent of all deaths
to be those of children. With moderately high mortality (life expectancy about 50
years), then perhaps 20 per cent would be children and in relatively low mortality
populations (life expectancy above 60 years), less than 10 per cent of deaths would be
to those under 10 years of age. Figure 3.1 shows these properties of typical mortality
structures. It also illustrates the fact that the rate of population growth, as well as the
level of mortality, will affect these proportions. For example, when life expectancy at
birth is 40 years and there is no population growth then 30 per cent of all deaths will
be to children, but if there were to be 1 per cent growth each year then the proportion
would rise to something in excess of 40 per cent. A further property of this way of
looking at mortality patterns is that the 0 per cent curve in figure 3.1 also expresses
the level of childhood mortality. When life expectancy at birth is 40 years, we would
expect 30 per cent of live-born infants not to reach their tenth birthdays. Only with
a life expectancy at 25 should this percentage rise to 50.

Of course, figure 3.1 offers only a generalised model. There will have been particular times and places in which more than half of all the live-born did not survive to
adulthood, but this would be under extreme and unusual circumstances. The note
to figure 3.1 explains briefly on what assumptions it is based. This is rather important because there are still many uncertainties concerning the pattern of mortality,

Figure 3.1 Framework to illustrate the likely proportion of all deaths occurring to children aged less than 10 years in populations with 0 and 1 per cent per year growth rates, organised by life expectancy at birth in years (*e*(0))

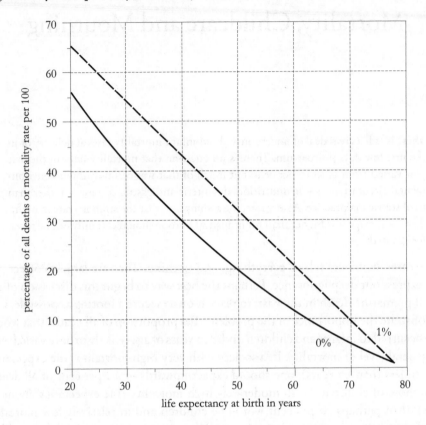

Note: constructed using Model West for females from Ansley J. Coale and Paul Demeny, *Regional Model Life Tables and Stable Populations* (Princeton, NJ: Princeton University Press, 1966). These Princeton models provide a useful way of describing the contribution of early-age mortality to the overall level of mortality. They are divided into four 'families' (North, South, East, West) that reflect distinctive age-specific mortality patterns. When mortality is high (life expectancy at birth (*e*(0)) is less than 40 years), then at least 30 per cent of all deaths will be to those aged under 10 years. If the population is growing slowly (0.5 per cent per year), then the under-10s will contribute at least 35–40 per cent. Figure 3.1 also provides a rough guide to the general level of mortality that may be anticipated in a population given a particular level of childhood mortality (here *q*(0–9) per 100 rather than per 1000). If in a population *q*(0–9) was thought to be about 20 (i.e. 200 per 1000), then life expectancy would be 50 years according to Princeton Model West. If only half of live-born infants survived to age 10 (i.e. *q*(0–9) was 50), then an *e*(0) of 25 years or less would be likely. Such an exceptionally high level of mortality would endanger the long-term survival of the population by seriously affecting its ability to reproduce itself. Although figure 3.1 relies on model mortality structures, it is reasonable to assume that the circumstances of actual historical societies would have fallen close to its predictions.

especially at early ages, in the past and how that pattern changed. It is also unclear how best to generalise the experience, to represent it in terms of survival models and life tables. This chapter is devoted to *la mort subie*: the changing and varying risk of dying at an early age. Specifically, it deals with fetal, infant and child mortality, that is, the risk of dying between conception and age 10 years. It attempts a comparison of experiences in France and England: the former because this will allow us to take up and consider in more detail some of the demographic observations raised by Philippe Ariès, and the latter because two of Michel Vovelle's three levels – *la mort vécue* and *les discours sur la mort*, which are influenced by *la mort subie* (see table 2.3, p. 25) – will be considered using mainly English examples. Chapter 3 concludes with short discussions of childcare behaviour (particularly the vexed issue of infant feeding), and the practice of mourning, again in France and England. These sections bring us towards *la mort vécue*.

The risk of dying at an early age

By convention, early-age mortality is defined and measured in the following ways. Infant mortality relates to the death of an infant during the twelve-month period between live birth and age one year. It is measured by taking the ratio of the number of infant deaths recorded as having occurred in a given year (the numerator) and the number of live births also recorded in that year (the denominator), and this is usually expressed in parts per 1000 (as opposed to parts per 100, that is, as a percentage). Here we shall refer to the infant mortality rate by the initials IMR (indicating that it is a rate per 1000) or by $q(0)$ (which means that it is in the form of a probability: if IMR is 200 then $q(0)$ will be 0.200). Age is denoted in brackets and refers to completed years; so the infant who has not reached his or her first birthday is regarded as aged 0 in completed years. Childhood will be divided into early and late; the early childhood mortality rate covers the four years from age 1 to age 5. The probability of dying between age 1 year and up to 5 years is $q(1-4)$ in completed years and in parts per 1000 it is ECMR. The probability of dying during the next five years is $q(5-9)$ and that between live birth and age 10 is $q(0-9)$ in completed years. We shall use the initials CMR to refer to the childhood mortality rate, that is $q(5-9)$ in parts per 1000 (or occasionally in parts per 100). Fetal mortality covers the period of development in the uterus between conception and miscarriage or stillbirth. The normal gestational age to a fetus's full term is taken to be 40 weeks since last menstrual period (LMP). Conception is likely to occur at 14 days LMP. Although the distinction between miscarriage and stillbirth has been rather fluid, we may regard stillbirths as those late-fetal deaths which take place after 28 weeks LMP where the fetus shows no vital signs at parturition. Perinatal mortality is used to refer to stillbirths and deaths during the first week after live birth in combination. One final demographic convention: $e(0)$ is used to represent life expectancy at birth in years ($e(20)$ will be life expectancy at age 20 in years, therefore).

Figure 3.2 **Infant and childhood mortality trends for France, 1806–2001**

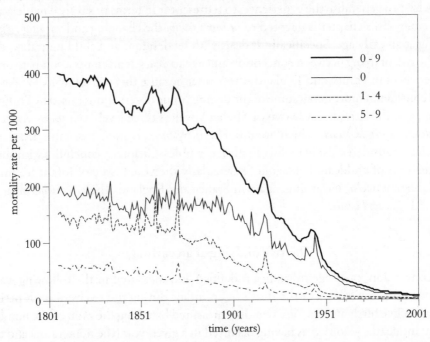

Note: infant mortality rate (o); early childhood mortality rate (1–4); late childhood mortality rate (5–9); infant and childhood mortality combined (o–9), this series has been smoothed using a 5-point moving mean.

Source: Jacques Vallin and France Meslé, *Tables de mortalité françaises pour les XIXe et XXe siècles et projections pour le XXI siècle* (Paris: INED, 2001), Annex I and II.

Of these various measures we shall find that the infant mortality rate is usually the most straightforward to derive and, partly for this reason, the factors that influence its variation have been the most intensively studied, even if they are as yet not fully understood. Once national civil authorities began the registration of live births and deaths distinguished by age (o, 1–4, 5–9, for example), the calculation of IMR became a relatively simple matter, although its accuracy was not guaranteed because, as we shall see, both the numerator and the denominator were subject to various forms of error. In France civil registration of vital events began in 1806 and in England and Wales the equivalent date was 1837 (1855 in Scotland). Prior to these dates IMRs need to be derived from ecclesiastical parish registers. This means either that entries in the baptism register must be traced on an individual by individual basis into the burial register so that the numerator becomes the sum of those infants whose burials are registered as having taken place within one year of their baptism, or the total number of infant deaths must be estimated. While both of these approaches are feasible, and have been employed on many occasions by historical demographers, the whole exercise is fraught with many dangers that tend to make parish register and civil registration based IMRs rather different animals. Of the other early-age mortality

Figure 3.3 Cumulative infant and childhood mortality trends for France, 1806–2001

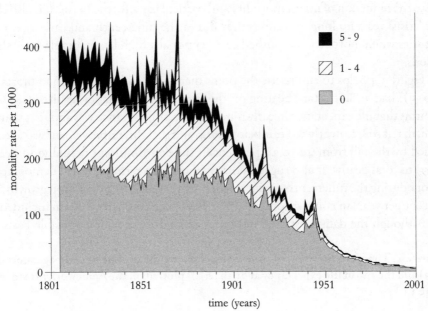

Note: infant mortality rate (o); early childhood mortality rate (1–4); late childhood mortality rate (5–9); infant and childhood mortality combined (o–9).

Source: see figure 3.2.

measures, ECMR and CMR in general may require the availability of a census that enumerates the age structure of the population in some detail, and at least in five-year age groups. Such censuses were first undertaken in both France and England during the early nineteenth century. Only nominal record linkage will provide the materials for these measures in the parish register period. Late-fetal mortality is particularly difficult to measure in the past and especially prior to the middle of the twentieth century. Even when it can be calculated directly, several confusions are possible over what constitutes a live birth and what the gestational age may have been.

Despite these many problems, historical demographers in France and England have been able to derive a range of early-age mortality measures, although their reliability and completeness will vary with period and place. We shall begin on what appears to be the safest ground and move towards the more conjectural.

Annual estimates of infant and the other childhood mortality rates have been derived for France from 1806 to 2001. These are illustrated in figures 3.2 and 3.3. The former shows the three time-series in the normal fashion while in the latter the rates are cumulated so that an impression is obtained of the sequence of risks children faced during their first ten years, and how those mortality risks changed during the two centuries. As a rough guide, in early nineteenth-century France 20 per cent of live-born infants died before reaching their first birthday and 40 per cent died before their tenth birthday. By 1901 childhood mortality had declined substantially, and during the twentieth century there were further dramatic improvements, especially due to the reduction of infant mortality and particularly after the 1940s. It is also clear that 'crisis' years no longer occur as they did in the nineteenth and early twentieth centuries when mortality was pushed to exceptionally high levels for relatively short periods.

Figure 3.4 helps to emphasise the point that the decline of childhood mortality ($q(0-9)$) had an important bearing on the rise in life expectancy at birth ($e(0)$). It confirms that life expectancy in early nineteenth-century France was about 35 years at birth, that it rose to nearly 50 years before 1914, and that this improvement was accompanied by the fall from 40 to 20 per cent in the contribution of childhood deaths (0–9) to total deaths. It also suggests that France had a rather unusual demographic history during the nineteenth century with only very modest population growth (0.5 per cent per year) in comparison with most European countries, Britain included.

Although the data illustrated in figures 3.2 and 3.3 provide a valuable basis for

Figure 3.4 Timepath for France, 1806–2001, showing the decline of early-age mortality (0–9) and the rise of life expectancy at birth ($e(0)$) plotted on the framework provided by figure 3.1

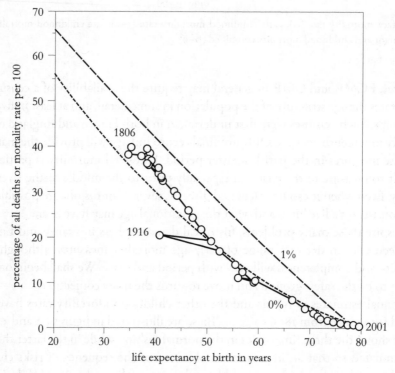

Note: the life expectancy and early-age mortality rate (0–9) series have been smoothed using 5-year moving means, and only index years at 5-year intervals (1806, 1811, 1816 etc.) have been plotted in the timepath.

See the note to figure 3.1 and the text for explanation.

discussion, they need to be complemented by estimates for the earlier centuries when parish registers offer the only source of demographic data. Table 3.1 gives a set of early-age mortality estimates drawn from the best available studies. They take us back to the 1680s and the revocation of the Edict of Nantes by Louis XIV in 1685 which re-confirmed Roman Catholicism as the only acceptable form of worship and gave its priests an important role in policing religious conformity through church attendance and the registration of baptisms, marriages and burials.[78] Between the revocation and the Revolution of 1789 one might expect French parish registers to be of exceptionally high quality, capable of withstanding the most rigorous of statistical analyses. This optimism was certainly important in encouraging pioneers such as Louis Henry to develop nominal record linkage methods suitable for application to historical parish registers.[79] The procedure came to be known as family reconstitution and its application to the listings provided in the registers of rural parishes has proved of remarkable value in the derivation particularly of early-age mortality measures.[80] Let us first take the mortality estimates reported in table 3.1 at their face value, and then consider the various problems that they raise.

Figure 3.5 traces the four mortality rates back into the eighteenth and seventeenth centuries using sources [1] and [2] from table 3.1. It suggests that while $q(5-9)$ remained roughly constant, the other mortality rates were even higher before the nineteenth century. During the late seventeenth and early eighteenth centuries $e(0)$ may have been 25 years; only 45 per cent of live-born infants survived to their tenth birthday; and perhaps 55 per cent of all deaths were those of infants and children. This would place Louis XIV's France at the top left extreme of the general mortality pattern described by figures 3.1 and 3.4. How could such a high level of mortality be sustained in an increasing population of 20 millions? Why did mortality decline? What effects were there on parental attitudes to infants and children? These are obvious questions to ask, but first it is necessary to look a little more closely at the mortality measures themselves.

Although good-quality parish registers do provide material appropriate for nominal record linkage, it is one thing to derive estimates for a single village and quite another to establish credible series for an entire country based on a relatively small sample of locations. Under normal conditions we should certainly expect early-age mortality to be higher in towns, where sanitary conditions were often poor and the childhood diseases endemic. This is suggested in table 3.1 by the differences between Crulai and Meulan, and between France as a whole and the three urban departments in the 1840s. So a rural sample would not necessarily capture the national picture, especially during a phase of urbanisation. Because of their size and the mobility of their populations, towns are notoriously difficult places on which to perform family reconstitution studies, even if the parish registers are of reasonably good quality. But as we have already heard from Philippe Ariès and others in Chapter 2, the practice of putting newly born infants out to be wet-nursed in the countryside was common, although not of course universal, in early modern France. These infants who were *la*

Table 3.1 Selected early-age mortality measures for France

	SBR	$q(0)$	$q(1-4)$	$q(5-9)$	$q(0-9)$	$e(0)$
Rural France [1]						
1690–1719		350	261	63	550	
1720–49		328	277	60	543	
1750–79		263	223	65	464	
France [2]						
1740–49		296	253	107	530	24.8
1750–59		277	239	87	498	27.9
1760–69		281	254	84	509	27.7
1770–79		273	236	83	491	28.9
1780–89		278	239	90	500	27.8
1790–99		254	219	72	459	F 32.1
1800–09		209	178	65	392	F 34.9
1810–19		198	167	59	371	F 37.5
1820–29		181	153	47	339	38.8
Crulai, 1688–1719 [3]		236	105	72	365	30.3
3 villages, 1600s [4]		277	262	89	528	
Meulan [5]						
1668–1739		244	312	92	528	
1740–89		226	269	55	465	
1790–1839		155	192	53	353	
3 villages, 1700–99 [6]		212	180			
17 parishes, 1774–94 [7]		177	201	87	400	
France, 1840s [8]	38	149	130	49	292	42.3
Seine (Paris)		191	221	79	420	31.1
Rhône (Lyon)		195	175	61	377	34.0
Bouche-du-Rhône (Marseilles)		173	230	65	404	32.9

Note: SBR, stillbirth rate per 1000 (stillbirths per 1000 total births (stillbirths plus live births))

Sources:

[1] Jacques Houdaille, 'La mortalité des enfants dans la France rurale de 1690 à 1779', *Population* 39 (1984), pp. 77–106, table 5.

[2] Corrected estimates for France by decades: Jacques Dupâquier *et al.* (eds), *Histoire de la population française: 3, De 1789 à 1914* (Paris: Presses Universitaires de France, 1988), p. 287, table 31, based on Yves Blayo, 'La mortalité en France de 1740 à 1829', *Population* 30 (Numero special) (1975), pp. 123–42, Annex tables 11–16. Estimates are for sexes combined, but *e*(0)s for 1790–1819 are for females only.

[3] Crulai (Orne), Normandy: Etienne Gautier and Louis Henry, *La population de Crulai, paroisse normande. Étude historique*, INED, Travaux et documents, Cahier No. 33 (Paris: Presses Universitaires de France, 1958), pp. 163 and 191.

[4] Three villages, mainly seventeenth century: Coulomiers et Chailly-en-Bière (Seine-et-Marne), 1557–1715; Rosny-sous-Bois (Seine-Saint-Denis), 1640–89; Tourouvre-au-Perche (Orne), 1670–

mise en nourrice (*les nourrissons*) tended to be children of the bourgeoisie who were sent away from the towns. Such a practice, as well as endangering the health and survival chances of the infant, can also lead to important distortions in the registration of baptisms and burials. The number of burials–deaths is inflated in the countryside but reduced in the towns, so that rural mortality appears higher and urban lower than it might otherwise have been without the practice, since 'place of birth' or 'normal place of residence' are not being allowed for. It seems reasonable to speculate that if eighteenth-century France had possessed the most effective modern vital registration system then its infant mortality rate would still have shown a substantial 'wet-nursing penalty', perhaps an additional 50 or even 100 parts per 1000 (around 25 to 50 per cent higher). But even in those cases where *les nourrissons* can be excluded from village studies (source [7] in table 3.1), the infant mortality rate is still rather high compared with France in the 1840s.[81]

The practice of putting infants out to be wet-nursed had social, geographical and demographic dimensions and implications, therefore. Mortality would increase if the practice became more fashionable; urban bourgeois fertility might also increase since the intervals between conceptions would not be extended by maternal breastfeeding; infant mortality in the villages on the outskirts of the large cities, especially Paris and Lyon, would be exacerbated. Although these points are reasonably well documented, it is far more difficult to assess the extent of the practice of wet-nursing. How many infants were affected? One estimate for the late eighteenth century suggests that of those Paris-born infants who died, about 30 per cent died in the countryside round the capital.[82] It has also been estimated that by the 1880s and 1890s around 30 per cent of Paris-born infants were still being placed with wet-nurses.[83] The scale of the practice was obviously substantial, therefore, and had been so for several centuries,

1719: Jacques Dupâquier *et al.* (eds), *Histoire de la population française: 2, De la Renaissance à 1789* (Paris: Presses Universitaires de France, 1988), p. 224, table 6.

[5] Meulan (Yvelines), small town northwest of Paris: Marcel Lachiver, *La population de Meulan du XVIIe au XIXe siècle. Étude de démographie historique* (Paris: SEVPEN, 1969), pp. 199 and 203.

[6] Three villages in the Ile-de-France, 1700–99: Jean Ganiage, *Trois villages d'Ile-de-France au XVIIIe siècle. Étude démographique*, INED, Travaux et documents, Cahier No. 40 (Paris: Presses Universitaires de France, 1963), p. 106.

[7] 17 parishes on the southern outskirts of Paris, 1774–94, excluding *nourrissons*: Paul Galliano, 'La mortalité infantile (indigènes et nourrissons) dans la banlieue sud de Paris à la fin du XVIIIe siècle (1774–1794)', *Annales de Démographie Historique* (1966), pp. 139–77, table 3.

[8] France, 1840s: SBR for 1853: Jacques Dupâquier, 'Pour une histoire de la prématurité', *Annales de Démographie Historique* (1994), pp. 187–202, Table 5; remaining measures for France: see figure 3.2. Jacques Bertillon, 'Mort-né', in *Dictionnaire Encyclopédique des Sciences Médicales, Tome Dixième* (Paris, 1876), pp. 2–28, discusses the problems associated with estimating SBR for France, and other European countries in the nineteenth century. His table VI suggests the following SBRs for France: whole country 43.3, rural areas 37.7, towns 52.2..

Three urban departments of France, 1840s: Samuel H. Preston and Etienne van de Walle, 'Urban French mortality in the nineteenth century', *Population Studies* 32 (1978), pp. 275–97, tables 1 and 5. Two departments (Orne and Sarthe) had *e*(0)s greater than 50 in the 1840s. Estimates for the female population only.

Figure 3.5 Infant and childhood mortality trends for France, 1680s to 1851

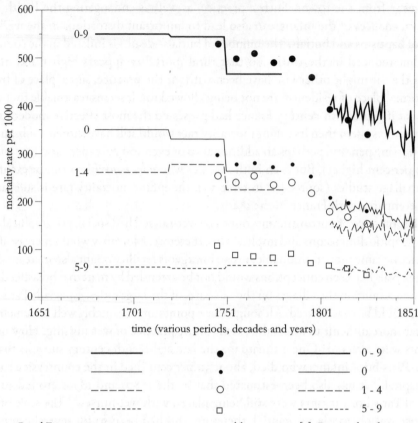

Sources: Rural France, 1680–1719, 1720–49, 1750–79: table 3.1, source [1]; France, decades 1740–49 to 1820–29: table 3.1, source [2]; France, post-1806: figure 3.2.

but it was socially and geographically localised. The establishment of a civil registration system and the division of France into departments allows a reasonably detailed map to be drawn of variations in infant mortality during the early nineteenth century. Figure 3.6 shows IMR ($q(0)$ per 1000) for 1806–10.[84] Mortality is highest in the north, excluding Normandy, and lowest in the south, excluding Provence. In the best conditions infant mortality might be 100 and in the worst 300 per 1000 live births. It is clear that the southwest represented the former and the area to the east of Paris the latter. Unfortunately, it is not possible to draw such maps for earlier periods. But there is some evidence to suggest that the regional patterns illustrated in figure 3.6 had a long history. For the eighteenth century, regional estimates indicate that the southwest had an IMR of 191 whereas the northeast and northwest had rates around 246–249.[85] Clearly, if these estimates are correct there were other practices and patterns of behaviour with a regional, and not just local, dimension that underlay the diversity of survival chances for the newly born.

Apart from the effects of breastfeeding (especially its duration and intensity) and the level of marital fertility (including contraception), factors to which we shall return later, there is one other important influence on early-age mortality that needs to be taken into account. A perfect vital registration system would make and apply a clear definition of 'live birth' based on 'vital signs' (breathing, crying, moving etc.) that it would use to distinguish such births from stillbirths and miscarriages. Only true live births would be registered. Their subsequent experience of life or death could then be traced in the death registration system. However, the Roman Catholic church placed special emphasis on the need for a newborn to be Christened quickly in order to avoid the possibility that an infant might die unbaptised, that is before being admitted to God's church. Such pressure could lead to the baptism of a fetus while still *in utero* or during parturition and thus the Christening of what may have proved to be a stillborn infant. These 'provisional or emergency baptisms', often conducted by the midwife (*les sages-femmes*), the surgeon or physician, appear to have been quite common.[86] They led to the creation of a special category: *les ondoyés décédés* as distinct from *les mort-nés*. The precise extent of this practice of 'provisional baptism' has proved difficult to judge. For example, in the Normandy parish of Crulai ([3] in table 3.1) there were 331 deaths under one year of which 99 infants (30 per cent) died on the same day as either their baptism or their 'provisional baptism.'[87] The consequences of this commitment to early, even premature, baptism are that the number of stillbirths will be reduced while the numbers of live births and infant deaths will be inflated. The net effect will be to raise the apparent level of IMR, but especially that element of infant mortality often labelled endogenous to distinguish it from the exogenous causes of death associated with the infectious diseases of childhood. Endogenous mortality is linked especially to the complications of childbirth as well as congenital malformations. If the practice of 'provisional baptism' were to decline in popularity then infant mortality would fall. Such a fall could be further accentuated if the baptism of live-born infants was conducted with less haste, if days or weeks were allowed to pass and only the survivors were Christened and registered.

Given these problems it is hardly surprising that some specialists have despaired of ever providing 'true' indicators of early-age mortality for France before 1806. Some, Jacques Dupâquier included, prefer to measure mortality in terms of life expectancy at ages 5 or 20 thereby removing the contribution of that illusive infant and early childhood component.[88]

Family reconstitution techniques have also proved especially useful tools when applied to English parish registers. For England, what might be called the 'parish register period' is longer than in France – 1538–1837 rather than 1680s–1806 – so that it has been possible to derive estimates for the key early-age mortality measures spanning at least four centuries by combining the results of parish reconstitutions and those using the full post-1837 civil registration system.[89] We shall look at these results first and then consider the inevitable problems.

Table 3.2 shows some of the early-age mortality estimates that have been derived during the past few years. In terms of the framework provided by figure 3.1, early

Figure 3.6 **Infant mortality variations in France, 1806–10 (q(0) per 1000)**

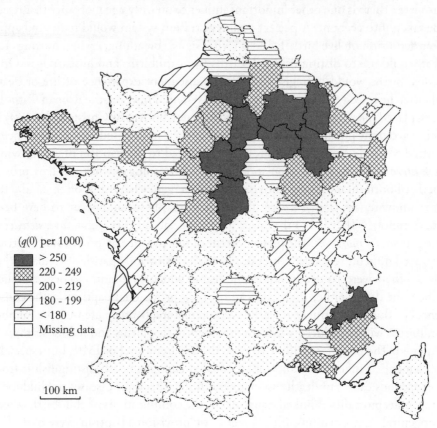

(q(0) per 1000)
- > 250
- 220 - 249
- 200 - 219
- 180 - 199
- < 180
- Missing data

100 km

Source: see note 84.

modern England sits where life expectancy at birth is in the high 30s (35–39 years) and the proportion of all deaths occurring to children is in the upper 20s or low 30s (27–32 per cent), and this was still approximately the case even in the 1840s. While English childhood mortality was certainly not constant over the centuries, it did tend to vary within quite a narrow range and, at least compared with France, the mean level was substantially lower. Figure 3.7 helps to illustrate these points more forcefully. In general, and from the best available estimates, it appears that 20 to 30 per cent of all live-born infants are likely to have died before reaching their first birthday while 30 to 35 per cent would have died before reaching their tenth birthdays, and that these proportions applied in England (and Wales) up to the end of the nineteenth century. In London and the towns in general, the situation was much worse. Infant mortality (q(0) per 1000) only passed into a phase of secular decline during the early years of the twentieth century while for early childhood mortality (q(1–4) per 1000) the origins of secular decline can be dated from the mid-nineteenth century. For the last 150 years early-age mortality levels and trends have been approximately the same in

England and France, but before the 1850s this was certainly not the case.

If this was the average level for mortality, then table 3.2 also gives several examples of extreme conditions. In north Devon, the parish of Hartland appears to have experienced exceptionally low infant mortality during the late sixteenth and early seventeenth centuries. Rates below 100 are certainly unusual in a pre-industrial society, but are they to be trusted? At the other end of the range come the towns and cities. The small Lincolnshire town of Gainsborough suffered much worse. There mortality was perhaps twice the level of Hartland, but in the cities of York and London it was closer to three times as high. It is not difficult to explain the cause of these rural–urban mortality differentials; they are only too evident in the nineteenth century when they can be examined in greater detail. Before the advances in medical science that came during the twentieth century, infants and children living in urban centres were particularly vulnerable to both the common infections of childhood, and the water- and food-borne diseases. Bubonic plague made matters worse in the towns and, occasionally, in the countryside prior to its withdrawal in the late seventeenth century. The aptly named 'urban graveyard effect' was above all the consequence of heightened risk to child survival. Among the London Quakers losses were on a scale equivalent to those in eighteenth-century France; half died before reaching their tenth birthdays, on a par with Victorian Liverpool and Manchester.

The second most important lesson that we learn from table 3.2 is that early-age mortality could vary substantially between disease environments in the past, but especially rural and urban places. This simple fact has an important bearing on the way in which supposedly representative examples are selected, and on the way in which parish studies are combined or pooled in order to capture the broader picture. Reference has already been made in the previous chapter to the widely held belief that childhood mortality must always have been ruinously high in earlier centuries.[90] Table 3.2 offers a forceful counter to this view, but it also helps to chart the history of attempts to measure the average rate of childhood mortality for England. Moving from sources [3] to [2] to [1] takes us from a summary of knowledge available in the 1970s through the 1980s to that provided by the most recent effort at national generalisation: *English Population History from Family Reconstitution, 1580–1837* (1997). The first two sources use the arithmetic means of mortality measures from, respectively, eight and twelve family reconstitution studies. They are close, but not exactly the same. The procedure used to derive the estimates in source [1] is far more sophisticated, however. It involves pooling the data from 26 family reconstitution studies so that the resulting summary measures behave more like a weighted mean than a simple average. The intention is that this will allow for the different population sizes of the selected parishes, thereby replicating more closely different levels of urbanisation within the settlement hierarchy. The resulting estimates have also been checked against equivalent measures from the post-1837 civil registration system (as in figure 3.7) and the findings from an earlier 'back projection' model.[91] One of the problems with the eight- and twelve-parish measures is that they appear to suggest

Table 3.2 Selected early-age mortality measures for England (and Wales)

	SBR	$q(0)$	$q(1-4)$	$q(5-9)$	$q(0-9)$	$e(0)$
England [1]						
1580–99	55	177	85	46	282	38
1600–24	56	171	82	36	266	39
1625–49	58	157	100	48	277	38
1650–74	64	169	111	51	299	37
1675–99	61	189	108	46	310	35
1700–24	57	195	108	46	315	37
1725–49	55	196	121	50	328	37
1750–74	50	170	107	41	289	40
1775–99	50	166	108	35	282	40
1800–24	45	144	98	26	248	40
1825–37	42	152	98	35	263	41
12 English parishes [2]						
1550–99		135	62	30	213	42–48
1600–49		133	85	40	237	41–46
1650–99		142	99	42	260	40–44
1700–49		158	96	41	270	39–43
1750–99		129	87	31	229	42–47
8 English parishes [3]						
1550–99		131	70	30	216	42–48
1600–49		127	90	41	239	41–46
Hartland (Devon)						
1550–99		92	38	22	146	46–54
1600–49		85	49	30	156	46–53
Gainsborough (Lincs.)						
1550–99		166	102	28	272	39–43
1600–49		224	134	65	372	34–35
York [4]						
1561–1720		248	162	89	426	31–32
London [5]						
1580–1650		228	190	82	426	28 31–32
London Bills [6]						
1728–49		277			486	27
1750–74		247			477	27
1775–99		213			472	28
1800–24		184			432	31
London Quakers [7]						
1650–99		260	244	67	478	28–27
1700–49		342	298	95	582	22–19
1750–99		276	253	57	490	27–26
England & Wales, 1840s [8]	40	149	125	47	297	41
Surrey		122	98	48	246	45
London		163	184	50	351	37
Manchester		268	296	74	524	26
Liverpool		253	301	76	518	26

Note: SBR, stillbirth rate (stillbirths per 1000 total births (stillbirths plus live births)); the $e(o)$s shown in italics are estimates derived from the association between $e(o)$ and $q(o-9)$ reported in source [1] (first number of pair), and Princeton Model West (second number). The exception is London Bills [6] which uses Model North. See the note to figure 3.1, p. 34.

Sources:

[1] England, 1580–1837: E. A. Wrigley, R. S. Davies, J. E. Oeppen and R. S. Schofield, *English Population History from Family Reconstitution, 1580–1837* (Cambridge: Cambridge University Press, 1997), table 6.2, p. 219 (for $q(o)$), and table 6.1, p. 215 (estimates for decades are also given in table 6.1), and table 6.21, p. 295. The estimates of SBR in italics are derived from maternal mortality rates, Robert Woods, 'The measurement of historical trends in fetal mortality in England and Wales', *Population Studies* 59 (2005), pp. 147–62, table 1, p. 149.

[2] Twelve English parishes, 1550–1799: E. A. Wrigley and R. S. Schofield, *The Population History of England, 1541–1871: A Reconstruction* (London: Edward Arnold, 1981), table 7.19, p. 249. The means of the twelve parishes are shown.

[3] Eight English parishes, 1550–1649s: Roger Schofield and E. A. Wrigley, 'Infant and child mortality in England in the late Tudor and early Stuart period', in Charles Webster (ed.), *Health, Medicine and Mortality in the Sixteenth Century* (Cambridge: Cambridge University Press, 1979), pp. 61–95, table 5, p. 66. Hartland and Gainsborough are two of the eight parishes representing the lowest and highest levels of mortality, respectively.

[4] York, 1561–1720: derived from data for two parishes, Chris Galley, *The Demography of Early Modern Towns: York in the Sixteenth and Seventeenth Centuries* (Liverpool: Liverpool University Press, 1998), table 4.4, p. 92.

[5] London, 1580–1650: based on the mean of four parishes, Roger Finlay, *The Demography of London, 1580–1650* (Cambridge: Cambridge University Press, 1981), table 5.15, p. 107.

[6] London Bills, 1728–1824: estimated from data provided by the London Bills of Mortality summarised in John Marshall, *Mortality of the Metropolis* (London: Treuttel, Würtz, and Richter, 1832). Here, Princeton Model North has been used to derive $q(o)$ from mortality among those aged 2–4 (i.e. burials aged 2–4 / baptisms – burials aged 0–1 years), and both $q(o-9)$ and $e(o)$ from the percentage of burials aged less than 10 years. Estimates based exclusively on burials aged 0–1 appear to exaggerate the level of infant mortality in the early eighteenth century.

[7] London Quakers, 1650–1799: based on the experience of the Peel and Southwark Quaker Meetings, John Landers, *Death and the Metropolis: Studies in the Demographic History of London, 1670–1830* (Cambridge: Cambridge University Press, 1993), table 4.3, p. 136. See also Robert Woods, 'Urban–rural mortality differentials: an unresolved debate', *Population and Development Review* 29 (2003), pp. 29–46, on the difference between urban and rural mortality levels in the past.

[8] England and Wales, 1840s: English Life Table No. 3 (ELT3) for 1838–54; and for 1841, Surrey (non-metropolitan), London and Liverpool are taken from the Registrar General's *Fifth Annual Report* for 1841, while Manchester comes from the *Seventh Annual Report* for 1843 and 1844. Dr William Farr, Statistical Superintendent at the General Register Office, London, suggested the SBR. See William Farr, *Vital Statistics*, edited by Noel A. Humphreys (London: Sanitary Institute of Great Britain, 1885), p. 107.

rather low levels of early-age mortality that are consistent with $e(o)$s in the low 40s. In the 26-parish exercise the $e(o)$s are in the upper 30s, and childhood mortality is rather higher and perhaps more realistic in consequence.

Of the various ways in which the results of English family reconstitution studies could be distorted, one of the most important stems from the lengthening interval between live birth and baptism. A second relates to the effects of migration, but especially the role of urbanisation when there is a strong rural–urban mortality gradient. The rise of non-conformity and secularisation in general, and thus the

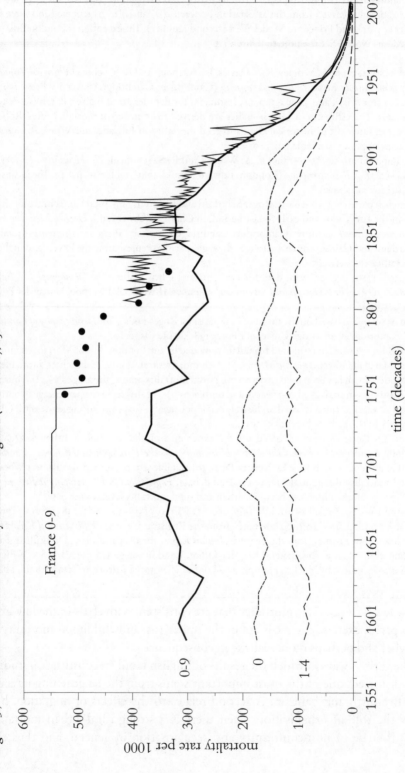

Figure 3.7 **Infant and childhood mortality trends for England (and Wales), 1580s to 2001**

Note: estimates of $q(0-9)$ are also shown for France from figures 3.2 and 3.5.

Source: see table 3.2.

declining influence of the established Church of England, represent a third set of factors which are also likely to have had a deleterious effect on the quality of the ecclesiastical registration system. The combined influence of these three problems will have been to reduce the proportion of live births entering baptism registers; to increase the average age at which an infant is baptised; and to reduce the likelihood that a subsequent registerable event will take place in the same parish as the original baptism. The assumption has been that early-age mortality measures become both less accurate and less representative especially as one moves through the eighteenth and into the nineteenth century. In short, it is important to be cautious about the apparent decline in infant mortality, for example, during the eighteenth century simply because the ecclesiastical registration system was in a state of decline during these years and on into the following century.[92]

Table 3.2 also gives estimates of the stillbirth rate for England during the parish register period, as well as for England and Wales in the mid-nineteenth century. Their derivation raises several new issues concerning the pattern of mortality in the early modern period. One of these relates to maternal mortality and, since in this case the stillbirth rate (SBR) has been derived from the maternal mortality rate (MMR), we shall consider, first, those special risks faced by women during pregnancy, at and immediately after childbirth, before looking at fetal mortality itself. Roger Schofield's classic study 'Did the mothers really die?' addresses all of the relevant problems and produces estimates that are still credible.[93] Some of his findings, together with more recent revisions, are displayed in table 3.3 and illustrated by figure 3.8. During the second half of the seventeenth century when maternal mortality is believed to have been at its highest, the risk of death associated with any one pregnancy is likely to have been between 0.0170 and 0.0242. If the average woman had six or seven pregnancies, the cumulative risk is likely to have been from 10 to 17 per cent. But these were the worst years. The more likely level of additional risk to a woman through her reproductive career was 5 to 6 per cent. Schofield has also attempted an ingenious calculation of heightened risk according to maternal age. Here he suggests that for women aged 25–34 perhaps 20 per cent of deaths may have been associated with a pregnancy. This is a substantial figure that it is plausible to speculate must have had a bearing on the collective psyche; if not fear, then at least a heightened state of apprehension will have been palpable.[94]

Schofield was able to judge the level of stillbirth mortality by using family reconstitution data for five parishes in southern Sweden during the late eighteenth and early nineteenth centuries, and by assuming that the English and Swedish historical mortality regimes were sufficiently close that knowledge of one might reasonably be substituted for ignorance of the other. These Swedish data indicate a stillbirth rate of 33 per 1000 birth events (live births plus stillbirths) with a range of 26 to 44. This method provided Schofield with the adjustment factors necessary to correct the estimates of maternal mortality based solely on deaths of mothers of live-born infants (shown as [4] in table 3.3), but they also encourage further speculation about

Table 3.3 Maternal mortality rates for England (and Wales)

	MMR France [1]	MMR England 'best estimate' [2]	MMR England 'maximal' [3]		MMR England (and Wales) [4]	0–6 days mortality rate [5]	Endogenous mortality rate [6]
1550–99		93	141				
				1580–99	123	64	78
1600–49		116	178	1600–24	128	75	89
				1625–49	140	69	80
1650–99		157	242	1650–74	170	76	87
				1675–99	156	78	88
1700–49	120	113	173	1700–24	134	65	84
				1725–49	123	63	81
1750–99	105	77	115	1750–74	95	50	61
				1775–99	90	47	53
1800–49	98	55	82	1800–24	63	34	41
				1825–37	47	23	33
				1850–74	49		24
				1875–99	48		22
				1900–24	40		23
				1925–49	31		22
				1950–74	4		13

Note: the maternal mortality rate (MMR) is given in parts per 10,000 birth events or births. It relates to those deaths occurring to pregnant females which are either directly connected with that pregnancy or occur within 60 days of childbirth and are the consequence of recently having given birth. The mortality rate for the first 0–6 days after live birth and the endogenous mortality rate (last two columns) are in parts per 1000.

Sources:

[1] Hector Gutierrez and Jacques Houdaille, 'La mortalité maternelle en France au XVIIIe siècle', *Population* 38 (1983), pp. 974–94, table 1, p. 978. These estimates apply to the following periods: 1700–49, 1750–89, 1790–1829. They have been revised by Schofield to make them directly comparable with his estimates; see [2], note 45, p. 250. The original MMRs were: 129, 111, 105. See also Alain Bideau, 'Accouchement 'naturel' et accouchement à 'haut risqué', *Annales de Démographie Historique* (1981), pp. 49–66.

[2] Roger Schofield, 'Did the mothers really die? Three centuries of maternal mortality in "The World We Have Lost"', in Lloyd Bonfield, Richard M. Smith and Keith Wrightson (eds), *The World We Have Gained: Histories of Population and Social Structure* (Oxford: Basil Blackwell, 1986), pp. 231–60, table 9.5, p. 248, based on 13 English parishes.

[3] As for [2]. 'Maximal' is Schofield's highest MMR series.

[4] England, 1580–1837: E. A. Wrigley, R. S. Davies, J. E. Oeppen and R. S. Schofield, *English Population History from Family Reconstitution, 1580–1837* (Cambridge: Cambridge University Press, 1997), table 6.29, column (3), p. 313. The MMR has been corrected to allow for background mortality, for stillbirth and no birth. It is expressed in parts per 10,000 birth events. England and Wales, post-1850: Irvine Loudon, *Death in Childbirth: An International Study of Maternal Care and Maternal Mortality,*

late-fetal mortality during the parish register period. One series of estimates is given in table 3.2 (SBR) and illustrated in figure 3.8.[95] These particular estimates are based on the maternal mortality rate (series [4] in table 3.3) and the assumption that the association between SBR and MMR that applied among the local administrative areas in England and Wales in 1931 also held in earlier decades and centuries. Like Schofield's point about equivalence between the mortality regimes of Sweden and England, this assumption is a large and rather critical one. Figure 3.8 shows that the registration of stillbirths was not begun in England and Wales until 1927, but it also suggests that the stillbirth rate may have changed very little during the nineteenth century, that it only began a significant secular decline in the late 1930s, and that this was also the time that maternal mortality began its own sharp fall. In other words, for the first ten years of registration the stillbirth rate appears to have been on a high plateau that stretched back into the more distant past. However, we must also accept that the 'plateau' might need to be raised or lowered depending on which series for maternal mortality proves to be the most reliable (between [2] and [3] in table 3.3, for example). It must also be acknowledged that there will appear to be some circularity of argument here. Maternal mortality estimates require knowledge of stillbirths, but SBR is being derived from MMR. Despite this problem, it still seems reasonable to conclude that from 4 to 6 per cent of fetuses that had survived to 28 weeks gestation were born dead or died with their mothers. Reading from left to right along the rows in table 3.2, this would indicate that in the late seventeenth and early eighteenth centuries when early-age mortality was at its worst in England, about 6 per cent might died in the late-fetal stage of development, a further 19 per cent in infancy; 11 per cent in early childhood and 5 per cent in later childhood. Each of these percentages would have been lower before 1650 and after 1750, but they would not have been very substantially lower until the twentieth century, and especially after 1950.

Although we started this discussion of mortality patterns and trends by looking at France in the nineteenth and twentieth centuries, as we moved back to the parish register period it became obvious that England, rather than France, offered better prospects for reconstructing both longer-run series of early-age mortality measures, and a more detailed picture. For example, revised estimates of the maternal mortality rate for France are given in table 3.3 and illustrated in figure 3.8, and certainly they correspond well with what is believed to be the experience of mothers in England. However, it has not proved possible to judge the level of stillbirth mortality in France, mainly because of the problems mentioned above.[96] It is possible to make a fuller

1800–1950 (Oxford: Clarendon Press, 1992), Appendix 6, table 1, pp. 542–45, based on Registrar General's *Annual Reports* and *Annual Statistical Reviews*.

[5] Wrigley *et al.*, *English Population History* (1997), table 6.5, p. 236.

[6] As for [5]. England and Wales, post-1850: Chris Galley, Naomi Williams and Robert Woods, 'Detection without correction: problems in assessing the quality of English ecclesiastical and civil registration', *Annales de Démographie Historique* (1995), pp. 161–83, table 7, p. 175.

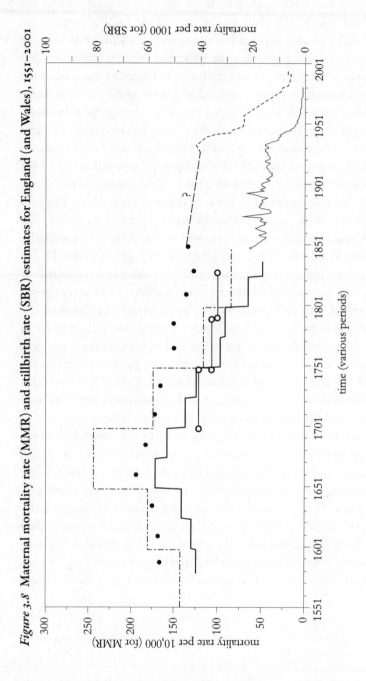

Figure 3.8 Maternal mortality rate (MMR) and stillbirth rate (SBR) estimates for England (and Wales), 1551–2001

Legend:
- – – – MMR England 'maximal' [3]
- ——— MMR England and Wales, 1847- [4]
- • SBR England (table 3.2 [1])
- ——— MMR England [2]
- —o— MMR France [1]
- – – – – SBR England and Wales, 1927- [4]

Note: MMR estimates are also shown for France. MMR is expressed per 10,000 birth events or births (left axis) while SBR is given per 1000 total births (live births plus stillbirths) (right axis).

Sources: see table 3.3; sources [1], [2], [3] and [4].

comparison of England with some other northern European countries – especially Norway, Denmark, and, as we have already seen, Sweden – although it is not possible to do this for periods before the mid-eighteenth century. Figure 3.9 uses the infant mortality rate (IMR, $q(0)$ per 1000 live births) and the stillbirth rate (SBR per 1000 total births, live and stillborn) to chart temporal and geographical variations. The two timepaths (lines linking observations for specific points in time) for England and Sweden are intended to show how SBR and IMR changed over time. In the case of Sweden post-1750, there was very little change in the stillbirth rate yet infant mortality fell almost continuously. For England between the 1580s and the 1850s, SBR did alter somewhat as did IMR, but the range of movement was quite confined. The evidence for Norway and Denmark in the nineteenth century also helps to support the argument that England, and northern Europe in general, did tend to have similar mortality regimes. The two remaining examples, international variations in the 1920s and 1930s, and less developed countries in more recent decades, also help to encourage the belief that late-fetal mortality was far less variable than infant mortality, and to set the upper limits on what rates might be credible for a high mortality society either in the past or today. It is also obvious that seventeenth- and eighteenth-century France ([1] and [2] in table 3.1 at least) would fall beyond the range with IMRs in excess of 250.

These observations about very early-age mortality and maternal mortality, but especially the contrasts between France and England, lead us naturally enough to a consideration of fertility within marriage. Not surprisingly, this is the point at which Philippe Ariès also began his demographic studies in the 1940s.[97] The issues are these. There appears to have been a particularly high rate of marital fertility in France during the seventeenth and early eighteenth centuries. This is consistent with short birth intervals that are likely to have resulted when a significant proportion of mothers did not breastfeed their own infants but put them out to be wet-nursed. During the second part of the eighteenth century, and certainly before the French Revolution, there are indications that marital fertility started to decline, suggesting that it might have been reduced deliberately by couples adopting some form or forms of contraception, and encouraging the speculation that such practices coincided with new attitudes and sentiments within marriage favouring the health and well-being of mothers and their children, along with the secularisation of society in general (see figure 2.2, p. 30). A substantial decline in marital fertility would also have encouraged a reduction in infant mortality, and vice-versa. It has also been proposed that France may have been alone in experiencing such a collection of changes during the eighteenth century or, rather, that a section of its population employed particular forms of birth control in order to solve a problem caused by repeated pregnancies and that these practices only became common among the European population in general during the late nineteenth century. France and England had different fertility regimes in the late eighteenth century, therefore, just as they appear to have experienced different levels of infant mortality. Ariès argued that the practice of contraception could be

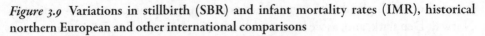

Figure 3.9 **Variations in stillbirth (SBR) and infant mortality rates (IMR), historical northern European and other international comparisons**

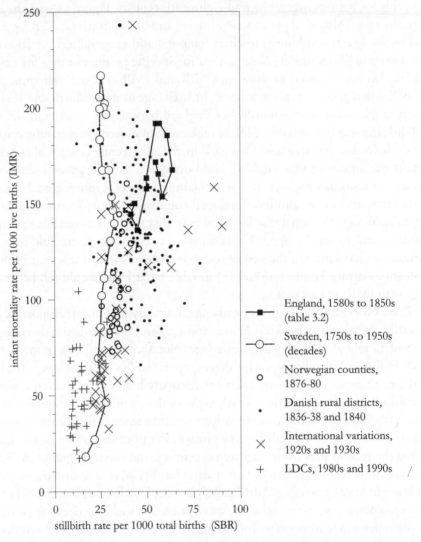

Note: the timepath for England moves from right to left, and that for Sweden from top to bottom. The less developed countries (LDCs) are drawn from Africa, Asia and Latin America where there has been a recent Demographic and Health Survey (DHS).

Source: based on figure 8 in Robert Woods, 'The measurement of historical trends in fetal mortality in England and Wales', *Population Studies* 59 (2005), p. 159.

taken as an indicator of a caring relationship within marriage and sought evidence for its existence in literature, diaries, memoirs etc. This search still continues and has had some success.[98] However, the demographic evidence provided by age- and duration-specific marital fertility rates derived from local family reconstitution studies tells a rather confused story about the extent of fertility decline prior to the Revolution and thus the likelihood that contraceptive practices were in any sense general and widespread. For example, there appear to have been marked inter-regional and urban–rural differences in the level and timing of fertility decline during the eighteenth century. While the region southeast of Paris had early and rapid decline, other districts in the west and south were far slower. In broad terms, the urban centres seem to have been more precipitant than the rural. Two additional considerations make the matter even more complicated. First, France did join with other European populations in the late nineteenth-century fertility decline, although it started from a lower average level. Secondly, although it is clear that there was fertility decline in parts of France before 1789, it cannot be demonstrated that this was the direct consequence of the general use of contraceptives among the populations affected. Rather, it appears that in terms of Louis Henry's concept of 'natural fertility' France merely achieved a lower level of natural fertility by the end of the eighteenth century and that fertility was not being deliberately regulated within marriage in such a way that some pre-determined ideal family size would be achieved. In other words, birth control practices were not being used in a way that depended on the number of live births a woman had already had. Marital fertility could fall because the intervals between births were lengthened and this would happen if more women breastfed their own infants and did so for longer: nine, twelve, eighteen months. If this interpretation of the available demographic material is correct, then it seems most likely that fertility decline in eighteenth-century France was more to do with childcare than contraception.[99]

Childcare in France and England

This too is an immense topic with which we shall be highly selective in our treatment. Ideally, we should like to know the following.[100] How did midwives operate and how successful were they in terms of delivery and survival? What were the common conventions and practices of childrearing? What proportion of mothers breastfed their own infants and for how long? How were young children socialised by their parents in terms of learning to walk and talk, being toilet trained and encouraged to play etc.? How did parents respond to childhood illnesses, to accidents in and outside the home? In considering these questions it is especially important to separate advice from actual behaviour, and to distinguish the particular instance from the general situation. Our concern here is with common patterns of behaviour, just as it has been with trends in average risk of dying or surviving.[101]

There is now some degree of consensus about these matters based largely on a very substantial amount of evidence drawn from individual cases. Care for the fetus, the infant and the young child can be distinguished.[102]

Most women who were pregnant were not 'with child' for the first time; they knew what to expect. For the first-timers there was advice from mothers, neighbours and peers. Certainly women knew from when they 'quickened' that they were pregnant and there was some general appreciation of what was necessary for conception to take place, but the complexities of human reproductive biology were not understood until the twentieth century. The possibility of miscarriage, that a fetus might be born dead and of the additional risks to multiple conceptions, were certainly recognised, but not in any precise way. As the pregnancy progressed, arrangements would be made for the time of labour. The local midwife was engaged or, in higher social circles, the physician was appointed. Of course, midwives and physicians varied in their knowledge, experience and practical skills, yet before the more widespread availability of forceps in the eighteenth century and effective Caesarean sections under anaesthetic in the nineteenth, it is difficult to see how the role of a birth attendant, male or female, learned or just experienced, could have been very much more than one of support and encouragement. The health of the fetus and that of the pregnant woman were largely beyond the beneficial influence of health professionals until the 1940s and 1950s. The health of mother and fetus could be adversely affected by poor nutrition, alcohol consumption, repeated pregnancy, poor maternal physiology (the effects of rickets or tuberculosis, for example), infectious diseases such as smallpox and rubella, and sexually transmitted infections. Variations in fetal and maternal mortality before the twentieth century are more likely to have been due to some combination of epidemiological and economic factors than the benefits of medical knowledge or even individual behaviour.[103]

Once a live birth had taken place, and assuming that it was not unduly premature, then there were various ways in which mother, relatives and society could influence health and ultimately survival chances during the first year. The most obvious of these relates to infant feeding practices. At the extremes, one could attempt to feed an infant on cow or goat milk with some solids and water right from the start. This would involve high risk to survival, but it was the convention in several parts of Europe not to breastfeed. At the other extreme, a mother could breastfeed her own infant without recourse to supplements well beyond the normal age at dentition, up to eighteen months perhaps. This behaviour is likely to have resulted in the lowest infant mortality, other factors considered, and to help to extend birth intervals. The duration of breastfeeding could be reduced to nine months perhaps and the introduction to the infant diet of solid foods would also be possible, so potentially affecting survival chances, but not necessarily too adversely. An intermediate possibility might involve the employment of a wet-nurse to care for the infant. There is no real reason why this should automatically adversely affect survival chances so long as the nurse is healthy, competent and resident in the parental home. But as we have already noted, wet-nurses usually cared for their charges in their own establishment and in ways that were unregulated and unobserved by parents. The use of wet-nurses was a common practice in France, although far from universal, and far more unusual in England where maternal breastfeeding was the norm.[104]

As well as being fed, infants needed to be cared for in several other ways. The practice of swaddling the newborn was intended to protect fragile limbs and to replicate the tightly confined environment of the womb. It became unfashionable as it was appreciated that the growing body needed room to stretch and exercise. Infants also need to be kept clean and warm, away from danger, and to be stimulated by close contact with other human beings. All of these are challenging for the modern parent, but in the past they were especially so. Exposure to infections and to accidents posed the most important problems that could not always be guarded against or coped with. However, there were aspects of child rearing in which there appear to have been deliberate choices to treat certain children differently. Perhaps the best example of this is the way in which boys and girls were cared for and socialised, but especially what expectations there were for their subsequent careers. Boys were to become leaders, workers, husbands, fathers, heads of households while girls might be expected to take on subservient roles as servants, wives, mothers, carers. Of course these are stereotypical roles which did not always apply, but they would have conditioned the ways in which childrearing was managed. How children were dressed, the games they played, their formal and informal education, all of these were gendered. But is it also the case that there was a significant gender divide in terms of material care and emotional support? Were boys better fed, breastfed longer for instance? Were girls taught to be modest, to stand back, be quiet and humble? Certainly boys were more likely to be sent to school and a substantial discrepancy existed in both England and France between literacy rates, signified by the ability to sign a marriage register, up until the end of the nineteenth century. However, while the traditional assumptions about gendered roles are obvious and persistent, it is far more difficult to establish credible and substantial evidence on material care. The sex ratio at birth in western Europe in the past was sufficiently close to the biologically determined norm for systematic social interference to have been unlikely; girls were not deliberately neglected and ill-treated merely because they were female. The evidence of age- and sex-specific survival rates would also support this conclusion; male mortality was higher at nearly every age apart from the late teens and twenties when women were exposed to the additional hazards of reproduction. Whether the emotional attachment of parents differed between boys and girls remains the open question.[105]

Mourning practices

Despite what appear to have been parents' best efforts, miscarriages, stillbirths, infant and child deaths did occur in large numbers and at high rates; how did they react, what in particular were the social conventions that conditioned their behaviour? What did the church permit and local custom encourage? These are large and difficult questions that, as we have already seen in Chapter 2 and as far as mourning for and by adults is concerned, have already been considered by many scholars, Ariès and Vovelle included. Again, our problem is that we wish to focus on the generality of experience rather than the individual instance that may turn out to have been an extreme event, an outpouring of exceptionally intensely felt emotions. How might we characterise normal behaviour in these matters?

Ralph Houlbrooke has summarised what may be taken as the consensus in relation to early modern England. This will provide a convenient starting point, although its concern is principally with grief rather than mourning.

> Children's deaths were, after those of marriage partners, the ones that left the deepest imprint on diaries and letters. However, reactions varied, above all according to the child's age and the strength of the previous relationship between parent and child. The numbers of survivors, and the chances of begetting more children also influenced parental feelings. In some cases the child's sex was important, especially in the upper classes, where the desire to leave at least one son to continue the name and line was especially strong. It was well known that the deaths of infants and young children made up a high proportion of all mortality, but this did not make bereavement any less painful to an individual parent. Children's deaths were always felt to be premature. Running through many expressions of grief at their loss is the sense of promise cut off.

> Writers said little of stillbirths or the deaths of newly born children.

> The growth of attachment, together with children's acquisition of skills and distinctive individual personalities, sharpened grief.

> Deaths in later childhood were far less frequent than in infancy and early childhood, and often harder to bear.

> The deaths of adolescents and young adults, especially those who were their parents' confidants, or prospective successors to their social roles, were very deeply felt.

> The loss of more than one child in quick succession (which often happened during epidemics) was especially hard to bear.

> The sharing of grief with a spouse equally affected by bereavement was a mitigating circumstance for parents who suffered the loss of children.[106]

The impression given by these statements must be that while expressions of grief can be detected, there were no special mourning rituals associated with the deaths of infants and children; indeed the public display via funerals and subsequent commemoration may have been rather muted at this time. Certainly, baptised infants were accorded Christian burial in consecrated ground outside the church or in family vaults within, but before the nineteenth century these were most likely to have been simple affairs in which only close relatives would participate.[107]

A particular question remains over the treatment of the stillborn and those infants who, although born alive, died without being baptised. Conventional wisdom has it that only those admitted to the church via the Christening ceremony (involving naming and the appointment of Godparents) could subsequently be buried in consecrated ground. But we have also noted that in both Protestant northern and Catholic southern Europe a midwife or other birth attendant could baptise an infant, and that an unborn fetus could be so treated if necessity demanded. What remain unclear are how the deaths of the newly born (live and still) were mourned, and what funeral and burial practices were adopted. It seems that midwives were usually left to dispose of stillborn fetuses and this they are likely to have done discreetly, but without ceremony. When the mother also died in childbirth, then the fetus could be buried with her. As far as the unbaptised are concerned, in England it became more and more common for such infants to be buried in the churchyard alongside the baptised and thus for the traditional discrimination against chrisom infants to be relaxed or abandoned entirely.[108] If it is generally believed that the newly born arrive in this world innocent of sin then it follows that even if death occurs before baptism then admission to heaven will be guaranteed; but if the notion of original sin is accepted then baptism is required and even then the newly dead may pass to heaven or hell or purgatory from which their souls may be saved for heaven by the intercession of the living, especially parents. The post-Reformation rejection by Protestants of both original sin and purgatory (a kind of intermediate holding area from which salvation was still possible) was especially important in establishing new principles of faith as well as different practices in relation to baptism and burial. It also conditioned the public expression of mourning.[109]

These distinctions are far too simple, of course. Among the New England Puritans there was a deep concern for sin and death, for doing God's will and following His laws. As far as children were concerned, the phrase 'innocent vipers' has been used to describe infants of the time. This paradoxical attitude appears to stem from the notion that 'to the Puritan the child was more than a loved one extremely vulnerable to the ravages of the environment; he was also a loved one polluted with sin and natural depravity'. This could involve original as well as acquired sin, the presence of which would encourage parents to maintain a 'due emotional distance' between themselves and their offspring; partly a response to such ungodly pollution and partly an insulation against the prospect of a child's early death.[110] The case of the Puritan child helps to highlight the ambiguous nature of the relationship between parents and children: a mixture of love and fear, affection and concern. In New England these intense personal religious feelings were manifest at the community level, a situation that cannot be anticipated in England or France.

* * *

I became interested in demographic phenomena not so much for the phenomena per se, nor for the science they inspired, nor for their political, economic, and social effects, but as signs. For they are the invisible signs of what has been happening below the surface and reveal collective attitudes toward life and death, at times almost subconscious and usually kept hidden. Birth and fertility rates are among the most meaningful of such signs. What do they reveal?[111]

Philippe Ariès made these remarks in 1980, towards the end of his career. He related them to trends in fertility, but it may be equally as appropriate to think in terms of mortality and the signs that such demographic series reveal about collective attitudes.

In this chapter we have been at pains to describe the course of infant and childhood mortality in England and France as they appear after scientific analyses of the available vital statistics. We have considered maternal and late-fetal mortality series, but these required even more sophisticated demographic conjuring tricks before they could be illustrated. And we have reviewed, albeit in a rather cursory manner, some issues of childrearing and what might be general forms of mourning practices specific to the deaths of children particularly in the early modern period. The mortality series summarised here can also be used to represent what Michel Vovelle has called *la mort subie* (see table 2.3, p. 25), that is, suffered, biological death; the generalised experience of an entire population or, before the nineteenth century, at least a substantial minority of the total population. Comparison of *les courbes démographiques* with our notes on childcare and mourning (*la mort vécue*) seems to suggest that, as many commentators have concluded, there was in the past, and perhaps still is, some connection between the risk of premature death and the responses as manifested in the behaviour of individuals (parents, families, siblings) and the practices condoned by the dominant cultural norms of the period.[112] Ariès's hypothesis of demographically conditioned parental indifference is simply an extreme form of such an argument. But to take the comparison further it must be acknowledged that dominant childcare practices, especially with respect to infant feeding, are bound to have an important bearing on survival chances and that mourning rituals for the dead fetus, infant or young child appear not only to have been very simple and rarely articulated, but also to offer thereby a rather inadequate device by which to analyse the emotional reactions of parents to the deaths of children. To put these points more bluntly: indifference is too strong a word to be applied in this context, and collective mourning rituals are poor expressions of the grief felt by individuals.[113]

The quantitative data presented in this chapter offer the best available evidence on the risk of dying at an early age, among mothers and the unborn. They provide our mortality series, the conditioning variable in the terms of Ariès's hypothesis (and a signifier of collective attitudes), and the base in Vovelle's three-levels model. Their appearance in the form of graphs and tables should not encourage their acceptance at face value, but they do offer a general view of average risk, the ways it changed and varied by period, place and age-group. We now need to explore other ways in which adults could express their feelings about children in general and their own offspring in particular. In Chapter 4 we consider children in portraits, on their own and in family groups, and in the three chapters that follow we turn to the feelings of grief etc. contained in English poetry. In numbers, pictures and words we shall have parallel histories of children's experiences and adults' responses.

4

Children in Pictures and Monuments

Pictures, especially paintings and even some photographs, have proved a tantalising source of evidence for historians. Their attraction is obvious; they appear to give an immediate visualisation of what it was like in the past, how our ancestors looked, how they lived, significant events, their environment, and so forth. But several generations of art historians have also counselled caution, advice that has generally been taken seriously by other specialists to the extent that some would not now regard visual images as offering suitable materials for historical analysis. This chapter takes the advice offered by Francis Haskell, however, and adopts the middle ground between uncritical over-optimism (paintings as documents) and the belief that only text documents will do (art is for the tourists). 'What we choose to call art is indeed best interpreted by the historian when it is studied in conjunction with other available testimony, but it does have a "language" of its own which can be understood only by those who seek to fathom its varying purposes, conventions, styles and techniques.'[114] The business of fathoming needs to be taken very seriously, therefore, but it is also best taken with a considerable amount of imagination and not a little speculation. Here we shall consider 20 paintings, mostly of children, sometimes of family groups or a single parent and child, executed between the 1520s and 1901 by Europeans or Americans. Although each will be considered in its own right, the principal objective will be to link them into a series so that some meaningful observations can be made concerning the ways in which the language of representation changed, and thereby the purpose intended for the image by contemporaries. Although the analysis will focus on the images selected for display in this hypothetical gallery, other paintings, monuments and pictures will also be referred to in passing. In general, original photographic images will not be considered since they are only available for the last 150 years or so and the series will not be extended into the twentieth century when film, television and video transformed our visual culture.

Historians, pictures and the deceased

Andor Pigler's great survey 'Portraying the dead' sets out to catalogue the various approaches to memorialising the dead adopted by European artists in past centuries.[115] Focusing specifically on funeral paintings, rather than funeral monuments in general, he outlines the following arguments. First, the rise to popularity of funeral paintings can be dated from the second half of the fifteenth century and their fall from favour occurred by the middle of the nineteenth century. Secondly, there are three features characteristic of this type of mortuary representation: 'the desire to proclaim the eternal idea of the vanity and transience of human existence, by representing the end of the individual's earthly life', and to create 'a realistic representation of the optical sensation' which might at some future date be used as a model for a funeral monument; but every portrait also 'expresses with greater or less clarity the ineradicable desire of the living to retain contact with those members of the community who had changed their essence and become unapproachable'.[116] Thirdly, although the number of examples is relatively small there seems to be no strong evidence to regard funeral portraits as principally a Protestant form; since there are sufficient examples from Catholic Europe, they are 'above denominational limits'. Fourthly, in the case of the seventeenth-century Netherlands, 'funeral portraits of dead children were by no means a rarity, though very few have come down to us, owing to the indifference and natural repugnance felt by succeeding centuries'.[117] Pigler's survey provides an invaluable marker in terms of geography and history. From it we may appreciate the extent of funeral portraiture in space and time – western Europe in the sixteenth, seventeenth and eighteenth centuries – as well as the subject matter – members of royal families, the aristocracy, the higher clergy, but also some other adults and children. We may also list the key motifs: eyes closed and downcast, calm facial expression, hands clasped if the picture is half- or full-length, flowers, candles, crosses and death's heads. But the survey also establishes that there were too few funeral portraits of children, or too few have survived, to permit the construction of a series of images from which some interpretation of changing attitudes might be attempted. In this sense the funeral portraits could have been regarded as part of what Michel Vovelle called *les discours sur la mort*, which included both literary and media discourses, but we shall be obliged to consider the presence of children rather than their absence, the living rather than the dead.

It has also been noted in Chapter 2 that although Philippe Ariès was especially interested in using the evidence of paintings and monuments in his history of death, he did not explore these materials for children. His arguments in *Images of Man and Death* (1985) were based almost entirely on the attitudes of adults to the deaths of other adults.[118] However, the first edition of *L'enfant et la vie familiale sous l'Ancien Régime* (1960) was illustrated by 26 black and white photographs of paintings, mostly family groups, children or young persons at school or work, as well as some etchings and illuminated manuscripts dating from the medieval period to the seventeenth century. Although Ariès was not systematic in his analysis of these images, they did form an integral part of his original study and they were discussed at some length, especially in his chapter on 'Les images de la famille'.[119] For example, Ariès reproduced the following paintings, among others: *Virgin and child with the family of Burgomaster Meyer*, 1528 (Hans Holbein, 1497–1543); *The van Berghem family*, 1561

(Frans Floris, c.1516–70); *Portrait of Antonius Anselmus, his wife and their children*, 1577 (Martin de Vos, c.1532–1600); *The young card players*, 1630s (Antoine Le Nain, c.1600–48); *The feast of St Nicholas*, 1663–65 (Jan Steen, c.1625–79); *The children of Henri-Louis Habert de Montmors*, 1660s (Philippe de Champaigne, 1602–74); *The family of Louis XIV*, 1670 (Jean Nocret, 1617–72). These he used to illustrate several significant points: the importance of recording age, even in paintings (de Vos); the representation of children with their parents (especially Floris and de Vos, all but Le Nain); how the dress of young children, particularly boys, changed with their age (de Vos and de Champaigne); the involvement of children in games (card playing, Le Nain) and seasonal festivities (Christmas, Steen); the gathering together of the family group round a table to eat or make music (Floris); the family united in devotion (Holbein); and the inclusion, as though still living, of dead children or adults (Holbein and Nocret).[120]

'Les images de la famille' became 'Pictures of the family' in *Centuries of Childhood* and it is to this chapter that we must turn for a fuller account of Ariès's general argument that iconography enables us to trace the emergence of the concept of the conjugal family from silence in the medieval period, 'when the feelings of artists and poets were insufficiently awakened', to its manifestation in the seventeenth century.

> The concept of the family, which thus emerges in the sixteenth and seventeenth centuries, is inseparable from the concept of childhood. The interest taken in childhood, is only one form, one particular expression of this more general concept – that of the family. An analysis of iconography leads us to conclude that the concept of the family was unknown in the Middle Ages, that it originated in the fifteenth and sixteenth centuries, and that it reached its full expression in the seventeenth century.[121]

This hypothesis is critical to the case: the concepts of childhood and the conjugal family are inextricably linked, they only rise to prominence during the sixteenth century, and pictures reflect their importance. Ariès highlights several examples of the ways in which a new iconography emerged. The family came to be depicted in its own private, interior homescape, devoid of devotional display and religious symbolism. Even weddings and Christenings were shown as popular, celebratory occasions in which the social far outweighed the ecclesiastical. Childbirth and deathbed scenes also emerged as popular themes. All the conjugal family members, both alive and recently deceased, became involved in the group picture which by the seventeenth century, and especially in the hands of Dutch artists, had turned into a subject painting; the concert after the family meal, for example.

> Henceforth, the family was depicted as in a snapshot, at a moment in its everyday life: the men gathered round the fire, the women taking a cauldron off the fire, a girl feeding her little brothers. Henceforth, it is difficult to tell a family portrait from a subject painting depicting family life.[122]

It will not come as a surprise to find that most aspects of Ariès's argument have been the subject of close critical scrutiny. However, it is to Ariès's lasting credit that many of the challengers have also begun by assuming that the analysis of iconography is a valid way to explore attitudes to the family, to childhood and children in the past. Their scepticism has focused on three particular issues: whether the Middle Ages were different; what significance the new representations of family groups actually had for the concept of childhood and the treatment of children; and whether 'full expression' was indeed achieved in the seventeenth century.[123]

We can dispense with the first issue quite quickly. In the 1970s Ilene H. Forsyth demonstrated convincingly by using art from the ninth to the twelfth century that 'children do appear in early medieval art and that their portrayal there, which is often handled with wit and understanding of a dramatic, even poignant sort, reflects a particular awareness of this phase of life and a keen rapport with its special quali-ties'.[124] This opposite thesis has also been echoed in the splendidly illustrated *Medieval Children* (2001) where Nicholas Orme surveys recent interpretations of childhood, especially in English society.

> So it cannot be over-emphasised that there is nothing to be said for Ariès's view
> of childhood in the middle ages, nor indeed of a major shift in its history during
> the sixteenth and seventeenth centuries, as opposed to changes of detail. The main
> difference, as one proceeds through the centuries, is the survival of evidence.[125]

Let us proceed directly to the third issue: whether the iconography of the seven-teenth century did indeed reflect the full expression of the concept of the conjugal family and thus of childhood. James Christen Steward's extensive exhibition catalogue and historical commentary *The New Child: British Art and the Origins of Modern Childhood, 1730–1830* (1995) clearly offers a different perspective, one that focuses on the eighteenth century, and especially the 1760s, as an artistic turning-point. When Steward looks back at pre-1730 paintings he sees the following:

> From the early Renaissance we have examples of children in portraiture, although
> these are almost exclusively dynastic portraits in which the children represented
> are heirs to wealth and power, and in which the children are usually seen with one
> or both parents. The children serve as reminders of the parents', particularly the
> father's, successful insurance of the family line and title, especially in countries such
> as England where laws of primogeniture dominated. Further, the figures of children
> in these portraits generally lack psychological and narrative interest, a narrative that
> is possible in multi-figure groups but denied in this format by the lack of interac-
> tion between figures. The artists choose, if anything, to capture the appearance of
> the sitters, the richness of clothing, accoutrement, and setting, rather than their
> character. The children are rigid and immobile, scarcely individuated in their physi-
> ognomies from each other or from their parents.[126]

But among eighteenth-century artists, particularly Gainsborough, Morland and Reynolds, Steward identifies many new themes. There is a distinctive 'childlike' nature given to children, also a sense of spontaneity and freedom; 'the child in the family group shifts from periphery to central position suggesting an inherently greater narrative importance'; the child in art begins to have an emblematic value (playing cards); to be illustrated playing with toys or learning lessons; and to be used as a means of delivering moral lessons usually against the behaviour of parents (not breastfeeding infants, harsh child labour). In short, 'Georgian artists fully discovered the complexities of children in their work'.[127]

Steward is not alone in claiming that eighteenth-century artists gave new and special significance to the lives of children. Karin Calvert has analysed the content, style and meaning (the visual language of material culture) in 900 American family portraits depicting 1330 children dated from 1670 to 1870.[128] She identifies three distinct periods in the perceptions of family structure and the nature of childhood: 1670–1750, 1750–1830 and 1830–70. In the late eighteenth century artists developed a new vocabulary that emphasised informality and playfulness as well as illustrating the distinctive artefacts of childhood (toys and other playthings), but during the 1670–1750 period no distinctive artefacts of childhood were represented, no children's furniture and no schoolbooks.

> The stock poses give no signs of play or playfulness, and the faces of children are as solemn as those of their elders. Childhood had no positive attributes of its own considered worthy of expression. A child was merely an adult in the making, and childhood, as a period of physical and spiritual vulnerability, was a deficiency to be overcome.[129]

However, it may be that Colonial America represented some form of special case, for as Calvert also points out, none of her pre-1730 portraits is of a nuclear family and even between 1730 and 1770 only a very small proportion were of such a group.

Many art historians have singled out seventeenth-century Holland as a further special case, particularly with respect to the popularity of paintings showing parents and children at home. But there have also been differences of opinion over how such genre paintings are to be read. For example, Mary Frances Durantini has argued that although children do appear more frequently their role is to present adult issues, such as proper upbringing; there is little concern for the depiction of childhood for its own sake, even by Jan Steen.

> Although there was no fundamental interest in childhood, no attempt to understand, to define or depict the life of children as an end in itself, the art does reveal an awareness of the complexity of the child's nature to an extent not found earlier. The child responds to natural impulses as well as to outside influences. He can laugh or cry, get into mischief or express deep piety. We are presented here with an increased range of topics and of reactions which all focus upon the anonymous individual, upon the ordinary child.[130]

Simon Schama's chapter 'In the Republic of Children' echoes, but then complicates, this idea that childhood provided a cipher by which adult preoccupations could be expressed. His analysis draws two conclusions:

First, that the boundaries between the concerns of the adult world and that of the children on whom they lavished so much time and attention were extremely weak. So that when we see children running riot or temporarily becalmed in some household chore, we are not merely glimpsing snapshots from the family album, but scenes from the interior of the Dutch mental world. Projecting onto children the anxieties and inner conflicts of their elders does not, of course, preclude the possibility that as a culture the Dutch were genuinely besotted with the children.

The second conclusion is that the great dominating theme of the treatment of children – in art and in letters – was the polarity between the ludic and the didactic, between play and learning, between liberty and obedience, between independence and safety.[131]

These two conclusions help to remind us again how perilous is our task of reading from pictures. Even, perhaps especially, in the Dutch Republic where the painting of everyday life appeared to blossom so fully for the first time, there were deep political and psychological anxieties. If the vulnerability people felt was symbolised by the more frequent representation of children, did not these pictures also help to remind parents of their responsibilities, their duty of care to the young?[132]

Of the three issues mentioned on page 64 – whether the Middle Ages were different; what significance the new representations of family groups actually had for the concept of childhood and the treatment of children; and whether 'full expression' was indeed achieved in the seventeenth century – only on the first and third can we offer some form of consensus view at this stage. Certainly there were shifts of artistic convention and popular motifs between the fifteenth and sixteenth centuries, and then again during the eighteenth century at least in western Europe. What remain to be demonstrated convincingly are whether and how such shifts reflected changes in the mental world of parents and whether (here we turn finally to the second issue) there were equally important movements between the sixteenth and the mid-eighteenth centuries.

There is, however, an important additional issue that needs to be emphasised at this point: the question of patronage, that is the relationship between the patron (the person who commissions and pays for the painting as an artistic product), the artist and the subject. In our case the subject will be a child, children, all or part (especially mother and child) of a family group, and the artistic product will be a portrait (head, half-body, full-length). In most cases we would expect the patron and the subject to be connected, to be part of the subject group perhaps or a parent of the subject. Here the commercial arrangement between patron and artist will be quite straightforward – the latter is commissioned by the former to make a painting – but what is less obvious is the extent to which the artist is under the instruction of the patron in terms of the detail of the composition. In certain cases, particularly where some form of text (inscription, age, relationship, name, date) appears on the margins of the portrait, it is probably reasonable to infer that this is the result of the patron's direct instruction, but in other cases such inference would be merely speculative. There are examples, even from the seventeenth century and certainly from the eighteenth, in which the relationship between the patron and the artist is well documented at least in terms of sittings and accounts, but in general it is unusual to have any direct evidence on a patron's instructions other than the picture itself.

There are, of course, other instances in which there is no patron. The artist chooses his subject, he is not commissioned, there is no pre-arranged buyer, and he is in a sense his own patron. The self-portrait is the simplest example, yet the purpose of such pictures is not clear-cut (practice, samples, self-image perhaps). Where the artist paints members of his own family or of an adopted family, can we regard this as the most secure evidence for artistic expression since it is outside the influence of a patron and may, like the self-portrait, not be executed for sale but for personal satisfaction? In those cases in which the artist is unknown, it might still be possible to learn something of the patron's purpose from the subject. When the artist is known but the subject is not, then all must rely on a reading of the painting itself, its form, content, style etc. Ideally, our objective should be to recover the patron–artist–subject relationship at the time of execution, yet this would still not give us the full account. For example, it is important to note the role of secondary or subsequent patrons; those who own the painting as a unique object and those who use the image as a model for their own work or for other purposes. These secondary patrons will not only secure the survival of a particular picture, they may also promote its interpretation in new ways quite at odds with the original patron's intentions. It is also worth emphasising here that in a formal sense we are considering images derived from unique artistic products; such images only became available relatively recently in colour printed form, and with the development of black and white photography in the middle of the nineteenth century.[133] We must also remind ourselves about the importance of artistic reputation and the license which eminence, popular demand, and being in fashion give to the painter. Whether we are dealing with Sir Joshua Reynolds at the height of his powers, or an artistic genius such as Vincent van Gogh who sold only one painting in his lifetime, or an anonymous provincial painter of modest technical ability who made a reasonable living from local patronage must have a marked influence on the patron–artist–subject relationship (not to mention secondary patrons). And, finally, if every picture tells a story not only must we attempt to learn that story; we need to ask whose story it is: patron, artist, or subject?

The changing representation of children, and what it signifies

The 20 images selected for display and detailed analysis as a series are listed in table 4.1 together with a further set, making 38 in all, which will be referred to but not illustrated. Each one has been given a letter (**A–Q** in bold) as an aid to reference, although **Ci** and **Cii** will be considered as a pair, and a number (1–36). The criteria for selection are not systematic. Each image must be of interest in its own right and its original completion dated with a reasonable degree of accuracy. It would certainly

Table 4.1 Example pictures of children and families from the sixteenth to the nineteenth centuries arranged in chronological order

Ref.	Title	Date	Artist	Location	Description
1 **A**	A little girl	**1520s**	Jan Gossaert (also known as Mabuse) (c.1478-1532)	National Gallery, London	single young girl facing the viewer
2	Clarice Strozzi	**1542**	Titian (1488-1576)	Gemäldegalerie, Berlin	single standing girl, aged 2, holding a puppy
3 **B**	William Brooke, 10th Lord Cobham and his family	**1567**	Unknown British artist (Master of the Countess of Warwick)	Longleat House, Warminster, Wiltshire (Marquis of Bath)	man and woman standing, a second woman seated, child on lap, with 5 other children round a table
4	Edward, 3rd Lord Windsor and his family		Unknown British artist (Master of the Countess of Warwick)	Mount Stuart, Isle of Bute, Scotland (Marquis of Bute)	standing father (aged 35), mother (25) and older woman (61); 4 seated boys playing chess and cards, aged 8, 6, 3, 2
5 **Ci**	Mary Rogers, Lady Harington	**1592**	Marcus Gheeraerts the Younger (c.1561-1636)	Tate Britain, London	single standing woman
6 **Cii**	Portrait of an unknown lady	**c.1595**	Marcus Gheeraerts the Younger (c.1561-1636)	Tate Britain, London	single standing, obviously pregnant, woman
7 **D**	Barbara Gamage and her six children	**1596**	Marcus Gheeraerts the Younger (c.1561-1636)	Penshurst Place, Tonbridge, Kent (Viscount De L'Isle)	single standing woman with 6 children
37 **Ri**	Lady Margaret Legh	**1600**	Marcus Gheeraerts the Younger (c.1561-1636)	Private collection	single standing woman
38 **Rii**	Monument to Lady Margaret Legh	after **1605**	Perhaps associated with Maximilian Colt	Fulham church, London	seated woman with two swaddled infants
8 **E**	The Cholmondeley ladies	**1600-10**	Unknown British artist	Tate Britain, London	two women sitting upright in a bed holding their swaddled infants
9	Margaret and John Russell	**1623**	Unknown British artist	Woburn Abbey, Bedfordshire (Duke of Bedford)	standing girl (aged 5) and seated boy (3) with small dog

10	*Deborah Kip, wife of Sir Balthasar Gerbier, and her children*	**1630**	Sir Peter Paul Rubens (1577-1640)	Andrew W. Mellon Fund, National Gallery of Art, Washington DC	seated woman holding infant with 3 standing children on right, a parrot perching on her chair
11	*Venetia Stanley, Lady Digby, on her deathbed*	**1633**	Sir Anthony Van Dyck (1599-1641)	Dulwich Picture Gallery, London	woman, eyes closed and with right hand supporting her head, lies in bed
F	*Sir Thomas Aston at the deathbed of his wife*	**1635**	John Souch (1594-c.1645)	Manchester City Art Galleries	standing man and young boy to left, 1 woman with closed eyes lying in bed and a second woman seated
G	*The Saltonstall family*	*c.***1637**	David Des Granges (1611-c.1675)	Tate Britain, London	standing man with 2 standing children to his right; a woman lying in bed, eyes open, and a second woman seated, holding a swaddled infant to his left
H	*The Streatfield family*	*c.***1640**	William Dobson (1611-46)	Yale Center for British Art, New Haven	man and woman standing with three children clustered before them
15	*Arthur Capel, 1st Baron Capel, and his family*	*c.***1641**	Cornelius Johnson (1593-1661)	National Portrait Gallery, London	seated man and woman, 2 boys stand by father on left, 2 girls by mother on right, an infant sits on mother's knee
I	*Elizabeth Clarke Freake and baby Mary*	**1671-1674**	Unknown American artist	Gift of Mr and Mrs Albert W. Rice, Worcester Art Museum, Massachusetts	infant girl held on mother's knee
17	*The Graham children*	**1742**	William Hogarth (1697-1764)	National Gallery, London	4 children in a drawing room; a seated boy plays a small organ, 2 standing girls, one holding the hand of her younger sister who sits in a baby carriage, a tabby cat and a caged goldfinch attend
18	*Pamela telling nursery tales*	*c.***1744**	Joseph Highmore (1691-1780)	Fitzwilliam Museum, Cambridge	a nursery scene with 5 women clustered round 4 children
19	*Robert Guillym, of Atherton, and his family*	*c.***1746**	Arthur Devis (1712-87)	Paul Mellon Collection, Yale Center for British Art, New Haven	4 standing men in parkland with house prominent in centre; to the right a seated woman has 4 young children clustered round her, 1 infant sits on her lap

Ref.	Title	Date	Artist	Location	Description
20 J	The James family	1751	Arthur Devis (1712-87)	Tate Britain, London	a man and a woman stand to the left, separated from 2 young women, their daughters, who stand to the right
21 K	The painter's daughters chasing a butterfly	c.1756	Thomas Gainsborough (1727-88)	National Gallery, London	2 female children with linked hands chase a butterfly
22	The Bradshaw family	c.1769	Johan Zoffany (1733-1810)	Tate Britain, London	4 children cluster round 2 seated women and a standing man; set in a landscape with one boy holding a pony and a second flying a kite
23	Mehetabel Patrick, Mrs Stratford Canning, and child	c.1778	George Romney (1734-1802)	Fyvie Castle, Aberdeenshire (National Trust for Scotland)	young smiling girl embraces her mother round the neck and is held by her mother round the waist
24	The Wedgwood family	c.1780	George Stubbs (1724-1806)	Wedgwood Museum, Burslem, Staffordshire	a man and woman mounted on horses accompanied by two boys on ponies stand in wooded parkland; they are accompanied by a couple seated on a bench and 3 children, the eldest pulls one in a 4-wheeled baby carriage
25	Miss Juliana Willoughby	1782-83	George Romney (1734-1802)	Andrew W. Mellon Collection, National Gallery of Art, Washington DC	single standing girl, aged about 6, wearing a large straw hat
26 L	A visit to the child at nurse	c.1788	George Morland (1763-1804)	Fitzwilliam Museum, Cambridge	a woman, accompanied by a young girl, bends over an infant who is held on the lap of a second woman; about them in the room are 2 further children
27 M	Penelope Boothby	1788	Sir Joshua Reynolds (1723-92)	Ashmolean Museum, Oxford (Private collection)	a young girl wearing a large mob cap sits patiently with her arms folded on her lap

	Title	Date	Artist	Location	Description
28	*The Wood children*	1789	Joseph Wright of Derby (1734–97)	Derby Museums and Art Gallery	3 children bat and ball prepare for a game of cricket
N 29	*Monument to Penelope Boothby*	1793	Thomas Banks (1735–1805)	Ashbourne church, Derbyshire	a young girl lies full-length as though asleep; both hands up to her face, she wears a dress, but her feet are bare
O 30	*Five children of the Budd family*	c.1818	Unknown American artist	Gift of Edgar William and Bernice Chrysler Garbisch, National Gallery of Art, Washington DC	5 children sit or stand; the eldest in the centre holds open a book, the youngest sits at her feet holding a kitten
31	*Baby in wicker basket*	c.1840	Joseph Whiting Stock (1815–55)	Gift of Edgar William and Bernice Chrysler Garbisch, National Gallery of Art, Washington DC	single infant girl seated on a large pillow in a basket full-face to the viewer
32	*Baby at play*	1876	Thomas Eakins (1844–1916)	John Hay Whitney Collection, National Gallery of Art, Washington DC	single young girl playing with toy building blocks on the brick floor of a back yard
33	*Little girl in a blue armchair*	1878	Mary Cassatt (1844–1926)	Collection of Mr and Mrs Paul Mellon, National Gallery of Art, Washington DC	single young girl lounges, left arm behind head and legs apart, on a large, blue armchair
P 34	*Roulin's baby*	1888	Vincent van Gogh (1853–90)	Chester Dale Collection, National Gallery of Art, Washington DC	the head, arms and hands of a baby
35	*Child with toys: Gabrielle and the artist's son, Jean*	1896	Auguste Renoir (1841–96)	Collection of Mr and Mrs Paul Mellon, National Gallery of Art, Washington DC	seated woman and young boy play with toy farm animals and farmer
Q 36	*Child with a dove*	1901	Pablo Picasso (1881–1973)	National Gallery, London (Private collection)	a child stands holding a dove in both hands, a ball at her feet

help if all the artists, their patrons and subjects were known, but this is not always possible. In most cases each one has been identified and a biographical sketch can be drawn. These are outlined briefly in the following pages.

A *A little girl*, 1520s, Jan Gossaert (also known as Mabuse) (*c.*1478–1532), National Gallery, London

Gossaert was a Flemish painter active from 1503 (admitted to the Antwerp guild of painters) in the Burgundian court. He visited Italy in 1508 and displayed a significant Italianate influence thereafter. Gossaert painted many Madonna and child pictures. The identity of *The little girl* is not known for certain, but it may be Jacqueline, the youngest daughter of Adolphe de Bourgogne and Anne de Bergues, also painted by Gossaert. They married in 1509 and Jacqueline was born in 1523. She holds upside down an armillary sphere, used to represent the movements of the planets. She appears in front of a painted picture frame that gives the impression that she is emerging from the picture, a style adopted after 1525. Gossaert also painted *The three children of Christian II of Denmark* (Hampton Court Palace, London).[134]

B *William Brooke, 10th Lord Cobham and his family*, 1567, unknown British artist, Longleat House, Warminster, Wiltshire (Marquis of Bath)

William Brooke, 10th Lord Cobham (1527–96) was Lord Warden of the Cinque Ports, Lord Chamberlain of Queen Elizabeth's household and Lord Lieutenant of Kent, 1558–96. He is shown with his second wife Frances, daughter of Sir John Newton, whom he married in 1560. Frances's sister Johanna is usually identified as the woman seated on the far left, but it is just as likely to be Dorothy Neville, Cobham's first wife who died in September 1559, although none of her offspring are shown. The six children are, from left to right: Henry (birth order 7, aged 2), William (8, 1), Maximillian (3, 6), Elizabeth (4, 5) (who married Robert Cecil, 1563–1612, 1st Earl of Salisbury), her twin sister Frances (5, 5) and Margaret (6, 4). (There was a son, George (9), born in 1568; as well as two children by Dorothy Neville, Dorothy (1) and Frances (2).)[135]

Ci *Mary Rogers, Lady Harington*, 1592, Marcus Gheeraerts the Younger (*c.*1561–1636), Tate Britain, London

One of the earliest known works by Marcus Gheeraerts the Younger, this painting of 1592 may be Mary Rogers, wife of Sir John Harington (1560–1612), the courtier, poet and translator, of Kelston near Bath. In her left hand she holds strings of pearls threaded into four knots. These knots and the distinctive black-and-white diagonal patterns on her dress suggest the Harington arms. The inscription in the top left-hand corner of the picture indicates that the subject was aged 23 in 1592. It is not known when Mary was born (she died in 1634) or when the Haringtons married. If it was 1583, as is usually supposed, then Mary would have been only 14 or 15, but her first son was not born until 1587 and the pair appear to have celebrated their fourteenth wedding anniversary in 1597. Queen Elizabeth is known to have visited Kelston in 1592 and this picture may commemorate that event.[136] Roy Strong's *The English Icon*

(1969), picture 162, copies a painting of Sir John and his wife by an unknown artist dated 1590–95, but known to originate from Kelston Hall, which bears a reasonable facial likeness to Gheeraerts's portrait. (Some of Sir John's poems to Lady Mary are discussed in Chapter 5, pp. 110-12.)

Cii *Portrait of an unknown lady*, *c.*1595, Marcus Gheeraerts the Younger (*c.*1561–1636), Tate Britain, London

The unknown lady is obviously heavily pregnant and, most unusually, she is smiling. Her richly decorated dress makes clear her elevated social station and her enlarged abdomen, with resting hand, illustrate her condition.[137]

D *Barbara Gamage and her six children*, 1596, Marcus Gheeraerts the Younger (*c.*1561–1636), Penshurst Place, Tonbridge, Kent (Viscount De L'Isle)

In the portrait of *Barbara Gamage and her six children* dated 1596, Lady Sidney touches her two sons, William (birth order 3, age 6) and Robert (7, nearly 1), while the four daughters are linked in pairs from left to right – Elizabeth (5, 4) and Phillippa (6, 2), Mary (1, 10) and Katherine (2, 7). Table 4.2 shows her birth history in full. Henry had died in infancy in 1591. In all Barbara bore eleven children, only three of whom survived her, although five married. In late 1596 she was pregnant with her eighth child, Bridget, while her husband, Sir Robert Sidney, was away in the Netherlands as governor of Flushing. Strong's *The English Icon* (1969), picture 299, copies a painting of *Barbara Gamage* dated *c.*1595, also at Penshurst, showing the subject's left hand entwined in a waist-length necklace resting on her stomach in the characteristic pose of a pregnant woman.

Lady Barbara's accomplishments as a hostess and 'housewife', as well as a mother, are celebrated in Ben Jonson's poem 'To Penshurst' (1612).[138]

> That found King James, when hunting late, this way,
> With his brave son, the prince, they saw thy fires
> Shine bright on every hearth as the desires
> Of thy Penates had been set on flame,
> To entertain them; or the country came,
> With all their zeal, to warm their welcome here.
> What (great, I will not say, but) sudden cheer
> Didst thou, then, make them! And what praise was heaped
> On thy good lady, then! Who, therein, reaped
> The just reward of her high huswifery;
> To have her linen, plate, and all things nigh,
> When she was far: and not a room, but dressed,
> As if it had expected such a guest!
> These, Penshurst, are thy praise, and yet not all.
> Thy lady's noble, fruitful, chaste withal.
> His children thy great lord may call his own:
> A fortune, in this age, but rarely known.
> They are, and have been taught religion: thence

Table *4.2* The birth history of Barbara Gamage, Lady Barbara Sidney, Countess of Leicester, from 1584

Name	Born	Married	Died	Comments
Sir Robert Sidney	1563	twice	13 July 1626	brother of the poet Sir Philip Sidney; knighted (1586), created Baron Sidney of Penshurst (1603), Viscount Lisle (1605), Earl of Leicester (1618); m Lady Sarah Smythe in 1626.
Barbara Gamage	1562	23 September 1584	May 1621	daughter of John Gamage of Coity, Glamorgan
1 Mary	18 October 1587	27 September 1604	1653	m Sir Robert Wroth, poet Mary Wroth
2 Katherine	1589	yes	1616	m Sir Lewis Maunsel
3 William	10 November 1590		2 December 1612	born at Flushing, knighted 8 January 1611
4 Henry	1591?		1591?	died in infancy at Flushing
5 Elizabeth	1592		1605	
6 Philip(pa)	18 August 1594	yes	1620	m Sir John Hobart
7 Robert	1 December 1595	yes	1677	m Lady Dorothy Percy
8 Bridget	February 1597		1599	
9 Alice	1598		1599	
10 Barbara	1599	1622	1643	m Sir Thomas Smythe
11 Vere	1602		July 1606	

Note: c baptised; *m* married; *b* buried

Sources: Millicent V. Hay, *The Life of Robert Sidney, Earl of Leicester (1563–1626)* (Washington, DC: Folger Books, 1984), records of the Sidney family at Penshurst Place, Kent.

Their gentler spirits have sucked innocence.
Each morn, and even, they are taught to pray,
With the whole household, and may, every day,
Read, in their virtuous parents' noble parts,
The mysteries of manners, arms, and arts.[139]

Lady Barbara was fifty in 1612 and six of her eleven children were still alive, although her eldest son, Sir William Sidney, died in December that year.

E *The Cholmondeley ladies*, 1600–10, unknown British artist, Tate Britain, London

The identity of the artist and of the sitters remains a mystery. But on the basis of the clothes worn and certain antiquarian references, the picture is believed to date from the first decade of the seventeenth century and to show members of the Cholmondeley family from Cheshire. One tradition has it that they are twin sisters, another that they were born and married on the same day. Recent research has argued that the ladies are Lettice Grosvenor (1585–1612) and Mary Calveley (died 1616) who were the daughters of Sir Hugh Cholmondeley (1552–1601) and Mary Holford (1563–1625), but this is still not certain.[140]

F *Sir Thomas Aston at the deathbed of his wife*, 1635, John Souch (1594–*c.*1645; active 1616–36), Manchester City Art Galleries

John Souch was active in Chester as a heraldic artist and portrait painter for the local gentry. In this painting the subjects are Sir Thomas Aston, Bart. (1600–46), of Aston Hall near Crewe, Cheshire; his wife Lady Magdalene Aston, a member of the Poultney family, who died in childbirth on 2 June 1635; their only surviving child, Thomas, aged 3 years and 9 months; and a further seated woman who is most likely to be Lady Aston when she was younger or a close relative, a sister perhaps, even Lady Jane Crewe (née Poultney) who died in 1639, also in childbirth.[141] One of the inscriptions dates the painting at 30 September 1635 when Sir Thomas was aged 35.[142] The following epitaph appeared on Lady Aston's monument in Aston chapel.

> The lady Magdalen Aston
> daughter and coheyre of Sir John Pultney of Pultney
> com. Leicester, kt
> dyed the 2d of June 1635.
> Had issue Jane, Robert, Thomas, and Elizabeth,
> (three of which early saynts dyed in her life)
> Thomas (a chyld of great hope) survived her,
> but soone left her inheritance for her grave.
> He dyed the 23d of January, 1637, ae'tis sexto
> to whose memories
> her sad husband, his father,
> Sir Thomas Aston, baronett,
> dedicates this sacred
> amoris ergo.
> Heere, reader, in this sad but glorious cell

Of death lyes shrind a double miracle,
Of Woman and of wife, and each soe best,
Shee may be fame's fayre coppy to the rest;
The virgin heere a blush so chaste might learne,
Till through the blood shee virtue did discerne;
Heere might the byrde upon her wedding day
At once both knowe to love and to obey,
Till shee grewe wife so perfect and refynd,
To be but body to her husband's mynd;
The tender Mother heere might learne such love
And care as shames the pelicane and dove.
But, fame and truth, noe more, for should you fynd
And bring each grace and beauty of her mynd,
Wonder and envy both would make this grave
Theyr court, and blast that peace her ashes have.[143]

G *The Saltonstall family*, c.1637, David Des Granges (1611–c.1675), Tate Britain, London

David Des Granges is best known as a miniaturist and for his Royalist connections, but here we have a full-scale painting that is believed to be the family of Sir Richard Saltonstall (1595–1650) of Chipping Warden near Banbury, Oxfordshire. Sir Richard's first wife, Elizabeth Basse, died in 1630 and it is she who appears lying in bed. Sir Richard remarried in 1633 and his second wife, Mary Parker, is pictured holding a male child wrapped in swaddling clothes who may be either John (born 1634, died in infancy) or Philip (born 1636). The two older children standing to the left are Elizabeth's surviving offspring, Richard (who has not yet been put into breeches) and Ann.

H *The Streatfield family*, c.1640, William Dobson (1611–46), Yale Center for British Art, New Haven

William Dobson was a well-known Royalist artist who flourished in the 1630s and early 1640s. This is said to be a painting of the Streatfield family of Chiddingstone Castle, Kent, but very little is known about either the artist or the family.[144]

I *Elizabeth Clarke Freake and baby Mary*, 1671–74, unknown American artist (known as the Freake-Gibbs painter), Gift of Mr and Mrs Albert W. Rice, Worcester Art Museum, Massachusetts

Elizabeth Clarke (22 May 1642–3 February 1713) married the Boston merchant John Freake (1635–75) on 28 May 1661. Elizabeth was 29 in 1671 when the picture was first painted, one of a pair with husband on the left and wife on the right. By the end of 1674 6-month-old Mary (6 May 1674–1752), one of eight children born to Elizabeth and John between 1662 and 1674, had been inserted.[145]

J *The James family*, 1751, Arthur Devis (1712–87), Tate Britain, London

This is the family of Robert James (1700–94), who served for many years as

Secretary to the East India Company, his wife, Mary, and daughters, Elizabeth and Ann.

K *The painter's daughters chasing a butterfly*, c.1756, Thomas Gainsborough (1727–88), National Gallery, London

Gainsborough's unfinished painting is of his two daughters, Mary (baptised 3 February 1750) and Margaret (baptised 22 August 1751). Gainsborough married Margaret Burr in July 1746 and their first child, Mary, died in 1748. *Portrait of the artist with his wife and daughter* (c.1748) shows Thomas, Margaret and Mary as a family group, while *The painter's daughters with a cat* (c.1760–61) shows the second Mary and Margaret again (both in the National Gallery, London). Gainsborough is among a rather small group of artists who regularly painted their own children. There are perhaps three other surviving examples.[146]

L *A visit to the child at nurse*, c.1788, George Morland (1763–1804), Fitzwilliam Museum, Cambridge

Although based for much of his career in London, Morland specialised in rustic scenes. In 1786 he married Anne, the sister of William Ward, the engraver. Morland led a reckless, self-indulgent life, often getting into debt. This picture has a companion, *The visit to the boarding school*, in the Wallace Collection, London. Morland has been credited with providing a rather more realistic view of the eighteenth-century rural poor than is often achieved by contemporary artists such as George Stubbs or Gainsborough.[147]

M *Penelope Boothby*, 1788, Sir Joshua Reynolds (1723–92), Ashmolean Museum, Oxford (Private collection)

Penelope Boothby (11 April 1785–19 March 1791) was the only child of Sir Brooke Boothby, Bart., of Ashbourne Hall, Derbyshire. Sir Brooke, a well-known member of the Lichfield literary circle and himself a subject of paintings by Reynolds and Joseph Wright of Derby (shown reclining in woodland holding a copy of Rousseau), had married Susannah Bristoe in 1784. Penelope, aged 3, sat for Reynolds on four occasions during July 1788. After her death in 1791, a month before her sixth birthday, Penelope's parents were so grief-stricken that it is said they parted company. Sir Brooke commissioned a monument for Ashbourne church by the sculptor Thomas Banks (**N**), a model of which was shown at the Royal Academy in 1793 to great acclaim. He also wrote a sonnet sequence entitled *Sorrows Sacred to the Memory of Penelope* that was illustrated by the engraver Henry Fuseli and published in 1796.[148]

N *Monument to Penelope Boothby*, 1793, Thomas Banks (1735–1805), Ashbourne church, Derbyshire

The sculpture by Thomas Banks of Penelope Boothby, who died in 1791 aged 5, shows her apparently asleep and lying on her right side. One of the inscriptions reads:

'She was in form and intellect most exquisite. The unfortunate parents ventured their all on this frail bark, and the wreck was total.' In Nicholas Penny's opinion, this is 'the first notable monument to a child erected in eighteenth-century England'.[149]

O *Five children of the Budd family*, c.1818, unknown American artist, Gift of Edgar William and Bernice Chrysler Garbisch, National Gallery of Art, Washington DC.

This picture by an unknown artist is believed to have originated in or near Lancaster, Pennsylvania, in the early nineteenth century and to be of five (there were at least ten) children of Samuel Woolston Budd. It remained in the Budd, and then by marriage the Hull, families until the 1950s.

P *Roulin's baby*, 1888, Vincent van Gogh (1853–90), Chester Dale Collection, National Gallery of Art, Washington DC.

Among many other works executed during 1888 at Arles in southern France, van Gogh painted three pictures of Marcelle Roulin (31 July 1888–22 February 1980), the 3-month-old daughter of the local postman, Joseph Roulin. The paintings are almost identical, suggesting that two are copies of the first. Van Gogh also painted two dissimilar versions of Marcelle with her mother, Augustine, as well as individual paintings of her father (six versions) and mother and brothers, Armand and Camille.[150]

Q *Child with a dove*, 1901, Pablo Picasso (1881–1973), National Gallery, London (Private collection)

Picasso painted *Child with a dove* while living in Paris in 1901. Several pictures of that year have women and children as their subjects; they reflect Paris low life and the poverty their creator experienced as a young artist.[151]

These eighteen images are highly suggestive in very many ways, and each viewer-reader will be able to create their own linking narrative. Here we shall focus on the images as a form of discourse, one that reflects not only childhood, but also more importantly the ways in which patron-parents and artists regarded their offspring in their lifetimes.

The first thing to note, and still perhaps the most important point, is that from at least the sixteenth century there are examples of young children, not just eligible young women involved in the marriage market, being the subjects of portraits in their own right (**A**, 2, 9, 17, 21, 25, **M**, 28, **O**, 31, 32, 33, **P**, **Q**). In this sense at least there is little difference between **A**, 2, and 25, **M**, despite the intervening 250 years. Titian in Venice painted Clarice Strozzi, 1540–81, the daughter of a Florentine banker, in 1542, aged 2. This painting (2) has recently been called a 'sensational and novel image of childhood', and 'one of the most engaging images of childhood produced in the Renaissance'.[152] Similarly, and as Ariès illustrated, there was an obvious desire to incorporate children of all ages in family group portraits of a 'line-up and face the camera' kind (**B**, 4, **D**, **G**, **H**, 15, 19, **J**, 22, 24). The 'mother and child' painting was also still important, at least in the seventeenth century (**E**, **I**, 23). These three formats – children without adults (on their own or in small groups), children with their parents in the family group, and parent plus child (usually in the Madonna and infant Jesus tradition) – can each be thought of as celebrations of children, of reproductive success, of hope for the future. Or to make the point more forcibly by considering its opposite; it would be unreasonable to argue from any one, particularly the first, or all of these formats that children were not well regarded and valued by their aristocratic or gentry parents in and from at least the sixteenth century. Parental indifference should have rendered them invisible.

And yet, of course, this is neither a new story nor the whole story.[153] Let us consider **D** (10 has a similar mother and children format, although more animated) in a little more detail. We know the identity of the patron (Sir Robert Sidney), the artist and each of the seven subjects as well as the year of execution (1596, when Sir Robert was away at Flushing) and the subsequent history of the painting. Lady Barbara occupies the higher ground, but not quite the centre of the picture; she both dominates and conducts us to her children. She touches her two sons who are kept close by. William, who is nearly 6, stands in the middle; he wears a sword and holds a hat decorated with badges matching those down the front of his mother's skirt and a beautiful red plume, but he has not yet been put into breeches. As the eldest son, he is the focus of family expectations. The second surviving son, Robert, who has not reached his first birthday, sits to his mother's right on a raised, red cushion. In his right hand he holds a plaything suspended from a red cord round his neck and in his left a bunch of cherries. The four daughters are also arranged carefully in pairs. Mary, the eldest child aged 9, stands at a little distance from her mother. She wears fashionable adult female attire, including a long rope of pearls knotted in the middle. Her sister Katherine, aged 6 or 7, holds her left hand. The remaining two daughters, Elizabeth and Philippa, stand together in the left foreground of the picture. There is a studied formality about this group, one that reflects power and authority, some wealth, but also considerable pride. Clearly, sons are favoured, yet daughters are not neglected. Of the symbols displayed, William's sword of power and authority of approaching manhood is matched by Mary's pearls of purity and beauty, but Robert's cherries are an enduring symbol of vitality, virginity, vigour and health, also a toy.[154] The expressionless formality and gendered arrangement of this image might encourage us to think of it solely in terms of its function as a record of achievement in the struggle for dynastic survival, but it also seems reasonable to speculate, with the additional assistance of Ben Jonson's testimony, that Lady Barbara was not only a good housewife but a loving wife and mother who cared for the material and spiritual well-being of her offspring. Sir Robert's dynastic ambitions may have proved successful under the patronage of James I, yet they were built on his marriage to a significant heiress and her abilities as estate manager and mother.[155]

None of the other images is quite as austere as **D**; even the *Cholmondeley ladies* (**E**), who may be celebrating a joint Christening, are enlivened by the red of their infants' shawls. The painting of Lord Cobham and his family (**B**, also 4) is positively animated by comparison, although its function is ostensibly similar. The large Latin inscription makes that plain. It has been translated as follows.

> See here the noble father, the most excellent mother. Seated around them spreads
> a throng worthy of their parents. Such was once the family of the patriarch Jacob,
> such the progeny gathered about the pious Job. God grant that the line of Cobham
> beget many offspring such as Joseph, and flourish like the seed of Job restored. Much
> has been given to the noble race of Cobham. Long may their joys endure.[156]

Round the table sit the six Cobham children, but it is not mealtime and they are
certainly not being taught any recognisable form of table manners. One holds a
puppy, another a tethered goldfinch, a third has a marmoset on her pewter plate,
while a parrot stands in the middle of the table-cloth. Some are engaged in eating
– apples, pears, grapes and cherries again – but there also appears to be a plate of nuts
for the monkey and parrot. The animals may not only be pets for the children but,
like the fruit, symbols of the Cobhams' capacity to 'beget many offspring'. The cup of
plenty also sits in the centre of the table. The idea that Elizabethan children should
be regarded as their parents' 'seeds' is entirely consistent with the sense of care and
nurture of the young.

The three paintings shown as **F**, **G** and **H** (also 15) – the Aston, Saltonstall
and Streatfield families – have offered several teasing challenges to social and art
historians over the years. These relate partly to the use of obvious symbols of death
and mourning, as well as to the presence of a second adult female in two of them.
William Dobson's painting of two adults and three children is believed to be that of
the Streatfield family; however, very little is known about the picture and the artist in
general. The iconography is also far from straightforward, despite first impressions.
In the top right-hand corner four skulls rest on a broken column. Below, a mother
points to her young boy whose left shoulder she also clasps. The boy is draped rather
than clothed; he looks directly at us and the hint of a smile plays on his face. Two
of his siblings stand towards the left of the group; the elder also looks at us and rests
his arm on the younger child's shoulder, she looks towards her mother while offering
her father a bunch of three cherries. The father is distracted by the skulls. The usual
interpretation is that the young boy has already died, that the cherries represent the
three children, and that the four skulls signify the inevitability of death for those
now living. This may be so, yet there is more to be learned from the expressions on
the five faces which, apart from collars, cuffs and the little girl's dress, seem to provide
the painting's only source of light. While the mother projects a serene beauty, her
husband is drawn away from this family by thoughts of mortality. His remaining
children appear apprehensive, unable to engage with their distracted parents. Only
for the young boy is there a sense of peace. Is this one of the first paintings of a family
in mourning, disturbed, unsure of what to do and think, unable to reconcile the way
they have been taught to feel with their actual response to untimely death?

Unlike **B**, and the same unknown artist's painting of Lord Windsor's family (4),
F and **G** show deathbed scenes in which the patron's first wife has died in childbirth.

It may seem strange that two women are shown, but it was quite common for the several wives of a deceased magnate to be represented on his funeral monument at this time.[157] Of the two, **G** appears the most straightforward in terms of iconography. This is not a mourning painting. Its dominant colour is red and although the rather elongated figure of Sir Richard Saltonstall, which dominates the centre of the picture, is dressed mainly in black, his stylish, gold-embroidered jacket with slashed sleeves, lace-trimmed collar and cuffs gives him an elegant demeanour. Young Richard grips his sister's wrist firmly while his father holds his left hand lightly. In his gloved left hand Sir Richard holds his other glove and gestures towards his second wife, Lady Mary, who holds their youngest child still in swaddling clothes. Lady Elizabeth, eyes wide open though pale and clearly on her deathbed, gestures past her husband to her children. Her death had broken a link in the family chain, but this has now been repaired and the arrival of a new addition can be celebrated. The way the baby is held is reminiscent of the *Cholmondeley ladies* (**E**) who also proudly cradle their wide-awake infants in their right arms; wrapped in red cloth, all three are displayed to perfection against their mothers' pale dresses.

While **E** and **G** celebrate birth, survival and family continuity; **F** is massively sombre, overwhelmingly mournful. Lady Magdalene Aston has died in childbirth. The wicker crib is draped in black and a skull, held by Sir Thomas, is placed at its head. Below is the inscription: 'He who sows hope in flesh reaps bones'.[158] Young Thomas is linked to his father by the cross staff which they both hold. The inscription on this navigational device, used for fixing latitude by taking the angle of the sun and the stars, reads: 'He telleth the number of the stars [Psalm 147]; He set a compass on the face of the deep [Proverbs 8]; Thou hast set all the borders of the earth [Psalm 74]; my grief is immeasurable'. Above the head of Thomas appear an unstringed lute and a globe with assorted creatures, while adjacent to his father's head there is the inscription: 'The sorrows of death compassed me [Psalm 116] in the year of grief 30 September 1635, aged 35. Though I walk through the valley of death, I will fear no evil; thy rod and thy staff comfort me [Psalm 23].' Apart from the inscriptions and the conspicuous symbolism, which is most likely to have been contrived by Sir Thomas himself, the artist also conveys grief and mourning by a number of other devices. The blackness of the huge 203 x 215 centimetre canvas imposes a gloomy, funereal quality. Only Lady Magdalene is at peace in the centre of her luminous bedclothes and pillow (as was Lady Venetia in 11); the rest, even her youthful persona, are in deep mourning. Sir Thomas leans backwards as if rocked by the assaults of family deaths: his wife, her unborn child and, perhaps, the other three children – Jane, Robert and Elizabeth – who predeceased Thomas. By 1646 when Sir Thomas himself died, a casualty of the Civil War, his wife, all his children and even his sister-in-law, Lady Jane Crewe, were already dead.

The remaining seventeenth-century picture comes from the artist known as the Freake-Gibbs painter or limner. He was responsible for a number of portraits executed in the early 1670s including *Elizabeth Clarke Freake and baby Mary* (**I**).[159]

There are two particular aspects of **I** that are especially interesting. First, the original painting of 1671 was intended to be one of a pair: Elizabeth alongside husband, John Freake. Only later in 1674 was the 6-month-old baby, Mary, inserted in the painting to create a mother and child portrait. Mary appears to be standing on her mother's lap; Elizabeth supports her daughter on the right shoulder and on her stomach. Apart from the introduction of Mary herself, there has been some remodelling of Elizabeth in terms of arms and hands; she may originally have held a fan in both hands on her lap. But the question remains, why was baby Mary included? In the following year, 1675, John Freake was killed in an accident so that Mary was the last of his eight children. Why not a new family portrait rather than a modification by the original artist?[160] Secondly, the Freakes were strict New England Puritans by religion and culture yet Elizabeth and Mary wear brightly coloured clothes – greens, reds and a vibrant lemon – which, when compared with the sober black of John Freake's portrait, not to mention the Gibbs and Mason children, establishes an even more dramatic contrast. We cannot answer these questions with any assurance; however, it is clear that *Elizabeth Clarke Freake and baby Mary* remains an early American icon which takes us back to sixteenth- and early seventeenth-century England, to **E** rather than **H**.

Studies such as Steward's *The New Child* (1995) encourage us to believe that a revolutionary change occurred during the middle of the eighteenth century: modern childhood was born. There are, however, several ways in which eighteenth-century artists merely continued the styles of expression adopted by their predecessors. The work of Arthur Devis (19, **J**) offers some examples from the 1740s and 1750s. His painting of Robert James, his wife, Mary, and daughters, Elizabeth and Ann (1751), shows a conventional enough family group. The subjects are placed outdoors in a way that conveys an association with parkland and property, wealth and status (as in 19). This device was also being used by seventeenth-century painters (15, for example, where the backdrop to the family group comprises interior wall hangings and exterior formal gardens). What is interesting about **J** is the formality of the group and the separation between parents and children, but this 'wide spacing' appears in many of Devis's paintings, 19 included. It is also a feature of 24, in which horses and ponies have to be accommodated, but not of 22. How should we interpret this 'wide spacing'; does it signify emotional separation or merely a desire to ensure that property is fully illustrated?

William Hogarth's *The Graham children* (17) and Joseph Highmore's *Pamela telling nursery tales* (18) both show a small group of children amusing themselves or being entertained. In the case of 17 there is a mixture of joyful animation (at the combination of caged bird and cat) and formal display (especially the studied poses of the two older girls who show off their dresses). The eldest girl holds a bunch of cherries harking back to earlier symbolic references (**H** and **D**).[161] In 18 we are placed in a bedroom rather than a drawing room; Pamela is telling stories to four children but she is accompanied by four other women who form a circle round their charges.

Both of these paintings date from the 1740s and in certain respects they do reveal childhood in a new light, yet they are also consistent with a style of representing children that we have already associated with Dutch seventeenth-century art. They suggest adult anxieties: the tensions between play and display, education and entertainment, freedom and control.

It is often claimed that Thomas Gainsborough's portrait of his two daughters chasing a butterfly (**K**) takes us on to a higher plain of sensitivity towards children. Coming in the mid-1750s, it marks a watershed in Georgian art. However, in sociological terms what is important about **K** is the fact that these are the painter's own children, and that they often appeared in his work. In artistic terms the picture shows two young girls at play with nature; it has vitality and animation, colour and great beauty. It is also unfinished, a practice piece perhaps, and certainly one without a commissioning patron. Above all this painting expresses tenderness and vulnerability in the way it shows the sisters' faces; in this sense it is unprecedented.[162]

George Romney's painting of Mehetabel Canning and her daughter in a loving embrace, child smiling broadly, also marks a new high point of emotional engagement (23). There is no hand holding or shoulder touching here, no one-way parent-to-child link; rather the little girl seated on her mother's lap leans towards and hugs her mother round the neck; they are cheek to cheek yet still facing the viewer. This painting from the late 1770s is obviously intended as an unambiguous display of mutual affection.

In the following decade Romney painted Juliana Willoughby who was 6 by the time of its final completion in 1783 (25). He shows her in white dress, pink waist sash, broad-brimmed bonnet, standing, head slightly tilted, in a rural scene. There is an intelligent, quizzical expression on her face suggesting a rather spirited character and an independence of mind. There are several striking contrasts between Juliana and Penelope Boothby, aged 3 in 1788 (**M**). In white dress with blue sash and a large mob cap, Penelope sits, arms folded on her lap, in a darkened interior. She looks to one side, a palpable sadness in her expression. Is she just resigned to having to pose for the famous artist, or has Sir Joshua captured in this portrait a lack of vitality and childish spirit, a seriousness beyond her years, a mournful debility presaging premature demise?[163] Certainly Reynolds's other fashionable child portraits of the 1780s adopt the 'rosy-cheeked cherub' image of childhood, one full of energy and not a little mischief.[164] *Penelope Boothby* is different. When Penelope died in 1791 her parents, but most conspicuously Sir Brooke, an ardent follower of Rousseau, went into a protracted period of mourning for their only child whose memory he sought to commemorate in several ways. Thomas Banks's monument to her in Ashbourne church (**N**) was said by contemporaries to be so life-like that it made them weep when they realised she had died so young.[165]

Also from the 1780s, George Morland's *A visit to the child at nurse* (**L**) may convey a message for maternal morality. Steward, for example, suggests that: 'Morland is here describing and indeed criticising the social pretensions of the mother and the hollowness of her values which have allowed her the luxury of emotion without the responsibility'.[166] However, a closer reading of the painting reveals some interesting ambiguities. Certainly, the lady in blue is fashionably dressed; her plumed hat is particularly majestic, as is the child who accompanies her, but they are not visiting a mean, rustic hovel. There are pewter plates on the rack; the nurse wears a handsome, striped house-coat over her dress; there are toys for the children, including a remarkably fine wooden horse and cart; there are places for the little ones to rest; and they all wear shoes – even the baby has pretty pink booties. If this is indeed the home of a wet-nurse, she runs a high-class establishment. But in the foreground on a stool stands a pewter gravy boat and spoon; does this contain the baby's food? Is she not being breastfed? Morland is well known for his apparently moralising paintings. For example, *The comforts of industry* and *The miseries of idleness* (both 1790, National Galleries of Scotland, Edinburgh) illustrate the dos and don'ts of rural life. In each case there are five subjects – mother, father and three children. In 'idleness' there is clear evidence of alcohol and tobacco, the baby is left to scream unattended in his basket while the adults snooze; but in 'industry' the baby sleeps peacefully on her mother's lap, and the little girl plays with her doll. If this is the simple point Morland wishes to make, then the nurse must also represent industry, good behaviour and moral rectitude. Is the mother, the lady in blue, to be castigated for leaving her infant in such good care?[167]

On the face of it, and certainly compared with earlier periods, the six nineteenth-century paintings listed in table 4.1, including the three selected for illustration (**O**, **P**, **Q**), offer few challenges to interpretation. Children of various ages, singly and in groups, without or with an adult, are pictured playing, being themselves, being childlike. Their presence and activities do not surprise the viewer; examples abound, and they are commonplace, everyday. For the artist there are new challenges: how to compete with the photographer; how to create new images of children that the dealer, as well as the patron-parent, will wish to buy; whether to give children a special position as artistic subjects; how to use the new, enhanced range of manufactured colour paints; whether to abandon the old figurative conventions of portrait painting and move towards abstraction.

This said **O**, *Five children of the Budd family*, seems to refer back to an earlier style of portraiture. The painting is thought to date from around 1818 and to come from Pennsylvania where until the 1950s it remained in the possession of the Budd and Hull families. It shows five very serious children, one seated on a high-backed chair holding an open book; another, the youngest, sits on the floor with a kitten on her lap; the remaining three stand clustered round the chair. Arms, hands and gestures establish a clockwise, circular frame from top right round towards bottom left. The children are physically linked as well as juxtaposed. They are plainly dressed and well shod; the eldest girl wears a necklace, but the rest is very simple, although the child on the right wears an all-in-one trouser suit, buttoned at the front in a deep russet colour. However, the proportions of the children's heads and their faces will strike

A *A little girl*, 1520s, Jan Gossaert (also known as Mabuse) (*c.*1478–1532), National Gallery, London

B *William Brooke, 10th Lord Cobham and his family*, 1567, unknown British artist (Master of the Countess of Warwick), Longleat House, Warminster, Wiltshire (Marquis of Bath)

Cii *Portrait of an unknown lady*, c.1595, Marcus Gheeraerts the Younger (c.1561–1636), Tate Britain, London

Ci *Mary Rogers, Lady Harington*, 1592, Marcus Gheeraerts the Younger (c.1561–1636), Tate Britain, London

D *Barbara Gamage and her six children*, 1596, Marcus Gheeraerts the Younger (*c*.1561–1636), Penshurst Place, Tonbridge, Kent (Viscount De L'Isle)

E *The Cholmondeley ladies*, 1600–10, unknown British artist, Tate Britain, London

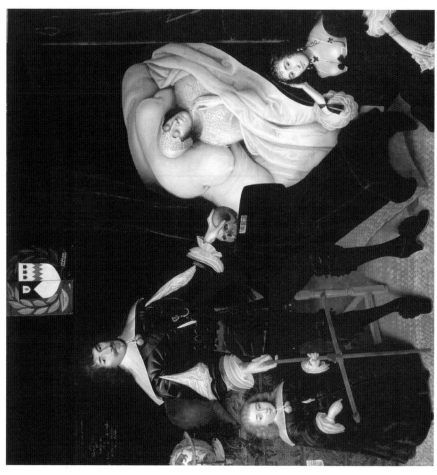

F *Sir Thomas Aston at the deathbed of his wife*, 1635, John Souch (1594–c.1645),
Manchester City Art Galleries

G *The Saltonstall family, c.1637*, David Des Granges (1611–c.1675). Tate Britain, London

H *The Streatfield family, c.*1640, William Dobson (1611–46), Yale Center for British Art, New Haven

1 *Elizabeth Clarke Freake and baby Mary*, 1671 to 1674 (completed), unknown American artist, Gift of Mr and Mrs Albert W. Rice, Worcester Art Museum, Massachusetts

J *The James family*, 1751, Arthur Devis (1712–87), Tate Britain, London

K *The painter's daughters chasing a butterfly*, c.1756, Thomas Gainsborough (1727–88),
National Gallery, London

L *A visit to the child at nurse*, c.1788, George Morland (1763–1804), Fitzwilliam Museum, Cambridge

M *Penelope Boothby*, 1788, Sir Joshua Reynolds (1723–92), Ashmolean Museum, Oxford (private collection)

N *Monument to Penelope Boothby*, 1793, Thomas Banks (1735–1805), Ashbourne church, Derbyshire (author's photograph)

O *Five children of the Budd family*, *c.*1818, unknown American artist, Gift of Edgar William and Bernice Chrysler Garbisch, National Gallery of Art, Washington DC

P *Roulin's baby*, 1888, Vincent van Gogh (1853–90), Chester Dale Collection, National Gallery of Art, Washington DC

Q *Child with a dove*, 1901, Pablo Picasso (1881–1973), National Gallery, London (private collection)

the twenty-first-century viewer. These may appear exaggerated, naive, poorly crafted perhaps; or they may be taken to signify the cerebral aspirations of parents, where the book is at the centre of a no-frills, no-toys childhood.[168] Several other American paintings of the period gathered together in the Garbisch collection at the National Gallery of Art also suggest this impression that children are intended to be seen as little adults, including Joseph Whiting Stock's *Baby in wicker basket* (31).

Compared with **O** and 31, 32 and 35 show children free of worldly adult cares; they are absorbed in play with complete disregard for the viewer. These are paintings from the late nineteenth century (1876 and 1896), from a world that we would now think of as classic, careless childhood. Both appear off-guard, unposed, natural; how could children behave in any other way? And yet there are other stories here. Thomas Eakins, who has been called an American realist, gives us a picture of his niece, Ella Crowell, at play. Children appear in many of his paintings, but although Eakins married in 1884 he had no children.[169] The subjects of 35 are Jean Renoir (1894–1979), who became the famous film director, and Gabrielle Renard, who joined the household in 1894 to help Renoir's wife, Aline, while she was pregnant with Jean. Gabrielle became one of the artist's most famous models. This is not, then, an image of mother and child; rather, like 18 and **L**, we see the childminder at work, a child left to the care of others.

Like Eakins, Mary Cassatt never had children, although she is best known as *the* female American impressionist and for her numerous paintings of children and of women holding infants. The pictures display a deep emotional attachment to children that may be thought to sentimentalise their position, and certainly they are celebratory of childhood and motherhood.[170] Cassatt, with Eakins and Renoir, created an idealised image of childhood that was comfortable, warm, bright, clean, healthy and untroubled. But in 33, *Little girl in a blue armchair*, we have a painting which has attracted considerable controversy. It was painted after Cassatt had settled permanently in Paris, but rejected for exhibition in 1878. The picture shows a young girl, the daughter of Edgar Degas's friends, sprawled in a large armchair. Is she a youthful Lolita, a dancer in the making; or merely an unselfconscious innocent lounging because she's hot, tired, bored? If the former, then is it the viewer-reader who is responsible for making her sexuality explicit, not the artist?[171]

The paintings by van Gogh and Picasso (**P** and **Q**), which complete our main illustrated series, are not of the nineteenth century in the way 32, 35 and even 33 clearly are. They look forward to a new age, but in rather different ways. Vincent van Gogh spent 1888–89 in Arles, painting feverishly and coping to various degrees with a variety of crises: mental, sexual, alcoholic, artistic. One of his few friends at that time was the local postman, Joseph Roulin, whom van Gogh painted along with his wife and their children. Van Gogh liked children. He had wanted to marry and establish a family himself, but on the one occasion when this seemed possible he had been persuaded out of it by parental pressure. By the time he reached Arles his alcoholic indulgence, and perhaps also his earlier treatment for syphilis, had made him impotent. In **P** we have one of three portraits of Marcelle Roulin, then 3 months old. Is this a real baby or van Gogh's own child? The colouring is the artist's yet she sits full square, solid, reliable, aged, as her father does in his portraits. Perhaps she is not a baby at all, but an old woman who, while she retains her chubby hands and arms, her Christening ring and bracelet, has begun to lose her memories, to be dulled by the passage of time. There is in the darkness of the eyes and the blankness of expression a pathos that could not be acquired in three months, although it could in the artist's own lifetime.

By 1901 Picasso was absorbed in colours, shapes, and symbols. His *Child with a dove* (**Q**), in its print form the most popular of the illustrated paintings, conveys a charming simplicity. A young girl in white dress and sash stands outdoors, the sky is blue and the grass is green. She holds in both hands a dove: which may symbolise purity or peace or death. Her hair is striking, close cropped and bright ginger. At her feet there is a large ball with segments – white, yellow, red, green, blue – just like a colour chart. Perspective is poorly developed; only the little girl's arms and the folds in her dress suggest three-dimensional mass. Picasso was 20 in 1901, struggling to begin his professional career as an artist in Paris. The painting illustrated as **Q** can be read in several ways. First, it is an expression of childhood innocence and purity; this is surely the quality the print sellers exploit. Secondly, it represents an experiment in the reduction of detail, the simplification, the abstraction of shapes that still allows objects to be recognised. The ball is a sphere, the shoes have laces, the tail feathers, and the head has hairs upon it, but none of this is made explicit, merely suggested, and the viewer does the rest. Thirdly, we may also have an experiment in colour composition, even a critique of contemporary colour theory. Orange against deep blue, white against pale green; large areas of canvas are given the same colour and the effect is striking; conventions are to be broken.[172] The child merely provides Picasso with a vehicle to challenge the older generation of established artists, those who paint with small dots and dashes of colour.

It should now be possible to draw together some preliminary, summary observations that relate to the broad sweep of four hundred years. First, and a point which is worth repeating, we have available a very wide variety of examples of children as portrait subjects in European art from at least the early sixteenth century. These are children of both genders, all ages, singly, in sibling groups, with a single adult, parents or carers. Children held significant places in the lives and emotions of adults throughout these centuries; they were represented and memorialised in ways that contemporaries appreciated and which we can still see, even if we cannot now fully understand their individual iconography.

Secondly, it is also a matter of debate whether we are seeing children as individual human beings or as the property of parents, available for celebratory display but also the source of adult concerns and anxieties (will they survive, what is the proper way to bring them up, to educate them?). Certainly **K** is rather different; here the artist is the father, and therefore it offers a special case. Before the 1750s our illustrated examples tend to show a stiffness of body, a formality of relationship that could be taken to signify the existence of a coolness between parents and children, a distance that is so obvious in **J**, for instance. Yet **H** offers a counter-point; here there is closeness, tenderness and concern, anxiety for the future. There is no good reason to believe on the basis of this pictorial series alone that there was in the 1750s or 1760s a revolutionary change in the attitudes of parents to their children: more caring, more sensitive, more inclined to appreciate their individual personalities. There was some shift towards the sentimental, the romantic, perhaps, and a tendency to emphasise the innocence of childhood, its playfulness (as in 32 and 35, many of Cassatt's paintings, even **Q** at one level). Periodisation that is so simple and straightforward is unlikely to be convincing.

Thirdly, it is also important to remember that the commercial arrangements governing the production of **K**, 32, 33, **P**, 35, **Q** were either non-existent or at least substantially different from the patron–artist–subject relationship which applied to all the other examples listed in table 4.1. Renoir was taken up by a dealer; van Gogh and Cassatt had no regard for market, although for different reasons; Gainsborough was probably content to hone his artistic skills with family subjects; Picasso was experimenting. This leads us to the general issue of artistic influence. Some of our painters were provincial limners who were obviously under close instruction from their clients: insert a baby here (**I**), an inscription and ages there (**B, F**), property in the background (**J**). Some were international migrants drawn to a new market for portraiture (**D**) or who had been exposed to artistic developments in other countries, especially Italy (**A**) and France (33). Others had acquired such a reputation and influential client list that they became artistic aristocracy in their own right (10, 11, **M**).

Fourthly, there are a number of apparently minor details – props, text, colours, for example – that have a significant history in their own right. The association of animals, especially kittens and puppies, with children was common from the sixteenth to the nineteenth centuries. On the one hand they provide pets to be played with, and on the other they underscore the untrained but not completely wild nature of childhood. Cherries appear with a surprising frequency (**B, D, H**, 17). They are probably intended to convey youthful vitality, purity, a plaything, although they are also attractive objects for an artist to enliven a dark canvas. What do children wear? Is there a strong gender divide and at what age does it change? What cultural meanings do costumes convey? Who goes bareheaded? These questions have attracted too much attention.

Fifthly, the patrons and their subjects tend to be drawn from a rather restricted social class, although this did widen during the centuries by encompassing royalty, aristocracy, gentry and wealthy merchants. Only with the development of photography from the mid-nineteenth century did the portrait of the entire family, the individual child or children become cheap enough to encompass mass society and popular culture. Even the reception of our paintings was confined to subsequent generations of the patron class until the twentieth century when many found their way into public museums and art galleries, and on to the internet. It must be remembered and repeatedly emphasised that the history of children's appearances in paintings can only reflect the intentions of the social élite and their artistic collaborators, and then only with numerous ambiguities.

Funeral memorials to departed children and their mothers

Up to this point we have mainly considered the iconography of paintings as potential historical evidence, although both **N** and several passing references to the presence of children in family monuments remind us that other forms of plastic representations have been at least as common in the past as portraits. Here we turn to a brief discussion of children's appearances in funeral monuments and of the distinctive commemoration in tomb effigies of mothers who died in childbirth. However, just as Pigler's survey concluded that paintings of dead children were unusual, or rarely survived, so Nigel Llewellyn has observed that there are 'comparatively few post-Reformation funeral monuments to children' in England.[173] Children certainly do appear in church monuments, but they are generally kneeling in devotional prayer below or at the feet of their dead parents or they are held as infants in their mother's arms or they represent special, often royal, cases. For instance, James I's daughter Sophia, who died in 1606 at 3 days old, was commemorated by a monument erected the following year in Westminster Abbey showing her apparently asleep, lying in her cradle.[174]

The second example, funeral memorials to the deaths of mother and infant in childbirth, offers another perspective on the changing styles by which children were commemorated, one that does suggest a contrast between the late-eighteenth and earlier centuries. It has been argued that in terms of English sculptured tombs, as distinct from brasses or tablets, the first to show an infant wrapped in swaddling clothes lying beside the feet of its mother who in turn rests in the traditional medieval pose alongside her husband dates from the 1570s. But the motif of the swaddled child held by the effigy of its mother, which appears to indicate that both died in childbirth, was most common in the 1620s and 1630s. The following argument has also been proposed:

> On the later [seventeenth-century childbirth] tombs the woman and swaddled child are more intimately associated, and death in childbirth is usually mentioned in the inscription. By referring directly to the cause of death, these tombs commemorate the deceased woman in a fashion more personal and intimate than had hitherto been attempted. They therefore seem to reflect the changing importance and value accorded the woman as wife and mother. At the same time, these tombs anticipate attitudes suggested in later seventeenth-, eighteenth- and even nineteenth-century tombs, where the expression of grief by the surviving family becomes a major theme.[175]

Of these childbirth tombs possibly the most emblematic is that to Lady Margaret Legh who was buried on 3 (or 23 or 29) July 1603 (All Saints church, Fulham,

Middlesex, now London, tomb monument dating from 1605 or later).[176] She sits facing the viewer; her left hand touches her breast while her right holds a swaddled infant; to her left, placed vertically, there is a second swaddled infant and to her right an hourglass (illustration **Rii**). Although the iconography seems straightforward, the inscription is not as informative as it might have been.

To y[e] memory
of
what dearer remayneth of that virteous lady, la. Margaret Legh,
daughter
of him y[e] sometimes was s'r Gilbert Gerrard, knt. and m'r of y[e]
rolles in y[e] highe court of chancery,
wife
to sir Peter Legh, of Lyme in the county of Chester, kt. and by him
y[e] mother of seven sons, Pierce, Frauncis, Radcliffe, Thomas, Peter, Gilbert,
and John, with two daughters, Anne and Catherine, of w'h Radcliffe, Gilbert,
John, deceased infants, the rest yet surviving to the happy increase of
their house: y[e] years she enjoyed were 33, yt her
husband enjoyed her 17, at which period she yielded her soul to the
blessedness of long rest, and her body to the earth, July 3 1603.
This inscription, in y[e] note of piety and love,
by her sad husband is here
devotedly placed.[177]

Lady Margaret was probably born in 1570 and certainly married in September 1585. During her seventeen years of marriage she had nine children of whom the eighth and ninth may have been Gilbert and John since at least one of her two daughters had been born in the 1590s (Anne was born in 1595). It has not been recorded whether Gilbert and John were twins, but if they were and she did indeed die in childbirth, then it is more likely that Lady Margaret would have been depicted holding both deceased infants. Alternatively, Lady Margaret may have died giving birth to John, and Gilbert also died during the dangerous, plague-ridden summer of 1603, after the death of Elizabeth I in March. Table 4.3 helps to piece together Lady Margaret Legh's birth history, but the positions of Katherine, Gilbert and John cannot be established. It is even possible that Katherine was the last-born child and that at least one of the infants shown in the Fulham monument did survive into childhood.

The story of Lady Margaret Legh is worth pursuing on at least two further points. A full-length painting, said to be by Marcus Gheeraerts the Younger about 1600, shows Lady Margaret in the same dress as her funeral monument, suggesting that at least on this occasion such monuments to the dead followed life portraits (illustration **Ri**). Also, as table 4.3 makes clear, Lady Margaret's husband remarried within twelve months of becoming a widower. Lady Dorothy Legh, a wealthy widow with no surviving children, was also the subject of a Gheeraerts portrait dated 1615 in which she wears her predecessor's magnificent strings of pearls.[178]

Table 4.3 **The birth history of Lady Margaret Legh**

Name	Born	Married	Died	Comments
Sir Peter Legh	1563	twice	17 February 1636	knighted 1598
Margaret Gerard	1570?	1585	3? July 1603	daughter of Sir Gilbert Gerard, Master of the Rolls
Dorothy Egerton	1560?	1604	April 1639	daughter of Sir Richard Egerton and widow of Richard Brereton
1 Piers	1588	1618	1624	*m* Ann, daughter of Sir John Savile
2 Francis	1590	1630	2 February 1643	*m* Anne, daughter of Sir Edmund Fenner
3 Radcliffe				died in infancy
4 Thomas	1594	yes	1639	*m* Lettice, daughter of Sir George Calveley
5 Anne	1595	3 January 1613	1642	*m* Richard Bold
6 Peter	1599	yes	1641	*m* twice
Katherine			1617	
Gilbert				
John			1603?	

Note: *c* baptised; *m* married; *b* buried

Source: based on Evelyn, Lady Newton, *The House of Lyme From its Foundation to the End of the Eighteenth Century* (London: Heinemann, 1917).

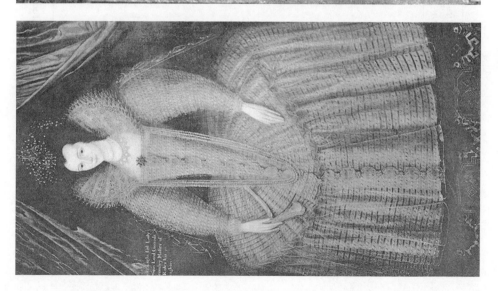

Ri (*left*) Lady Margaret Legh, 1600, Marcus Gheeraerts the Younger (c.1561–1636), private collection

Rii (*right*) Monument to Lady Margaret Legh, after 1605, perhaps associated with Maximilian Colt, Fulham church, London (author's photograph)

Table 4.4 Styles of American gravestones

Period	Style or motif	Principal attitude towards death	Hijiya's observations
1. 1640–1710	Plain style	Resignation	minimal inscription (names, dates, 'here lies . . .'); significance of technical and fiscal constraints; artless gravestones, humble, meek; unworthy of conspicuous commemoration; calm, resigned, almost absent-minded attitude towards death; between passive resignation and mystical trust
2. 1670–1770	Death's head	Awe	skull flanked by extended wings; intended as a reminder to keep death in mind; reflects Puritan ambivalence to death; death as gateway to both torment and bliss, damnation and salvation; terror plus hope lead to awe (fearful reverence)
3. 1740–1820	Angel	Confidence	human face with wings (often cherub-like); confidence in salvation; simple anticipation of endless happiness
4. 1780–1850	Urn and/or willow	Mourning	most important turning point; urn and/or willow often accompanied by weeping woman; willow used to symbolise grief over someone's death; cultivation of mourning which supplanted fear and hope
5. 1840–1920	Monumentalism	Defiance	no single motif; reminder of past life of particular person; e.g. lambs, doves, cradles used on children's graves; reluctance to let go of dead
6. 1900–2001	Modern plain style	Ignorance	absence of ornament and minimum of inscription, plain and inconspicuous; persistence of traditional, resigned attitude towards death (studied ignorance); less sorrow over deaths of old, who form the overwhelming majority

Source: James A. Hijiya, 'American gravestones and attitudes toward death: a brief history', Proceedings of the American Philosophical Society 127 (1983), pp. 339–63, especially the table on p. 341.

Placing the portrait alongside the funeral monument and noting their connection gives the story of Lady Margaret's life and death greater poignancy, but her case also demonstrates quite clearly how difficult it is to draw firm conclusions about experiences and feelings. What does the monument actually tell us about the circumstances of the subjects' deaths and the responses of those who remain? Here is Catherine Belsey's version of the story based on monument and inscription:

> Text and image together constitute a perfect representation of the emergent family, fruitful, pious, loving – and potentially tragic. The serenity of the whole can be read as an affirmation of triumph over loss, but the loss is evident in the sad husband's tribute to motherhood as the patient endurance of sorrow. Daughter, wife and mother, Margaret Legh is memorialised as an ideal woman according to family values. Her death, if it occurred while giving birth to her ninth child at the age of 33, is the outcome of marital love, and her loss is experienced as tragic in direct proportion to its cause.[179]

Table 4.3 offers a different account; one of marriage at 15 or 16, of repeated pregnancies, of early death, and of a husband who remarried quickly, before the monument was begun. It is short on 'marital love' and harsh in terms of demographic reality.

Returning to childbirth tombs in general, Nicholas Penny has considered this theme in some detail for the period 1780–1835. He identifies and illustrates two distinctive conventions in the representation of women who died in childbirth during these decades: the first portrays the woman as she dies, and the second shows 'the spirits of the mother and her child ascending to Heaven, sometimes leaving a draped body and draped mourners behind'.[180] Compared with their early seventeenth-century equivalents, the monuments from 1780 to 1835 tend to be far more naturalistic, more dynamic; they are likely to involve mourners, full-bodied angels, to strike poses; to focus almost exclusively on the mother and, as a consequence, to omit or minimise the presence of the dead infant. Penny speculates on the reasons such monuments came to popularity at this time – the influence of Rousseau, greater frequency of love-matches, death in childbirth declining among the upper classes – and why by 1850 they had passed from fashion – general decline in church monuments, further decline in maternal mortality, or even 'a squeamishness [which] had gradually grown up around the whole subject'.[181]

Pictorial ambiguities?

Before attempting to draw together some concluding observations we shall offer one final example, an apparently optimistic one, of the use of plastic material to interpret changing attitudes towards death. James A. Hijiya has provided a remarkably clear and imaginative commentary on the styles and motifs of American tombstones since the mid-seventeenth century.[182] His conclusions are summarised in table 4.4. It is important to note that the styles and motifs have phases when they move into fashion and are then abandoned, that the periods therefore are not sharply defined. It is also significant that Hijiya feels confident enough to draw implications in terms of prevailing attitudes to death and to summarise each of them by a single word: resignation, awe, confidence, mourning, defiance, ignorance. If only it was this straightforward. On closer examination, it appears that Hijiya has actually made a rather simple distinction between the period before 1800, during which grave markers were used to encourage the living to prepare for death, and the post-1800 years when they were used to look back on a life lived, to commemorate.[183]

The detailed classification in table 4.4 and illustrations **Ri** and **Rii** give two important warnings on the problems of generalisation; of reading too much into a picture; of inventing an interesting narrative; of turning an instance into a fashion, an entire artistic movement even; or of making a time-series out of style changes.

What would Ariès and Vovelle have made of this plastic evidence for the presence of children. As we have seen, the former would probably have applauded the exercise since it follows the example he set in *L'enfant*, although it employs a longer perspective and is more systematic. Vovelle, himself a user of images in his *L'heure du grand passage* (1993), would have been more sceptical of the value of portraits as historical evidence, especially their use to chart emotional attachment, although he did once attempt, not entirely successfully, to develop a 'serial history' from an analysis of the epitaphs on American tombstones and other memorials.[184] Both would probably have been surprised by the apparent continuity, and one might have been encouraged to persist in his belief that this was, at least in part, due to the comparatively favourable chances of child survival among the English.

5

Emotions and Literature

Shakespeare's 11-year-old twin son, Hamnet, was buried on 11 August 1596. How did his father react to the death? Did he express his grief, and if so in what way? To what extent can his work be seen to be autobiographical or biographical? If Shakespeare did express his own feelings of loss and regret, were other poets and playwrights so moved by their experiences?[185] Chapter 5 explores some of these questions, but it will also conduct an experiment to see whether it is possible to use literary works as a way of describing changing attitudes to the deaths of children since the sixteenth century. It deals mainly with elegies, a form of poetry intended for the intense expression of emotions. It is a compressed form so that illustrations can be viewed in their entirety, and it is a form of literary discourse that, unlike the novel, has a long and continuous history, especially in English.[186]

This will not be an experiment without its problems. Let us consider just a few. Selection is required; there can be no sense of a representative sample and thus what is expressive and illuminating must be privileged over what may be said to be typical. The 'materials' on which this chapter is based comprise 69 poems written between the 1570s and the 1990s; they are printed in full in Chapter 6. They have been selected to reflect differences in sentiment, forms of expression, authorship, relationship, purpose and audience. Most deal directly with the deaths of children, but some have been chosen to reflect other sentiments or purposes. There is no attempt to make the 69 equally representative of the centuries: the eighteenth century is distinctly under-represented and in the nineteenth century other literary forms, the novel in particular, took the place of the poem as the most popular literary medium. Indeed, several studies have been undertaken using nineteenth-century novels as a means of reflecting popular feelings of grief over the deaths of children.[187]

Many of the authors are parents lamenting the loss of their own child. There are also sufficient examples for some form of distinction to be drawn in terms of gender differences: mother and father, daughter and son. The poems of mothers will prove especially informative. But others relate to the deaths of children in general or a particular child with whom the poet was familiar. There are also some examples that deal with the deaths of older people, especially mothers, but the mortality of other adults has largely been ignored. Several of the poems are well known, often appearing in anthologies, or at least they are by poets who are well known, but the obscure and anonymous are also represented. Some can bear comparison with the best from their times, while others are devoid of literary merit although their social comment may still be of value.

The styles and forms of expression, as well as the subject matter, passed through cycles of popularity and relative neglect. The sonnet, epigram and epitaph each had particular periods when they were in vogue. For example, the commercial market for epitaphs by famous professional poets was especially important in the eighteenth century while epigrams were popular in the sixteenth and seventeenth, and the sonnet form fell into neglect during the seventeenth century. The use of classical allusions and styles, especially the influence of Latin verse, had a marked impact on the work of some, but especially those classically trained male poets writing for their similarly educated friends and patrons. These precedents had at times profound effects on how a poet might represent feelings to the extent that such expressions often appear heavily over-stylised, rather forced, even remote and uncaring. This becomes an important problem for the interpretation of text as comment when it is appreciated that the Romantic movement of the late eighteenth century is claimed to have adopted the subject of children, their perceptions and experiences, as one of its central themes.[188] As we saw in Chapter 4, portraits were supposed to have become more naturalistic, more child-like in their reflection on life. It would be anticipated that during this period the premature deaths of children also took on a new meaning as a cause for concern, anger as well as grief.

These various problems will be considered again in more detail as we conduct our experiment. This chapter sets the scene for interpretation, and justifies the selection of the 69 poems that will be analysed in detail in Chapter 7. It deals with the ways in which grief, as one of the emotions, and psychologists, anthropologists, historians and literary specialists have considered mourning. It offers an outline of reception theory, the ways in which readers receive texts. And it discusses the various forms of autobiographical writing, especially the possibility of using imaginative literature as a source of historical evidence. It also makes a case for a more thoughtful and positive appreciation of the potential of such material while being sceptical about the traditional historical sources, especially diaries, and sensitive to their limitations as a device for charting the varying emotional responses of adults, particularly parents, to the deaths of children. In this chapter we are clearly on Vovelle's level 3, considering discourses on death, particularly those developed in certain forms of literature, especially the elegy.[189]

Grief and other emotions

Charles Darwin's *The Expression of the Emotions in Man and Animals* (1872) is a remarkable book in several respects.[190] It was one of the first to contain photographic plates; it combined the results of direct observation of the expressions of human beings and animals with those from an international questionnaire; and it helped to initiate what has come to be a long-running debate on the relative importance of biology and culture in the human sciences (between the 'universalists' and the 'relativists', between emotion as 'universal bodily feeling' and 'cultural meaning'). Although the study is mainly concerned with physiological expressions, those that appear in obvious facial contortions (joy and weeping) and other physical signs, Darwin did touch on grief as an emotion:

> When a mother suddenly loses her child, sometimes she is frantic with grief, and must be considered to be in an excited state; she walks wildly about, tears her hair or clothes, and wrings her hands. This latter action is perhaps due to the principle of antithesis, betraying an inward sense of helplessness that nothing can be done. The other wild and violent movements may be in part explained by the relief experienced through muscular exertion, and in part by the undirected flow of nerve-force from the excited sensorium. But under the sudden loss of a beloved person, one of the first and commonest thoughts which occurs, is that something more might have been done to save the lost one. An excellent observer, in describing the behaviour of a girl at the sudden death of her father, says she 'went about the house wringing her hands like a creature demented, saying "it was her fault;" "I should never have left him;" "If I had only sat up with him,"' &c. With such ideas vividly presented before the mind, there would arise, through the principle of associated habit, the strongest tendency to energetic action of some kind.[191]

In his paper entitled 'Mourning and melancholia' (1917), Sigmund Freud developed a rather sketchy outline of what he called 'the normal emotion of grief, and its expression in mourning'. Grief could be characterised as involving a feeling of pain, dejection, loss of interest in the outside world, loss of the capacity to love. In time these features are relieved by the work of mourning.[192] If Freud only scratched the surface, he did so in a highly provocative way. First, if grief can be thought of as normal then absence of grief must be abnormal. Secondly, the symptoms of normal grief can be overcome by what, following Freud, is termed 'mourning work' or 'grief work'. We shall leave the question of death without grief until Chapter 7 (p. 200), and focus here on the notion of 'grief work'.

Paul C. Rosenblatt has provided an especially accessible outline of the concept of 'grief work', together with the various factors that are likely to influence its intensity and duration.[193] Of particular significance is the interplay between the effects of 'memories' and 'hopes'. The former will be most important when the deceased is an adult and has been co-resident for a long period with the subject, while hopes will be at their height for children and the younger ages in general. Memories are likely to encourage discontinuous grieving, while hopes may generate a more continuous response. 'Grief work' is required by the subject in order to detach him or herself from the person who has been lost and this requires energy, effort and a willingness to face up to pain. The notion of a 'rate of grief work' which can be assessed in terms of the length of time needed to disconnect hopes and memories is also helpful since it suggests the possibility that simple models of the various patterns of grief intensity

Figure 5.1 'Grief work' models

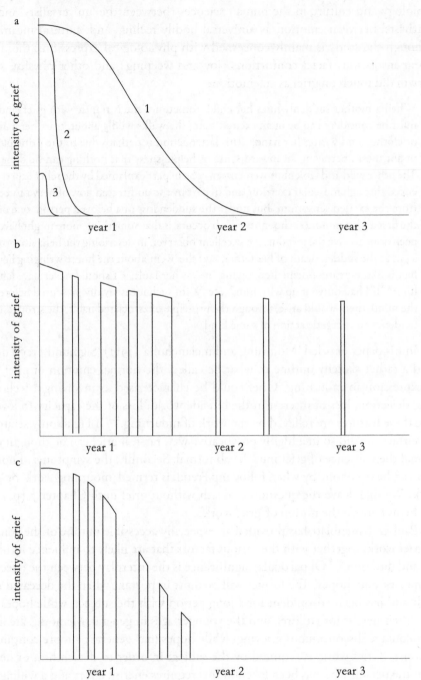

Note: see text for explanation.

and duration may be developed. Some examples of these models are shown in figure 5.1.

Figure 5.1a illustrates three possibilities for the decline of grief intensity with time. Curve 1 suggests very intense grief that only begins to fade after a year; curve 2 starts from a similarly intense point, but fades very rapidly; curve 3 shows low intensity and short duration. The model in figure 5.1b, on the other hand, represents discontinuous grief the intensity of which plateaus at a rather high level, but recurs in ever shorter episodes. Finally, figure 5.1c has grief expressed in episodes, but the rate of decline matches that of curve 1 in figure 5.1a. Figure 5.1b is probably most appropriate in representing the pattern of grief intensity for a spouse (a single partner), or possibly a sibling, one with whom there has been close contact (co-residence) over a long period of time and for whom there is a substantial accumulation of memories. Figure 5.1a may be more appropriate as a means of illustrating the intensity of grief shown in the case of child deaths where hopes and memories combine, but the former are more significant than the latter which have had less time to accumulate. In this case there will be a curve for each child prematurely lost and these curves may overlap. Curve 3 in figure 5.1a can be used to illustrate Ariès's parental indifference hypothesis discussed in chapter 2. Finally, figure 5.1c offers a more appropriate model of the way in which grief is expressed or displayed when hopes rather than memories are dominant, but when incidents or memories spark emotions.

The models in figure 5.1 also suggest some interesting supplementary questions about the ways in which the rate of 'grief work' might be judged. For example, we need to consider the role of language in the expression of grief and what has been done in comparative linguistics to tease out the extent of change in and variation between societies. However, there is also a need to be wary of applying these new psychological theories and methods to historical situations. The remainder of this section briefly considers parental grief and pregnancy loss; the use of emotion keywords; and the writing of emotion histories. The following sections take us from language into literature.

It has been recognised in recent decades that miscarriage, stillbirth and the death of a young baby can lead to intense parental grief. It has also been claimed that the death of an infant should be regarded as no less an important loss than that of an older child or an adult. Further, it has been argued that the response to pre-natal deaths can be analysed in the same ways as post-natal ones. There is, in short, no significant relationship in the form or intensity or duration of parental grief in terms of fetal-infant age. Outside the fields of psychology and bereavement counselling, a number of anthropologists have also pointed to the relative neglect of the subject in their own and related disciplines. They have even expressed their surprise at the neglect of pregnancy loss in literary works generally.[194] Given today's ambiguous cultural practices – the development of IVF treatment and the legalisation of abortion, for example – these reactions are not surprising, but they do not necessarily help us understand how parental responses to very early deaths have changed in the long term especially now that the risks of maternal mortality are so low in the West. However, they do warn us about the dangers of 'presentism', of taking the models in figure 5.1, for instance, and expecting them to be equally appropriate, or otherwise, in past centuries.

Among anthropologists and cultural psychologists there has been much debate in recent years on the ways in which emotions are expressed in different societies and the possibility that study of certain keywords, their use and variation across languages, may prove a useful way of comparing cultural practices.[195] For example, Catherine A. Lutz in her *Unnatural Emotions* (1988) argues that 'emotional meaning is fundamentally structured by particular cultural systems and particular social and material environments'; that emotional experience is pre-eminently cultural, not precultural; that emotions are not simply 'bio-psychological events'; and that the translation of emotion words between languages must also be combined with comparison of 'ethnotheoretical ideas and the scenes they are encoded in', that is, with actions or ideological practices.[196] Although Lutz is principally concerned with the differences between cultures, her focus on language is helpful here in at least two respects. First, it offers an illustration of the potential, but also the possible pitfalls, of such a cross-cultural comparative analysis, one emphasising language, ideas, actions together (known as 'situated speech practices'). Secondly, it provides a well-aimed critique of contemporary Western, as opposed to indigenous, models that also tend to have strong bio-psychological roots. Anna Wierzbicka has considered some of these issues from the perspective of comparative linguistics. She suggests that both word frequencies (she uses the example of 'homeland') and keywords can be helpful in cultural comparisons, but that the selection of such words to focus on cannot be an 'objective discovery procedure', but must be subjective, even 'inspired'. Once again, the intention is to compare cultures through the device of word use, lexicons and vocabulary in general since the last mentioned can be thought of as a 'sensitive index of the culture of a people'.[197] However, our objective in this study is to consider change over the long term in one culture; we are interested in how the expression of emotions, but especially grief, changed and thus how language and vocabulary shifted during the centuries. It is possible, we shall see in Chapter 7, that the analysis of word frequencies and the selection of keywords or word-groups can also play useful roles in this historical experiment, yet it also needs to be remembered that the very concept of 'the emotions' has a relatively short pedigree.[198]

Some historians have also turned their attentions to dealing with emotions explicitly. Here is one example of such a discussion:

> Prior to the early modern transition, Western norms did not stress intense, recip-
> rocal affection between parents and children, and positively discouraged romance
> – especially in the upper classes – as the basis for family formation. Anger was freely
> and publicly expressed as part of social and familial hierarchy, and also as a function
> of an emphasis on shame as the chief emotional means of community discipline.
> Vocabulary itself inhibited discussion of many emotional niceties that would subse-

quently become commonplace. With varying levels of contrast, historians have painted a premodern society, and individuals within it, quite different emotionally from the patterns with which we are familiar.

Then, during a roughly 150-year span, beginning in the second half of the 17th century, the intensity of various emotional relationships within the family increased. 'Love' became increasingly approved as a basis for courtship and marriage, and its absence a reason for dissolution of marriage. Here, again, was a shift in attitudes that carried over into emotion behaviour and perceptions and possibly to the frequency and intensity of certain kinds of feeling states. Children were increasingly seen as recipients and providers of affection. Anger, particularly within the family, became newly identified and reproved.[199]

The popularity of 'psychohistory' with its particular interest in love, shame, guilt, jealousy and anger as well as the psychological state of famous individuals (especially the highly original, the thoroughly evil and charismatic) seems to have peaked in the 1980s. But there have been a number of more recent attempts to reinvigorate the field by, for example, developing a general framework for the history of emotions and attempting an emotional history of the United States.[200] Neither of these quite work. They fail to demonstrate by example how one might recover the changing history of emotions, and not just at a point in past time, 1789 for instance. This may be because the enterprise is too ambitious; emotions, collectively rather than individually, are too varied and complex as a category of feelings to be treated empirically and in the long term. As the passage quoted above tends to demonstrate, the temptation to broad generalisation and simple periodisation is too great.

Reception and contextual literary history

Most of the remainder of this chapter re-focuses our attention on grief, rather than the emotions in more general terms, and on literature, rather than language or vocabulary. We need to be confident that literature is capable of providing some form of historical evidence, to be aware of the ways in which historians have employed such materials, but also of the approaches scholars of literature have adopted to history.

Reception theory offers both a reminder and an interesting starting point for discussion. While writers create texts, their meanings are established by readers (viewers have been said to operate in the same way). This line of argument has been developed from debates on the nature of discourse and owes much to the early work in linguistics by Ferdinand de Saussure and in literary theory by Roman Jakobson.[201] The three parts of figure 5.2 attempt a diagrammatic summary of some of their ideas and place them alongside a similarly simplistic representation of reception theory's principal contention. Figure 5.2a draws the distinction between form and content, between signifier and signified, sound image and concept, sound and meaning, means of representation and what is represented. In figure 5.2b the distinction is between addresser and addressee in terms of the communication of a message, but the circumstances in which the message is communicated, the possibility that the message is in some form of code and the general context in which the interchange is conducted are also highlighted. Finally, figure 5.2c deals with the distinction between production and reception. The thought process finds expression in speech and in writing. They both produce, or can be translated into, texts which have form and content, and which can be received by being listened to or read. While

    (a) speaking → listening

and

    (b) writing → text → reading

are both direct, one-to-one, forms,

    (c) speaking → transcript text → reading

and

    (d) writing → text → reading aloud → listening

are also distinctive and common forms of communication which are indirect; they require a transcriber or a reader to act as intermediary between addresser and addressee. In all but the first case both the form and the content of the text influence reception, but the meaning that is given to the text is also affected by who the individual reader or listener is, their physical and mental abilities, their expectations and experiences, and so forth. In the particular case of literary texts (b) is the most likely, but for poetry (d) is also common (writer as reader). The process of

Figure 5.2 Linguistic and reception theory models

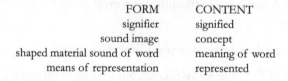

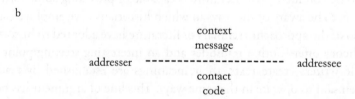

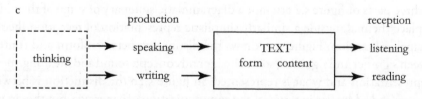

Note: see text for explanation.

text production by transcription, printing and publishing may also be of significance especially if the author has died before publication and agents, editors, typesetters etc. play unchecked roles. In none of our cases may it be assumed that the author's intentions (thoughts, feelings) can be simply and directly derived by a reader from the text produced. The appreciation of this point is both salutary and challenging, but it should not become destructive.

The rise to prominence of 'new historicism' in the 1980s and 1990s placed special emphasis on the historical context of literature. It was not possible to interpret a text fully until the social, political, economic and cultural circumstances of its production had been properly appreciated. This went beyond asking who was in the audience, what did the patrons want, and what was the market for poetry books and novels to an analysis of literary works as political devices and cultural artefacts.[202] However, this is neither an entirely new approach nor one that has ever gone without challenge. For example, A. C. Bradley's *Shakespearean Tragedy* (1904) contains some notes on Macbeth that reflect on his possible age and the fact that he appears to have had no children (otherwise, it is thought, he would not have ordered the murder of Macduff's). L. C. Knight's subsequent essay asks *How Many Children had Lady Macbeth?* (1933). His answer, of course, is that we should not be asking the question: 'the only profitable approach to Shakespeare is a consideration of his plays as dramatic poems, or his use of language to obtain a total complex emotional response'.[203]

We shall return to this contest in the next section, but first it is worth taking a brief look at some examples of the new historicism at work, just to acquaint ourselves with the possibilities offered. Beginning with the use of text to elaborate context, Virginia Mason Vaughan's *Othello: A Contextual History* (1994) offers interesting illustrations. Vaughan uses the play to analyse four different forms of discourse: the geo-political involving the relationship between Venetians and Turks; the military, knights and mercenaries; the racial, black and white; and the marital, husbands and wives. In similar fashion, Catherine Belsey's *Shakespeare and the Loss of Eden* (1999) explores early modern desire, marriage, parenthood and sibling rivalry via, respectively, *Love's Labour's Lost* and *As You Like It, Cymberline, The Winter's Tale* and *Hamlet*. Her approach is more critical of new historicism, claiming that there has been a tendency to treat texts uncritically, as though they are relatively transparent; to avoid proper emphasis on power and dissent; and to neglect change, why certain cultural values do not survive.[204] The use of historical context to illuminate texts is well illustrated by Jonathan Goldberg's *James I and the Politics of Literature* (1983). Here we find detailed analysis of family relations, especially fatherly authority, and its reflection in the patriarchal state, as seen in *Romeo and Juliet* and *King Lear*, but also Ben Jonson's court masques.[205] Two additional examples illustrate broader, perhaps more tentative approaches of a literary scholar to history and of an historian to literature. In both cases, the texts are poems. Lauro Martines has argued the case for 'social literary analysis'. He sees poetry as giving voice to historical and social realities, and in its Renaissance form of providing 'the chief gateway to certain zones in experience'.

Cleanth Brooks, on the other hand, is perhaps a little cautious, though nonetheless positive about the potential of finding historical evidence in seventeenth-century poetry. However, he also warns us: 'To be blunt, one can know all about an author and the circumstances under which his poem was written and still not grasp the meaning of the poem'.[206]

Autobiographical writing

The traditional sources used by historians to recover the life experiences, feelings and emotions of our ancestors are letters, diaries, and, in certain cases, wills. Letters offer an especially important perspective if both sides of the correspondence, between husband and wife for example, have survived, but even here the couple would need to be parted on a regular basis for the correspondence to be required. More generally, letters offer a fitful and often one-sided picture. Vovelle, as we have already seen (pp. 29–30), has used wills to very good effect to chart the secularisation of Provençal society during the eighteenth century, yet wills are very particular legal documents intended to apportion material goods. They follow a distinct formula of words that does not lend itself to emotional outpourings. Diaries, however, should provide important, continuous and highly revealing sources for the study of events and feelings alike.

Linda A. Pollock's *Forgotten Children* (1983) demonstrates this point to the full. Her analysis of 194 diaries written by British and 105 by American adults (also, respectively, 93 and 28 autobiographies) draws her to the following conclusions:[207]

There is no change in the extent of parental grief over the centuries and no support at all for the argument that parents before the 18th century were indifferent to the death of their young offspring, whereas after the 18th century they grieved deeply. (pp. 141–42)

It seems as if parents grieved at the death of a baby for what that infant would have become whereas, at the death of an older child, they grieved not only for what that child would have become, but also for what the child had been. (p. 141)

The texts examined reveal that even parents who regarded their children as innocent could still be ambivalent to them – many parents found the amount of time and attention that children took up both wearisome and exasperating. It seems as if it was the strength of parental affection and involvement in their own children that produced this state of mind. (p. 141)

Contrary to the belief of such authors as Ariès, there was a concept of childhood in the 16th century. This may have become more elaborated through the centuries but, none the less, the 16th-century writers studied did appreciate that children were different from adults and were also aware of the ways in which children were different ... (pp. 267-68)

The sources used reveal that there have been very few changes in parental care and child life from the 16th to the 19th century in the home, apart from social changes and technological improvements. Nearly all children were wanted, such developmental changes as weaning and teething aroused interest and concern and parents revealed anxiety and distress at the illness or death of a child. (p. 268)

Clearly, these are important findings that rest almost entirely on the interpretation of a single source. Pollock herself provides a very detailed and highly critical evaluation of the diary as historical evidence under three headings: representation, censorship and generalisation. On the first, it must be noted that although 8 per cent of the British adult diaries are classified as from the sixteenth century, with a further 20 per cent from the seventeenth (table 5, p. 92), in fact only 11 of the 20 texts cover any years prior to 1600 and then only two of the 11 are recorded as having been written by a person who had children who died (Appendix table, p. 272). For the seventeenth century, there are 49 texts, 23 of whose authors experienced the deaths of one or more children. The 49 produced 265 children (four had no children) and there were 72 child deaths giving a 27 per cent mortality rate, a not unreasonable figure for a population with moderate mortality (see figure 3.1, p. 34). In terms of representation, while the seventeenth century may be secure the sixteenth century is, to say the least, poorly covered.

Since the publication of *Forgotten Children*, literary scholars and historians have become even more acutely aware that historical texts, diaries included, can be read in many different ways, and that as with other forms of autobiographical writing the reader must consider the problem of author 'self-fashioning'.[208] The use of self-invention by the writer, only too obvious in such fictional autobiographies as *Jane Eyre*, can also apply in apparently objective, factual accounts such as diaries, even those which take the form of a dialogue with the self, a spur to greater acts of faith and Godly behaviour. Brigitte Glaser, for instance, has even suggested that seventeenth-century English diaries 'exhibit traces of having been influenced by literary conventions and of the writers' experimentation with the construction of their own lives along fictional lines'.[209] Such a line of thinking encourages the reclassification of diaries and letters, but not wills, as literary constructs, ones in which self-representation combines with self-censorship. Pollock's third heading, generalisation, is of particular importance because, as we have seen, neither the temporal nor the geographical coverage of the available diaries make definitive conclusions possible even for the literate, God-fearing, Protestant English.[210]

These observations, and Pollock's general conclusions, can be placed in sharper focus by examining two examples of autobiographical writing from the early seventeenth century: those of Nehemiah Wallington (1598–1658) and Ralph Josselin (1617–83). Wallington was a London artisan of a markedly Puritan persuasion who between 1618 and 1654 wrote a series of memoirs, letters and religious reflections as well as a spiritual diary. Some of the key events in his life are illustrated in table 5.1 including his marriage to Grace and the birth of their five children, only one of whom survived beyond childhood. Josselin was vicar of Earls Colne, Essex, between 1641 and 1683 during which time he kept a detailed, almost daily diary. The birth

Table 5.1 The birth history of Grace Wallington from 1621 to 1632

Name	Born	Married	Died	Comments
Nehemiah Wallington	1598	once	1658	wood turner of Eastcheap, London
Grace Rampaigne		1621		died after 1658
1 Elizabeth	1622		11 October 1625	
2 John	January 1624		5 April 1626	
3 Nehemiah	December 1625		November 1628	
miscarriage	5 June 1626			fright after gable end of house fell down
4 Sarah	December 1627	20 July 1647		*m* John Houghton, twins born 1649, son 1654
5 Samuel	February 1629		October 1630	died away at wet nurse
miscarriage	1630			fright caused by debt collectors calling

Note: c baptised; *m* married; *b* buried

Source: Paul S. Seaver, *Wallington's World: A Puritan Artisan in Seventeenth-Century London* (London: Methuen, 1985).

Table 5.2 **The birth history of Jane Josselin from 1640 to 1663**

Name	Born	Married	Died	Comments
Ralph Josselin	26 January 1617	once	b 30 August 1683	clergyman of Earls Colne, Essex
Jane Constable	c 26 November 1621	28 October 1640	1693	
1 Mary	12 April 1642		27 May 1650	
2 Thomas	30 December 1643		15 June 1673	
3 Jane	25 November 1645	30 August 1670		
4 Ralph	11 February 1648		21 February 1648	
5 Ralph	6 May 1649		2 June 1650	
6 John	19 September 1651	October 1681		
7 Anne	20 June 1654		31 July 1673	
miscarriage	June 1656			
8 Mary	14 January 1658	10 April 1683		
miscarriage	May 1659			
9 Elizabeth	20 June 1660	5 June 1677		
3 miscarriages	by December 1661			
10 Rebecka	26 November 1663	6 May 1683		

Note: c baptised; m married; b buried
Source: Alan Macfarlane, *The Family Life of Ralph Josselin: A Seventeenth-Century Clergyman* (Cambridge: Cambridge University Press, 1970).

history of his wife Jane is shown in table 5.2. Of their ten children, seven survived into adulthood and five are known to have married. Grace had two recorded miscarriages and Jane had perhaps five.

Wallington was openly grief-stricken at the deaths of his four children and, but to a lesser extent, when Grace miscarried. It is clear from Paul Seaver's account not only that Wallington had to be consoled by his wife, but also that such crises challenged his faith, the way that he knew he should behave in these circumstances, and that he allowed himself to be overwhelmed by inordinate grief at these times.[211] The relationship between Nehemiah and Grace appears to have been a deeply loving and supportive one. That between the Wallingtons and their children was strengthened by Grace nursing them at home, apart, that is, from the last child, Samuel, who was only sent away to be wet-nursed as a last desperate measure. Samuel's death and Grace's miscarriage generated particularly intense emotions in 1630. This year also marked the end of childbearing for Grace.

Although the Josselins were more fortunate than the Wallingtons in terms of childbearing, they too had to face repeated deaths.[212] Of the ten live-born children, five survived to marry and the others died at the following ages: 10 days, 13 months, 8 years and 1 month, 19 years and 1 month, 29 years and 6 months. Three may be said to have died in infancy or childhood, therefore. Of the deaths, two occurred within seven days of one another in May–June 1650 and a further pair (the young adults) happened in June–July 1673. Josselin's diary entries for the period 11 February (Ralph's birth) to 22 February 1648 (his burial) are a mixture of everyday events: Josselin was ill with a fever and regaining his health only slowly; his wife was recovering from the birth (unaided by a midwife); daughter Jane who had fallen in the fire, pushed a pair of scissors in her brother Thomas's eyebrow; but young Ralph sickened from birth and was always very quiet. Ralph's death is recorded with this entry:

21 February 1648
This day my deare babe Ralph, quietly fell a sleepe, and is at rest with the lord, the Lord in mercy sanctifie his hand unto mee, and doe mee good by it and teach mee how to walke more closely with him: I blesse god for any measure of patience, and submission to his will. oh Lord spare the rest of us that are living for thy name sake wee entreate thee; this correction though sad was seasoned with present goodnes. for first the lord had given it us untill both my selfe and wife had gotten strength, and so more fitt to beare it, than in the depth of our sickness; and lord gave us time to bury it in our thoughts, we lookt on it as a dying child, 3 or 4 dayes: 2 it dyed quietly without schreekes, or sobs or sad groanes, it breathd out the soule with 9 gaspes and dyed; it was the youngest, and our affections not so wonted unto it: the lord, ever the lord learne mee wisedome and to knowe his mind in this chastisement. (pp. 113-14)[213]

The diary entries for the days of the remaining deaths are as follows:

27 May 1650
This day a quarter past two in the afternoone my Mary fell asleepe in the Lord, her

soule past into that rest where the body of Jesus, and the soules of the saints are, shee was: 8 yeares and 45 dayes old when shee dyed, my soule had aboundant cause to blesse god for her, and was our first fruites, and those god would have offered to him, and this I freely resigned up to him, it was a pretious child, a bundle of myrrhe, a bundle of sweetnes, shee was a child of ten thousand, full of wisedome, woman-like gravity, knowledge, sweet expressions of god, apt in her learning, tender hearted and loving, an obedient child to us it was free from rudeness of little children, it was to us as a boxe of sweet ointment, which now its broken smells more deliciously than it did before, Lord I rejoyce I had such a present for thee, it was patient in the sicknesse, thankefull to admiracion; it lived desired and dyed lamented, thy memory is and will bee sweete unto mee (p. 203)

2 June 1650
... my deare Ralph before midnight fell asleepe whose body Jesus shall awaken, his life was continuall sorrow and trouble, happy he who is at rest in the lord, my deare wife, ill as if she would have dyed, the lord revived her againe for which his holy name bee praised, it was one of the most lovely corpses that ever was seene (p. 205)

15 June 1673
about one a clocke in the morning my eldest sonne Thomas and my most deare child ascended early hence to keepe his everlasting Sabbath with his heavenly father, and Saviour with the church above, his end was comfortable, and his death calme, not muche of pain til the Satturday afore. in my course this morning I read Josh; I: which had words of comfort, god making his word my counsellour and comfort. He was my hope. but some yeares I have feared his life, god hath taken all my first brood but Jane. lett all live in thy sight sanctified. a wett morning, the heavens for some time have mourned over us (p. 567)

31 July 1673
This morning after 2 of the clocke my deare Ann in her twentieth year died with mee at Colne. a good child, following her brother to London. and from thence hither, to lie in his grave, loving in their lives and in their deaths they were not divided. lying in the same grave. twenty three yeares before god opened the grave and Mary first the eldest of that brood and Ralph the youngest after, lay in the same grave. god hath taken 5 of 10. lord lett it bee enough, and spare that we may recover strength; bee reconciled in the blood of thy son my saviour and make all mine thine as I hope thou wilt and shine upon mee for the Lords sake in mercy. (p. 568)

There can be no doubt that Ralph Josselin felt deeply about the untimely deaths of his children, whether they were infants or adults. These five extracts are in one sense conclusive evidence, and they can be supplemented by mention of other occasions on which Josselin recorded his memory of them after their deaths.[214] But it is also clear that the diary is not just a record of humdrum events in a busy vicar's life; it is not even a set of incidental observations and opinions. Rather, Josselin's diary is a work of devotion, almost a continuous prayer to the Almighty for support and guidance to help bring the author closer to the Godly ways of living, to righteous self-improvement. Like Wallington, Josselin often struggled to contain his emotions but the Lord's will is never seriously questioned; even the observation that five out of ten should be enough is turned into a plea – let it be so. For this reason, and despite its frequent use as an historical source, Josselin's diary needs to be treated with much care; it is a devotional Puritan text, a dialogue with the Lord and not simply a reflective account.[215]

Autobiographical writing offers a body of material in the form of diaries and letters, for example, which while highly revealing, cannot be taken at their face value. They may not be counted as literature, but as texts they pose several of the challenges to interpretation that one would expect to encounter in a poem or a novel. In the remainder of this section we shall consider examples of literary works that are, first, explicitly autobiographical and, secondly, in which the autobiographical content is ambiguous and contested.[216]

It has proved difficult to document fully the family life of Sir John Harington of Kelston, Somerset (1560–1612), the Elizabethan courtier, adventurer and poet, but through his letters and especially his book of epigrams it is possible to gain some sense of his feelings for his wife, Mary Rogers (**Ci**), and their many children.[217] Harington's *Epigrams both Pleasant and Serious* were first collected and published in 1615 after his death, although they must have been written mainly in the 1580s and 1590s. Here are some examples.[218]

4 OF A POINTED DIAMOND GIVEN BY THE AUTHOR TO HIS WIFE,
AT THE BIRTH OF HIS ELDEST SON

Dear, I to thee this Diamond commend,
In which, a model of thy self I send,
How just unto thy joints this circlet sitteth,
So just thy face and shape my fancy fitteth.
The touch will try this Ring of purest gold,
My touch tries thee as pure, though softer mold.
That metal precious is, the stone is true,
As true, as then how much more precious you?
The Gem is clear, and hath nor deeds a foil,
Thy face, nay more, thy fame is free from soil.
You'll deem this deer, because from me you have it,
I deem your faith more deer, because you gave it.
This pointed Diamond cuts glass and steel,
But this, as all things else, time wastes with wearing,
Where you, my Jewels multiply with bearing.

25 THE AUTHOR TO HIS WIFE, OF A WOMAN'S ELOQUENCE

My Mall, I mark that when you mean to prove me
To buy a velvet gown, or some such rich border,
Thou callst me good sweet heart, thou swearst to love me,
Thy locks, thy lips, thy looks, speak all in order,

Thou think'st, and right thou think'st, that these do move me,
That all these severally thy suit do further:
But shall I tell thee what most thy suit advances?
Thy fair smooth words? no, no, thy fair smooth haunches.

Addition 24 To MALL, TO COMFORT HER FOR THE LOSS OF A CHILD

When at the window thou thy doves are feeding,
Then think I shortly my Dove will be breeding,
Like will love like, and so my liking like thee,
As I to doves in many things can like thee.
Both of you love your lodgings dry and warm,
Both of you do your neighbours little harm,
Both love to feed upon the finest grain,
Both of your livings take but little pain,
Both murmur kindly, both are often billing,
Yet both to Venus sports will seem unwilling;
Both do delight to look your selves in Glasses,
You both love your own houses as it passes;
Both fruitful are, but yet the Dove is wiser,
For, though she have no friend that can advise her,
She, patiently can take her young ones loss,
Thou, too impatiently do bear such cross.

72 To HIS WIFE AFTER THEY HAD BEEN MARRIED 14 YEARS

Two Prenticeships with thee I now have been,
Mad times, sad times, glad times, our life hath seen,
Souls we have wrought four pair since our first meeting
Of which, two souls, sweet souls, were to to fleeting.
My workmanship so well doth please thee still,
Thou wouldst not grant me freedom by thy will:
A I'll confess such usage I have found,
Mine heart yet ne're desired to be unbound.
But though my self am thus thy prentice vowed,
My dearest Mall, yet thereof be not proud,
Nor claim no Rule thereby; there's no such cause:
For Plowden, who was father of the Laws
Which yet are read and ruled by his Enditings,
Doth name himself a Prentice in his writings,
And I, if you should challenge undue place,
Could learn of him to alter so the case:
I plain would prove, I still keep due priority,
And that good wives are still in their minority:
But far from thee, my dear, be such Audacity:
I doubt more thou dost blame my dull Capacity,
That though I travail true in my vocation,
I grow yet worse and worse at the occupation.

45 THE AUTHOR TO HIS WIFE

Mall, once in pleasant company by chance,
I whished that you for company would dance,
Which you refused, and said, your years require,
Now, Matron-like, both manners and attire.
Well, Mall, if needs thou wilt be Matron-like,
Then trust to this, I will a Matron like:
Yet so to you my love may never lessen,
As you for Church, house, bed, observe this lesson.
Sit in the Church as solemn as a Saint,
No deed, word, thought, your due devotion taint.
Vail (if you will) your head, your soul reveal
To him, that only wounded souls can heal.
Be in my house as busy as a Bee,
Having a sting for every one but me,
Buzzing in every corner, gathering honey.
Let nothing waste, that costs or yieldeth money.
And when thou seest my heart to mirth incline,
The tongue, wit, blood, warm with good cheer and wine,
And that by lawful fancy I am led,
To climb my nearest, thy undefiled bed
Then of sweet sports let no occasion scape,
But be as wanton, toying as an Ape.

There is much loving playfulness in these examples, as well as commemoration of family events (first son John's birth in 1587? (Epigram 4); fourteen years of marriage in 1597? (Epigram 72)); also some consolation for the loss of children (Epigrams 24 and 72). Dearest Mall is also teased for not wishing to dance; for being a busy bee about the house; for being parsimonious; for not being a wanton, but a matron (Epigram 45). She is also cast as a sexual object, a plaything, a body to be admired, to be used to bear more offspring (his jewels). There is a rich complexity of feelings and emotions even in these five illustrations. The reader learns of Sir John's desires, his regrets and sense of frustration.[219] Factually less helpful than most diaries, yet more revealing of the author's emotional state, these consciously autobiographical poems encourage the belief that from ones such as these can be recovered other parental sentiments. But what of those contentious autobiographical writings, the ones that may be deliberately obtuse or evasive to lead the reader on, perhaps?

A. L. Rowse has argued, in a way that has tended to irritate rather than convince literary scholars, that Shakespeare's *Sonnets* 'were autobiography before they became literature,'[220] and that if we wish to explore their autobiographical nature more fully, only one method is appropriate:

> As I have said all along, the proper method is an historical one: to take each poem one after the other, to follow it line by line, watching for every piece of internal information for its coherence with what is happening in the external world, checking for

consistency at every point, accumulating patiently every fact and what may legiti-
mately be inferred, until the whole structure stands forth clear. I said originally that
the historian's account of the matter could not be imputed.[221]

Rowse overplays his hand of course, but he also places in sharp focus the problem
of inferring autobiographical or biographical references in cases where they are not
made directly explicit. Here is an apparently undisputed example: Shakespeare's great
rival, Christopher Marlowe, died in a tavern brawl on 30 May 1593 and in *As You Like
It* we have Touchstone remarking to Audrey:

> When a man's verses cannot be understood, nor a man's good wit seconded with the
> forward child, understanding, it strikes a man more dead than a great reckoning in
> a little room.
> (*As You Like It*, 3.3.10).[222]

But this is too simple. We have no instances, as we do in Sir Philip Sidney's sonnet
sequence *Astrophil and Stella*, of the author virtually telling us the identity of his
principals and upon whom his thoughts are dwelling. Shakespeare's *Sonnets* are more
challenging historically yet, and perhaps thereby, most sublime poetically. Those
sonnets that have been mentioned in connection with his own emotions, as opposed
to character identity, remain at least opaque if not obscure compared with Sidney's.
But even here, William A. Ringler has remarked that:

> *Astrophil and Stella* is in no sense a diary, for in it Sidney did not write about the full
> range of his interests and activities, but only about those directly concerned with his
> love for Stella. His emotion may or may not have been recollected in tranquillity,
> but he was obviously in full command of himself and his materials while he was
> writing. Everything in his poem is focused on his relations with Stella; everything
> in his experience during those months [probably the summer of 1582] which did
> not directly relate to his central theme he ruthlessly excluded. Therefore, though
> the substance of his poem was autobiographical, mere fact was made subservient to
> the requirement of art.[223]

At least two of Shakespeare's *Sonnets* have been associated with either the period of
Hamnet's death or with the loss itself. Edgar I. Fripp in his *Shakespeare: Man and
Artist* (1938) links Sonnet 77 with the period 1587–95 and the increasingly infrequent
visits of Shakespeare to his wife and children in Stratford-upon-Avon, but when we
consider the sonnet in full the connection may appear rather more tenuous.[224]

> The glass will show thee how thy beauties wear,
> Thy dial how thy precious minutes waste,
> The vacant leaves thy mind's imprint will bear,
> And of this book, this learning mayst thou taste:
> The wrinkles which thy glass will truly show
> Of mouthed graves will give thee memory;
> Thou by the dial's shady stealth mayst know
> Time's thievish progress to eternity;

Look what thy memory cannot contain,
Commit to these waste blanks, and thou shalt find
Those children nursed, delivered from thy brain,
To take a new acquaintance of thy mind.
    These offices, so oft as thou wilt look,
    Shall profit thee, and much enrich thy book.
    (*Shakespeare's Sonnets*, 77)[225]

Most editors, Rowse included, ignore the reference to children and emphasise the theme of time, three gifts and the author's relationship with his young friend whom he appears to be presenting with a blank book for him to write down his thoughts.[226] Park Honan, a recent biographer of Shakespeare, favours Sonnet 37.[227]

As a decrepit father takes delight
To see his active child do deeds of youth,
So I, made lame by fortune's dearest spite,
Take all my comfort of thy worth and truth:
For whether beauty, birth, or wealth, or wit,
Or any of these all, or all, or more,
Entitled in thy parts do crowned sit,
I make my love engrafted to this store:
So then I am not lame, poor, nor despised,
Whilst that this shadow doth such substance give
That I in thy abundance am sufficed,
And by a part of all thy glory live:
    Look what is best, that best I wish in thee;
    This wish I have, then ten times happy me.
    (*Shakespeare's Sonnets*, 37)[228]

But once again it seems clear from the tone of the full sonnet, as well as its relationship to others in the early part of the collection, that Shakespeare is speaking metaphorically, that the young friend is being thought of as a son whose love (and abundance) will revitalise the poet (as well as relieving his poverty and feeling of social inferiority). The first 126 of Shakespeare's 154 sonnet collection are addressed to the beautiful, young, noble friend and the first 17 are intended to persuade the friend to marry and have children.[229] Sonnet 9 provides a good example that has even more allusions to marriage, bereavement and the need for children than 37 or 77.

Is it for fear to wet a widow's eye
That thou consum'st thyself in single life?
Ah, if thou issueless shalt hap to die,
The world will wail thee like a makeless wife;
The world will be thy widow and still weep
And thou no form of thee hast left behind,
When every private widow well may keep,
By children's eyes, her husband's shape in mind:
Look what an unthrift in the world doth spend,

Shifts but his place, for still the world enjoys it;
But beauty's waste hath in the world an end,
And kept unused the user so destroys it:
    No love toward others in that bosom sits
    That on himself such murd'rous shame commits.
(*Shakespeare's Sonnets*, 9)[230]

Dover Wilson surmises that poet and friend first met on 8 April 1597 at Wilton House, Wiltshire, that is on Lord William Herbert's seventeenth birthday, hence the 17 sonnets, and that they were written on the encouragement of Lord William's mother, the Countess of Pembroke.[231] This all seems rather fanciful, taking Rowse's historical method and close internal reading to a higher level. What we can say of *Shakespeare's Sonnets* is what Ringler said of *Astrophil and Stella*; while some of the substance and sentiment may have been autobiographical, mere fact was always made subservient to the requirement of art.[232]

Apart from the *Sonnets*, *The Tempest* and *King John* have been the subject of some discussion over their autobiographical qualities, the former in terms of its general characterisation and the latter in relation to a specific passage. Let us begin with the much later and far greater play, *The Tempest*. Is there a sense in which the relationship between Miranda and her father, Prospero, could reflect that between Susanna or Judith as they mature and seek a marriage partner, and as they are watched over by their father William? Susanna Shakespeare was born in 1583 and married in 1607 while Judith, the twin sister of Hamnet, was born in 1585 and married in 1616, a few months before her father's death and five years after the first performance of *The Tempest* in 1611 (see table 5.3).

In a lecture to the English Association entitled 'The impersonal aspect of Shakespeare's art', delivered on 11 June 1909, the distinguished biographer Sir Sidney Lee concluded that Shakespeare's 'work discovered the omnipotence of his imaginative faculty, his all-absorbing devotion to art. In his work he did not air his own woes.'[233] To illustrate his point Lee used the example of Miranda whom, he argued, 'was suggested by no episode in Shakespeare's private experience, but by popular romantic stories, for the time in general vogue, of girl princesses torn in infancy from home and civilised society and flung desolate by misfortune on the mercies of nature'.[234] His scorn of the 'personal theorist' was directed at Morton Luce whose edition of *The Tempest* had been published in 1902.[235] It is probably the following passage in Luce's 'Introduction' that Lee objected to most.

> No imaginative writer, not even the dramatist, if his period of authorship is a long one, and more especially if he writes in verse – not even a dramatist as impersonal as Shakespeare, can altogether stand aside from his work; at least his shadow will fall here and there on the pages as he bends over them; and those who read the many and varied dramatic productions of Shakespeare from one end of them to the other, and with the aid of the Sonnets and the poems, will get more than a glimpse of the great artist himself.

Table 5.3 The birth history of Anne Shakespeare

Name	Born	Married	Died	Comments
William Shakespeare	c 26 April 1564	once	23 April 1616	
Anne Hathaway	1556?	27 November 1582	6 August 1623	3 months pregnant when married
1 Susanna	c 26 May 1583	5 June 1607	11 July 1649	m Dr John Hall (1575?–1635), 1 child: Elizabeth (1608–70)
2 Hamnet twin	c 2 February 1585		b 11 August 1596	
3 Judith twin	c 2 February 1585	10 February 1616	9 February 1662	m Thomas Quiney (1589–1663?), 3 children: Shakespeare Quiney (1616–17, died aged 6 months), Richard (1618–39), Thomas (1619–39)

Note: c baptised; m married; b buried

Critics who contend for an absolute objectivity in the dramatic work of Shake-speare forget that they are making a man into a machine; that they are offering an insult to the wisdom of one who was the very wisest of their kind; and they deny him those attributes of a fully endowed mind which at other times they are over-anxious to concede.[236]

However, Luce's autobiographical argument was more subtle than Lee chose to acknowledge.

But, again, there is no need to insist upon any deliberate introduction of the bare facts of Shakespeare's life into *The Tempest* or any other of his plays; I merely repeat that the man – such as he was at the time of writing – will be present, consciously or unconsciously, in his work.[237]

In the 1930s the personal theorists found at least a partial champion in John Dover Wilson, whose thinly veiled attack on the 'scientific school of Shakespearean biography' singled out Lee's *A Life of William Shakespeare* for special attention.[238] In *The Essential Shakespeare: A Biographical Adventure* (1932) Dover Wilson was particularly critical of those who set aside the plays and poems, claiming that they are impersonal and therefore of no value as evidence, while relying entirely on external sources without appreciating that as such it has itself been selected to fortify the biographer's 'own implicit conception of the poet'. And that 'With most imagina-tive writers, memories of childhood and the natural scenes amid which they grew up are a primary source of later inspiration. It was so with Wordsworth; it was so with a very different writer, Dickens. It was certainly so also with Shakespeare.'[239] More recent editors and critics have shown themselves reluctant to follow Dover Wilson in terms of their approach to *The Tempest*. For example, in the introduction to his 1954 edition Frank Kermode remarks rather ruefully that 'Morton Luce ... gave what may be the best account of the autobiographical interpretation, as of so much else; it is my loss that I find his approach incompatible with my own'.[240] He prefers to emphasise 'the opposition of Nature and Art', the importance of place and magic, and of the play as a 'pastoral tragicomedy'. The American critic Harold Bloom still has a romantic spot for Shakespeare as father as Prospero, although not for Judith as daughter as Miranda, and certainly not for the ideology-driven bespoilers (Marxists, multiculturalists, feminists, *nouveau* historicists).[241] Indeed, it is the feminists who are now more inclined to see *The Tempest* in terms of family relations and sexual politics.[242] Miranda is the good daughter who remains chaste and chooses a partner who is also her father's choice; like Susanna, the physician's wife, she marries well. But Judith does not. In Edward Bond's play *Bingo* she is the only daughter, a rather difficult child, estranged from her father; and even in William Black's Victorian romance *Judith Shakespeare*, 'the fairest maid in Warwickshire', she is to say the least a scheming young lady.[243]

Finally, let us turn to the passage in *King John* that many think directly links to the death of Hamnet. It is reproduced below (p. 131) as poem **2**. Constance grieves for the loss of her young son Arthur. The play, though in existence in the early 1590s, could have been revised in 1596; there is no problem with dating therefore. Historian Rowse is entirely convinced, but editor Dover Wilson is rather more sceptical, if not dismissive.[244]

> It [*King John*] is full also of lines and passages which only Shakespeare could have penned. Yet we seldom feel that the pen was dipped in his own heart's blood; and if the much-praised, and over-praised, portrait of the boy Arthur be really the dramatist's obituary notice of his own son, as many have supposed, his paternal affection must have been conventional and frigid to a degree which is very difficult to reconcile with the tender and passionate nature that gives warmth and reality to his later dramas. Indeed, if the death of Hamnet Shakespeare in 1596 meant anything to Shakespeare, Constance's lamentation must surely have been written before that event taught him what true grief was.[245]

Here we must draw our third, and undoubtedly most complicated, set of examples to a close and take stock. If Shakespeare will be part of our experiment, then the rest may follow. None of the illustrations we have considered are without their problems. While it is difficult to believe that Shakespeare was able to stand completely aloof from his own experiences – to smother up his feelings from the world – it is clear that through his characters he could convey the full range of human emotions without their needing to reflect on him personally. So many biographies have obscured autobiography. Even in the *Sonnets* we have no instances to parallel 'Stella is Rich' and, in general, little to support the extreme view that they should be read first and foremost as autobiography. What we do have, however, are a mother's heart-rending grief over the loss of her young boy whom she is sure is dead; and the confusion of feelings about family relationships and the expectations one generation has for the next, father and daughter if not father and son. We also have some glorious instances of how fluid literary criticism can be. Scientific biography, personal theorists, the historical method, 'language is all' and feminist theorists have each made their mark, yet Shakespeare's plays and poems remain elusive, a home for every theorist. In terms of our experiment, it cannot be claimed that Shakespeare's response to the death of his son Hamnet in 1596 has been revealed clearly by his works or indeed that his attitude to parenthood is conveyed in explicit terms. However, what we do have are some partial glimpses into Shakespeare's feelings and some clear warnings concerning interpretation, method and theory, especially their mutability. We can be encouraged by this case while being made wary of the scope for misunderstanding.

Selection

The next chapter reproduces 69 poems written between the 1570s and the 1990s. Most relate to the deaths of children and have been written by one of their parents, but there are also examples of epitaphs for adults and pieces by non-relatives. This is neither a sample, in the statistical sense at least, nor a comprehensive collection of all poems written in English on the subject of early-age death during the last five hundred years. Rather it is a selection chosen to reflect what is available in terms of age of deceased, gender, relationship and so forth. Not every period is evenly represented, but then the popularity of the theme among poets is one of the issues under consideration. Two further points are worth repeating here. Although poetry is often thought of as a medium of the literary elite, this perspective owes more to the position of the genre in the nineteenth and especially the twentieth centuries after the rise to prominence of the novel. Poetry could be heard as well as read and, if only the latter, then this might still include as readership up to a third of the population of England.[246] Secondly, despite the impression that would still be gained from the largest and most popular anthologies, poetry writing was not a solely male preserve. Thanks to recent generations of feminist literary scholars we now have several excellent anthologies devoted exclusively to the work of female poets. Their work is reflected in this selection, as might be expected of maternal concerns.

The brief notes that follow introduce each of the 69 poems and their authors. For ease of reference the poems are numbered **1** to **69** in bold type.

'An epicedium by Elizabeth Hoby, their mother, on the death of her two daughters Elizabeth and Anne' (poem number **1**) by Lady Elizabeth Hoby (1540–1609) was originally inscribed in Latin on a Hoby family monument in Bisham church, Berkshire. Their father Sir Thomas Hoby, a noted traveller and translator, died in 1566, while both daughters died in February 1570.[247]

Number **2** is taken from Shakespeare's *King John*, Act III, Scene 4 [3.4.93]: Constance's lines 'Grief fills the room up of my absent child: ... '. It has already been mentioned above.

Poems **3**, **4** and **5** are taken from Ben Jonson's *Epigrams*, first published in 1616. Two are concerned with the deaths of his children, Mary and Benjamin, and the third with Salomon Pavy. Jonson married Anne Lewis on 14 November 1594 and their first child, Mary, was probably born and died in 1595, although this is not certain. Benjamin was born in 1596 and died aged 7 during a severe plague outbreak in May 1603.[248] There were perhaps a further four children fathered by Jonson, but only two whose mother was Anne. None of these children appear to have survived to marry or were alive at Jonson's death in 1637.[249] Salomon Pavy, a boy actor with Queen Elizabeth's Revels, died in July 1602 in his thirteenth year. He had performed in Jonson's *Cynthia's Revels* (1600) and *Poetaster* (1601).[250] The choice of these three epigrams requires little justification: they are direct and explicit expressions of loss by a father for two of his offspring and an admired colleague; the events to which they relate can be dated with relative ease and the poems themselves were probably written shortly after the events; they are also frequently anthologised.[251]

These claims cannot be made for **6**, John Donne's holy or divine Sonnet 17. Here the subject is generally agreed to be Ann Donne, who died on 15 August 1617, having recently given birth to a stillborn child. Ann's birth history is discussed in Chapter

7 and illustrated in table 7.9 (p. 204). It shows that she was probably only 16 when she married and 32 when she died; that she was pregnant for more than half of her married life; that in the fifteen years between mid-1602 and mid-1617 she had 12 confinements producing ten live-born children, seven of whom survived to adulthood. Apart from Ann and the two stillborn, four children died during Donne's lifetime with three dying while their mother was still alive.[252] Donne was no stranger to both childhood and maternal mortality, therefore. Poem 6 was probably written a few years after 1617, but it was not published until the late nineteenth century.

Poem 7 is a wife's epitaph for her husband, Lady Katherine (c.1600–54) for Sir William Dyer. Sir William died in 1621 at the age of 36 and in 1641 Lady Katherine erected a monument to his name in Colmworth church, Bedfordshire.[253]

John Milton's poem 'On the death of a fair infant dying of a cough' (8) may have been written in 1625 or 1626 when he was 17. If this dating is correct it was prompted by the death of a niece, an infant daughter of Milton's sister, but this is uncertain. The poem is the first Milton wrote in English and it was composed while he was still a Cambridge undergraduate, although it was not published until 1673, the year before his death. Milton was married three times and had five children, two of whom died in infancy (see table 7.6, p. 191). His first wife, Mary Powell, died shortly after giving birth to their fourth child. Poem 8 cannot be said to stem directly, therefore, from parental experience, although that of a close relative may have prompted it. Its date is known and its precocity obvious, as are its classical influences. Number 9 (Sonnet 19 (or 23)) probably dates from 1658 and the death in February of Milton's second wife, Katherine, whom he married in November 1656 and who gave birth to a daughter, also Katherine, in October 1657. Milton became totally blind in 1652.[254]

Relatively little is known about Henry King other than that from 1642 he was Bishop of Chichester, a post which he was unable to occupy from 1643 until 1660 and the restoration of the Anglican bishops to their sees. He was a friend of Ben Jonson and John Donne, to both of whom he wrote elegies. He married Anne Berkeley in 1617 and had five children, two of whom died in infancy, and two sons survived him. Anne died in January 1624 aged 23. King's 'On two children, dying of one disease, and buried in one grave' (10) probably relates to his own experience and is likely to have been written in the early 1620s, although it was not published until 1657.[255]

Like Henry King, Robert Herrick was also a Royalist clergyman, although far less well connected. He was forced from his Devon living during the interregnum, and he collected his poems for publication in these lean years. But Herrick was a lifelong bachelor who is not known to have fathered any children unless, that is, one believes the doubtless scurrilous accusation that Tomasin Parsons (*Hesperides* 981, i below) bore his child.[256] The importance of Herrick's collection *Hesperides*, published under his supervision in 1648, is that it is obviously autobiographical and reflects in ways that are not always straightforward the experiences of a Devon clergyman from the mid-1620s to the mid-1640s.[257] It is full of characters, reflections and observations, some malicious and most witty. Eleven poems have been selected from *Hesperides* (numbers 11 to 21), and a further ten (a to j) are reproduced below. Group A illustrates Herrick's friendship with the Crewe family of Cheshire. Herrick first met Sir Clipsby Crewe (a) when he was a student at St John's College, Cambridge, in 1613. Number 11 laments the death of a child of theirs and 12 is an epitaph to Lady Jane herself.[258] Group B covers 13 and 14 and is given the title 'Jibes' to reflect the rather more earthy side of reproductive life in the seventeenth-century countryside (other examples are given below at b to h). Group C covers 15 to 17 (j below) and deals with the experiences of mothers and motherhood in general; while group D relate explicitly to the deaths of infants (numbers 18 to 21).[259]

a To Sir Clipsebie Crew
Since to th'Country first I came,
I have lost my former flame:
And, methinks, I not inherit,
As I did, my ravisht spirit.
If I write a Verse, or two,
'Tis with very much ado;
In regard I want that Wine,
Which sho'd conjure up a line.
Yet, though now of Muse bereft,
I have still the manners left
For to thanke you (Noble Sir)
For those gifts you do conferre
Upon him who only can
Be in Prose a *gratefull man*.
Hesperides 491 Martin 182

b Upon Doll. Epig.
Doll she so soone began the wanton trade;
She ne'r remembers that she was a maide.
Hesperides 379 Martin 149

c Kissing and Bussing
Kissing and bussing differ in this;
We busse our Wantons, but our Wives we kisse.
Hesperides 514 Martin 189

d Upon Skoles. Epig.
Skoles stinks so deadly, that his Breeches loath
His dampish Buttocks furthermore to cloath:
Cloy'd they are up with Arse; but hope, one blast
Will whirle about, and blow them thence at last.
Hesperides 652 Martin 226

e Upon Gander. Epig.
Since *Gander* did his prettie Youngling wed;
Gander (they say) doth each night pisse a Bed:

What is the cause? Why *Gander* will reply,
No Goose layes good eggs that is trodden drye.
Hesperides 638 Martin 223

f UPON DUNDRIGE
Dundrige his Issue hath; but is not styl'd
For all his Issue, Father of one Child.
Hesperides 535 Martin 195

g UPON JOLLY AND JILLY, EPIG.
Jolly and *Jillie*, bite and scratch all day,
But yet get children (as the neighbours say.)
The reason is, though all the day they fight,
They cling and close, some minutes of the night.
Hesperides 412 Martin 156

h ABSTINENCE
Against diseases here the strongest fence
Is the defensive vertue, Abstinence.
Hesperides 1119 Martin 333

i ON TOMASIN PARSONS
Grow up in Beauty, as thou do'st begin,
And be of all admired, *Tomasin.*
Hesperides 981 Martin 304

j UPON A LADY FAIRE, BUT FRUITLESSE
Twice has *Pudica* been a Bride, and led
By holy *Himen* to the Nuptiall Bed.
Two Youths sha's known, twice two, and twice 3. yeares;
Yet not a Lillie from the Bed appeares;
Nor will; for why, *Pudica*, this may know,
Trees never beare, unlesse they first do blow.
Hesperides 479 Martin 180

Little is known of Thomas Jordan (1612?–1685?). His 'An elegie on the death of a male-child drown'd in ice' (**22**) appeared in *Love's Dialect* (London, 1646).

Poem **23**, 'Mrs Thimelby, on the death of her only child', was probably written in the 1640s. Gertrude Aston married Henry Thimelby in the late 1630s or early 1640s. Both only child and husband died young. After their deaths she retired to a convent in Louvain, Flanders. The Astons were a devout Catholic family from Tixall in Staffordshire.[260]

Numbers **24** and **25**, by Thomas Philipott (c.1616–82), first appeared in his *Poems* (London, 1646). Philipott also published *Elegies* (1641) and *Aesop's Fables* (1687).

Poems **26** to **30** have, with one possible exception, been written by mothers about their own or a close relative's experiences of maternity. Relatively little is known about Mary Carey. She was the daughter of Sir John Jackson of Berwick-upon-Tweed,

Northumberland, and married, first, Sir Pelham Carey and, secondly, George Payler of Nun Monkton, Yorkshire. Numbers **26** and **27** relate to Lady Mary's pregnancies in the 1650s. Peregrine Payler, Mary's fifth child, was buried on 14 May 1652 and the miscarriage or stillbirth relates to December 1657.[261]

Elizabeth Egerton (née Cavendish, daughter of the first Duke of Newcastle) married aged 15. On 6 June 1656 Elizabeth bore a son, Henry, who died 29 days later (**28**). Over a period of seventeen years from 1646 she gave birth to nine children, six of whom survived her while three (Frances, Henry and Catherine) died in infancy. She died in (premature) childbirth, 14 June 1663, which is the subject of her sister Jane Cheyne's poem (**29**). Jane Cavendish married Charles Cheyne (later Viscount Newhaven) in 1654. They had three children: Elizabeth (1656), William (1657) and Catherine (1658). Jane suffered a series of epileptic seizures in 1668 and died on 8 October 1669.[262] She was present at her sister Elizabeth's death in 1663.

Katherine Philips (1631–64) was the daughter of a London merchant, John Fowler, and was brought up in what has been called a typical middle-class London Puritan family. She married Colonel James Philips of Cardigan in 1648 when still only 16 (her widower husband was 54). Hector Philips, her first child, was born on 23 April 1655 and died on 2 May (or June) 1655. The church mentioned in **30** is St Bene't Sherehog at the end of Syth's Lane. It was burnt down in the fire of London in 1666. Katherine Philips's *Poems* were circulated in an unauthorised form just before she died from smallpox in London in 1664, and were published in an authorised version in 1667.[263]

Matthew Stevenson's (*fl.* 1654–85) 'Upon a lady at York dying in child-birth' (**31**) is from *Poems* (London, 1665).

Anne Dudley (a distant relative of Sir Philip Sidney) married Simon Bradstreet probably in 1628. In 1630 they left England for America, arriving in Salem on 12 June. The first of Anne's eight children (Samuel) was born in 1633, the same year that her father, Thomas Dudley, became Governor of Massachusetts. Her last child was born on 22 July 1652. Of the Bradstreets' eight children, all survived into adulthood and only one pre-deceased Anne, and then only by a matter of months. She died at Andover on 16 September 1672. Samuel Bradstreet (who practised as a physician in Boston) married Mercy Tyng, and of their five children only one survived infancy. Three of Mercy's children became the subjects of elegies by Anne, as did the mother herself when she died shortly after childbirth in 1670. The Simon Bradstreet who is remembered in **32** was one of the children of Mercy and Samuel.[264]

Little is known of Aphra Behn's personal details. She may have been born Aphra Johnson in Canterbury in 1640 and married John Behn sometime in the 1660s. She was certainly active as a playwright in London from 1670 and died on 16 April 1689. Aphra Behn is not known to have had children, so **33** may have been a commissioned epitaph.[265]

Thomas Flatman (1637–88) is perhaps better known as a miniaturist than a poet, although he was at some time a scholar of Winchester College and a fellow of

New College, Oxford. The epitaph (**35**) is in St Bride's church, Fleet Street, London, and relates to Thomas, the eldest son of Thomas and Hannah Flatman (married 8 December 1672), who died on 28 December 1682 in his tenth year. The coridon (**34**) is also said to refer to young Thomas.

Number **36**, Alexander Pope's epitaph to Mrs Corbett, provides a marker for a new century. It has been selected to illustrate the commercial epitaph business, towards the upper end of the market. Elizabeth Corbett was the sister of Sir Richard Corbett who commissioned the epitaph from Pope. She died on 1 March 1725 and is buried in St Margaret's church, Westminster. Pope himself did not marry, but lived in quiet seclusion as a semi-invalid (the result of Pott's disease, tuberculosis of the bones, which led to stunted growth; he measured little more than 1.4 metres with a severe stoop) with his mother in Twickenham near London. Children do not figure in his poetical works and most of his epitaphs are for distinguished or noble men buried in Westminster Abbey.[266]

Hetty Wesley was the sister of the Methodist, John Wesley. Forced to marry on 13 October 1725 after various affairs, she lived with her husband John Wright, a London plumber. Although **37** does not mention a particular child by name, its sentiments may relate to a number of premature deaths between 1725 and 1733. Apparently, Mrs Wright was convinced that her husband's lead works caused the early deaths of her children.

Nothing is known of Elizabeth Boyd except that she worked in London between 1727 and 1745, and that her collection *The Humorous Miscellany* was published in 1733. It is from this that **38** is drawn.

Jane Colman Turell (1708–35) spent all her life in or near Boston, Massachusetts. She was the daughter of a well-known minister (Benjamin Colman) and married the minister of Medford, Ebenezer Turell, in August 1726. At the time of her death in 1735 only one of her children, Samuel Turell (1730–36), was still alive. Poem **39** reflects Jane Turell's experience of repeated fruitless pregnancies and her deep piety.[267]

Poem number **40** was published in the *Gentleman's Magazine* in 1740 and relates to the experience of the poet herself.

'On the death of an only child, of very pregnant parts' (**41**) by Samuel Bowden comes from his *Poems on Various Subjects* (1754). Bowden was a physician from Frome in Somerset.

Thomas Gray's (1716–71) 'Epitaph on a child' (**42**) is believed to be for Robert (Robin) Wharton, the son of Dr Thomas Wharton, an old Cambridge friend. Robin was born in 1753 and died in April 1758.

Jane Cave's poem (**43**) appears to have been written just before labour; a happy outcome may be assumed. The first edition of her *Poems* was published in Winchester in 1783; by 1786 she was married to an excise man, Mr Winscom, and living in Bristol. She died in January 1813 at the age of 58.

Helen Leigh lived in Middlewich, Cheshire, and was the wife of a curate there. She was active in the 1780s and died in 1795, but her poem 'The natural child' (**44**) surely is one of social comment rather than personal experience, although she is thought to have had seven children herself.

Robert Burns's 'On the birth of a posthumous child, born in peculiar circumstances of family-distress' (45) was first printed in the Edinburgh edition of his works in 1793. The first child of Susan Henri (daughter of Mrs Dunlop and sister of Sir Thomas Wallace) was born in November 1790. His father had died in June of that year. Mrs Dunlop and her daughter were family friends of Burns.

Although William Blake was happily married, it seems to have been a source of deep regret that he and his wife Catherine Boucher (married 1782) had no children. The two chimney sweep poems (numbers 46 and 47) from the illustrated *Songs of Innocence and of Experience,* which date from the late 1780s and early 1790s, have been included because they are believed to mark a turning point in the way in which children were represented in literature. Little Tom Dacre was, in a sense, one of the Blakes' children.[268]

Sir Brooke Boothby's *Sorrows Sacred to the Memory of Penelope* (London, 1796) contains 24 sonnets, plus other miscellaneous poetry, dedicated to the memory of his daughter Penelope (1785–91). With engravings of the portrait of Penelope by Sir Joshua Reynolds (1788) and her tomb monument by Thomas Banks (1793) in Ashbourne church, Derbyshire (N), Sonnet I (48) is selected here. Penelope's portrait by Reynolds (M) was discussed in Chapter 4 (pp. 77 and 83).

Poem number 49 comes from a letter by Samuel Taylor Coleridge to his wife Sara dated Göttingen, 8 April 1799. Berkeley, the Coleridges' second child, was born on 15 May 1798 and died on 10 February 1799.

Numbers 50 and 51 are said to be, respectively, a picture of Wordsworth's daughter Catharine who died the following year aged 3, and a remembrance of her written in 1813–14. Both of Catharine's parents were away from home when she died. Thomas, the Wordsworths' third child, also died in 1812. The cause was measles complicated by pneumonia. Table 7.7 (p. 197) illustrates Mary Wordsworth's birth history.[269]

William Shelley (the subject of 52 and 53) was born to Mary Godwin on 24 January 1816 and died at Rome on 7 June 1819. An infant daughter, Clara (2 September 1817–24 September 1818), had died in Venice and Mary's first child by Shelley had also died in infancy in London (an unnamed girl probably conceived shortly after their elopement on 28 July 1814 and born two months prematurely on 22 February 1815, who died on 6 March 1815). Shelley's first wife, Harriet Westbrook, by whom he had two children in 1813 and 1814, committed suicide by drowning on 9 November 1816 while she was pregnant.[270] Table 7.8 (p. 199) illustrates the birth history of Shelley's various children.

What is especially interesting about the Wordsworths and the Shelleys is that they also kept journals and wrote copious letters, many of which have survived.[271]

Amelia Alderson Opie's (1769–1853) 'On the death of a child' (54) comes from her collection *Lays for the Dead* (London, 1834). Opie was the daughter of a Norwich dissenting minister who subsequently became a Quaker. She was as well known in her time as Jane Austen and Sir Walter Scott.

Mary Ann Browne spent much of her life in Ireland. She married James Gray in 1842 and they settled in Cork. Poem number **55** dates from the early 1830s.

It is possible to link Fanny Verchild, the subject of poem number **56**, with Dorothy Lyttleton, a childhood friend of Walter Savage Landor (1775–1864) and his sister, Elizabeth. Dorothy married in 1795 and died in 1811. She is buried in Studley church, Warwickshire.[272]

John Clare spent the last twenty-two years of his life in Northampton General Lunatic Asylum and it is from this period (June 1844) that poem number **57** is taken. Clare married Patty Turner in 1820 and they had at least seven children (Anna Maria, June 1820; Eliza Louisa, June 1822; Frederick, January 1824; John, June 1826; William Parker, May 1828; Sophia, 1830; Charles, December 1832). Three of the children (Anna Maria, 1844; Frederick, 1843; Charles, 1852) died in early adulthood, probably as a result of tuberculosis. No deaths in childhood are known. Clare's lengthy period of incarceration in various lunatic asylums was obviously not a happy one, although accounts of his condition and the extent to which he was cared for by his friends and relatives vary. It seems most likely that he was suffering from manic-depression, exacerbated perhaps by his being locked away. He certainly experienced delusions that, for example, he was a prize fighter and that the first love of his youth, Mary Joyce, was with him still.[273]

Louisa married Edwin Horsfield in about 1855. She came from a Primitive Methodist family who lived in the Barnsley area of west Yorkshire. *The Cottage Lyre* (from which number **58** is taken) was her only published work.

Alexander Anderson's (1845–1909) 'The dead child' (**59**) comes from his collection *A Song of Labour, and other Poems* (Dundee, 1873).

'To a child dead as soon as born' (**60**) is taken from Edward Dowden, *Poems* (London, 1877). Dowden (1843–1913), a professor at Trinity College, Dublin, was a distinguished Shakespeare scholar and biographer of Shelley.[274]

Robert Bridges qualified with an MB from St Bartholomew's Hospital in 1874 and was for a short period from 1878 Assistant Physician at the Hospital for Sick Children, Great Ormond Street, London. He gave up medical practice in 1881 and married in 1882. Poem **61** dates from the late 1870s when Bridges was still in medical practice.

Poem **62** was written in December 1912, days after the death of Thomas Hardy's first wife, Emma Gifford, from whom he had been estranged for several years. 'The voice' remembers an earlier meeting, during their courtship in Cornwall, in the summer of 1870.

In 1945, towards the end of the Second World War, Dylan Thomas was living in London with his wife and two young children (born 1939 and 1943; a third child was born in 1949). Poem number **63** dates from this time; it is personal, but not autobiographical.[275]

'On the death of a child' (**64**) is taken from D. J. Enright's *The Laughing Hyena* *and Other Poems* (London, 1953).

'For a child born dead' (**65**) comes from Elizabeth Jennings's early collection *A Way of Looking* (1955).

Sylvia Plath and Ted Hughes were married in June 1956. Their first child, Frieda, was born on 1 April 1960; there was a miscarriage in February 1961; and Nicholas was born on 17 January 1962. Sylvia Plath committed suicide on 11 February 1963. 'Stillborn' (**66**) probably dates from mid-1960, after the birth of her daughter, and reflects not only Plath's striving for her unborn poems, but also her often repeated death wish.[276]

Seamus Heaney's 'Elegy for a still-born child' (**67**) comes from *Door into the Dark* (London, 1969).

Poem **68** is taken from Paula Meehan's 1991 collection *The Man Who Was Marked by Winter*. Meehan was born, educated and lives in Dublin. Her other collections include *Pillow Talk* (1994).

The last poem (**69**) is by Nina Bogin. It comes from her collection *The Winter Orchards* (2001). Its subject is her stillborn son.

The various characteristics of the 69 poems are listed in table 5.4.

Table 5.4 *Some characteristics of the 69 poems*

No.	Name of poet	Date	Lines	Poet	Subject	Relationship
1	Hoby	1570s	17	F mother	F 2 daughters Elizabeth & Anne	own children in teens
2	Shakespeare	1590s	13	M father	M son Hamnet?	own child aged 11
3	Jonson	1590s	12	M father	F daughter Mary	own child aged 6 months
4	Jonson	1600s	12	M father	M son Benjamin	own child aged 6
5	Jonson	1600s	24	M playwright	M actor	friend aged 13
6	Donne	1620s	14	M husband	F wife Ann	wife
7	Dyer	1620s	30	F wife	M husband William	husband
8	Milton	1620s	14 (77)	M uncle	F niece	sister's infant daughter
9	Milton	1650s	14	M husband	F wife Katherine	wife aged
10	King	1620s	20	M father	U 2 infants	own children, died in infancy, sex unknown
11	Herrick	1630s	8	M	U infant	death of Lady Crewe's child
12	Herrick	1630s	6	M	F wife of friend	death of Lady Crewe in 1639
13	Herrick	1630s	2	M	M	jibe on Batt
14	Herrick	1630s	2	M	M	jibe on Gubbs
15	Herrick	1630s	4	M	F	young mother
16	Herrick	1630s	8	M	F	epitaph to a sober matron
17	Herrick	1630s	11	M	F	lady dying in childbirth
18	Herrick	1630s	6	M	U	child that died
19	Herrick	1630s	8	M	U	child that died
20	Herrick	1630s	6	M	F	baby
21	Herrick	1630s	4	M	U	baby
22	Jordan	1640s	26	M	M	boy drowned on ice
23	Thimelby	1640s	16	F mother	U	death of only child
24	Philipott	1640s	12	M	F	lady in childbirth
25	Philipott	1640s	22	M	U 5 children	farmer's 5 children who died of plague

26	Carey	1650s	10	F mother	M son	Peregrine Payler
27	Carey	1650s	6	F mother	U stillbirth	
28	Egerton	1650s	10	F mother	M son Henry	infant few days old
29	Cheyne	1660s	18	F	F sister Elizabeth	death in childbirth of sister, Countess of Bridgewater, 1663
30	Philips	1660s	22	F mother	M son Hector	death of few weeks old infant
31	Stevenson	1660s	31	M	F	lady dying in childbirth
32	Bradstreet	1660s	12	F grandmother	M grandson Simon	infant died a few weeks old
33	Behn	1670s	14	F	M	epitaph
34	Flatman	1680s	26	M father	M son Thomas	boy aged 9
35	Flatman	1680s	8	M father	M son Thomas	boy aged 9
36	Pope	1720s	10	M	F	Elizabeth Corbett died 1725
37	Wright	1720s	20	F	U	own premature infant?
38	Boyd	1720s	22	F	U	own stillborn infant?
39	Turell	1730s	28	F mother	U, M	several perinatal deaths
40	Anonymous	1730s	18	F	U	abortion
41	Bowden	1750s	10	M	F	possibly own daughter
42	Gray	1750s	6	M	M	son of friend aged 5
43	Cave	1780s	16	F	F	ante-natal prayer
44	Leigh	1780s	44		U	illegitimate child
45	Burns	1790s	24	M	M?	child of family friend whose father had pre-deceased him
46	Blake	1780s	24	M	M	chimney sweeper
47	Blake	1790s	12	M	M	chimney sweeper
48	Boothby	1790s	14	M father	F daughter Penelope	daughter died aged 8
49	Coleridge	1790s	6	M father	M son Berkeley	death of infant son
50	Wordsworth	1810s	21	M father	F daughter Catharine	Catharine (aged 3) and Thomas (6) both died in 1812
51	Wordsworth	1810s	14	M father	F daughter Catharine	
52	Shelley	1810s	18	M father	M son William	son (aged 3) died in 1819

No.	Name of poet	Date	Lines	Poet	Subject	Relationship
53	Shelley	1810s	6	M father	M son William	
54	Opie	1820s	24	F	M	widow and her son
55	Browne	1830s	24	F mother	M son	
56	Landor	1830s	28	M	F	childhood friend
57	Clare	1840s	18	M		children in general
58	Horsfield	1850s	16	F mother	U	baby
59	Anderson	1860s	46	M	U	
60	Dowden	1870s	14	M father	M son	infant
61	Bridges	1870s	28	M	M	boy
62	Hardy	1910s	16	M husband	F wife	estranged first wife
63	Thomas	1940s	24	M	F	girl killed in air-raid
64	Enright	1950s	10	M	U	baby
65	Jennings	1950s	18	F	U	stillborn
66	Plath	1960s	14	F		stillborn
67	Heaney	1960s	20	M father	U	stillborn
68	Meehan	1980s	32	F mother	M probably	young child
69	Bogin	1990s	18	F mother	M son	stillborn

6

Poems, Mainly of Child Loss

Lady Elizabeth Hoby (1540–1609)

1

AN EPICEDIUM BY ELIZABETH HOBY, THEIR MOTHER,
ON THE DEATH OF HER TWO DAUGHTERS ELIZABETH AND ANNE

Elizabeth lies here (alas for my heart), thus fated:
    You lie here, scarecely mature, a tender virgin
When you lived, you were a daughter dear to her mother
    Now, live dear to God and your father.
Your death was cruel, but there was one still crueller:
    the one which cut down your younger sister Anna with you.
Anna, you were the glory of your father and mother; after your sister's end
    and after your mother's grief, here you lie, golden virgin!
There was one mother, one father, one death, for the pair
    And this one stone hides both their bodies.
Thus I, their mother, wanted to unite them in a single tomb,
    weeping, whom I once carried in the same happy womb
These two noble and most hopeful sisters
in the same Year, i.e. 1570
In the same Month, i.e. February
only a few days apart,
slept in the Lord.

William Shakespeare (1564–1616)

2

KING JOHN
Act III, Scene 4 [3.4.93]

CONSTANCE
Grief fills the room up of my absent child:
Lies in his bed, walks up and down with me,
Puts on his pretty looks, repeats his words,
Remembers me of all his gracious parts,

131

Stuffs out his vacant garments with his form;
Then have I reason to be fond of grief!
Fare you well: had you such a loss as I,
I could give better comfort than you do.
I will not keep this form upon my head,
When there is such disorder in my wit... [*she tears her hair again*
O Lord! my boy, my Arthur, my fair son!
My life, my joy, my food, my all the world!
My widow-comfort, and my sorrows' cure! [*she runs forth*

Ben Jonson (1572–1637)

3
Epigram 22
ON MY FIRST DAUGHTER

Here lyes to each her parents ruth,
Mary, the daughter of their youth;
Yet, all hevens gifts, being heavens due,
It makes the father, lesse, to rue.
At six months end, shee parted hence
With safetie of her innocence;
Whose soule heavens Queene, (whose name shee beares)
In comfort of her mothers teares,
Hath plac'd amongst her virgin-traine:
Where, while that seuer'd doth remaine,
This graue partakes the fleshy birth,
Which couer lightly, gentle earth.

4
Epigram 45
ON MY FIRST SON

Farewell, thou child of my right hand, and ioy;
    My sinne was too much hope of thee, lou'd boy.
Seven yeeres tho'wert lent to me, and I thee pay,
    Exacted by thy fate, on the iust day.
O, could I loose all father, now. For why
    Will man lament the state he should enui?
To have so soon scap'd worlds, and fleshes rage,
    And, if no other miserie, yet age?
Rest in soft peace, and, ask'd, say here doth lye
    BEN. IONSON his best piece of *poetrie*;
For whose sake, hence-forth, all his vowes be such,
    As what he loues may neuer like too much.

5
Epigram 120
EPITAPH ON S[ALOMON] P[AVY]
A CHILD OF Q[UEEN] EL[IZABETH'S] CHAPEL

Weepe with me all you that read
 This little storie,
And know, for whom a teare you shed,
 Death's selfe is sorry.
'Twas a child, that so did thriue
 In grace, and feature,
As *Heauen* and *Nature* seem'd to striue
 Which own'd the creature.
Yeeres he numbred scarse thirteene
 When *Fates* turn'd cruell,
Yet three fill'd *Zodiackes* had he beene
 The stages iewell,
And did act (what now we mone)
 Old men so duely,
As, sooth, the *Parcæ* thought him one,
 He plai'd so truely.
So, by error, to his fate
 They all consented;
But viewing him since (alas, too late)
 They haue repented.
And haue sought (to giue new birth)
 In bathes to steepe him;
But, being so much too good for earth,
 Heauen vowes to keepe him.

John Donne (1572–1631)
6
Holy Sonnet 17

Since she whom I lov'd hath payd her last debt
To Nature, and to hers, and my good is dead,
And her Soule early into heaven ravished,
Wholly in heavenly things my mind is sett.
Here the admyring her my mind did whett
To seeke thee God; so streames do shew their head,
But thou I have found thee, and thou my thirst hast fed,
A holy thirsty dropsy melts mee yett.
But why should I begg more Love, when as thou
Dost wooe my soule for hers; offring all thine:

And dost not only feare least I allow
My Love to Saints and Angels things devine,
But in thy tender jealosy dost doubt
Least the World, Fleshe, yea Devill putt thee out.

Lady Katherine Dyer (c.1600–54)

7

M.S. Sir Will: Dyer, Kt:
Who put on Immortality Aprill th 29th Anno Domini 1621

If a large hart: Joyned with a Noble minde
Shewing true worth, unto all good inclin'd,
If faith in friendship, Justice unto all,
Leave such a Memory as we may call
Happy, Thine is: Then pious Marble keepe
His Just Fame waking, Though his lov'd dost sleepe.
And though Death can devoure all that hath breath,
And Monuments them selves have had a Death,
Nature shan't suffer this, to ruinate,
Nor time demolish't, nor an envious fate,
Rais'd by a Just hand not vaine glorious pride
Who'd be conceal'd, wer't modesty to hide
Such an affection did so long survive
The object of 't: yet lov'd It as alive.
And this grate Blessing to his Name doth give
To make It by his Tombe, and Issue live.
My dearest dust could not thy hasty day
Afford thy drowzy patience leave to stay
One hower longer; so that we might either
 Sate up, or gone to bedd together?
But since thy finisht labor hath possest
 Thy weary limbs with early rest,
Enjoy it sweetly; and thy widdowe bride
Shall soone repose her by thy slumbering side;
Whose business, now is only to prepare
 My nightly dress, and call to prayre;
Mine eyes wax heavy and the day growes old
 The dew falls thick, my bloud growes cold;
Draw, draw the closed curtaynes: and make roome;
My deare, my dearest dust; I come, I come.

John Milton (1608–74)

8

ON THE DEATH OF A FAIR INFANT DYING OF A COUGH

I

O fairest flower no sooner blown but blasted,
Soft silken primrose fading timelessly,
Summer's chief honour if thou hadst outlasted
Bleak winter's force that made thy blossom dry;
For he being amorous on that lovely dye
   That did thy cheek envermeil, thought to kiss
But killed alas, and then bewailed his fatal bliss.

II

For since grim Aquilo his charioteer
By boisterous rape the Athenian damsel got,
He thought it touched his deity full near,
If likewise he some fair one wedded not,
Thereby to wipe away the infamous blot
   Of long-uncoupled bed, and childless eld,
Which 'mongst the wanton gods a foul reproach was held.

III

So mounting up in icy-pearled car,
Through middle empire of the freezing air
He wandered long, till thee he spied from far,
There ended was his quest, there ceased his care,
Down he descended from his snow-soft chair,
   But all unwares with his cold-kind embrace
Unhoused thy virgin soul from her fair biding-place.

IV

Yet art thou not inglorious in thy fate;
For so Apollo, with unweeting hand
Whilom did slay his dearly-loved mate
Young Hyacinth born on Eurotas' strand
Young Hyacinth the pride of Spartan land;
   But then transformed him to a purple flower
Alack that so to change thee winter had no power.

V

Yet can I not persuade me thou art dead
Or that thy corse corrupts in earth's dark womb,
Or that thy beauties lie in wormy bed,
Hid from the world in a low-delved tomb;
Could heaven for pity thee so strictly doom?

O no! for something in thy face did shine
Above mortality that showed thou wast divine.

VI

Resolve me then O soul most surely blest
(If so it be that thou these plaints dost hear)
Tell me bright spirit where'er thou hoverest
Whether above that high first-moving sphere
Or in the Elysian fields (if such there were)
 O say me true if thou wert mortal wight
And why from us so quickly thou didst take thy flight.

VII

Wert thou some star which from the ruined roof
Of shaked Olympus by mischance didst fall;
Which careful Jove in nature's true behoof
Took up, and fit place did reinstall?
Or did of late Earth's sons besiege the wall
 Of sheeny heaven, and thou some goddess fled,
Amongst us here below to hide thy nectared head?

VIII

Or wert thou that just maid who once before
Forsook the hated earth, O tell me sooth
And cam'st again to visit us once more?
Or wert thou that sweet smiling youth?
Or that crowned matron sage white-robed Truth?
 Or any other of that heavenly brood
Let down in cloudy throne to do the world some good?

IX

Or wert thou of the golden-winged host,
Who having clad thyself in human weed,
To earth from thy prefixed seat didst post,
And after short abode fly back with speed,
As if to show what creatures heaven doth breed,
 Thereby to set the hearts of men on fire
To scorn the sordid world, and unto heaven aspire?

X

But O why didst thou not stay here below
To bless us with thy heaven-loved innocence,
To slake his wrath whom sin hath made our foe
To turn swift-rushing black perdition hence,
Or drive away the slaughtering pestilence,
 To stand 'twixt us and our deserved smart?
But thou canst best perform that office where thou art.

XI

Then thou the mother of so sweet a child
Her false imagined loss cease to lament,
And wisely learn to curb thy sorrows wild;
Think what a present thou to God hast sent,
And render him with patience what he lent;
   This if thou do he will an offspring give,
That till the world's last end shall make thy name to live.

9
Sonnet 19 (or 23)

Methought I saw my late espoused saint
   Brought to me like Alcestis from the grave,
    Whom Jove's great son to her glad husband gave,
    Rescued from death by force though pale and faint.
Mine as whom washed from spot of childbed taint,
   Purification in the old Law did save,
   And such, as yet once more I trust to have
Full sight of her in heaven without restraint,
Came vested all in white, pure as her mind:
   Her face was veiled, yet to my fancied sight,
   Love, sweetness, goodness in her person shined
So clear, as in no face with more delight.
   But O as to embrace me she inclined
   I waked, she fled, and day brought back my night.

Henry King (1592–1669)
10
ON TWO CHILDREN, DYING OF ONE DISEASE,
AND BURIED IN ONE GRAVE

   Brought forth in sorrow, and bred up in Care,
Two tender Children here entombed are:
One Place, one Sire, one Womb their being gave,
They had one mortall Sicknesse, and one Grave.
And though they cannot number many Yeeres
In their Account, yet with their Parent's teares
This comfort mingles. Though their Dayes were few,
They scarcely Sinne, but never Sorrow, knew:
So that they well might boast, they carry'd hence,
What riper Ages loose, their Innocence.
   You Pretty Losses, that revive the fate
Which in your Mother, Death did Antedate,

O let my high-swol'n grief Distill on You
The saddest dropps of a Parentall Dew:
You ask no other Dowre then what my eyes
Lay out on your untimely Exequyes:
When once I have discharg'd that mournfull skoare,
Heav'n hath decreed you ne're shall cost mee more,
Since you release, and quitt my borrow'd trust,
By taking this Inheritance of Dust.

Robert Herrick (1591–1674)
Group A. Crewe family
11
To The Lady Crew, Upon The Death Of Her Child

Why, Madam, will ye longer weep,
When as your Baby's lull'd asleep?
And (pretty Child) feeles now no more
Those paines it lately felt before.
All now is silent; groanes are fled:
Your Child lyes still, yet is not dead:
But rather like a flower hid here
To spring againe another yeare.
Hesperides 516 Martin 189

12
Upon the Lady Crew

This Stone can tell the storie of my life,
What was my Birth, to whom I was a Wife:
In teeming years, how soon my Sun was set,
Where now I rest, these may be known by *Jet.*
For other things, my many Children be
The best and truest *Chronicles* of me.
Hesperides 980 Martin 304

Group B. Jibes
13
Upon Batt

Batt he gets children, not for love to reare 'em;
But out of hope his wife might die to beare 'em.
Hesperides 184 Martin 72

14

UPON GUBBS. EPIG.

Gubbs call's his children *Kitlings*: and wo'd bound
(Some say) for joy, to see those Kitlings drown'd.
Hesperides 200 Martin 80

Group C. Mothers

15

UPON A YOUNG MOTHER OF MANY CHILDREN

Let all chaste Matrons, when they chance to see
My num'rous issue: Praise, and pitty me.
Praise me, for having such a fruitfull wombe;
Pity me too, who found so soone a Tomb.
Hesperides 151 Martin 58

16

AN EPITAPH UPON A SOBER MATRON

With blamelesse carriage, I liv'd here,
To'th' (almost) sev'n and fortieth yeare.
Stout sons I had, and those twice three;
One onely daughter lent to me:
The which was made a happy Bride,
But thrice three Moones before she dy'd.
My modest wedlock, that was known
Contented with the bed of one.
Hesperides 116 Martin 41

17

UPON A LADY THAT DYED IN CHILD-BED,
AND LEFT A DAUGHTER BEHIND HER

As Gilly flowers do but stay
To blow, and seed, and so away;
So you sweet Lady (sweet as May)
The gardens-glory liv'd a while,
To lend the world your scent and smile,
But when your own faire print was set
Once in a Virgin *Flosculet*,
(Sweet as your selfe, and newly blown)
To give that life, resign'd your own:
But so, as still the mothers power
Lives in the pretty Lady-flower.
Hesperides 318 Martin 126

Group D. Infants
18
AN EPITAPH UPON A CHILD

Virgins promis'd when I dy'd,
That they wo'd each Primrose-tide,
Duely, Morne and Ev'ning, come,
And with flowers dresse my Tomb.
Having promis'd, pay your debts,
Maids, and here strew Violets.
Hesperides 125 Martin 44

19
UPON A CHILD. AN EPITAPH

But borne, and like a short Delight,
I glided by my Parents sight.
That done, the harder Fates deny'd
My longer stay, and so I dy'd.
If pittying my sad Parents Teares,
You'l spil a tear, or two with theirs:
And with some flowrs my grave bestrew,
Love and they'l thank you for't. Adieu.
Hesperides 180 Martin 69

20
UPON A CHILD THAT DYED

Here she lies, a pretty bud,
Lately made of flesh and blood:
Who, as soone, fell fast asleep,
As her little eyes did peep.
Give her strewings; but not stir
The earth, that lightly covers her.
Hesperides 310 Martin 123

21
UPON A CHILD

Here a pretty Baby lies
Sung asleep with Lullabies:
Pray be silent, and not stirre
Th'easie earth that covers her.
Hesperides 642 Martin 224

Thomas Jordan (1612?–85?)

22

AN ELEGIE ON THE DEATH OF A MALE-CHILD DROWN'D IN ICE

Blest *Infant* to thy *Marble* I am sent
By pittying fate and my owne discontent,
To be resolv'd, why (in thy budding youth)
Thou wert thus rudely ravish'd, that the truth
Unto thy mourning friends I may relate,
Who with their tears thy cold *urne* consecrate.
How didst thou get thy ruine? What fate sent
Thy beautious body to that element
Devoures those it embraceth? couldst thou be
Flatter'd to hugge the infidelity
Of wanton *Thetis*? sure it was not so,
Twas thy owne *Beauty* wrought thy overthrow,
Shee was enamor'd of thee, and could finde
No way but this to state her ravenous mind.
She did convert to *Christall*, for shee saw
None but thy *beauty*, could thy *beauty* draw.
For there thy eyes surpriz'd by their owne sight
Eclips'd each other, making midday, night:
Blacke night, worse waters, may ye ever be
Us'd to make beauty blacke, so curs'd be me,
May never discontents or *sorrowes* rise
In griefe-afflicted *bosomes*, if their eyes
Bannish you thence, for when your floods are spent,
There shall not be a cause for discontent:
　　Rest peaceably (sweete boy) though to us dead,
　　love shall for thee exchange *Ganemed*.

Gertrude Thimelby (c.1615–c.1670)

23

MRS THIMELBY, ON THE DEATH OF HER ONLY CHILD

Deare Infant, 'twas thy mother's fault
So soone inclos'd thee in a vault:
And fathers good, that in such hast
Has my sweet child in heaven plac'd.
I'le weepe the first as my offence,
Then joy that he made recompence:
Yet must confesse my frailty such
My joy by griefe's exceeded much:
Though I, in reason, know thy blisse

Can not be wish'd more than it is,
Yet this selfe love orerules me soe;
I'de have thee here, or with thee goe,
But since that now neyther can be,
A vertue of necessitie
I yet may make, now all my pelf
Content for thee, though not myselfe.

Thomas Philipott (c.1616–82)

24

ON A GENTLEWOMAN DYING IN CHILD-BED OF AN ABORTIVE DAUGHTER

What neare alliance was between the grave
Of this dead infant, and the place that gave
First life to't? Here was a sad mysterie
Work'd up it selfe, both Life and Death, we see,
Were Inmates in one house, making the womb,
At once become a Birth-place and a Tomb?
The mother too, as if she meant t'improve,
In everie fatall circumstance her love,
When this unpollisht infant di'd, her breath
Resign'd, that she might wait on it in death:
And in one Monument might sleep by her,
To whom before she was a Sepulcher.

25

ON A FARMER, WHO HAVING BURIED FIVE OF HIS CHILDREN OF THE PLAGUE, PLANTED ON EACH OF THEIR GRAVES AN APPLE-TREE

You whose bold thoughts do prompt you on to glorie
I'th number of your issue, view the storie
Of this afflicted Villager, since he
Was by th' increase of a faire Progenie
Made happy, till just God, for mans offence,
Imploy'd th' infection of a Pestilence
T'annoy the world, which five of's children gave
Up to th' possession of the lavish grave.
But see what glorious pietie can dwell
I'th' narrow circuit of an humble Cell,
To preserve life in their remembrance, hee
Establishes on each grave an apple-tree,
By that quaint Hieroglyphick to declare
He was their tree, and they his apples were,
Which in his estimate did farre outvie

In tendernesse the apple of his age;
And though sterne death had been so much unkind,
To pluck the fruit and leave the tree behind,
Yet in that action, he did but show,
That they untimely to their graves did go.
To shew in time, what we must likewise do,
Branches, Trunk, Root, and all must follow too.

Lady Mary Carey (fl. 1643–80)

26

Wretten By Me At The Death Of My 4th Son And 5th Child Perigrene Payler

I thought my all was given before
But mercy ordered me one more:
A Perigrene; my God me sent
Him back againe I doe present.
As a Love-Token; 'mongst my others
One Daughter; and her four deare Brothers;
To my Lord Christ; my only bliss
Is, he is mine; and I am his:
My dearest Lord, hast thou fulfill'd thy will,
Thy Hand-Maid's pleas'd, compleatly happy still
Grove-Street, May 12th, 1652 Mary Carey

27

What birth is this: a poore despissed creature?
    A little Embrio; voyd of life, and feature:
Seven tymes I went my tyme; when mercy giving
    deliverance unto me; & mine all living:
Stronge, right-proportioned, lovely Girles, & boyes
    There fathers; Mother's present hope't for Joyes:
                                        [continues

Elizabeth Egerton, Countess of Bridgewater (1626–63)

28

On My Boy Henry

Here lyes a Boy the finest child from me
Which makes my Heart and Soule sigh for to see
Nor can I think of any thought, but greeve,
For joy or pleasure could me not releeve,
It lived dayes as many as my years,
No more; which caused my greeved teares;
Twenty and Nine was the number;

And death hath parted us asunder,
But thou art happy, Sweet'st on High,
I mourne not for thy Birth, nor Cry.

Jane Cheyne, Vicountess Newhaven (1621–69)

29

ON THE DEATH OF MY DEARE SISTER THE COUNTESSE OF BRIDGEWATER DYING IN CHILDBED, DELIVERED OF A DEAD INFANT A SON, THE 14TH DAY OF JUNE 1663

O God thy Judgments unto sinfull eye
Were greate, when I did see my Sister dye,
Her last look was to heaven, from whence she came,
And thither going, she was still the same,
No Discomposure in her life or Death,
She lived to pray, prayer was her last Breath:
And when Deaths heavy hand had closed her eyes,
Me thought the World gave up it's Ghost in Cryes:
What ere relations choyce, or nature made
Lost their best light, and being in that Shade;
For none can give Example like her life,
To Friendship, Kindred, Family, or wife.
A greater Saint the Earth did never beare,
She lived to love, and her last thought was care;
Her new borne Child she asked for, which n'ere cryed,
Fearing to know its end she Bowed, and Dyed:
And her last Vale to Heaven appeared to all,
How much she knew her Glory in the call.

Katherine Philips (1632–64)

30

EPITAPH. ON HER SON *H.P.* AT ST. SYTH'S CHURCH WHERE HER BODY ALSO LIES INTERRED

What on Earth deserves out Trust?
Youth and Beauty both are dust.
Long we gathering are with pain,
What one Moment calls again.
Seaven years Childless, Marriage past,
A Son, A Son is born at last;
So exactly limm'd and Fair,
Full of good Spirits, Meen, and Aire,
As a long life promised;
Yet, in less than six weeks, dead.

Too promising, too great a Mind
In so small room to be confin'd:
Therefore, fit in Heav'n to dwell,
He quickly broke the Prison shell.
So the Subtle Alchymist,
Can't with Hermes' Seal resist
The Powerfull Spirit's subtler flight,
But 'twill bid him long good night.
And so the Sun, if it arise
Half so Glorious as his Ey's,
Like this Infant, takes a shroud,
Bury'd in a morning Cloud.

Matthew Stevenson (fl. 1654–85)

31

UPON A LADY AT YORK DYING IN CHILD-BIRTH

And, but Her fate was such, think ye that she
Could fall beneath these flags of Victory.
Not possible, but, ah! this Lilly-bed,
Was ashy Death mounted on his pale steed;
That Prince of terrors from the Sisters sent
To rifle and take down this silver Tent.
And, what was that to us, if Heaven thought meet,
That she should lay in, in Her Winding sheet?
Or that Her Son thus unaccustom'd wise,
Should *Phoenix* like from Her own ashes rise.
Or, that his Spring must needs her Autumn be,
And we have but a Pippin for a Tree?
All still to love is not lost that's crown'd with Fruit.
Nay, let us rather Heavens just praise proclaim,
That from a shadow such a substance came.
Not but her Years so fresh, so full of bloom,
Among the living might have still found room.
But that her soul which nought, but Heaven contents,
Became too volatile for its Elements.
Which, ('cause their centres, yet, contrary are)
Subsided, and became this falling Star.
Left here as pledge, till Earth shall kiss the Skies,
And dust in glory to its Consort rise.
Meanwhile thus White, thus all in brydal State,
To Her bright Spouse ascends Heaven's Candidate.
How then is Fate unkind? Death comes but right,

'Tis sickle-season when the Fields are white.
Yea, even her Bed did so all-white appear,
As if her innocence would still live here.
Thus Heaven, and Earth conspire a glorious day,
When Soul and Body go the milky way.

Anne Bradstreet (1613?–72)

32

ON MY DEAR GRANDCHILD SIMON BRADSTREET, WHO DIED ON
16 NOVEMBER, 1669, BEING BUT A MONTH, AND ONE DAY OLD

No sooner came, but gone, and fall'n asleep,
Acquaintance short, yet parting caused us weep;
Three flowers, two scarcely blown, the last i'th' bud,
Cropt by th' Almighty's hand; yet is He good,
With dreadful awe before Him let's be mute,
Such was His will, but why, let's not dispute,
With humble hearts and mouths put in the dust,
Let's say He's merciful as well as just.
He will return and make up all our losses,
And smile again after our bitter crosses
Go pretty babe, go rest with sisters twain;
Among the blest in endless joys remain.

Aphra Behn (1640?–89)

33

EPITAPH ON THE TOMBSTONE OF A CHILD,
THE LAST OF SEVEN THAT DIED BEFORE

This Little, Silent, Gloomy Monument,
Contains all that was sweet and innocent;
The softest pratler that e'er found a Tongue,
His voice was Musick and his Words a Song;
Which now each List'ning Angel smiling hears,
Such pretty Harmonies compose the Spheres;
Wanton as unfledg'd Cupids, ere their charms
Had learn'd the little arts of doing harms;
Fair as young Cherubins, as soft and kind,
And tho translated could not be refin'd;
The Seventh dear pledge the Nuptial Joys had given,
Toil'd here on Earth, retir'd to rest in Heaven;
Where they the shining Host of Angels fill,
Spread their gay wings before the Throne, and smile.

Thomas Flatman (1635?–88)

34

CORIDON ON THE DEATH OF HIS DEAR ALEXIS, OB. JAN. 28 1683.
PASTORAL SONG. SET BY DR. BLOW

Alexis! dear Alexis! lovely boy!
 O my Damon! O Palaemon! snatch'd away,
 To some far distant region gone,
Has left the miserable Coridon
Bereft of all his comforts, all alone!
 Have you not seen my gentle lad,
 Whom every swain did love,
 Cheerful, when every swain was sad,
 Beneath the melancholy grove?
His face was beauteous as the dawn of day,
 Broke through the gloomy shades of night:
 O my anguish! my delight!
 Him (ye kind shepherds) I bewail,
 Till my eyes and heart shall fail.
'Tis *He* that's landed on that distant shore,
And you and I shall see him here no more.
 Return, Alexis! O return!
 Return, return, in vain I cry;
Poor Coridon shall never cease to mourn
Thy too untimely, cruel destiny.
 Farewell for ever, charming boy!
And with *Thee*, all the transports of my joy!
Ye powers above, why should I longer live,
To waste a few uncomfortable years,
 To drown myself in tears,
For what my sighs and pray'rs can ne'er retrieve?

35

EPITAPH ON HIS ELDEST SON, THOMAS, 1682

Whoe'er thou art, that look'st upon,
And read'st what lies beneath this stone;
What Beauty, Goodness, Innocence,
In a sad hour was snatch'd from hence.
What reason canst thou have to prize
The dearst object of thine eyes?
Believe this, mortal, what thou valuest most,
And set'st thy soul upon, is soonest lost.

Alexander Pope (1688–1744)

36

ON MRS. CORBET
WHO DIED OF A CANCER IN HER BREAST

Here rests a Woman, good without pretence,
Blessed with plain Reason, and with sober Sense;
No Conquests she, but o'er herself, desir'd,
No Arts essay'd, but not to be admir'd.
Passion and Pride were to her soul unknown,
Convinc'd that Virtue only is our own.
So unaffected, so compos'd a mind;
So firm, yet soft; so strong, yet so refin'd;
Heav'n, as its purest gold, by Tortures try'd;
The Saint sustain'd it, but the Woman dy'd.

Mehetabel (Hetty) Wright (1697–1750)

37

TO AN INFANT EXPIRING THE SECOND DAY OF ITS BIRTH

Tender softness, infant mild,
Perfect, purest, brightest child;
Transient lustre, beauteous clay,
Smiling wonder of a day
Ere the last convulsive start
Rends the unresisting heart;
Ere the long-enduring swoon
Weighs thy precious eyelids down;
Oh! regard a mother's moan,
Anguish deeper than thy own!
Fairest eyes, whose dawning light
Late with rapture blessed my sight,
Ere your orbs extinguished be,
Bend their trembling beams on me,
Drooping sweetness, verdant flower,
Blooming, withering in an hour,
Ere thy gentle breast sustains
Latest, fiercest, vital pains,
Hear a suppliant! Let me be
Partner in thy destiny!

Elizabeth Boyd (fl. 1730–44)

38

ON THE DEATH OF AN INFANT OF FIVE DAYS OLD,
BEING A BEAUTIFUL BUT ABORTIVE BIRTH

How frail is human life! How fleet our breath,
Born with the symptoms of approaching death!
What dire convulsions rend a mother's breast,
When by a first-born son's decease distressed.
Although an embryo, an abortive boy,
Thy wond'rous beauties give a wond'rous joy:
Still flattering Hope a flattering idea gives,
And, whilst the birth can breathe, we say it lives.
With what kind warmth the dear-loved babe was pressed:
The darling man was with less love caressed!
How dear, how innocent, the final embrace!
The father's form all o'er, the father's face,
The sparkling eye, gay with a cherub smile,
Some flying hours the mother-pangs beguile;
The pretty mouth a Cupid's tale expressed,
In amorous murmurs, to the full-swoll'n breast.
If angel infancy can so endear,
Dear angel-infants must command a tear.
Oh! could the stern-souled sex but know the pain,
Or the soft mother's agonies sustain,
With tenderest love the obdurate heart would burn,
And the shocked father tear for tear return.

Jane Colman Turell (1708–35)

39

PHOEBUS HAS THRICE HIS YEARLY CIRCUIT RUN

Phoebus has thrice his yearly circuit run,
The winter's over, and the summer's done;
Since that bright day on which our hands were join'd,
And to Philander I my all resign'd.

    Thrice in my womb I've found the pleasing strife,
In the first struggles of my infant's life:
But oh how soon by heaven I'm call'd to mourn,
While from my womb a lifeless babe is torn!
Born to the grave 'ere it had seen the light,
Or with one smile had cheered my longing sight.

Again in travail pains my nerves are wreck'd.
My eye-balls start, my heart strings almost crack'd;
Now I forget my pains, and now I press
Philander's image to my panting breast.
Ten days I hold him in my joyful arms,
And feast my eyes upon his infant charms.
But then the king of terrors does advance
To pierce it's bosom with his iron lance.
It's soul releas'd, upward it takes it's flight,
Oh never more below to bless my sight!
Farewell sweet babes I hope to meet above,
And there with you sing the redeemer's love.

And now oh gracious saviour lend thine ear,
To this my earnest cry and humble prayer,
That when the hour arrives with painful throws,
Which shall my burden to the world disclose;
I may deliverance have, and joy to see
A living child, to dedicate to thee.

Anonymous

40

EPITAPH ON A CHILD KILLED BY PROCURED ABORTION

O thou, whose eyes were closed in death's pale night,
Ere fate revealed thee to my aching sight;
Ambiguous something, by no standard fixed,
Frail span, of naught and of existence mixed;
Embryo, imperfect as my tort'ring thought,
Sad outcast of existence and of naught;
Thou, who to guilty love first ow'st thy fame,
Whom guilty honour kills to hide its shame;
Dire offspring! formed by love's too pleasing pow'r!
Honour's dire victim in a luckless hour!
Soften the pangs that still revenge thy doom:
Nor, from the dark abyss of nature's womb,
Where back I cast thee, let revolving time
Call up past scenes to aggravate my crime.
Two adverse tyrants ruled thy wayward fate,
Thyself a helpless victim to their hate;
Love, spite of honour's dictates, gave thee breath;
Honour, in spite of love, pronounced thy death.

Samuel Bowden (fl. 1732–61)

41

On The Death Of An Only Child, Of Very Pregnant Parts

Ungentle Death with fatal dart,
Has pierc'd young *Phillis* to the heart.
Tyrannic death that wou'd not spare
The wise, the witty, and the fair.
She blossom'd with so quick a shoot,
You had the bloom, but heav'n the fruit.
(Young plants, thus loaded, often drop,
Kill'd with their own luxuriant crop.)
Transplanted to that happy shore,
Where sickly Winters blast no more.

Thomas Gray (1716–71)

42

Epitaph On A Child

Here, freed from pain, secure from misery, lies,
A child, the darling of his parents' eyes:
A gentler lamb ne'er sported on the plain,
A fairer flower will never bloom again.
Few were the days allotted to his breath;
Now let him sleep in peace his night of death.

Jane Cave (c.1754–1813)

43

Written A Few Hours Before The Birth Of A Child

My God, prepare me for the hour
    When most thy aid I want;
Uphold me by thy mighty power,
    Nor let my spirits faint.

I ask not life, I ask not ease,
    But patience to submit
To what shall best thy goodness please,
    Then come what thou seest fit.

Come pain, or agony, or death,
    If such the will divine;
With joy shall I give up my breath,
    If resignation's mine.

One wish to name I'd humbly dare,
    If death thy pleasure be;
O may the harmless babe I bear
    Haply expire with me.

Helen Leigh (fl. 1780–95)

44

THE NATURAL CHILD

Let not the title of my verse offend,
    Nor let the prude contract her rigid brow;
That hapless Innocence demands a friend,
    Virtue herself will cheerfully allow:

And should my pencil prove too weak to point
    The ills attendant on the babe ere born,
Whose parents swerved from Virtue's mild restraint,
    Forgive th'attempt, nor treat the muse with scorn.

Yon rural farm, where Mirth was wont to dwell,
    Of Melancholy now appears the seat;
Solemn and silent as the hermit's cell –
    Say what, my muse, has caused a change so great?

This hapless morn, an infant first saw light,
    Whose innocence a better fate might claim
Than to be shunned as hateful to the sight,
    And banished soon as it receives a name.

No joy attends its entrance into life,
    No smile upon its mother's face appears.
She cannot smile, alas! she is no wife,
    But vents the sorrow of her heart in tears.

No father flies to clasp it to his breast;
    And bless the power that gave it to his arms;
To see his form, in miniature, expressed,
    Or trace, with ecstasy, its mother's charms.

Unhappy babe! thy father is thy foe!
    Oft shall he wish thee numbered with the dead,
His crime entails on thee a load of woe,
    And sorrow heaps on thy devoted head.

Torn from its mother's breast, by shame or pride –
    No matter which – to hireling hands assigned;
A parent's tenderness when thus denied,
    Can it be thought its nurse is over-kind?

Too many like this infant we may see,
   Exposed, Abandoned, helpless and forlorn;
Till death, misfortune's friend, has set them free
   From a rude world, which gave them naught but scorn.

Too many mothers – horrid to relate!
   Soon as their infants breathe the vital air,
Deaf to their plaintive cries, their helpless state,
   Led on by shame, and driven by despair.

Fell murderers become – Here cease, my pen,
   And leave these wretched victims of despair;
But ah! what punishments await the men,
   Who, in such depths of misery, plunge the fair?

Robert Burns (1759–96)

45

ON THE BIRTH OF A POSTHUMOUS CHILD,
BORN IN PECULIAR CIRCUMSTANCES OF FAMILY-DISTRESS

Sweet flow'ret, pledge o'meikle love,
And ward o'mony a prayer,
What heart o'stane wad thou na move,
Sae helpless, sweet, and fair.

November hirples o'er the lea,
Chill, on thy lovely form;
And gane, alas! the shelt'ring tree,
Should shield thee frae the storm.

May He who gives the rain to pour,
And wings the blast to blaw
Protect thee frae the driving show'r,
The bitter frost and snaw!

May He, the friend of Woe and Want,
Who heals life's various stounds,
Protect and guard the mother plant,
And heal her cruel wounds.

But late she flourished, rooted fast,
Fair on the summer morn:
Now, feebly bends she, in the blast,
Unsheltered and forlorn.

Blest be thy bloom, thou lovely gem,
Unscath'd by ruffian hand!

And from thee many a parent stem
Arise to deck our land.

William Blake (1757–1827)

46

THE CHIMNEY-SWEEPER *Songs of Innocence*

When my mother died I was very young,
And my father sold me while yet my tongue,
Could scarcely cry weep weep weep weep.
So your chimneys I sweep & in soot I sleep.

Theres little Tom Dacre, who cried when his head
That curl'd like a lambs back, was shav'd, so I said,
Hush Tom never mind it, for when your head's bare,
You know that the soot cannot spoil your white hair.

And so he was quiet, & that very night,
As Tom was a sleeping he had such a sight,
That thousands of sweepers Dick, Joe, Ned & Jack
Were all of them lock'd up in coffins of black,

And by came an Angel who had a bright key,
And he open'd the coffins & set them all free.
Then down a green plain leaping laughing they run,
And wash in a river and shine in the Sun.

Then naked & white, all their bags left behind,
They rise upon clouds, and sport in the wind.
And the Angel told Tom, if he'd be a good boy,
He'd have God for his father & never want joy.

And so Tom awoke and we rose in the dark
And got with our bags & our brushes to work.
Tho' the morning was cold, Tom was happy & warm.
So if all do their duty, they need not fear harm.

47

THE CHIMNEY-SWEEPER *Songs of Experience*

A little black thing among the snow:
Crying weep, weep, in notes of woe!
Where are thy father & mother? say?
'They are both gone up to the church to pray.

Because I was happy upon the heath,
And smil'd among the winters snow:

They clothed me in the clothes of death,
And taught me to sing the notes of woe.

And because I am happy, & dance & sing,
They think they have done me no injury:
And are gone to praise God & his Priest & King,
Who make up a heaven of our misery.

Sir Brooke Boothby (1743–1824)
48
Sonnet I

Life's summer flown, the wint'ry tempest rude
Began to lower on the declining year;
When smiles celestial gilt the prospect dear,
Dispell'd the gloom, and joyful spring renew'd:
    Fresh flowers beneath her fairy feet were strew'd;
Again soft accents woo'd the enchanted ear;
In her bright form, as in a mirror clear,
Reflected, each gay scene of life I view'd.
    Young in her youth, and graceful in her grace,
In her's, I lived o'er every joy again;
Lived o'er the charms that beam'd upon her face,
    Where Hope and Love revived their smiling train.
Night o'er the scene her blackest veil has spread;
And Death's pale hand a tenfold horrour shed.

Samuel Taylor Coleridge (1772–1834)
49
On An Infant, Who Died Before Its Christening

Be rather than be *call'd* a Child of God!
Death whisper'd. With assenting Nod
Its head upon the Mother's breast,
The baby bow'd, and went without demur,
Of the kingdom of the blest
Possessor, not Inheritor.

William Wordsworth (1770–1850)

50

CHARACTERISTICS OF A CHILD THREE YEARS OLD

Loving she is, and tractable, though wild;
And Innocence hath privilege in her
To dignify arch looks and laughing eyes;
And feats of cunning; and the pretty round
Of trespasses, affected to provoke
Mock-chastisement and partnership in play.
And as a faggot sparkles on a hearth,
Not less if unattended and alone
Than when both young and old sit gathered round
And take delight in its activity;
Even so this happy Creature of herself
Is all sufficient; solitude to her
Is blithe society, who fills the air
With gladness and involuntary songs
Light are her sallies as the tripping Fawn's
Forth-startled from the fern where she lay couched;
Unthought-of, unexpected as the stir
Of the soft breeze ruffling the meadow flowers;
Or from before it chasing wantonly
The many-coloured images impressed
Upon the bosom of a placid lake.

51

Miscellaneous Sonnets XXVII

SURPRIZED BY JOY – IMPATIENT AS THE WIND

Surprized by joy – impatient as the Wind
I wished to share the transport – Oh! with whom
But Thee, long buried in the silent Tomb.
That spot which no vicissitude can find?
Love, faithful love recalled thee to my mind–
But how could I forget thee? – Through what power,
Even for the least division of an hour,
Have I been so beguiled as to be blind
To my most grievous loss? – That thought's return
Was the worst pang that sorrow ever bore,
Save one, one only, when I stood forlorn,
Knowing my heart's best treasure was no more;
That neither present time, nor years unborn
Could to my sight that heavenly face restore.

Percy Bysshe Shelley (1792–1822)

52

To William Shelley II

My lost William, thou in whom
   Some bright spirit lived, and did
That decaying robe consume
   Which its lustre faintly hid,–
Here its ashes find a tomb,
   But beneath this pyramid
Thou art not – if a thing divine
Like thee can die, thy funeral shrine
Is thy mother's grief and mine.

Where art thou, my gentle child?
   Let me think thy spirit feeds,
With its life intense and mild,
   The love of living leaves and weeds
Among these tombs and ruins wild;–
   Let me think and through low seeds
Of sweet flowers and sunny grass
Into their hues and scents may pass
A portion–

53

To William Shelley III

Thy little footsteps on the sands
 Of a remote and lonely shore;
The twinkling of thine infant hands,
 Where now the worm will feed no more;
Thy mingled look of love and glee
When we return to gaze on thee–

Amelia Alderson Opie (1769–1853)

54

On The Death Of A Child

And he is gone! that winning child
Whose eyes with varied meanings shone:
By turns the gay, the grave, the wild:
A child't was sweet to look upon!

Joy of a widow'd mother's breast;
But yet at times her anxious care!
Now with the tenderest love carest,
Now needy duty's frown severe.

For sure her heart some comforts felt
When, as she view'd the future years,
She for her boy in prayer has knelt,
Now flush'd with hope – now pale with fears.

But He, that God who 'heareth prayer,'
To her's a favouring answer gave;
And sav'd her child from every snare,
By – precious gift! – an early grave.

For mercy bids, when those we love
In childhood's morn of cloudless ray,
At once from life's dread snares remove,
And pass like early dews away!

So mourner! has thy darling pass'd,
And safely reach'd the destin'd bourne!
Then, though thy path clouds still o'ercast,
Let faith exult, though fondness mourn.

Mary Ann Browne (1812–44)

55

'My Baby! My Baby! They've Told Me He Is Dead'

My baby my baby! They've told me he is dead;
That they've ta'en him to the church-yard, and the funeral rite is said;
They have told me that his blue eyes have closed in their last sleep,
That his lips are lying silent there, and worms may o'er them creep;
My baby! my baby! and then to comfort me,
They say 't is gone away to rest, where sorrow cannot be!
I heed not, I care not, lay ashes on my head;
Let me lie down in silence too, mine only child is dead!

Who dared to speak of comfort? I tell thee, he is gone,
And I shall never see him more, my dear, my precious one;
I tell thee that these arms have clasped his young limbs o'er and o'er,
And I tell thee that these empty arms shall never clasp him more.
Who art thou, with solemn brow, who wouldst whisper words of peace?
They fall on me like dew on rocks, I pray, I pray thee, cease!
Thou never wast a mother, or thou never couldst have said,
There is comfort for a mother, whose only babe is dead!

Oh let me speak of sorrow, and nurture it with tears;
Let me think of all the hope with which I looked to future years;
Let me number up the treasures that in him were stored for me,
And try to find the bound of this my burning agony;

Thus weave around my spirit, o'erwearied with its task,
A hollow cloud of comfort, a mocking, specious mask;
Till my soul, awakening with a start, recoileth in its dread,
As again it echoeth the words, 'My child, my child is dead!'

Walter Savage Landor (1775–1864)
56
On The Dead

Thou in this wide cold church art laid
Close to the wall my little maid!
My little Fanny Verchild! thou
Sole idol of an infant vow!
My playmate in life's break of day,
When all we had to do was play!
Even then, if any other girl
To kiss my forehead seiz'd a curl,
Thou wouldst with sad dismay run in,
And stamp and call it shame and sin.
And should some rough, intrusive boy
Bring thee an orange, flower, or toy,
My tiny fist was at his frill,
I bore my jealousy so ill,
And felt my bosom beat so bold,
Altho' he might be six years old.
Against the marble slab mine eyes
Dwell fixt; and from below arise
Thoughts, not yet cold nor mute, of thee
It was their earliest joy to see.
One who had marcht o'er Minden's plain,
In thy young smile grew young again.
That stern one melted into love,
That father traced the line above.*
His Roman soul used Roman speech,
And taught (ah thou too, thou didst teach!)
How, soon as in our course we start,
Death follows with uplifted dart.

John Clare (1793–1864)

57

GRAVES OF INFANTS

Infants' graves are steps of angels, where
Earth's brightest gems of innocence repose.
God is their parent, so they need no tear;
He takes them to his bosom from earth's woes,
A bud their lifetime and a flower their close.
Their spirits are an Iris of the skies,
Needing no prayers; a sunset's happy close.
Gone are the bright rays of their soft blue eyes;
Flowers weep in dewdrops o'er them, and the gale gently sighs.

Their lives were nothing but a sunny shower,
Melting on flowers as tears melt from the eye.
Their deaths were dewdrops on heaven's amaranth bower,
And tolled on flowers as summer gales went by.
They bowed and trembled, and they left no sigh.
And the sun smiled to show their end was well.
Infants have naught to weep for ere they die;
All prayers are needless, beads they need not tell;
White flowers their mourners are, nature their passing-bell.

Louisa A. Horsfield (1830–65?)

58

TO MY DEPARTED BABY

The flowers will bud and bloom again,
    The leaves bedeck the forest-tree,
The grass enrobe the wither'd plain;–
    But thou wilt not return to me!

The black-bird and the thrush will sing
    Their songs of gushing melody,
To greet again the blushing Spring;–
    But thou wilt not return to me!

Ah no! thy blighted buds no more
    Shall blossom with returning Spring;
They bloom on yon celestial shore,
    To grave the palace of their King.

One fetter less hath earth for me,
    But heaven one bright attraction more;
My gather'd flower, I'll follow thee
    To Canaan's ever-blooming shore.

Alexander Anderson (1845–1909)

59

THE DEAD CHILD

There is an angel sleeping in this room,
A little angel, with the quietest bloom
Of white, all downy-like, upon the cheek
And round the brow, and yet it will not speak;
But in its silence seeming still a form
Cut by some sculptor when his mind was warm
With highest beauty. Look! I pull away
The little curtain, and you look on clay,
Yet clay so wrought to love's own rest that you
But weep to share the calm that meets your view;
Then worship, and with fingers fondly touch
The little brow that wakens not at such;
Put back the delicate wealth of silken hair,
And wonder why it keeps so fresh and fair;
Kiss the faint curved lips, and you the while,
A dupe to fancy, think they sweetly smile;
Press the shut eyelids, that, all white and even,
Like tiny clouds that hide blue spots of heaven,
Drop o'er those eyes, whose light has fled away,
To leave this human blossom to decay,
Like the few flowers that seem dewy fair
Within the little hands. We place them there,
As if to see how well their hues would keep,
A perfect type of its most innocent sleep.
But these will wither, and the grave will hide
Within its dull, dank, clasp our household pride,
And little feet will touch no more the hearth,
And little lips will laugh no more their mirth,
But silence, ever deeper when we miss
A cherub presence for its nightly kiss.
Yet in our hearts most sacred spot shall be
A little angel type of this we see–
Fair, pure, and heavenly, through the changing years,
And kept all golden with our sweetest tears,
Until the little form, not lost, but hid
For in our bosom like a golden thread,
Shall twine itself around our life till we
Bear lighter weight of sin and earth, and see
Before us all our paths shaped out of love,

And brighten'd with a shadow from above
Beneath whose balm and Hope's eternal love
The days but seem as links to guide us on.
Till, when we reach our pilgrimage of clay,
And all we had of each is passed away,
We find at least beyond the stars' abode
Our little wither'd bud full blown in God.

Edward Dowden (1843–1913)
60
TO A CHILD DEAD AS SOON AS BORN

A little wrath was on thy forehead, Boy,
Being thus defeated, the resolved will
Which death could not subdue, was threatened still
From lip and brow. I know that it was joy
No casual misadventure might destroy
To have lived, and fought and died. Therefore I kill
The pang for thee, unknown, nor count it ill
That thou hast entered swiftly on employ
Where Life would plant a warder keen and pure.
I thought to see a little piteous clay
The grave had need of, pale from light obscure
Of embryo dreams, thy face was as the day
Smit on by storm. Palms for my child, and bay!
Thus far thou hast done well, true son, endure.

Robert Bridges (1844–1930)
61
ON A DEAD CHILD

Perfect little body, without fault or stain on thee,
   With promise of strength and manhood full and fair!
     Though cold and stark and bare,
The bloom and the charm of life doth awhile remain on thee.

Thy mother's treasure wert thou; – alas! no longer
   To visit her heart with wondrous joy; to be
     Thy father's pride; – ah, he
Must gather his faith together, and his strength make stronger.

To me, as I move thee now in the last duty,
   Dost thou with a turn or gesture anon respond;
     Startling my fancy fond
With a chance attitude of the head, a freak of beauty.

Thy hand clasps, as 'twas wont, my finger, and holds it:
  But the grasp is the clasp of Death, heartbreaking and stiff;
    Yet feels to my hand as if
'Twas still thy will, thy pleasure and trust that enfolds it.

So I lay thee there, thy sunken eyelids closing,–
  Go lie thou there in thy coffin, thy last little bed!–
    Propping thy wise, sad head,
Thy firm, pale hands across thy chest disposing.

So quiet! doth the change content thee? – Death, wither hath he taken thee?
  To a world, do I think, that rights the disaster of this?
    The vision of which I miss,
Who weep for the body, and wish but to warm thee and awaken thee?

Ah! little at best can call our hopes avail us
  To lift this sorrow, or cheer us, when in the dark,
    Unwilling, alone we embark,
And the things we have seen and have known and have heard of, fail us.

Thomas Hardy (1840–1928)

62

THE VOICE

Woman much missed, how you call to me, call to me,
Saying that now you are not as you were
When you had changed from the one who was all to me,
But as at first, when our day was fair.

Can it be you that I hear? Let me view you, then,
Standing as when I drew near to the town
Where you wait for me: yes, as I knew you then,
Even to the original air-blue gown!

Or is it only the breeze, in its listlessness
Travelling across the wet mead to me here,
You being ever dissolved to wan wistlessness,
Heard no more again far or near?

    Thus I; faltering forward,
    Leaves around me falling,
Wind oozing thin through the thorn from norward
    And the woman calling.

Dylan Thomas (1914–53)

63

A REFUSAL TO MOURN THE DEATH,
BY FIRE, OF A CHILD IN LONDON

Never until the mankind making
Bird beast and flower
Fathering and all humbling darkness
Tells with silence the last light breaking
And the still hour
Is come of the sea tumbling in harness

And I must enter again the round
Zion of the water bead
And the synagogue of the ear of corn
Shall I let pray the shadow of a sound
Or sow my salt seed
In the least valley of sackcloth to mourn

The majesty and burning of the child's death.
I shall not murder
The mankind of her going with a grave truth
Nor blaspheme down the stations of the breath
With any further
Elegy of innocence and youth.

Deep with the first dead lies London's daughter,
Robed in the long friends,
The grains beyond age, the dark veins of her mother,
Secret by the unmourning water
Of the riding Thames.
After the first death, there is no other.

D. J. Enright (1920–2002)

64

ON THE DEATH OF A CHILD

The greatest griefs shall find themselves
    inside the smallest cage.
It's only then that we can hope to tame
    their rage.

The monsters we must live with. For
    it will not do
To hiss humanity because one human threw
    Us out of heart and home. Or part

At odds with life because one baby failed
   to live.
Indeed, as little as its subject, is
   the wreath we give –

The big words fail to fit. Like giant boxes
Round small bodies. Taking up improper room,
Where so much withering is, and so much bloom.

Elizabeth Jennings (1926–2001)
65
FOR A CHILD BORN DEAD

What ceremony can we fit
You into now? If you had come
Out of a warm and noisy room
To this, there'd be an opposite
For us to know you by. We could
Imagine you in lively mood.

And then look at the other side,
The mood drawn out of you, the breath
Defeated by the power of death.
But we have never seen you stride
Ambitiously the world we know.
You could not come and yet you go.

But there is nothing now to mar
Your clear refusal of our world.
Not in our memories can we mould
You or distort your character.
Then all our consolation is
That grief can be as pure as this.

Sylvia Plath (1932–63)
66
STILLBORN

These poems do not live: it's a sad diagnosis.
They grew their toes and fingers well enough,
Their little foreheads bulged with concentration.
If they missed out on walking about as people
It wasn't for any lack of mother-love.

O I cannot understand what happened to them!
They are proper in shape and number and every part.

They sit so nicely in the pickling fluid!
They smile and smile and smile and smile at me.
And still the lungs won't fill and the heart won't start.

They are not pigs, they are not even fish,
Though they have a piggy and a fishy air–
It would be better if they were alive, and that's what they were.
But they are dead, and their mother near dead with distraction,
And they stupidly stare, and do not speak of her.

Seamus Heaney (1939–)
67
ELEGY FOR A STILL-BORN CHILD
I
Your mother walks light as an empty creel
Unlearning the intimate nudge and pull.

Your trussed-up weight of seed-flesh and bone-curd
Had insisted on. The evicted world

Contracts round its history, its scar.
Doomsday struck when your collapsed sphere

Extinguished itself in your atmosphere,
Your mother heavy with the lightness in her.

II
For six months you stayed cartographer
Charting my friend from husband towards father.

He guessed a globe behind your steady mound.
Then the pole fell, shooting star, into the ground.

III
On lonely journeys I think of it all,
Birth of death, exhumation for burial,

A wreath of small clothes, a memorial pram,
And parents reaching for a phantom limb.

I drive by remote control on this bare road
Under a drizzling sky, a circling rook,

Past mountain fields, full to the brim with cloud,
White waves riding home on a wintry lough.

Paula Meehan (1955–)

68

CHILD BURIAL

Your coffin looked unreal,
fancy as a wedding cake.

I chose your grave clothes with care,
your favourite stripey shirt,

your blue cotton trousers.
They smelt of woodsmoke, of October,

your own smell there too.
I chose a gansy of handspun wool,

warm and fleecy for you. It is
so cold down in the dark.

No light can reach you and teach you
the paths of wild birds,

the names of the flowers,
the fishes, the creatures.

Ignorant you must remain
of the sun and its work,

my lamb, my calf, my eaglet,
my cub, my kid, my nestling,

my suckling, my colt. I would spin
time back, take you again

within my womb, your amniotic lair,
and further spin you back

through nine waxing months
to the split seeding moment

you chose to be made flesh,
word within me.

I'd cancel the love feast
the hot night of your making.

I would travel alone
to a quiet mossy place,

you would spill from me into the earth
drop by bright red drop.

Nina Bogin (1952–)

69

The Stillborn

The stillborn have no claim
on this world. They are quiet
and distant, taking care of themselves,
perfect as seashells,
as starfish navigating point by point
along the shallows,
as the smallest seahorses
grazing in the sands.

They have nothing in common with death.
No, it's as if a path
had been traced for them across a clean beach
with footprints ready for them to fall into step,
to walk into the dazzling wind of their lives.
And when they turned back,
remained crustacean,
slowly the footprints unmade themselves,
each grain of sand, one after the other,
tumbled back into the sea ...

7

The Vocabulary of Grief

Almost all of the 69 are elegies, 'mournful poems' for the dead, and several are also epitaphs, poems inscribed or purporting to be inscribed on tombs. Most are sincere expressions of feelings towards the recently departed; they signify bereavement, although in a few cases sincerity may be questioned and a commercial motive suspected. Usually the subject is a child, but infants, the unborn, and women who are about to or who have recently given birth also have a place. A small number of the subjects are spouses, mourned by their partners. How should we read these elegies?

Literary critics and historians have given elegies and epitaphs considerably more attention in recent years.[277] Their interest has tended to dwell on four particular areas. The first focuses on the purpose of elegies and poetic epitaphs as literary genre. It covers the various distinctions between mourning as a process; grief as an emotion of intense sorrow; the conflict between reason and emotion, between lamentation and praise; and their use as forms of consolation for the bereaved. The second stems from the recognition that the functions and forms of the genre changed; that these changes might be used to reflect how attitudes to mourning altered, as well as what people believed they should feel and what they actually did feel; that elegies were literary versions of certain specific social and psychological practices. In this they could provide insights on the conventions of consolation not only via their content, but also the way they moved in and out of fashion with poets and patrons. 'Intentionality' provides a convenient label for the third area. Are the author's intentions recoverable and if so by what means? For example, did the poet write as an act of self-consolation, part of 'mourning work'? The fourth sees elegies and especially epitaphs through their historical rather than literary contexts; how they are anchored to biography, fixed in time and place. Questions of historical significance and meaning are brought to the fore while language is moved to the background.[278]

The discussion in this chapter moves between several of these areas. While the principal objective is to explore the ways in which author-parents expressed their feelings, we are also concerned with their use of language, how that language changed and varied, and how they selected and used different vocabularies of grief.[279] Grief and the emotions are our target rather than mourning practices. But it is impossible to escape from the fact that elegies can provide consolation to authors and readers. The next section begins by considering emotion lexicons: the vocabulary that could be used to express the emotions, but especially grief. The following section uses a simple form of content analysis to establish the pattern of word use in the 69 poems in the anticipation that this will help to describe when and how the expression of emotions changed. The presumption is that these expressions were in some way shaped by demographic experience. Subsequent sections consider the ways in which relationships affected forms and styles of elegy. Finally, we turn to the challenging problem of silence: death without grief, 'mourning work' not completed.

Emotion lexicons

The second edition of the Oxford English Dictionary defines the various meanings and senses of 'emotion' and 'grief' in the following ways.

emotion
1 a moving out, migration, transference from one place to another
2 a moving, stirring, agitation, perturbation (in the physical sense)
3 a political or social agitation, a tumult, popular disturbance
4(a) any agitation or disturbance of mind, feeling, passion; any vehement or excited mental state
4(b) *psychology* a mental 'feeling' or 'affection' (e.g. of pleasure or pain, desire or aversion, surprise, hope or fear, etc.), as distinguished from cognitive or volitional states of consciousness; feeling as distinguished from the other classes of mental phenomena

grief
1 hardship, suffering; a kind, or cause, of hardship or suffering
2(a) hurt, harm, mischief or injury done or caused by another; damage inflicted or suffered; molestation, trouble, offence
2(b) a wrong or injury which is the subject of formal complaint or demand for formal redress = grievance
3 gravity, grievousness (of an offence)
4 feeling of offence; displeasure, anger
5(a) a bodily injury or ailment; a morbid affection of any part of the body; a sore, a wound; a blemish of the skin; a disease, sickness
5(b) the seat of disease; the diseased part; the sore place
6 physical pain or discomfort
7(a) mental pain, distress, or sorrow. In modern use in a more limited sense: deep or violent sorrow, caused by loss or trouble; a keen or bitter feeling of regret for something lost, remorse for something done, or sorrow for mishap to oneself or others.
7(b) a cause or subject of grief
also **grief** *adj.* and *adv.*
grievous, grave, troublesome, oppressive (of armour), grievously, excessively

grieve

contains the mental and physical aspects; to cause bodily pain or discomfort
to affect with grief or deep sorrow

formerly, in a wider sense: to vex, trouble, or oppress mentally; to cause pain,
anxiety, or vexation; to annoy

It is obvious from this list, as well as the discussion in Chapter 5, that the word
'emotion' and 'the emotions' as a collective term for a certain category of human
feelings has a complicated set of meanings which will require close interpretation
according to context; that 'grief', while unquestionably one of the emotions, also has
a rather unsettled meaning that has shifted during the centuries. This fluidity makes
the construction of a single, definitive lexicon extremely difficult. This is further illustrated in tables 7.1 and 7.2.

Table 7.1 focuses on 'emotion' and 'emotional'. It compares the definitions
offered in Dr Johnson's eighteenth-century dictionary; the first edition of Dr Roget's
thesaurus from the 1830s; as well as the most recent Oxford and Chambers diction-
aries. It also lists related words, including some opposites, upon which an emotion
lexicon could be based. Table 7.2 follows a similar pattern using 'grief' and 'mourning'.
It suggests that even in Dr Johnson's time 'grief' was still used to express physical
pain, just as it had been by Shakespeare, but that its modern sense is very much one of
mental anguish associated with bereavement or loss in general. Certainly it is a deeply
felt emotion, one that is often expressed in particular physical ways (wailing, weeping
etc.), and, in common with the other emotions, is distinct from cognition and will.
Table 7.2 provides the basis for the selection of keywords for which the 69 poems can
be searched. The changing density of occurrences may then give a rough indicator
of how intensely the poets expressed their grief, but also of how they modified their
vocabulary during the centuries.[280]

Some of the potential, as well as obvious limitations, of this approach via content
analysis can be illustrated with an example. Table 7.3 gives the entire word content of
four elegiac poems written by Anne Bradstreet (1613?–72) after the deaths of her three
grandchildren and her daughter-in-law, Mercy.[281] The poem to Simon is number 32.
The full alphabetical listing of words used, including frequency in the four poems,
suggests that the poet employed a similar vocabulary for each of her subjects, and
that references to God (He, His, Almighty, Saviour) and nature (flower, bud, plums,
apples, corn, grass, branches, root, tree, fruit) were especially prominent. However,
there are also some important sentiments that such a simple word-based analysis will
not detect. For example, the poem to Elizabeth (died August 1665 aged 18 months)
repeats 'farewell', and stresses impermanence via images from nature ('buds new
blown') and the idea that children are lent by God, that we should not bewail fate:
'His hand alone guides nature and fate'. In the poem to Anne (died June 1669 aged 43
months) delight is turned to sorrow and disappointment, although the poet acknowledges that experience should have made her wise, and again impermanence is linked
to nature (withering flower, a bubble, brittle glass, a shadow) and God's children are

Table 7.1 Emotion keywords

---

emotion *n.*

Johnson (1755): disturbance of mind; vehemence of passion, or pleasing or painful

Roget (1853): impression, sensation, affection, response, pathos, warmth, glow, vehemence, fervour, fervency, heartiness, cordiality, earnestness, ardor, zeal, eagerness, passion, enthusiasm

Oxford: a strong feeling deriving from one's circumstances, mood, or relationship with others [*orig.* mid 16th cent. denoting a public disturbance or commotion; mid 17th cent. mental agitation; early 19th cent. current general sense]

Chambers: a moving of the feelings, agitation of mind, any of the various phenomena of the mind (such as anger, joy, fear or sorrow), associated also with physical symptoms, feeling as distinguished from cognition and will.

anger ardor coldness *opp.* despair dread ecstasy excitement fear feeling fervour fieriness fire grief gut-feeling happiness hate heart inclination indifference *opp.* instinct intellect *opp.* intensity intuition joy passion reaction response sadness sensation sense sentiment sentimentality softness sorrow soul spirit tenderness vehemence warmth

emotional *adj.*

affecting apathetic *opp.* ardent calm *opp.* cold *opp.* delicate demonstrative detached *opp.* dry *opp.* emotionless *opp.* emotive enthusiastic excitable exciting feeling fervent fiery haunting heart-warming heated hot-blooded impassioned inner loving material *opp.* mawkish melodramatic moved moving of the heart overcharged passionate pathetic poignant powerful psychic psychological responsive roused sensitive sentimental soul-stirring spiritual stirring temperamental tempestuous tender thrilling touching tragic unemotional *opp.* unfeeling *opp.* warm zealous

---

lent. The sense of positive resignation is also repeated: 'Thou with thy Saviour art in endless bliss'. Expressions of impermanence and nature also appear in the poem to Simon (died November 1669 aged 1 month and 1 day), but here the resignation slips. There is for the first and only time the merest hint of a questioning doubt: 'Such was His will, but why, let's not dispute'. But again the poem ends on a positive note: 'Go pretty babe, go rest with sisters twain; | Among the blest in endless joys remain.' The fourth poem is addressed to Anne Bradstreet's son, Samuel, whose wife, Mercy, gave birth to their fifth child, also called Anne, on 3 September 1670. Mother and child died three days later. Anne commiserates with her son over his loss of tree and fruit, but it is the tone of positive resignation that still dominates the poem: 'So with her children four, she's now at rest, | All freed from grief (I trust) among the blest'; and in the poem's last line, 'He knows it is the best for thee and me'. Taken together these poems display a remarkable degree of self-control, and a joyful acceptance of God's fate. 'Grief' is used only twice and then in different senses: for Samuel's mourning and Mercy's release from physical pain.[282]

Table 7.2 **Grief and mourning keywords**

grief *n.*
Johnson (1755): 1 sorrow, trouble for something past; 2 grievance, harm; 3 pain, disease
Oxford: deep or intense sorrow, especially caused by someone's death [*orig.* Middle English]
Chambers: sorrow, distress, great mourning, affliction, a cause of sorrow, bodily pain
(Shakespeare)

affliction agony angst anguish bereavement dejection delight *opp.* depression desolation despair despondency distress dole dolour happiness *opp.* heartache heartbreak joy *opp.* lament lamentation misery mortification mournfulness mourning pain pining regret remorse sadness sorrow suffering torment tribulation trouble unhappiness woe

grief-stricken *adj.*
afflicted angst-ridden anguished bereaved crushed cut-up dejected delighted *opp.* depressed desolate despairing despondent devastated disconsolate dismal distressed doleful dolorous grieving gutted heartbroken heartsick inconsolable joyful *opp.* lamenting mortified mournful mourning overcome overjoyed *opp.* overwhelmed pained pining regretful remorseful sad sombre sorrowful sorrowing suffering tormented troubled upset woebegone woeful wretched

grieve *v.*
Johnson (1755): to afflict, to hurt, to be in pain for something past, to mourn, to sorrow, as for the death of friends
1 mourn
ache be happy *opp.* be miserable be mournful be sad be sorrowful cry keen lament rejoice *opp.* shed tears sob sorrow suffer wail weep
2 hurt
gall harrow pain sting wound
3 sorrow
ache brood cry lament mope mourn pine away regret rejoice *opp.* sob suffer wail weep
4 sadden
afflict break crush devastate dismay distress gladden *opp.* horrify hurt offend pain please *opp.* shock upset wound

mourning *n.*
anguish bereavement desolation despair despondency dole grief grieving heartache keening lament lamentation melancholy misery rejoicing *opp.* sadness sorrow sorrowing wailing weeping woefulness

mournful *adj.*
cheerful *opp.* cheerless dejected depressed desolate despondent disconsolate dismal doleful dolorous downcast elegiac forlorn funereal gloomy grief-stricken happy *opp.* heartbroken heavy-hearted joyful *opp.* joyless lugubrious melancholic melancholy mirthless miserable plaintive plangent rueful sad sombre sorrowful tragic unhappy woebegone woeful

mourn *v.*
bemoan bewail deplore grieve keen lament miss regret rejoice *opp.* rue sigh-over sorrow wail weep

Table 7.3 **Full content analysis of Anne Bradstreet's four poems to her grandchildren: Elizabeth (E), Anne (A) and Simon (S), and her daughter-in-law, Mercy (M)**

a 2 E a 4 A a 6 M above M according A acquaintance S after S again S ah M all S all 3 M Almighty's S alone E alone M along M amazing M among S among M an E an A and 8 E and 2 A and 4 S and 10 M apples E are 2 E arrive M art E art A as 4 A as 2 S asleep S at 3 M away E awe S

babe 3 E babe S babe M be E be S be 2 M bear M because M before A before S before M being M below A best M bewail E bitter S bleeding M blest E blest S blest M bliss 2 A blown E blown S both E both M branches M brings E brittle A bruised M bubble A bud S buds E but E but 2 A but 2 S but 2 M by 2 E by S

came S caused S caused M changed A cheer M cheered A child A children M coast M come A content A corn E could M cropt S crosses S crushed M

date E daughter M days E dear E dear A dear 3 M delight A did 3 M disappointment A dispute S do 2 E down E down M dreadful S dust S dying M

endless A endless S eradicate E ere M eternity ever A ever M everlasting E experience A eye E fading A fainting M fair E fall E fall M fall'n S farewell 3 E farewell A fate 2 E fifth M flower E flower A flowers S fly M fool A for E for M foreign M found A four M freed M from M fruit M full M funeral M

glass A go A go 2 S go M gone A gone S gone 2 M good S grass E grief M griefs M grievous M grown E guides E

hadst M hand E hand A hand S hath 2 M have E have 4 A have M He 2 S He M He's S heart A heart 3 M heart's E heart's A hearts S heavens A heavens M heavy M her 5 M here A high M Him S Him M His E His S hither M hopes A hour 2 A how M humble S

I E I 6 A I 6 M i'th' S if A ignorant M impermanent A in 2 E in 2 A in 2 S in 4 M is 2 E is S is 2 M it A it 5 M

joy A joy M joys S just S

knew A knows M

last S last 3 M lent E lent A let's 3 S lies M life M like 2 A live M lived M long M longer 2 M look A lopped M losses S lost 3 M love M loved M

made A make S may M me 2 A me 5 M mean A merciful S met A might A might M mine E mine A misery M mixture A more A more M mouths S mown E much E mute S my E my 3 A my M

nature 2 E nature M ne'er A new 2 E no S no 2 M not S not M now 2 M

O A of E of A of M oft A oh M on 2 A on M once E once M one 2 M only M or E or 2 A our 2 S own A own M

pain M part M parting S passed M perfect A perhaps A plants E pleasure E pledge M plums E pretty S price A put S

reason M relations M remain S rest S rest M return S riches M ripe E root M rot E

sad 2 M sailing M Saviour A saw M say S scarcely S seas M season E second M see M seemed M sent M set E set A settled E shadow A shall 2 A she A she 6 M she'd M she's M short E short S should E sigh E sisters S sith E smart M smile S so 2 E so 3 M soared M sobbing M son 2 M song M soon E soon M sooner S sorrow A sorrows M soul M sound M space E stable A state E still 2 M stood M strike M strokes M strong E such S survive 2 M sweet E sympathise M

ta'en E tall E terminate E th' S than M that 2 E that A that 2 M that's A the E the 2 A the 3 S the 7 M thee A thee 5 M their E their A then E then A then 2 M they E things 2 A this 2 A

this 2 M thoroughly E those M thou E thou 2 A thou 6 M though M three S throbbing A
thus A thy 2 E thy A thy 4 M tidings M time E time A to 2 E to 6 A to 6 M today A tone M
too E too M tree 2 M trees E trembling A troubled A trust M turning A twain S two S
unto E up A up S up M us S
value A vouchsafe M
wailing M was E was 4 A was S was M week M weep S well S were E what E what 2 M
when E when 2 A while A who 2 M why E why S wife M will 2 S wise A with 4 A with 3 S
with 4 M withal M withering A without A woe A woe 2 M wonder M would M write A
write M yet 2 A yet 2 S yet 2

How language changed

Despite these difficulties and the recognition that content analysis on its own
provides a very crude picture, as the Bradstreet example illustrates, it may still prove
useful to have a general overview of when certain keywords, or groups of words, were
used and how the frequency of their use changed. Table 7.4 lists ten categories of
keywords. These lists have been developed partly by using table 7.2 and also, but to
a lesser extent, table 7.1 and taking a retrospective view, and partly from a reading of
the poems themselves. The ten word-groups have been chosen to reflect particular
aspects of the vocabulary employed, mostly in relation to grief and mourning.

Group 1 (death, grief) is straightforward in its composition and stems directly
from table 7.2. It focuses on both the experience of death and the expression of feelings
after the event or events. Group 2 (tomb) concentrates on words associated with the
funeral ceremony and burial practices, but since there are several occasions in which
'tomb' is paired with 'womb', the latter is also included. The third group (heaven)
covers religious references, especially to God, worship and faith. It may provide a
proxy indicator of the secularisation of English society. Group 4 (innocence) selects
words associated with the innocence of childhood as it is now conceived in Western
society (sweet, pure, gentle, meek, mild). Since infants and young children have not
always been viewed in this light, group 4 could give an interesting perspective on the
rise of the so-called 'new childhood'. Group 5 (relationship) focuses on the use of
relationship terms while group 6 (age) deals with the various ways of expressing age
or stage in the life course. Groups 7 (seeing) and 8 (hearing) can be paired because
they both deal with vital signs. Group 9 (flower) involves references to the signs of
nature, flowers and fruits included. Finally, group 10 (joy) reflects the opposites of
group 1, life rather than death, joy rather than grief.

Users of content analysis are inevitably faced with the difficult problem of how
to display results to their maximum advantage. Here we shall simply graph the
density of occurrences, that is, the number of times any member of a word-group is
used per 1000 words in each of the 69 poems. Each of the poems has been allocated
a composition date; although on occasions this dating procedure has made some
rather arbitrary assumptions. It has also been necessary to modernise and standardise
spellings so that the keywords in table 7.4 can all be searched for throughout the

Table 7.4 Ten word-groups

1 death grief
abort absent afflict agonies agony alas anguish bereft bitter care cries cried cropped cruel cry dead death decay decease despair die dismay distraction distress drown dying empty end expire fatal fate forlorn gloomy grief grieve grievous groan kill lament loss lost melancholy miserable misery moan mortal mourn murder pain pang part pity rage rue ruth sad shed sigh solemn sorrow sorry suffer tear terror vacant wail weep woe wrath wretched

2 tomb
ash bell burial buried bury ceremony clay coffin cold consecrate decay dust earth exequies funeral grave jet lie marble memorial monument repose rest sepulchre sheet shrine shroud slab sleep slept slumber stone tomb urn vault winding womb worm wreath

3 heaven
almighty angel bless Christ church divine faith ghost God heaven Lord pious praise pray priest redeemer saint saviour sin soul spirit worship

4 innocence
beauty blameless blest chaste cherub fair frail gentle good grace harmless innocence innocent jewel lamb maid pretty pure soft sweet tender true virgin virtue winning

5 relationship
bride bridal brother daughter family father friend husband mother parent sister son spouse widow wife

6 age
autumn babe baby birth boy child embryo girl infancy infant issue lad offspring old spring summer winter wintry young youth

7 seeing
black blind dark day eye gaze light night orb saw see shade sight white

8 hearing
deaf ear hear mute peace quiet silence silent still

9 flower
apple blast bloom blossom blown bower bud flower fruit grass iris leaf leaves lily nature plant primrose scent seed shoot smell strew tree violet weed

10 joy
affection bliss charming cheer comfort consolation content darling dear delight ecstasy flesh fond gay glad glee glory glorious happy heart hope joy life like live living love loving please pleasure rapture smile smiling thrive

full set of poems. (The 69 poems have 1130 lines and 8378 words in total.)[283] The distributions of word occurrences are illustrated in figure 7.1 against the backdrop provided by the pattern of early-age mortality variation outlined in Chapter 3 (figure 3.7, p. 48). Although obvious, it must always be borne in mind that the poems are not uniformly distributed in time nor are they of equal length. It is also important that the differences between those poems written during any single period should be made clear and not 'averaged out' in some way.

The group 1 words (death, grief) were at their most popular in the early seventeenth century, although even then there were some poems among the 69 in which they were used only sparingly or not at all. After this period, and even during the nineteenth century, there appears to have been a steady falling-off, but not a total disappearance. While the most extreme use of group 2 words, those relating to the funeral ceremony, to burial and memorial, also occurred in the early seventeenth century their occurrence was fairly regular and consistent thereafter. The historically interesting, although poetically dull, pairing of 'womb' with 'tomb' occurs in 1, 10, 15 and 24, while 'tomb' on its own is used in 7, 18, 33, 51, 52, and 'womb' in 39, 40 and 68. The last pairing dates from the 1640s.[284] The group 3 words reflecting Christian faith and religious conformity taper off in popularity after 1851, and pass out of favour completely in the twentieth century. Words associated with childhood innocence, captured by group 4, have a greater prominence before 1751 than after. This is rather surprising since it might have been anticipated that poets of the Romantic era would have emphasised such traits. Reference to kin and relationships (group 5) are at their least obvious during the nineteenth century. Those to age or position in the life course (group 6) are subdued apart from a couple of cases in the late eighteenth and a handful more in the early seventeenth century. The two senses of seeing and hearing are reflected in groups 7 and 8, with the former more prominent than the latter. In neither case are distinctive patterns discernible. References to flowers and other symbols of nature (group 9) are especially prominent in a small number of particular poems (18, 41, 58), but are not uniformly favoured. Group 10 (joy) has an irregular distribution with even less sign of downward trend over the centuries than its opposite, group 1.

The analysis of Anne Bradstreet's four poems indicated the presence of a deeply held form of what was termed 'positive resignation', that is, an acceptance that God only lends children, that they may be restored to Him at any time, and that in being returned they are going to heaven. References to 'lent', 'sent', 'restored' or 'returned' appear in the following poems: 4, 6, 8, 16, 17, 18, 22, 26, 31 and 32, while the notion of contentment or resignation is to be found in 16, 22, 23 and 31. Mention of 'mercy' ('merciful') or 'justice' (being 'just') occurs in 4, 7, 25, 26, 27, 31 and 32. These concepts do not find favour after the 1660s (32 is Bradstreet's elegy to her grandson). However, the counter view that children are 'stolen' or 'snatched', that parents have been 'robbed' in some way and that in general the deaths of children may be thought of as 'untimely' appears to have coincided with 'positive resignation'

Figure 7.1 Word-group occurrence patterns

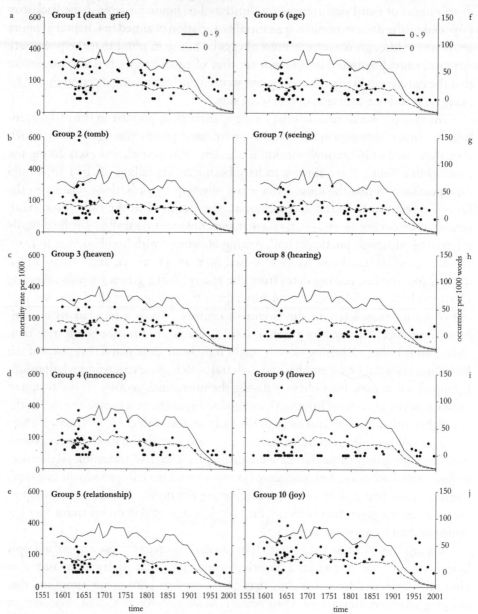

Note: see table 7.4 and text for explanation.

to some extent.[285] These words are used in **10, 25, 34** and **35**. The idea that child deaths are untimely may also be linked to that of a child being permanently lost to his or her parents, that there will be 'no return' to them and their secular world. This perspective is conveyed in the following poems: **34, 38, 39, 51, 53** and **58** (1680s to 1820s).

The distributions shown by figure 7.1 suggest a number of general points. First, few very clear and obvious patterns emerge. Certainly there is a falling-off in group 1 words from the early seventeenth century (figure 7.1a) and the distribution of group 3 words is particularly marked (figure 7.1c), indicating a secularisation of language, but there is also a high degree of variability within each period. For example, and with the possible exception of the group 10 words (figure 7.1j), the late eighteenth and early nineteenth century does not stand out as a period of special innovation in terms of the vocabulary used by poets in their work on children and child deaths. Secondly, on the basis of the evidence provided in figure 7.1 alone it cannot be argued that variations in mortality have had a marked bearing on choice of vocabulary. Rather, the continuity over several centuries is most apparent. 'Mourning work' was done by poets using grief words. Thirdly, this form of content analysis is very crude; it is only capable of revealing broad outlines.

Relationships

The 69 poems can also be used to consider the possibility that grief was expressed in different ways depending on the relationship between poet and subject. Is it important whether the poet was a mother or father writing about her or his own daughter or son? How did the same poet deal with different relationships? How did the circumstances of the death and the age of the deceased affect the choice of language? Were there certain periods, the Romantic era for example, in which new sensitivities came to the fore and are evident in the individual poems?

Table 7.5 classifies the poems in terms of relationship between author and subject. It provides a useful checklist for reference purposes. It will be used to select cases in which poets wrote about their own children; other people's children; about deaths in childbirth; late-fetal deaths; and where the subject was a spouse. This section will also compare those poems by Ben Jonson and Robert Herrick that have been included in the 69 because they enable us to consider the same poet's different responses. Finally, it will discuss nine of the selected poems drawn from the Romantic era. Do they represent a special case?

Own children
1, 10, 23, 26, 28, 30, 32, 34, 35, 37, 39, 43, 55, 58, 59, 60, 64, 68 (considered elsewhere: 2, 3, 4, 48, 49, 50, 51, 52, 53)

Lady Elizabeth Hoby's epitaph (1) for her two teenage daughters, Elizabeth and Anne, touches on several of the most important themes in memorial poetry. It is explicit about its expression of grief over the 'cruel' deaths; it links the mother's 'womb' and the children's 'tomb'; it mentions both parents; God is present; the lost futures of the 'most hopeful sisters' is stressed; and the poem is very particular concerning names and dates (February 1570). Henry King also mourns for the loss of two, albeit younger, children (10). He makes two additional allusions: first, to the

Table 7.5 **Authors and subjects of the selected poems**

Subject	Male poet	Female poet
Son	2 Shakespeare 1590s 4 Jonson 1600s 34 35 Flatman 1680s 49 Coleridge 1790s 52 53 Shelley 1810s 60 Dowden 1870s	26 Carey 1650s 28 Egerton 1650s 30 Philips 1650s 38 Boyd 1730s 39 Turell 1730s 55 Browne 1830s 68 Meehan 1980s 69 Bogin 1990s
Daughter	3 Jonson 1590s 48 Boothby 1790s 50 51 Wordsworth 1810s	1 Hoby 1570s
Own child: sex not stated	10 King 1620s 59 Anderson 1870s 67 Heaney 1960s	23 Thimelby 1640s 37 Wright 1730s 43 Cave 1770s 58 Horsfield 1850s
Relative: male		7 Dyer (husband) 1620s 32 Bradstreet (grandson) 1660s
Relative: female	6 Donne (wife) 1610s 8 Milton (niece) 1620s 9 Milton (wife) 1650s 62 Hardy (wife) 1910s	29 Cheyne (sister) 1660
Friend: male	5 Jonson 1600s *Many epitaphs*	
Friend: female	12 Herrick 1630s 56 Landor 1840s	
Other: child: male	22 Jordan 1640s 42 Gray 1750s 45 Burns 1790s 46 47 Blake 1780s	33 Behn 1670s 54 Opie 1830s
Other: child: female	41 Bowden 1750s 62 Thomas 1940s	
Other: child: sex not stated	10 18–21 Herrick 1630s, 1640s 44 Leigh 1780s 57 Clare 1840s 61 Bridges 1870s 64 Enright 1950s	
Other: adult: male	*Most epitaphs*	
Other: adult: female	15–17 Herrick 1630s & 1640s 24 Philipott 1649s 31 Stevenson 1660s 36 Pope 1720s	

Note: not all of the 69 poems have been classified.

idea that since the children died so young they preserved their innocence because they scarcely had opportunity to sin and were ignorant of sorrow and, secondly, that their funeral rite (exequy) was untimely. Gertrude Thimelby's elegy for her only child (**23**) conveys not only her intense grief, but also a sense of guilt ('mother's fault', 'my offence'). She acknowledges that her self-love has disturbed her reason, that her child has reached a state of bliss, but still 'I'de have thee here, or with thee goe'. She accepts that she must make a virtue of necessity and while she cannot herself feel content, her sweet child has at least found a place in heaven. There are several mixed emotions here, including not a little bitterness. After the death of her husband and child Mrs Thimelby retreated to a convent. Mary Carey's poem for her fourth son (**26**) displays a high degree of devotion and 'positive resignation'. God has sent her Perigrene Payler, but as a token of her love she has returned him and is 'completely happy still' in the belief that her Lord's will has been done although, as she says, 'I thought my all was given before'. Henry Egerton died aged 28 days in 1655. In his mother's elegy (**28**) Henry is 'the finest child from me', and although the Countess grieves, she closes with the conventional topos 'But thou art happy, Sweet'st on High, | I mourne not for thy Birth, nor Cry'. Katherine Philips endured seven years of childless marriage before the birth of her son, Hector, in 1655, but in less than six weeks he died. There is little sign of God's will in **30**; no lent–returned theme and no refusal to grieve. What we do find is a small picture of a mother's initial happiness ('A Son, A Son is born at last'), of her infant's beauty and great promise, of his confinement and escape to heaven in a morning cloud. Her collection *Poems* (1667, pp. 148–49) also contains 'Orinda upon little Hector Philips' which expresses similar sentiments in a very natural style.

ORINDA UPON LITTLE HECTOR PHILIPS

1.
Twice forty months of Wedlock I did stay,
Then had my vows crown'd with a lovely boy,
And yet in forty days he dropt away,
O swift Visissitude of humane joy.

2.
I did but see him and he disappear'd,
I did but pluck the Rose-bud and it fell,
A sorrow unforeseen and fearcely fear'd,
For ill can mortals their afflictions spell.

3.
And now (sweet Babe) that can my trembling heart
Suggest to right my doleful fate or thee,
Tears are my Muse and sorrow all my Art,
So piercing groans must be my Elogy.

4.
Thus whilst no eye is witness to my mone,
I grieve thy loss (Ah boy too dear to live)
And let the unconcerned World alone,
Who neither will, nor can refreshment give.

5.
An Offring too for thy sad Tomb I have,
Too just a tribute to thy early Herse,
Receive these gasping numbers to thy grave,
That last of thy unhappy Mothers Verse.

We have already discussed Anne Bradstreet's elegy to her grandson, Simon (32). It returns us to God's will and 'positive resignation'.

These seven own-children poems (2, 3, 4 could also be included) from the late sixteenth and seventeenth centuries display certain consistent themes and styles of expression, though they are by no means undifferentiated. What is most striking about them is their authors' belief that their dead children have gone to a better place, which is heaven. Even if there is no mention of the 'lent–returned' idea, it is still acknowledged that God is merciful even in his omnipotence. Certainly, strong emotions are conveyed to the reader. The mothers (most of the poets happen to be mothers although none are as dramatic as Constance in 2) express their grief with great force, and sometimes this is mixed with a feeling of guilt, of regret, of personal despair, of promise unfulfilled. Occasionally, doubts are aired ('untimely' 10, 'but why' 32), yet there is in general a convincing sincerity and this despite the likelihood that certain stylistic conventions are being employed. In the late seventeenth and eighteenth centuries these beliefs appear to have been modified and new topoi introduced.

Thomas Flatman's coridon (34) and epitaph (35) for his eldest son who died in 1682 aged 9 develop alternative ways of expressing parental grief. God, the Almighty, He and His, are dispensed with, although there are still 'powers above'; even the value of prayer is questioned. Instead, the virtues of the deceased are extolled (the lovely, charming, gentle boy); his destination becomes 'that distant shore' from which no return is possible; his departure is 'too untimely', the result of 'cruel destiny'. There are echoes in the epitaph: the beauty, goodness, innocence of Thomas; his being snatched away, beyond reason; and, finally, the old adage that what is most valued will be soonest lost is repeated. There is no resignation here, just bitterness. Hetty Wright's poem (37) uses very simple language and obvious rhyme to contrast the first appearance of the perfect infant with symptoms of its illness (the 'long-enduring swoon' and the 'convulsive start') and loss of vital signs (closing eyes). The transient nature of life for the newborn is like a flower: 'Blooming, withering in an hour'. The mother's plea to be the infant's partner in destiny is the poem's last refrain (echoed in 43). Jane Turell's elegy for her three stillborn offspring and her 10-day-old son (39) is highly emotional: 'Again in travail pains my nerves are wreck'd. | My eye-balls start, my heart strings almost crack'd; | Now I forget my pains, and now I press | Philander's image to my panting breast.' But the 'king of terrors' returns to take away even this 'sweet babe'. The mother's final wish is that 'I may deliverance have, and joy to see | A living child, to dedicate to thee.' Poem **39** was written in New England during the 1720s. In some respects it harks back to Anne Bradstreet's work of the 1660s since it displays due deference to God, but its tone is not one of unquestioning acceptance and this despite the all-pervading Puritan culture into which the author was born and married. Indeed, Jane Turell conveys not only her love for her husband and her redeemer, but also her desperate desire for the earthly joy that would be provided by surviving children. These three poems from the late seventeenth and early eighteenth centuries show a less accepting side to untimely death.

By the 1830s 'positive resignation' was even less in evidence. Mary Ann Browne's poem (**55**) is a cry of despair, a 'burning agony' of grief at the death of her infant son. The anger is directed at those who would console her: 'They say't is gone away to rest, where sorrow cannot be! | I heed not, I care not, lay ashes on my head; | Let me lie down in silence too, mine only child is dead!'

> Who art thou, with solemn brow, who wouldst whisper words of peace?
> They fall on me like dew on rocks, I pray, I pray thee, cease!
> Thou never wast a mother, or thou never couldst have said,
> There is comfort for a mother, whose only babe is dead!

Part of the mother's bitterness stems from her expectations for her child and herself in the times to come: 'Let me think of all the hope with which I looked to future years; | Let me number up the treasures that in him were stored for me'. Louisa A. Horsfield's poem to her baby (**58**) repeats the refrain 'But thou will not return to me!' It combines images from nature (flowers, song-birds, the spring that will return) and the child's departure to the 'celestial shore' with the often-repeated request of a parent to join an offspring in heaven. Again, there is little sign of acceptance here, just an expression of the loss that is final. Although Alexander Anderson's poem (**59**) from the 1870s concludes with a reference to God, it is mainly preoccupied with silence and absence. The sculptor's angel, the missed nightly kiss, the golden thread of memory alive still in the poet's heart and twined around his life, these are the conjured images. The modern reader may find this too sentimental, too contrived, mawkish even, but Anderson's poem reflects the culture of death said to be prominent in high Victorian art.[286] By comparison, Edward Dowden's elegy to his dead son (**60**) appears deliberately obscure. The literary scholar does not express himself in a way that is either direct or immediate. How does he really feel? Is he grief-stricken, at a loss for words, his 'embryo dreams' shattered?

Several of the 'own children' poems from the twentieth century have the stillborn as their subjects, but **64** and **68** give voice to the grief of a father in the late forties or early fifties and a mother in the 1980s. They contrast markedly with those from the

nineteenth century. A simple rearrangement of D. J. Enright's poem will help us to
see the ways in which he used traditional motifs in conjunction with new idioms.

> The greatest griefs shall find themselves inside the smallest cage.
> It's only then that we can hope to tame their rage.
> The monsters we must live with.
> For it will not do to hiss humanity because one human threw us out of heart and
> home.
> Or part at odds with life because one baby failed to live.
> Indeed, as little as its subject, is the wreath we give –
> The big words fail to fit.
> Like giant boxes round small bodies.
> Taking up improper room, where so much withering is, and so much bloom.

The floral metaphor is employed as is that of imprisonment and release. But the poem
is dominated by contrasts: greatest–smallest, humanity–one human, life–failed to
live, little–big, giant–small, cage–room, wither–bloom. There are monsters to live
with and rage that cannot be tamed. There is also, and perhaps for the first time
among the 69, a sense in which the poet is conscious of the inadequacy of language to
convey his emotions. The big words are like coffins, they fail to fit, they are improper.
Paula Meehan's 'Child burial' (68) has a beautifully sensuous lyricism. We have the
smell of wood smoke in autumn, of warm wool. But there is also darkness, ignorance
and regret; a wish to 'spin time back', to have not conceived perhaps. Again (and like
66), it is suggested that flesh and the word were made together in the author's fertile
womb. Grief is not made explicit here, that is left to another poem.[287]

The children of others, and children in general
8, 22, 25, 33, 41, 42, 44, 45, 54, 56, 57, 61, 63 (considered elsewhere: **5, 11, 18–21, 46,
47**)

John Milton probably wrote **8** in 1625–26 when he was 17. If this is the case then
the subject is his infant niece and the poem was intended to console his sister. But
the piece is more a showcase for young Milton's classical learning, his wit and obvious
precocious talent as a poet. Only in the eleventh and final stanza does it turn to the
mother's feelings and then in a way that appears indifferent in its stress on the 'lent–
returned to God' theme and its strictures concerning lamentation.

> Then thou the mother of so sweet a child
> Her false imagined loss cease to lament,
> And wisely learn to curb thy sorrows wild;
> Think what a present thou to God hast sent,
> And render him with patience what he lent;
>   This if thou do he will an offspring give,
> That till the world's last end shall make thy name to live.

If anything, Thomas Jordan's elegy for a beautiful boy who drowned on ice is made even more remote by its allusions to Greek mythology. Although the youth does have 'mourning friends', the reason for his ruin is his very beauty and attractiveness to 'wanton' Thetis, the water nymph. He has become, like Ganymede, a victim of his own physical perfection, abducted into the service of the gods. A fanciful conceit to gloss a tragic accident, 22 is hardly a poem of grief and consolation. There is a great distance between subject and author. Thomas Philipott's sad tale of a farmer who in an act of remembrance and 'glorious piety' plants an apple tree on the grave of each of his five children is able to reduce that author–subject distance by drawing us closer to the bereaved father. Poem 25 plays off three themes: first, a just God punishes man's offence by sending a deadly disease (bubonic plague); secondly, nature, in the form of tree and fruit (father and children), is resilient, although in time all must succumb; and thirdly, in this case stern death has been unkind, as well as untimely. Aphra Behn's epitaph (33) manages to contrast the immediate appearance of the gloomy monument with an imagined scene in which a host of smiling angels listen to the music of the 'softest pratler'. No grief is shown here; rather the child, six of whose siblings have already died, has managed to escape toil on earth for rest in heaven, and to do so before he 'Had learn'd the little arts of doing harms'.

These four poems from the seventeenth century (1620s to 1670s) appear disengaged when compared with the 'own children' poems. The author does not grieve, he or she is remote; the subject is not named; mythology, nature, angels offer convenient distractions; they are unemotional, restrained yet not totally indifferent.

The poems by Samuel Bowden (41) and Thomas Gray (42) date from the 1750s. Both adopt the flower metaphor, blooming yet soon to die. Bowden's casts death as 'ungentle' and 'tyrannic'; unwilling to spare 'the wise, the witty and the fair', the most fruitful and promising whom it transports 'to that gentle shore'. Gray, on the other hand, who was probably writing for the parents of a particular child, stresses the release from pain and misery that lets him 'sleep in peace'. Another poem by Bowden in his 1754 collection also dwells on this theme (see p. 226).

A PARENT'S LAMENTATION,
ON THE DEATH OF AN ONLY PROMISING CHILD

Where art thou fled my hope, my joy,
What shade conceals my lovely boy?
Just as the dawn of life began,
The circle of thy race was run.
So dawns *Aurora* fair, and gay,
'Till clouds o'ercast the opening day.
Just as thy cheeks begun to bloom,
Thy feet to totter round the room;
With infant sounds thy tongue to prattle,
Thy hands to play with toys, and rattle,

Stern death—inexorable death,
Seal'd up thy eyes, and stop'd thy breath.
Nor didst thou know, unthinking boy!
That life itself was but a toy,
A painted dream, a gilded bubble,
Checquer'd with sorrow, care, and trouble.

Peace to thy shade, O! lovely child,
In death's cold arms how sweet he smil'd,
Lodg'd in the silent tomb he lies,
Eternal slumbers seal his eyes.
No more to murmur, cry, or crave,
Rock'd in the cradle of the grave.
O! happy child—in early age,
To quit this transitory stage:
Just in thy opening bloom to die,
And shoot, and ripen in the sky.
So tender flowers nurs'd up with care,
In colder climes, and northern air,
Transplanted with new beauty rise,
And flourish in indulgent skys.

While neither Bowden nor Gray can be said to extol the benefits of an early death, they do both provide some consolation by ending with the peaceful and the happy.

Equivalent poems from the nineteenth century, of which there are four among the 69, display a sense of remoteness from the actual experience of grief and mourning, but they also develop different ways of consoling the bereaved or of memorialising the departed. However, Amelia Opie's offering to a widowed mother (54) lacks the sympathy necessary to be effective. It harks back to a bygone age in which faith in God's purpose was all important: 'Let faith exalt, though fondness mourn'. The fourth stanza may appear to us even rather callous, especially so in comparison with Mary Ann Browne's poem (55) which was also written in the 1830s.

But He, that God who 'heareth prayer,'
To her's a favouring answer gave;
And sav'd her child from every snare,
By – precious gift! – an early grave.

Walter Savage Landor evokes the memory of a childhood playmate, Fanny Verchild, in his poem 'On the dead' (56). She comes to mind as he regards the marble slab of a memorial tablet in a 'wide cold church'. Like Wordsworth's sonnet (51), although with far less intensity, Landor is able to contrast the warmth of a remembered, joyful childhood with the reality of an early death and its commemoration in an obscure Latin inscription. The poem closes with its salutary lesson: 'How, soon as in our course we start, | Death follows with uplifted dart.' It is tempting to dismiss

John Clare's poem (**57**) in which he likens the graves of infants to the steps of angels as excessively romantic. Since 'God is their parent, so they need no tear; | He takes them to his bosom from earth's woes', infants can be mourned by nature, by the white flowers, and 'prayers are needless'. The earthly parents of dead infants have no role here. Clare offers an extreme form of 'positive resignation', one in which grief is banished, mourning unnecessary. God and God's nature will provide.

Unlike these three poems dating from the 1830s and 1840s, Robert Bridges's piece (**61**) engages directly and sympathetically with bereaved parents, but its tone is also one of despair, of unknowing. Doctor Bridges appears to be laying out in his coffin a dead boy, a child of great promise, his mother's treasure and father's pride. The child clasps his finger and, for a moment, the author fancies that he is alive again, 'But the grasp is the clasp of Death, heartbreaking and stiff'. The last two stanzas of the poem reject faith. They leave us in the dark, with sorrow and no hope, with disturbing and unanswered questions. Experience fails us.

> So quiet! doth the change content thee? – Death, wither hath he taken thee?
>   To a world, do I think, that rights the disaster of this?
>   The vision of which I miss,
> Who weep for the body, and wish but to warm thee and awaken thee?
>
> Ah! little at best can call our hopes avail us
>   To lift this sorrow, or cheer us, when in the dark,
>   Unwilling, alone we embark,
> And the things we have seen and have known and have heard of, fail us.

How would Victorian parents have responded to these poems? Might they prefer Opie's unquestioning faith, the comfort of believing that death is for the best, or Clare's assertion that there is no need to mourn, to Bridges's agnosticism?

Finally, Dylan Thomas makes a passionate plea for us not to mourn, as he refuses to, the death of a young girl killed by fire in London during the Second World War (**63**). Thomas's intentions are unclear. Surely he is not to be taken literally? Rather, he reminds the reader (better still, the listener) of the destruction of war; how can the death of one be singled out among so many? He does this using a stream of words uninterrupted by punctuation that tumble over one another like the flow of water, the riding Thames. But his point is also a personal one; he refuses to write an elegy.

> I shall not murder
> The mankind of her going with a grave truth
> Nor blaspheme down the stations of the breath
> With any further
> Elegy of innocence and youth.

Death in childbirth
12, 17, 24, 29, 31

Five of the 69 poems are directly concerned with death in childbirth. They all date from the mid-seventeenth century, roughly the 1630s to the 1660s. Only that by Jane Cheyne (**29**), whose subject is her sister, gives any sense of direct involvement. The remainder were written by male poets, and in all but one case the mother goes unnamed. In **24** and **29** there is also a stillborn child.

Robert Herrick's floral tribute to a lady who died in child-bed and who, in giving her daughter life, resigned her own is finely tooled yet remote (**17**). Similarly, Matthew Stevenson's elegy for a woman who died at York (**31**) appears distant from its subject as a result of its heavy use of conventional topoi. Here too the mother's fruit, her son, survives, but she herself was left to heaven. Death is symbolised by the prince of terrors, the lily-bed, the winding sheet, and the colour white is used repeatedly for bridal attire and death-bed sheets. There is no grief or even regret here: 'How then is Fate unkind? Death comes but right, | 'Tis sickle-season when the Fields are white.' By contrast, Jane Cheyne demonstrates a deep and obvious emotional intensity over the death of her sister, and her stillborn child. This is achieved despite the religious conventions: God's judgment, the saint on earth, and the call to glory. There is no anger here, no recrimination, simply acceptance.

Is it merely a coincidence that these examples all date from the middle of the seventeenth century? We have seen that maternal mortality was nearly as high in the eighteenth and nineteenth centuries (table 3.3 and figure 3.8, pp. 50 and 52), but it does not seem to have attracted so much concern among poets. It is possible that the seventeenth century was a period of heightened anxiety about death in child-bed; paintings **F** and **G** encourage this view. However, it is also conceivable that in subsequent centuries such deaths came to be feared even more and were, in consequence, subjected to a form of artistic denial, a poetic silence.

Abortion and stillbirth
24, 27, 29, 38, 39, 40, 65, 66, 67, 69

Jane Cheyne's tribute to her sister also records the stillbirth of the Countess's infant (**29**).

> She lived to love, and her last thought was care;
> Her new borne Child she asked for, which n'ere cryed,
> Fearing to know its end she Bowed, and Dyed.

The author is at pains to stress how peaceful these departures were, that there was 'No Discomposure in her life or Death'. The other poems that have an abortive or late-fetal death as their subject are far less tranquil. Thomas Philipott's account of a woman dying in childbirth with an abortive daughter (**24**) develops the womb–tomb association.

> Work'd up it selfe, both Life and Death, we see,
> Were Inmates in one house, making the womb,
> At once become a Birth-place and a Tomb?

But we also have here an issue of meaning and usage. It is unclear whether the poem's subject is a stillborn or a live-born infant who died very shortly after birth. The title refers to an 'abortive daughter' while the poem itself speaks of a dead infant, one for whom the womb that gave her life also formed her grave. There is a similar ambiguity in **38**, 'On the death of an infant of five days old, being a beautiful but abortive birth'. The question of definition is spelt out clearly here in lines five and eight: 'Although an embryo, an abortive boy', 'And, whilst the birth can breathe, we say it lives'. Should we take this to mean that as late as the 1720s the terms 'abortive' and 'embryo' were in common usage even for those infants who showed clear vital signs at birth, but who died (stopped breathing) shortly after (within a week perhaps)? The other poems from the seventeenth and eighteenth centuries do not contradict this view.[288] Poem **27** refers to 'A little Embrio; voyd of life, and feature', and in **39** the mother relates how 'While from my womb a lifeless babe is torn! | Born to the grave 'ere it had seen the light'. In an anonymous poem dating from the 1740s (**40**) the procured abortion of a fetus conceived out of wedlock is reported. The ambiguity of the fetal state is made quite explicit here:

> Ambiguous something, by no standard fixed,
> Frail span, of naught and of existence mixed;
> Embryo, imperfect as my tort'ring thought.

What is clear, however, is the emotional attachment of mothers even to the unborn embryo or to the abortive infant, and the obvious grief caused by their deaths. Take, as an example, Elizabeth Boyd's poem (**38**) which combines joy at the arrival of a beautiful first-born son with distress over his early death, and an apparent rebuke to the less sensitive father.

> Oh! could the stern-souled sex but know the pain,
> Or the soft mother's agonies sustain,
> With tenderest love the obdurate heart would burn,
> And the shocked father tear for tear return.

The death of an 'angel-infant' so mortified the mother in Thomas Philipott's poem (**24**) and Lady Bridgewater (**29**) that they both resigned their lives to be with their infants. Jane Turell was also distraught at producing three stillborn infants, none of whom had given her even one smile to cheer her 'longing sight'.

This deep attachment is also conveyed in several late twentieth-century poems. Nina Bogin's poem 'The stillborn' (**69**) is disturbingly modern, abstract, philosophical; there is no obvious grief. The stillborn have no claim on the world nor do they have anything in common with death. They are quiet and distant, shells on the seashore; or footprints on a beach, ready to be unmade by the sea. In 'Elegy for a still-born child' (**67**) Seamus Heaney is more obviously emotional both for himself and the mother. She 'walks light as an empty creel', yet is 'heavy with the lightness in her'. But the most telling part of the elegy is its capacity to evoke memories.

> On lonely journeys I think of it all,
> Birth of death, exhumation for burial,
> A wreath of small clothes, a memorial pram,
> And parents reaching for a phantom limb.

While poems **69** and **67** have been written as from the heart, they convey experienced emotions; **65** and **66** are, for different reasons, from the head. Elizabeth Jennings imagines the funeral of a stillborn infant; the difficulty of not being able to contrast a shared past life with a present death. Her point relates to the special circumstances of a death before birth, of a life too short and too obscured to generate full memories.

> Not in our memories can we mould
> You or distort your character.
> Then all our consolation is
> That grief can be as pure as this.

Number **66** is disturbing. Not elegies for the stillborn, but poems that refuse to be born: 'They sit so nicely in the pickling fluid!', smiling, unfinished, lifeless, their would-be mother 'near dead with distraction'. Sylvia Plath was certainly not the first author to think of her poems as children – Ben Jonson had done the same for the son who died in 1603 (**4**) – yet she was the first to take the metaphor to its extreme: stillborn for incomplete. Could this have been attempted before the 1960s?[289]

Spouses
6, 7, 9, 12, 36, 62

Ann Donne, Sir William Dyer, Lady Jane Crewe, Katherine Milton, Elizabeth Corbett and Emma Hardy are the subjects of poems that relate to the deaths of spouses, although only four of the six were written by the surviving partner. Their presence in the **69** may help us to see how the reactions of adults to the deaths of children compared with those among marriage partners, although the comparison attempted will be neither systematic nor detailed. Two further poems (**40** and **44**) also reflect on the importance of marriage because they deal with the pregnancies of unmarried women.

Holy or Divine Sonnet 17 (**6**) is generally agreed to have as its subject Ann Donne, the poet's wife, who died in 1617. There is little indication of mourning here, and yet it seems certain that Donne did love his wife and regretted her loss: 'my good is dead, | And her Soule early into heaven ravished'. One critic likens this sonnet (and in this it is unlike most of the others) to an 'unaccompanied song, sparse, ardent and deeply expressive – a kind of shaped self-communing'.[290] It is sad, slow, and halting, but deeply felt. We shall return to Donne in the section on 'Death without grief'. Milton's Sonnet 19 (**9**) is almost equally self-obsessed, but in this case its author is

Table 7.6 **The birth history of John Milton from 1645 to 1658**

Name	Born	Married	Died	Comments
John Milton	9 December 1608	three times	*b* 12 November 1674	February 1652 became totally blind
Mary Powell (M)	1625?	June 1642	5 May 1652	Mary was aged 17 when she married.
				She returned home in July 1642 and Milton contemplated divorce. Between 1642 and 1645 his name was linked with that of a Miss Davis. There was a reconciliation with Mary in 1645.
Katherine Woodcock (K)		12 November 1656	3 February 1658	
Elizabeth Minshull		24 February 1663		
1 Anne (M)	29 July 1646			
2 Mary (M)	25 October 1648			
3 John (M)	16 March 1651		16 June 1652	
4 Deborah (M)	2 May 1652			
5 Katherine (K)	19 October 1657		17 March 1658	

Note: *c* baptised; *m* married; *b* buried

Source: William Riley Parker, *Milton: A Biography* (Oxford: Clarendon Press, 1968).

most concerned for his physical disability and the tricks it plays upon his mind. There are at least some brief words of tribute to Katherine, 'my late espoused saint', whom he may never have seen (table 7.6). 'Her face was veiled, yet to my fancied sight, | Love, sweetness, goodness in her person shined'. In spite of the mythological and ecclesiastical allusions, Milton does manage to convey some feeling for his wife, although the dominant mood is one of self-pity.[291] If Lady Katherine Dyer's epitaph (7) to her husband who died in 1621 is less polished, less learned than either of the sonnets, it is at least both heartfelt and immediate in its sincerity. Sir William is lovingly regarded and sorely missed by his widow, so much so that she imagines herself joining him in the bed that is his tomb.

> Mine eyes wax heavy and the day growes old
>   The dew falls thick, my bloud growes cold;
> Draw, draw the closed curtaynes: and make roome;
>   My deare, my dearest dust; I come, I come.

The death of Thomas Hardy's first wife, Emma Gifford, in November 1912 may have prompted him to write 'The voice' (62). Once again, the poem is more to do with memory and its tricks than mourning. Hardy imagines his first wife as he originally knew her and before they became estranged. He hears her voice calling; sees her standing, waiting for him, wearing a blue dress. He will not grieve for her.

On another level entirely we have the short and formal epitaph for Lady Jane Crewe, who died in 1639, by Herrick (12), and the epitaph to Mrs Corbett, who died in 1725, by Pope (36). Both are likely to have been commissioned pieces. Pope is polite and complimentary, but he also mocks using opposites – firm–soft, strong–refined – how can the woman be both? Finally, although her goodness and virtue, her saint-like qualities helped her to sustain the tortures of her illness, as a mortal woman, she died. There is no care of poet for subject here. Pope illustrates for us the triumph of wit and reason over the emotions; no grief, no mourning, no pretence.

It is difficult to over-emphasise the importance of marriage for reproduction in the past. Infants born to mothers who were not married were especially at risk of early death through poverty, deliberate neglect or murder. In poems 40 and 44 we have particularly illuminating examples of what a premarital conception might lead to and thus what stigma and physical dangers were to be avoided by following society's conventions. Helen Leigh's poem from rural Cheshire in the 1780s (44) conveys several distinct messages. The innocence of the 'natural child' is contrasted with the sorrowful mother who vents her tears in melancholy surroundings, but it is the father's reaction that attracts most attention.

> Unhappy babe! thy father is thy foe!
>   Oft shall he wish thee numbered with the dead,
> His crime entails on thee a load of woe,
>   And sorrow heaps on thy devoted head.

The infant is to be taken away from its mother and placed in the 'hireling hands' of a nurse. Leigh turns her story of a particular instance into a general admonition of the consequences of 'swerving from Virtue's mild restraint'.

> Too many like this infant we may see,
>   Exposed, Abandoned, helpless and forlorn;
> Till death, misfortune's friend, has set them free
>   From a rude world, which gave them naught but scorn.

The abandoned mothers who 'Led on by shame, and driven by despair. | Fell murderers become' are, nonetheless, accorded some sympathy compared with their lovers: 'But ah! what punishments await the men, | Who, in such depths of misery, plunge the fair?'

The innocent babe as victim of male pride and honour is also the theme of poem 40. Here the hapless, anonymous woman is obliged to submit to a procured abortion so raising the vexed question of whom in this case the 'murderer' may be.

Ben Jonson and Robert Herrick

It is unusual to have several poems by the same author concerned with the deaths of children, but in the case of Ben Jonson and Robert Herrick such sequences do exist. Jonson wrote about his daughter and his son, as well as a young actor well known to him. Herrick not only wrote for, perhaps at the request of, members of the Crewe family, but also about his Devon parishioners, most of whom went unnamed. Both used the epigrammatic form that gives their poems an engaging immediacy through their pithy brevity. Jonson's first child, Mary, probably died in 1595 aged 6 months; his son Benjamin died in 1603 aged 7; and Salomon Pavy died in the previous year aged 12.[292] The elegy to Mary (3) is at one and the same time gentle, loving, heartfelt; parents' regrets (ruth, rue) and mother's tears are shown, but it also displays signs of 'positive resignation' on the principle that God's children are only lent ('all heavens gifts, being heavens due'). Mary retains her innocence by dying early. The elegy to Benjamin (4) is, by contrast, strident and assertive of his father's powers. But the acceptance that the boy was only lent is again made explicit. In the memorial epigram to Salomon Pavy we find a mixture of sorrow and praise, tears and plaudits for the stage's jewel. However, the little story becomes distracted by its borrowing from the Roman poet Martial of a myth about one of the fates, the Parcæ, who mistakenly believe the youth to be aged because of his ability to take the parts of old men. Once recognised, the error cannot be corrected even with the aid of life-restoring baths, so 'Heauen vowes to keepe him'.

These three poems span a range of emotions. Jonson clearly felt keenly the death of his infant daughter, a grief that he shared with his wife, but Anne is not partner in his response to their son's death which turns to self-pity and not a little arrogance. The reader and his audience are left to mourn the boy actor, less so the poet himself. Jonson also wrote epigrams celebrating the lives of others who were known to him,

Shakespeare and Donne included. However, the epitaph for Elizabeth Chute, who died a young child, illustrates his ability to write on demand.[293]

AN EPITAPH [ON ELIZABETH CHUTE]

What beauty would have lovely styled,
What manners pretty, nature mild,
What wonder perfect, all were filed,
Upon record, in this blest child.
  And till the coming of the soul
  To fetch the flesh, we keep the roll.

Much has been written about Jonson's 'family' epigrams, especially 'On my first son', but it is unusual for them to be read comparatively as we shall do here. Critics have commented on the tension between writing as a father and accepting 'heaven's fate' as a Christian, and how 'father Ben' resolves that conflict; whether, following one of Freud's distinctions, Jonson can be classified as possessing an 'anal personality', one showing excessive orderliness and restraint; the poet's egocentrism in regarding his child as his best piece of poetry; and Jonson's reliance on models derived from classical literature, especially Martial.[294] However, when the four poems (3, 4, 5 and Elizabeth Chute's epitaph) are treated as a set alternative readings become possible, ones that stress both the humanity of Jonson's language and the importance of biographical circumstance. Wesley Trimpi has commented on Jonson's use of 'plain style'.

> A poem in the plain style offers the reader the intimacy of a specific situation and its context of feeling. The generalizations, either stated or implied, arise out of particular detailed experience and are persuasive because the reader is encouraged to participate in the experience rather than simply to acquiesce in a moral precept.[295]

Trimpi uses 3, 4 and 5 to illustrate how the reader could be made to participate in the writer's experience by stressing the simplicity of expression and brevity of the poems.[296] The use of 'plain style' guides the reader back to the poet's experience, then. But what was that experience? The epigrams may be arranged in a series to reflect the intensity of Jonson's emotions. Their first daughter, Mary, died an infant early in the Jonsons' married life. His first son, Benjamin, died during a severe outbreak of bubonic plague in 1603 when Jonson was both estranged from his wife, whom he referred to as 'a shrew but honest', and safely out of London. Salomon Pavy was an admired colleague and Elizabeth Chute the daughter of an acquaintance or client or both. The epitaph to daughter Mary is the most expressive of shared grief; that to Benjamin has as its focus the relationship between father and son, thwarted expectations, self-worth and guilt; Salomon Pavy receives a regretful notice; and Elizabeth, who goes unnamed in the printed epigram, is turned into the idealised child.[297]

Critics over the years have not been kind to Robert Herrick; they place him at the margins, a Royalist incidental, or they ignore him altogether. Here is one example.

Herrick's epitaphs upon children differ sharply from those of his master Jonson: while the child is very much an 'other' to Jonson, an innocent foil to the adult man of experience, the child embodies in prettified, sentimental form Herrick's own retreat into the littleness of death.[298]

Taken at face value Herrick's epigrams have two strong themes: reproduction and death. Poems **11** to **21** (**a** to **j**, pp. 121–22) deal with one or the other, and in several cases both. But there are many characters in *Hesperides*, and more than one Herrick is at work. Some of the epigrams relate to named historical individuals, Tomasin Parsons (**i**) and members of the Crewe family, for example; others may be real enough, although they are dealt with in a satirical fashion (Batt and Gubbs; Doll, Skoles, Gander, Dundridge, Jolly and Jilly) while the 'young mother', the 'fruitful mother', the 'sober matron' and the 'lady who died in child-bed' (also the 'fruitless lady', **j**) are representatives of particular types. *Hesperides* also contains four epitaphs to young children (**18** to **21**), although it is unlikely that any of these were ever used on funeral monuments. It has become a point of debate whether Herrick's epigrams can be read autobiographically and which particular persona he was intending to project in each poem.[299] Emphasis on these questions will make Herrick appear insincere, even flippant, in his epitaph writing. His witty, satirical, artful qualities are stressed and, compared to Jonson, his tone may be sentimental. Herrick was neither married nor a parent. His exile in 'dull *Devon-shire*' may have improved his poetic productivity, but it did little for his temper (*Hesperides* 51, Martin 19). The world of his poems is an idealised one in which the peasants are even more rustic and lascivious, and nature is raw, but beautiful. Herrick's epitaphs are not for real infants, they do not come from experience or association, but from imagination. If they are touching it is because of their floral references (primrose, violets, flowers, strewing, bud); their stress on the senses (seeing, hearing, silence, lullabies); and their explicit reference to the grief of parents.[300] These are all very earthly, 'natural' and human preoccupations; there is no place for God, heaven, the soul, or the concept of loan. Although Herrick's view is more distanced than Jonson's and his tone of voice more modulated, he does, nonetheless, convey the reader's feelings for his dead subjects once they are in the tomb.

The Romantics

45 to 53

Although it is widely acknowledged that the Romantic poets played a critical role in the artistic and cultural movement of the same name, it is also accepted that Romanticism defies any simple definition. It is usual to stress the importance of 'emotional self-expression', of imagination, inspiration, subjectivity, of the 'primacy of the individual', and to say that the movement also represented a reaction to classicism, to the emphasis on reason and order that symbolised the eighteenth-century Enlightenment. If dates are required, then 1780 and 1840 can be taken as the outer limits, although much significance is also given to the social and political ideals of the French Revolution of 1789. The poets always mentioned are Wordsworth, Coleridge,

Byron, Shelley and Keats, but Burns and Blake are also important in the early years while Opie, Landor and Clare are associated more with the Victorian era. It must also be remembered that not all of the work of these poets is Romantic, and that the wider movement included art and music. What is interesting about the Romantics from the perspective of this study is that we might expect their poems to display a heightened sensitivity to untimely death; to express feelings of grief, mourning, and consolation in ways that were both new and particularly intense. Referring back to Philippe Ariès's 'mourning curve' (figure 2.1, p. 12), we find that point C1 is located at the height of the Romantic Movement and that this is also the curve's early apex. The nine poems by Burns, Blake, Boothby, Wordsworth, Coleridge and Shelley should help us to observe the full power of Romanticism as its exponents address childhood, children and child loss.[301]

There are, however, certain difficulties with these expectations. Only two of the nine poems appear in two of the three most recently published anthologies of Romantic verse and these are both by William Blake, a poet and artist of such originality that he is impossible to classify or associate with any particular movement. Wordsworth's sonnet 'Surprized by joy' (51) is included in one anthology, and one anthology has none of the nine. Clearly, the anthologists regard the other poems by Wordsworth, Coleridge and Shelley in our selection as unworthy to be included with the great Romantic poets' major works. Boothby does not appear in any of the anthologies and Burns, although he is included, remains a rather eccentric figure.[302] The Romantic poets were concerned with childhood and children, but grief and mourning did not preoccupy them, especially in their most significant works. Rather, Romanticism represented a reaction against that emphasis on sensibility in artistic works which had prevailed in the years 1740–70, and which was characterised by heightened sensitivity and the excessive arousal of pathos.[303] Among the nine are poems by Boothby, Coleridge and Shelley which have as their subject the death of an own child, while those by Wordsworth evoke memories of a child, or the poet's children, and those by Blake and Burns stress the dangers faced by children as they lose their innocence.

Poems 45 and 46 are addressed, respectively, to a real but unnamed infant whose father died before he was born, and an imagined but named child whose mother has died and whose father has sold him into work. In neither case do the prospects look promising. Burns prays that infant and mother will be protected from life's storm, yet he writes more in hope than expectation. Blake's two chimney-sweeper poems dwell on sharp contrasts: innocence and experience, fact and symbol, vision and disenchantment, soot and snow.[304] They are powerful pieces of contemporary social comment that satirise the establishment and its institutions, including the family. Little Tom Dacre the chimney sweep has a vision of thousands of other child sweeps being set free from their 'coffins of black' by an angel who shows them a pastoral idyll where they can run, laugh, and be clean in the sunshine. But the angel also tells Tom that 'if he'd be a good boy, | He'd have God for his father & never want joy'.

Table 7.7 **The birth history of Mary Wordsworth from 1802 to 1810**

Name	Born	Married	Died	Comments
William Wordsworth	7 April 1770	once	23 April 1850	Caroline born 15 December 1792 to Annette Vallon
Mary Hutchinson	16 August 1770	4 October 1802	1859	
1 John	18 June 1803	October 1830	1875	
2 Dora	16 August 1804	1841	9 July 1847	
3 Thomas	15 June 1806		1 December 1812	
4 Catharine	6 September 1808		4 June 1812	
5 William	12 May 1810	January 1847	1883	

Note: c baptised; *b* buried
Source: Stephen Gill, *William Wordsworth: A Life* (Oxford: Clarendon Press, 1989).

'The chimney-sweeper' in *Songs of Experience* feigns happiness and for his pains he is clothed in mourning black and taught to 'sing the notes of woe'.

> And becausee I am happy, & dance & sing,
> They think they have done me no injury:
> And are gone to praise God & his Priest & King,
> Who make up a heaven of our misery.

Sir Brooke Boothby's book of 24 sonnets to the memory of his daughter and only child, Penelope, who died aged 5 in 1791 cannot be counted among the pantheon of English poetry. The sonnets are mournful, highly sentimental, mawkish even. Certainly, Penelope's father was greatly affected by her death, but his way of expressing that feeling through her funeral monument (**N**) and especially this lavishly printed memorial volume may seem excessive. The language of the poems is over-blown with emotion, highly repetitive, and excessively contrived, and yet the pathos is touching and the grief obviously sincere. Here is another sonnet from the collection to illustrate the point.

Sonnet V

> Death! thy cold hand the brightest flower has chill'd,
> That e'er suffused Love's cheek with rosy dies;
> Quench'd the soft radiance of the loveliest eyes,
> And accents, tuned to sweetest musick, still'd;
>   The springing buds of hope and pleasure kill'd;
> Joy's cheerful measures changed to doleful sighs:
> Of fairest form, and fairest mind, the ties
> For ever rent in twain. — So Heaven has will'd!
>   Though in the bloom of health thy arrow fled,
> Sudden as sure; long had prophetick dread
> Hung o'er my heart, and all my thoughts depress'd.
>   Oft, when in flowery wreaths I saw her dress'd,
> A beauteous victim seem'd to meet my eyes,
> To early fate a destined sacrifice.

Boothby's Sonnets I and V bear interesting comparison with poems **50** and **51**. The Wordsworths lost two of their children in 1812. Catharine died in June aged 3 and Thomas in December aged 6 (table 7.7). 'Characteristics of a child three years old' offers a sketch of the wilful child. She is loving, tractable, wild, innocent, cunning, provoking, and playful; has laughing eyes and gives arch looks. Her presence is like an ember sparkling on a hearth, full of movement and song. And yet the poet father forgets his daughter, the 'heavenly face', his 'heart's best treasure' (**51**). When he does recall her, his remembering is made even more grievous by feelings of guilt:

Table 7.8 **The birth history of Percy Bysshe Shelley from 1812 to 1822**

Name	Born	Married	Died	Comments
Percy Bysshe Shelley	4 August 1792	twice	8 July 1822	drowned at sea
Harriet Westbrook (H)	1795	28 August 1811	November 1816	eloped aged 16; suicide by drowning while pregnant
Mary Godwin (M)	30 August 1797	30 December 1816	1 February 1851	mother, Mary Wollstonecraft, died from puerperal fever 10 September 1797; eloped with Shelley 28 July 1814
1 Ianthe Elizabeth (H)	23 June 1813	27 September 1837	18 June 1876	
2 Charles Bysshe (H)	30 November 1814		14 September 1826	died from tuberculosis aged 12
3 unnamed girl (M)	22 February 1815		6 March 1815	born 2 months prematurely
4 William (M)	24 January 1816		7 June 1819	died at Rome possibly from malaria
5 Clara Everina (M)	2 September 1817		24 September 1818	died at Venice from dysentery
6 Elena Adelaide	27 December 1818		9 June 1820	mother probably Elise Foggi
7 Percy Florence (M)	12 November 1819	22 June 1848	December 1889	inherited baronetcy 24 April 1844
miscarriage (M)	6 June 1822			

Note: c baptised; *m* married; *b* buried

Sources: R. Glynn Grylls, *Mary Shelley: A Biography* (London: Oxford University Press, 1938); Richard Holmes, *Shelley: The Pursuit* (London: Weidenfeld and Nicolson, 1974).

But how could I forget thee? – Through what power,
Even for the least division of an hour,
Have I been so beguiled as to be blind
To my most grievous loss? – That thought's return
Was the worst pang that sorrow ever bore.

If the subject of poems **50** and **51** is indeed Catharine Wordsworth, as seems most likely, how different is her father's response compared with the father of Penelope? Penelope is the sad rosebud, Catharine the crackling ember; Boothby the romantic sentimentalist, Wordsworth the creator of a natural realism.

The short poems by Coleridge and Shelley relate, respectively, to the deaths of their infant son Berkeley in 1799 (**49**) and 3-year-old son William in 1819 (**52** and **53**) (Table 7.8). Coleridge offers some consolation to his wife. Their baby 'went without demur', he is a 'Child of God', 'in the kingdom of the blest'. But Shelley appears tortured by the death of his son. He dwells on the remoteness and decay of death, the worms, the ashes and the funeral shrine; and these he compares with the bright spirit, the twinkling of infant hands, the 'look of love and glee' of their 'lost William'. Table 7.8 does little justice to the turbulence of Shelley's life, but it does catalogue the births, deaths, affairs, and the restless wanderings. Shelley was tormented by his passions, by poverty and illness, and by the deaths of those to whom he was close, children included. Grief and guilt combined.

Death without grief

Parents, adults, society in general hardly ever expressed marked indifference to the survival of children openly. Silence, sometimes palpable, was maintained. However, there are in literature just a few exceptions to this rule.

On a journey to visit Anna Karenina, Princess Darya Oblonskya (known as Dolly) brought to mind the following incident when thinking about her own last pregnancy and the death of her infant.

> And she recalled a talk she had had with a young woman at the halting-place. In answer to the question whether she had any children, the good-looking young peasant wife had cheerfully replied:
> 'I had one girl, but God released me. I buried her in Lent.'
> 'And are you very sorry?' asked Dolly.
> 'What's there to be sorry about? The old man has plenty of grandchildren as it is. They're nothing but worry. You can't work or anything. They're nothing but a tie …'
> This answer had seemed horrible to Dolly, despite the good-natured sweetness of the young woman's looks, but now she could not help recalling it. In those cynical words there was some truth.[305]

The other counter-examples are far less serious. This poem by Emmeline Grangerford, aged 14, is reported by Mark Twain in *The Adventures of Huckleberry Finn* (1885).

Ode to Stephen Dowling Bots, Dec'd

And did young Stephen sicken,
    And did young Stephen die?
And did the sad hearts thicken,
    And did the mourners cry?

No; such was the fate of
    Young Stephen Dowling Bots;
Though sad hearts round him thickened,
    'Twas not from sickness' shots.

No whooping-cough did rack his frame,
    Nor measles drear, with spots;
Not these impaired the sacred name
    Of Stephen Dowling Bots.

Despised love struck not with woe
    That head or curly knots,
Nor stomach troubles laid him low,
    Young Stephen Dowling Bots.

O no. Then list with tearful eye,
    Whilst I his fate do tell.
His soul did from this cold world fly,
    By falling down a well.

They got him out and emptied him;
    Alas it was too late;
His spirit was gone for to sport aloft
    In the realm of the good and great.[306]

Apparently, Emmeline 'could rattle off poetry like nothing. She didn't ever have to stop to think… She warn't particular, she could write about anything you chose to give her to write about, just so it was sadful. Every time a man died, or a woman died, or a child died, she would be on hand with her "tribute" before he was cold.'[307] Here Twain (Samuel Langhorne Clemens, 1835–1910) is apparently parodying Julia A. Moore (1847–1920) whose poems 'Little Libbie' and 'Little Andrew', also the victim of drowning, displayed excessive sentimentality but were nonetheless rather popular in America during the 1870s and 1880s.[308] Twain made light of untimely death in order to poke fun at over-sentimental authors, or to amuse children themselves by using the extremely unlikely events of tragicomedy. Could this poem have been published before the late nineteenth century?

During the early years of the twentieth century Freud's work on the subconscious began to consider the psychology of the emotions and in particular the 'normal emotion of grief, and its expression in mourning'.[309] What would be the consequences for mental health if 'grief work' or 'mourning work' were not undertaken effectively? Freud's answer was melancholia, by which he meant 'a profoundly painful dejection, abrogation of interest in the outside world, loss of the capacity to love, inhibition of all activity' and a lowering of self-esteem in general. Freud suspected that people with 'a morbid pathological disposition' were likely to be prone to melancholia.[310] The theme of 'death without grief' has been taken up in subsequent work both by those interested in the psychoanalytical implications and by those concerned to improve the quality of bereavement counselling, and thus the effectiveness of 'mourning work'.[311] In the remainder of this chapter we shall consider two further examples of 'absence of expression' in the past: how the vocabulary of 'death' was not mirrored by that of 'grief' in Shakespeare's plays, and how in the case of John Donne we have a poet who, although he experienced the deaths of several of his children and seems to have become obsessed with his own impending mortality, did not make the loss of his offspring the subject of his work.

John Donne, Ann Donne, undone

John Donne was a scholar, a soldier and adventurer; an aspirant to genteel status who sought favour at court; a preacher and clergyman, Dean of St Paul's; a poet of great wit whose works circulated among friends during his lifetime and were only published after his death. More important for the circumstances of his everyday life, he made a disastrous marriage in 1601 and in 1615, despite his upbringing as a Roman Catholic, he was ordained a priest in the Church of England – he became an apostate. During the years of his marriage (1601–17) Donne was racked by physical, psychological and financial torments. He appears to have experienced bouts of depression, even contemplating suicide; he certainly suffered periods of physical ill-health; and he was afflicted by guilt, doubt, disappointment and poverty.[312] But one critic has also observed that 'Donne is a maker of fictions and a trier-on of masks, and this perhaps applies as much to his life as his art'.[313]

We shall focus here on Donne's married life and his experience as a father, and reflect on why his parental role does not appear to have impinged upon his poetry as, for example, Ben Jonson's did. The demography of John Donne and Ann More's lives is summarised in table 7.9. When they married secretly in December 1601, Ann was probably 16. When the marriage was made public in February 1602 Donne was dismissed from the employment of Ann's guardian and briefly imprisoned. Ann was disinherited and Donne forfeited any prospect of early advancement at the Elizabethan court or of substantial patronage; he was 'undone'.[314] During the 188 months in which they were married, Ann was pregnant for perhaps 108 months. She was 'brought to bed' twelve times with ten live and two stillbirths. Of the ten, six survived their father and one her mother. An infant died in 1613 or 1614, and two young children died in 1614. It was not an unusual record.[315]

It is the case that one of Donne's epigrams, 'Niobe', does relate to the deaths of children.

Table 7.9 The birth history of Ann Donne from 1602 to 1617

Name	Born	Married	Died	Comments
John Donne	early 1572	once	31 March 1631	ordained January 1615; installed as Dean of St Paul's November 1621
Ann More	1585?	(5 December?) 1601	15 August 1617	m secretly aged 16?; marriage revealed 2 February 1602
1 Constance	early 1603	3 December 1623 24 June 1630		m Edward Alleyn, widower, 58
2 John	early 1604		January 1663	
3 George	c 9 May 1605	yes	early 1639	daughter c 22 March 1638
4 Francis	c 8 January 1607		b 10 November 1614	
5 Lucy	c 8 August 1608		b 9 January 1627	
6 Bridget	c 12 December 1609	1633?		m Thomas Gardiner, daughter born 7 March 1634
7 Mary stillborn	c 31 January 1611		b 18 May 1614 b 24 January 1612 in infancy?	
8 Nicholas	c 3 August 1613		3 October 1679	
9 Margaret	c 20 April 1615	1633		m Sir William Bowles
10 Elizabeth stillborn	c 14 June 1616 10 August 1617	18 May 1637	b 16 August 1617	m Dr Cornelius Laurence buried with Ann

Note: c baptised; *m* married; *b* buried

Source: R. C. Bald, *John Donne: A Life* (Oxford: Clarendon Press, 1970), pp. 547–56, 'Appendix B. Donne's Children'.

By childrens births, and death, I am become
So dry, that I am now mine owne sad tombe.[316]

Although the title leads one to suppose that Niobe herself is speaking, it could just as well be Ann or the poet. Donne did write more formal and far more substantial consolatory poems. When Elizabeth Drury died in December 1610 aged 14 he wrote 'A funeral elegy' for her now childless parents. Donne had never met the young lady although his sister, Anne, knew her. This was a speculative venture that paid off. Sir Robert Drury took Donne into his employ for a journey to the Continent (1611–12) and found the Donne household accommodation in Drury House, London.[317] To help cement the patronage arrangement Donne wrote two further poems on the death of Elizabeth: 'An anatomy of the world: The first anniversary' (1611) and 'On the progress of the soul: The second anniversary' (late 1611 or early 1612). The three poems were published together in 1612.[318] Donne did write other poems whose subjects were, at least notionally, the recently deceased. Bridget, Lady Markham (died May 1609 aged 30), and Cecelia Bulstrode (died August 1609 aged 25), both friends of the Countess of Bedford, were made the subjects of elegies in order to encourage the Countess's patronage. It has also been speculated that 'A valediction: forbidding mourning' was written for Ann and prompted by the poet's travelling abroad in 1611; and that 'A nocturnal upon St Lucy's Day, being the shortest day' relates to Ann's illness in 1611, or her death in 1617.[319] And then, of course, we have Holy Sonnet 17 (6).

None of these poems offers a direct expression of Donne's grief or an indication of his state of mourning for the dead. Rather, they provide him with the opportunity to write 'clever, paradoxical poetry', to indulge in self-dramatisation and to develop his egocentricity.[320] In his letters Donne did mention his wife and children, and their domestic arrangements, and in his sermons, especially that delivered in 1627 after the death of his daughter Lucy, he did raise the matter of grief and how it might improve his status in heaven as a martyr.[321] There is no grief in Holy Sonnet 17; rather, Ann's achievement of heaven has freed Donne from lust.[322] It is acknowledged that Donne became obsessed with death and that this is reflected in his preparations during his final illness in 1631; his last sermons; and some of his Holy Sonnets, particularly number 6: 'Death be not proud, though some have called thee | Mighty and dreadful, for, thou art not so'. But the first stanza of 'The dampe' also shows how in an instant Donne can turn us from the macabre to thoughts of love, and back to death. He plays with us.

When I am dead, and Doctors know not why,
    And my friends curiositie
Will have me cut up to survey each part,
When they shall finde your Picture in my heart,
    You thinke a sodaine dampe of love
    Will through all their senses move,
And worke on them as mee, and so preferre
Your murder, to the name of Massacre.[323]

Comparison of 'A funeral elegy' for Elizabeth Drury with the first and second 'Anniversaries' helps to illustrate how Donne moves away from his ostensible subject to considerations of the state of the world after her death and the progress of the soul to heaven. In 'A funeral elegy' the subject is clearly a young ('not yet fifteen'), unmarried female ('Clothed in her virgin white integrity'), whose pages in the 'book of destiny' relate 'How fair and chaste, humble and high she had been'. But the elegy also asks 'must we say she's dead?' and proceeds to liken her to a 'sundered clock' whose maker has taken it apart in order to reassemble 'without error'.[324]

It is not that Donne is unfeeling – his letters and sermons suggest otherwise although they are hardly stricken by emotion – rather his mind was set on higher matters, latterly 'Wholly in heavenly things'. He was preoccupied with death, but death was not an end, and not to be feared, but simply a route to heaven. Donne was also driven by ambition, dogged by disappointment and the guilt of failure especially during his married life. He was disparaging of his own poetic abilities and would not publish his work. The small amount that was printed in his lifetime was done so out of necessity, to please the Drurys. Bouts of suicidal depression and physical ill-health made him wretched for himself, Ann and their children. Donne did not express his feelings for named individuals, as Jonson did, yet his capacity to soar above the earthly and mundane set him apart. These flights of fancy make Donne appear uncaring, indifferent to his wife and children.[325]

'Death' and 'grief' in Shakespeare's plays

The group 1 words shown in table 7.4 include both 'death' and 'grief', but as we have already noted some of the uses of the latter (especially the association with physical pain) have shifted during the centuries. All of Shakespeare's plays involve some reference to 'death', yet they are not matched by mention of 'grief'. Figure 7.2 illustrates the varying occurrence of the two words.[326] Several of the comedies have very little 'death' and even less 'grief', but among the tragedies and history plays there are some interesting variations. A group of three plays that have been dated in the mid-1590s stand out because of their use of both 'death' and 'grief'. Romeo and Juliet, King John and Richard II have the highest density of references to 'grief' and are among the highest for references to 'death'. King John, as we have already noted, contains the scene in which Constance mourns for her son Arthur, whom she believes to be dead (2). Richard II bears comparison with Richard III, one of the very early history plays. In the latter there is much 'death', but precious little 'grief', while in Richard II 'grief' and the introspective scrutiny of one's own feelings that accompanies it abounds. Richard not only grieves for himself and the folly of his own demise, but there are also many references to images associated with death and dying, among them the 'hollow womb' and 'still-breeding thoughts'.[327] Although Romeo and Juliet is often portrayed as a love story, the dominant theme is death. Deaths occur as the result of a brawl, a duel and a fight; death is feigned; there are two suicides; a vital message is stopped by an outbreak of plague; a mother dies from grief; even Juliet's nurse has

Figure 7.2 Occurrence of the words 'death' and 'grief' in Shakespeare's plays

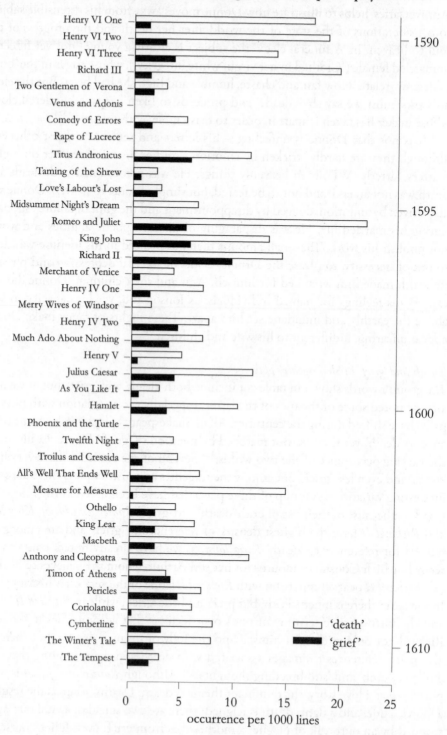

had a daughter who died young. All of these deaths are grieved over and mourned by the relatives who remain.[328] Here are some examples of the ways in which Shakespeare plays on the word 'grief'.

> Juliet's nurse
>> These griefs, these woes, these sorrows make me old. (3.2.89)
> Juliet
>> if sour woe delights in fellowship,
>> And needly will be ranked with other griefs, (3.2.116)
> Juliet's mother
>> Some grief shows much of love,
>> But much of grief shows still some want of wit. (3.5.72)
> Peter, a servant
>> When griping griefs the heart doth wound (4.4.48)
> Paris, Juliet's suitor, referring to Romeo and the cause of Juliet's death
>> This is that banished haughty Montague
>> That murdered my love's cousin, with which grief
>> It is supposed the fair creature died (5.3.49)
> Romeo's father
>> Alas, my liege, my wife is dead tonight;
>> Grief of my son's exile hath stopped her breath. (5.3.210)

And in the play's final scene, Friar Laurence's account of the proceedings even has Juliet besieged by grief (5.3.237).

Among Shakespeare's latter plays, *Measure for Measure* and *Antony and Cleopatra* stand out in figure 7.2 as dramas with much 'death', but very little 'grief'. In the case of the former, the explanation is that the play is concerned with moral judgements of sexual behaviour or intentions. Death is threatened, several are condemned, but no one actually dies. There is no need of grief. *Antony and Cleopatra*, on the other hand, does contain conspicuous deaths, yet there are none to grieve and mourn. Of Shakespeare's last plays, only *The Winter's Tale* deals with death to any extent and then in the case of Hermione it is a 'false death'. The real victim of the play is Mamillius, her young son, whose reported actual death causes Hermione to collapse. When her death is announced, the king-husband-father expresses pity for them both, but Mamillius does not attract deep mourning in his own right.[329]

Once again, we can be awed by the subtlety of Shakespeare's language and tantalised by the ambiguity of his autobiographical allusions. The deaths of Arthur and Mamillius stirred different emotions; King Richard's self-pity was grievous; and the waste of young lives in *Romeo and Juliet* is deeply felt. The expression of grief was fitful and profoundly complex.

*   *   *

This chapter has described how it is possible to chart the ways in which poets expressed their feelings over the deaths of children. It has done this using a simple form of content analysis that looks at the occurrence of words in selected groups. In general, this approach has emphasized continuity, a good deal of variability of vocabulary choice in any particular period, and certain specific instances of change ('lent–returned', 'untimely', and the word group labelled 'heaven', for example). As far as relationships are concerned, it has illustrated the differences between responses to 'own children' deaths and those in which other people's offspring were involved. Finally, the chapter has considered Donne's apparent failure to mourn and Shakespeare's use of 'death' and 'grief' words in his plays, and how their lack of coincidence focuses attention on the mid-1590s.

8

Parallel Histories: Experience and Expression

It has been said on several occasions that this study has been an experiment. Has it been successful? There are several reasons for optimism. First, it has proved possible to chart the risks of life and death in France and England as they affected infants, children and mothers, and to do this in such a way that differences between the two societies become obvious. This has not been a relatively simple task. It rests upon the cumulative findings of generations of historical demographers, not to mention a number of assumptions about the quality of statistical data and the justification for joining together estimates from different sources. What we have as a result is the pattern of level and trend that, although complete representation cannot be claimed, is at least based on large samples. It is as close as we are likely to come to describing the generality of mortality experience in the past. During the early modern period, the age of contention for family historians, it is possible that in France 50 per cent of infants did not survive to their tenth birthday while in England it is likely that the equivalent figure was 30 to 35 per cent. Half or a third would meet an untimely death.[330] If we compare these proportions with the experience of those ten individuals for whom we have shown birth histories, then 40 per cent would be closer to the mark. These were certainly high levels of mortality, a point which table 8.1 brings home even more effectively than say figure 3.7 (p. 48), but they were neither uniform nor constant.

Secondly, since very few paintings of dead children were completed, and even fewer have survived, we are obliged to use visual evidence on the presence of children rather than their absence. Although children were placed in English church funeral monuments, it is very unusual for them to be given individual status before the nineteenth century. **N** is the outstanding first example. The small gallery of portraits displayed in Chapter 4 or included in table 4.1 (p. 68) can be used to tell a story about parental attitudes, but it is not a simple story in which there are pivotal works or key turning points. The principal reason seems to be that artists have used children as their subjects to earn money from patrons; to make a moral or political point; to show their own talents; and to provide symbols, signs of innocence, what they have themselves already lost. Inferring artists' intentions is troublesome enough; detecting the purpose of the patron-parent is even more hazardous. And yet this has been attempted, especially by those who wish to see something new emerge in the eighteenth century. Are the parents of **M** more caring than those of **A**? Is the group

Table 8.1 Summary of early-age deaths among the ten birth histories

Subject	Birth date	Birth date of first child	Number of children dying under 10 years of age	Total number of live births	Table
Shakespeare	1556	1583	1	3	5.3
Sidney	1562	1587	5	11	4.2
Legh	1570	1588	4	9	4.3
Donne	1585	1603	3 (2)	10	7.9
Wallington	?	1622	4 (2)	5	5.1
Josselin	1621	1642	3 (5)	10	5.2
Milton	1625	1646	2	5	7.6
Wordsworth	1770	1803	2	5	7.7
Shelley	1795	1813	3 (1)	6	7.8
Brontë	1777	1814	0	6	2.2

Note: the table has been arranged in order of the birth date of the subject's first child. In the cases of Milton and Shelley, the birth date refers to that of their first wife while the deaths and births are from two wives. The numbers in brackets are the miscarriages plus stillbirths mentioned in the birth histories. Two Brontës and a Shelley died aged 10–12.

Source: see final column for table numbers.

in **J** less concerned with status and wealth, with ensuring family survival, than that in **D**? It is not that there weren't some changes, as well as much continuity; rather the visual evidence is profoundly ambiguous. While it helps to see the children, and their parents, they still cannot speak to us.

Thirdly, although the convention among historians is to use letters and diaries as means of giving voice, and to be sceptical of literary evidence, this study has, while not rejecting the accounts constructed from diaries, favoured the use of poetry as a medium to reflect the emotions.[331] The 69 poems selected, mostly elegies written in English between the 1570s and the 1980s, have been used to show the ways in which vocabularies of grief were formed, how emotional language changed during the centuries, and to highlight the role of relationships. This analysis has tended to emphasise the importance of continuities. Children were mourned, grief was felt in all five centuries, but the way those feelings were expressed did change. A form of 'positive resignation' was common in the sixteenth and seventeenth century up to the 1660s. Here God is often thanked for calling a child into heaven, and it is clearly understood that children are only lent by and must be returned to the Lord. They are not unqualified gifts. The counter view that the deaths of children may be thought of as 'untimely' appears to have overlapped with 'positive resignation' to some extent, but the notion of children being prematurely lost or stolen from their parents, never to return to their secular world, was current between the 1680s and the 1820s. There are no obvious turning points in the eighteenth century. The 1740s do not stand out and the Romantic era (1780–1840) holds no special significance in terms of the way grief was expressed or, presumably, the intensity with which it was felt. It may well be, as is often claimed, that a new sensitivity to children and the concept of childhood emerged round about 1800, but this is not manifest in the poets' responses to child death. Possibly during the late nineteenth and certainly in the twentieth century there are sufficient examples to encourage the argument that substantial changes have occurred, and even these are not straightforward. The vocabulary of grief became secular; little room for God, heaven, or 'going to a better place', and, in terms of subjects, the stillborn were far more prominent. Even when anger and bitterness were not projected, there was a refusal to accept fate, to be resigned to loss.

These are the three, parallel histories: demographic rates, artistic images and poetic language. How can they be fused? There are several instances in which at least two of the histories can be joined. Penelope Boothby is the subject of **M**, **N** and **48** (also Sonnet V, p. 198); Lady Jane Crewe (**11**, **12**) and Lady Magdalene Aston (**F**) are sisters; Ben Jonson writes about Penshurst and Lady Barbara Sidney (p. 73) who is the subject of **D** and for whom there is a birth history; and we have birth histories for five poets, as well as Lady Margaret Legh (**Ri** and **Rii**). However, this is insufficient to meet the requirements for 'corroborative comparison' or to allow numbers, pictures and words to tell the same story. Let us return to parent–child relations and the question of demographic conditioning.

Philippe Ariès's parental indifference hypothesis states that before the seventeenth century parents were largely indifferent to the fate of their young children because emotional investment could not be justified when the chances of their early death were so high; parental behaviour was conditioned by high childhood mortality. But a new sentimental attachment did develop by the late eighteenth century when the belief that infantile wastage was inevitable was abandoned. As we noted in Chapter 5, Linda Pollock has concluded that 'There is no change in the extent of parental grief over the centuries and no support at all for the argument that parents before the 18th century were indifferent to the death of their young offspring, whereas after the 18th century they grieved deeply'.[332] In general, this observation is still valid. There are, however, other questions concerning the hypothesis that remain puzzling. It is clear that Ariès and the many scholars who followed him, Lawrence Stone in particular, regarded the indifference hypothesis as at least plausible; why should parents who might lose 1 in 2 or 1 in 3 of their children make a strong emotional attachment? The higher the anticipated rate of return the greater the level of investment, they argued. The counter-argument being that parents who did not develop a close bond, who invested little or nothing, were displaying unnatural behaviour. Surely all human parents love their offspring and mourn their deaths. Couched in these terms, hypothesis and null-hypothesis, and with the bulk of evidence favouring the latter, how does the debate now stand?

It might be suggested that the real problem is one of false distinction; not either one or the other, but sometimes one and sometimes the other. Historical societies were made up of people with varying capacities to be loving parents living in material conditions that militated against the possibility of providing good-quality care. From among the relics of these people historians select example texts, pictures, artefacts etc., materials that just happen to have survived. They analyse and generalise: continuity / turning points, biology / culture. Past societies were heterogeneous in thought, word and deed, just as now. This would be a counsel of despair. It goes against the quest for order, pattern, generality, the need to extract meaning; it is post-modern.

Let us look at the problem in three other ways. What led Ariès to his hypothesis? What happened in societies where infanticide, child murder or abandonment were regularly practised? What will be the emotional response when early-age mortality is close to zero, the deaths of infants and children very rare?

It is probably no coincidence that early modern France seems to have experienced particularly high levels of infant and childhood mortality. Indications of these high rates were available to Ariès and the assumption that France was 'normal' would be a reasonable one to make in the 1940s and 1950s. If at least 1 in 2 infants died, deep emotional attachment could not be expected. Further, the apparent decline in mortality during the second half of the eighteenth century and its association with a contraceptive revolution unique in Europe, as it turns out, would only have helped to support the case for a transition from indifference to loving relations; a before and after type of hypothesis. But France was unusual in its demographic regime compared with northern Europe, England included. In France early-age mortality and marital fertility were both much higher, the extent of wastage greater, although 'effective fertility' need not have been higher, and the practice of sending infants away to be wet-nursed was more common. Ariès just happened to conduct his early demographic research on an anomaly. That Lawrence Stone and others followed his lead stems as much from their ignorance of the true demographic situation in England and New England as their commitment to the 'modernisation paradigm'. However, it must also be added in Ariès's favour that in privileging the cultural over the biological he stimulated much important research on historical and geographical differences.[333]

Infanticide conducted systematically is a selection process in which some are killed or left to die, while others are favoured, properly cared for and much loved. Those who are dispatched or ignored tend to be females; infants born with deformities or disabilities; high birth orders; those born in periods of particular stress because of food shortages, natural disasters, epidemics, extreme poverty; and those whose births break some social rule, especially illegitimates. Ancient Greece and Rome, and traditional China and Japan are usually singled out as examples. But for each of these cases discussion continues over the extent of the practice, its impact, and whether it should be seen as a demographic or economic regulator; whether, for instance, infanticide was always a response to poverty and despair or part of a deliberate strategy of betterment and hope.[334] It is difficult to judge the extent of infanticide in Europe in the past. The convention seems to be that it was not systematically practised during the early modern period; that although there were cases of child murder, accidental deaths and child abandonment were far more important. Major towns, especially in southern and Catholic Europe, all had substantial and long-standing foundling hospitals at which infants were abandoned.[335] As far as the parental indifference hypothesis is concerned, how should infanticide and abandonment be regarded? If those who are selected to survive are treated with care and affection by their parents, perhaps more loving care because they have been chosen, this could provide evidence of a child-oriented society, one in which the untimely death of a favoured one would be sorely felt.

In populations with exceptionally low infant and child mortality (less than 1 per cent dying before their tenth birthday), where the effects of prematurity and sudden infant death syndrome (SIDS) are the most important causes of death, it is assumed that all parents are, or should be, loving and caring to their offspring. Therefore, parental indifference is absent in the modern family; even though domestic living arrangements are such that 'marriage' and 'family' are now both fluid and contested concepts. The illustration of Ariès's 'mourning curve' shown in figure 2.1 (p. 12) has the following text to accompany phase D, the late twentieth century: 'prohibition of mourning, grief hidden from public, secret grief, unemotional self-control, fear of "cracking", exclusion of grandchildren, loneliness of hospital death, cremation as means of escaping cult of the dead'. This should apply to the deaths of adults, especially the aged, but because early-age deaths are now rare in the West, and parental expectations recognise the low risk, when such deaths do occur they are even more keenly grieved over and mourned. In this simple sense, at least, the 'parental indifference hypothesis' is valid. Rare events encourage more deeply felt emotional responses.

This is also an appropriate place to reflect on some of the other theoretical constructs that have influenced the study: Vovelle's 'three-levels model'; the concept of 'grief work'; and the position of reception theory, especially the way in which it affects our approach to evidence.

Vovelle's 'three-levels model' (table 2.3, p. 25) occupies an important position because it attempts to combine the expression of feelings and emotions with the experience of death and bereavement. Its focus on the demographic conditioning of behaviour is especially attractive. The model is not without its difficulties, however, as we suspected in Chapter 2. One of these relates to the terms that should be used to connect the three levels. It was proposed that while level 1 *shapes* level 2, level 3 *reflects* level 2. But it was also anticipated that a finer distinction would need to be made between grief and mourning. While the former could be private, internalised, kept out of sight, the latter was more likely to involve some culturally defined, permissible practices for public display, and that this is what Ariès had in mind when constructing his 'mourning curve'. It now seems more appropriate to think in terms of three simple models: one in which level 1, the 'brute facts of mortality', influences the group display of mourning (death rites, funerals etc.); a second where level 1 affects

Figure 8.1 **A triangular model: demography, grief and mourning**

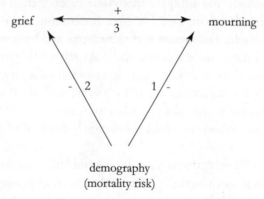

Note: see text for explanation.

the expression of grief by individuals and may be traced through their contribution to some collective discourse; and a third in which grief and mourning interact. In this way the three levels become a triangle with demography at the bottom, grief and mourning above. Sides 1 and 2 in the triangular arrangement illustrated by figure 8.1 are both given negative signs to reflect the 'indifference hypothesis', while side 3 (both directions) is given a positive sign.

The form of analysis discussed in Chapter 7 was directed towards side 2, the response to early-age mortality expressed in poetry. It is summarised in figure 8.2. It adopts the style often employed by environmental scientists to convey change over the long term. Time is displayed from top to bottom and mortality is set alongside the occurrence of certain groups of keywords. On this occasion the group 1 words (death, grief) are shown as a continuous series so that changes can be highlighted for comparison. Word groups 3 (heaven) and 10 (joy) are also illustrated.

The 'grief work' models illustrated in figure 5.1 (p. 98) were intended to help draw out the effects that age and relationship might have on the intensity and duration of grief. They use 'memories' and 'hopes' as ways of accounting for the quantity of 'grief work' required. Figure 5.1a may describe the intensity of grief shown in the case of child deaths where 'hopes' outweigh 'memories'; while curve 3 in figure 5.1a can be used to illustrate the 'parental indifference hypothesis'. Figure 5.1b is probably most useful in representing the pattern of grief intensity for a spouse, or possibly a sibling, and figure 5.1c shows what may happen when incidents or memories spark emotions. Although these models do serve a purpose in clarifying expectations, they are rather too sophisticated for the 'sample texts' provided by the 69 poems. What can be said is, first, that the 'own children' or close relative poems show deeper feelings of grief, and thus stronger attachment, than those elegies in which the subject is not well-known to the poet. Although this is only to be expected, the fact that it does emerge clearly in a comparative analysis of selected poems (those by Jonson and Herrick, for example) is encouraging. Secondly, there is no clear indication that the loss of male

Figure 8.2 Experience and expression compared: early-age mortality and word occurrence patterns

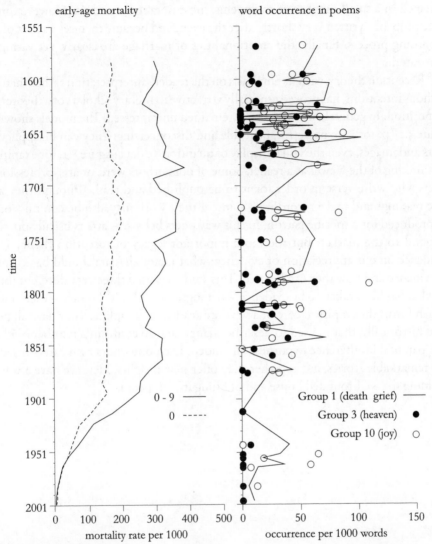

Source: based on figures 3.7 and 7.1.

offspring was especially felt, although there are several examples of mothers writing about their sons. Gender bias does not dominate. Thirdly, and of most interest, the subject's age appears to have been of negligible influence. The stillborn, infants and children were all grieved over. Late-fetal deaths, the inability to produce live-born infants and the double deaths of unborn and mother all appear in a number of the poems. Their occurrence suggests, no more, that the anticipation of 'hoped for joy' in parenthood was an especially strong emotion even when life had been extremely short. The notion that 'grief work' may be undertaken in a discontinuous way (figure 5.1b and c), that memories are likely to be evoked by stray thoughts or incidents, is reflected in a small number of the poems, most notably **51** and **62**. However, most were probably written very shortly after the event and became themselves part of the mourning process. Finally, the emotional ties of marriage are clearly, yet variously, illustrated.

Reception theory, with its emphasis on the reader's interpretation rather than the author's intentions, has proved especially attractive to literary scholars of a theoretical disposition. In general, historians have remained unimpressed. The models shown in figure 5.2 (p. 102) are powerful, plausible and disconcerting. They can be applied to texts and images, even the visual display of quantitative data (figure 8.2, for example), by thinking of the viewer as a reader. Some of our authors were, or are, 'professional' poets who write verse in order for it to be published and read, although they also give readings and make recordings. Some of their work may also be commissioned or produced for a specific patron. In this way poets behave as artists usually do, they respond to the market. But the more important legacy of reception theory is its influence on our appreciation of evidence; what materials/data should be accepted as evidence and how they can be used. This study has used three very different forms of what has been taken to be evidence – demographic, plastic, literary – each one of which forms the empirical core of a separate academic discipline. They have all been read historically, that is, used to describe change, and to confront a number of ideas, the 'parental indifference hypothesis' included. Each one on its own can be used to tell remarkable stories, but together they offer new insights. Here we have a way of building the well-founded house and of filling it with people.[336]

Acknowledgements

It has been particularly enjoyable and challenging to write this book. Enjoyable because it ignores disciplinary boundaries and makes free with many different forms of evidence. Challenging in the sense that several new competences have been demanded, although not necessarily acquired. I should like to thank the following for their support, advice and critical comments: Bernard Beatty, Godfried Croenen, Bill Gould, Sandra Mather, Eilidh Garrett, Chris Galley, Nicola Shelton, Eleanor Dickey, Jane Humphries, Frans van Poppel, Robin Bloxsidge and Richard M. Smith. The Wellcome Trust supported my research on *Fetal Health and Mortality in the Past*, which contributed especially to Chapter 3. The Warden and Fellows of All Souls College, Oxford, elected me to a Visiting Fellowship for the Michaelmas Term 2005. Alison, Rachel and Gavin were encouraging, as ever.

The following lists acknowledge permission to reproduce photographic images of paintings, and to reprint those poems still in copyright.

Images The National Gallery, London: **A**, **K** and **Q** (private collection); Tate Britain, London: **Ci**, **Cii**, **E**, **G** and **J**; Manchester City Art Gallery: **F**; The Marquis of Bath, Longleat House, Wiltshire: **B**; The Viscount De L'Isle, Penshurst Place, Kent: **D**; The Yale Center for British Art, New Haven, Connecticut; Bridgeman Art Library: **H**; The National Gallery of Art, Washington DC: **O** (Gift of Edgar William and Bernice Chrysler Garbisch) and **P** (Chester Dale collection); The Worcester Art Museum, Worcester, Massachusetts: **I** (Gift of Mr and Mrs Albert W. Rice); The Fitzwilliam Museum, Cambridge: **L**; The Ashmolean Museum, Oxford: **M** (private collection).

Poems **63** 'A refusal to mourn the death, by fire, of a child in London', Dylan Thomas, by kind permission of David Higham Associates, London; and the Trustees of the Copyrights of Dylan Thomas and New Directions Publishing, New York; from *The Poems of Dylan Thomas*; **64** 'On the death of a child', D. J. Enright, by kind permission of Watson, Little Limited, London; from *The Laughing Hyena* (1953); **65** 'For a child born dead', Elizabeth Jennings, by kind permission of David Higham Associates, London; from *A Way of Looking* (1955); **66** 'Stillborn', Sylvia Plath, by kind permission of Faber & Faber, London; and HarperCollins, New York; from *Crossing the*

Water (1971); **67** 'Elegy for a still-born child', Seamus Heaney, by kind permission of the author; Faber & Faber, London; and Farrar, Straus and Giroux, New York; from *Door into the Dark* (1969); **68** 'Child burial', Paula Meehan, by kind permission of the author and The Gallery Press, Oldcastle, County Meath, Ireland; from *The Man who was Marked by Winter* (1991); **69** 'The stillborn', Nina Bogin, by kind permission of the author and Anvil Press Poetry, London; from *The Winter Orchards* (2001).

Notes on the Sixty-Nine Poems

1

Lady Elizabeth Hoby (1540–1609)

An epicedium by Elizabeth Hoby, their mother, on the death of her two daughters Elizabeth and Anne

Elizabeth lies here (alas for my heart), thus fated

From Elias Ashmole, *The Antiquities of Berkshire, Volume 2* (London: Edmund Curll, 1719), pp. 470–71, reprinted in Jane Stevenson and Peter Davidson (eds), *Early Modern Women Poets: An Anthology* (Oxford: Oxford University Press, 2001), p. 47. Originally inscribed in Latin on a Hoby family monument in Bisham church, Berkshire. Sir Thomas Hoby had died in 1566.

2

William Shakespeare (1564–1616)

King John, Act III, Scene 4 [3.4.93]

Constance Grief fills the room up of my absent child

From John Dover Wilson (ed.), *King John* (Cambridge: Cambridge University Press, 1936), p. 49, and notes p. 151. E. A. J. Honigmann (ed.), *King John*, Arden Shakespeare, Second Series, 1954 (London: Routledge, 1994) notes 'Some editors think Shakespeare remembers the death of his son Hamnet (*ob.* 1596)' (p. 84), also in his 'Introduction', 'The death of Shakespeare's son Hamnet in 1596 once inclined the sentimental to suspect autobiography in Constance's laments for Arthur...' (p. xliii). Prince Arthur, the nephew of King John, is the son of John's deceased elder brother, Geoffrey. In the play he appears as a helpless child, but was aged about 15. Arthur is not dead, King John has captured him. He escapes blinding, but falls to his death (4.3.10) from castle walls in attempting to escape. On stage with Constance, Arthur's mother, is King Philip of France, Lewis the Dauphin and the Papal Legate, Cardinal Pandulph. Honigmann (1994) dates the play at 1590–91, but accepts that other authorities give a later date, 1593–96 (p. lviii). A. R. Braunmuller (ed.), *The Life and Death of King John* (Oxford: Clarendon Press, 1989) favours 1595–96 (p. 15).

3

Ben Jonson (1572–1637)

Epigram 22 On my first Daughter

Here lyes to each her parents ruth

4

Epigram 45 On my First Son

Farewell, thou child of my right hand, and ioy

5
Epigram 120 EPITAPH ON S[ALOMON] P[AVY] A CHILD OF Q[UEEN] EL[IZABETH'S]
CHAPEL
Weepe with me all you that read
Poems **3**, **4** and **5** reprinted in C. H. Herford, Percy and Evelyn Simpson (eds), *Ben Jonson,
Volume VIII, The Poems* (Oxford: Clarendon Press, 1954), pp. 33–34, 41 and 77. Ian Donaldson
(ed.), *Ben Jonson*, Oxford Authors (Oxford: Oxford University Press, 1985), pp. 229, 236–37
and 270, gives the modernised spelling and punctuation. A folio edition of Jonson's works
containing these epigrams was first published in 1616. Ben Jonson married Anne Lewis in 1594
and their first child, Mary, was probably born in 1595 although this is not certain. Benjamin
was born in 1596 and died during a severe plague outbreak in London in 1603 when his father
was both estranged from his mother and away from town. Salomon Pavy was a boy actor with
Queen Elizabeth's Revels who died in his thirteenth year in July 1602.

6
John Donne (1572–1631)
Holy Sonnet 17
Since she whom I lov'd hath payd her last debt
Reprinted in C. A. Patrides (ed.), *John Donne: The Complete English Poems* (London:
Everyman, J. M. Dent, second edition, 1994), pp. 349–50. The versions in Herbert J. C.
Grierson (ed.), *Donne: Poetical Works* (Oxford: Oxford University Press, 1929), p. 301, and
Helen Gardner (ed.), *John Donne: The Divine Poems* (Oxford: Clarendon Press, 1952), pp.
14–15, have some small differences. From the Westmoreland MS, New York Public Library,
first published in Edmund Gosse (ed.), *The Jacobean Poets* (London: John Murray, 1894), p.
59. Holy or Divine Sonnet 17 relates to John Donne's wife, Ann, who died on 15 August 1617
having recently given birth to a stillborn child, her twelfth confinement. The sonnet may have
been written a few years after 1617 and certainly remained in manuscript form until the late
nineteenth century.

7
Lady Katherine Dyer (*c.*1600–54)
M.S.SIR WILL: DYER, KT: WHO PUT ON IMMORTALITY APRILL TH 29TH ANNO DOMINI
1621
If a large hart: Joyned with a Noble minde
Reprinted in Jane Stevenson and Peter Davidson (eds), *Early Modern Women Poets: An
Anthology* (Oxford: Oxford University Press, 2001), pp. 223–24. Taken from the funeral
monument erected in 1641 in Colmworth church, Bedfordshire.

8
John Milton (1608–74)
ON THE DEATH OF A FAIR INFANT DYING OF A COUGH
O fairest flower no sooner blown but blasted
9
Sonnet 19 (or 23)
Methought I saw my late espoused saint
Reprinted in John Carey and Alastair Fowler (eds), *The Poems of John Milton* (London:
Longmans, 1968), pp. 14–18 and 415–16. Poem **8** is headed *Anno aetatis 17* and like **9** was

first published in 1673. Milton wrote **8** in 1625–26 or 1628 and it relates to the death of a niece, the infant daughter of his sister. He would only have been 17 at the time (1625–26) and this was the first poem in which English was favoured to Latin. However, it is also possible that the infant in question was Anne Phillips (12 January 1626–22 January 1628), in which case the date is misleading. Poem **9** probably dates from 1658 and the death in February of Milton's second wife, Katherine, whom he married in November 1656 and who gave birth to a daughter, also Katherine, in October 1657. Milton became totally blind in 1652.

10
Henry King (1592–1669)
ON TWO CHILDREN, DYING OF ONE DISEASE, AND BURIED IN ONE GRAVE
Brought forth in sorrow, and bred up in Care
Reprinted in Margaret Crum (ed.), *The Poems of Henry King* (Oxford: Clarendon Press, 1965), p. 72. Originally published in *Poems, Elegies, Paradoxes, and Sonnets* (London: Richard Marriet and Henry Herringman, 1657). Henry King had five children by his wife Anne Berkeley whom he married in 1617. Two of these children died in infancy and Anne herself died in 1624. This poem is likely to date from the early 1620s, therefore.

11
Robert Herrick (1591–1674)
TO THE LADY CREW, UPON THE DEATH OF HER CHILD
Why, Madam, will ye longer weep
Hesperides 516 Martin 189
12
UPON THE LADY CREW
This Stone can tell the storie of my life
Hesperides 980 Martin 304
13
UPON BATT
Batt he gets children, not for love to reare 'em
Hesperides 184 Martin 72
14
UPON GUBBS. EPIG.
Gubbs call's his children *Kitlings*: and wo'd bound
Hesperides 200 Martin 80
15
UPON A YOUNG MOTHER OF MANY CHILDREN
Let all chaste Matrons, when they chance to see
Hesperides 151 Martin 58
16
AN EPITAPH UPON A SOBER MATRON
With blamelesse carriage, I liv'd here
Hesperides 116 Martin 41
17
UPON A LADY THAT DYED IN CHILD-BED, AND LEFT A DAUGHTER BEHIND HER
As Gilly flowers do but stay
Hesperides 318 Martin 126

18

An Epitaph upon a child
Virgins promis'd when I dy'd
Hesperides 125 Martin 44

19

Upon a Child. An Epitaph
But borne, and like a short Delight
Hesperides 180 Martin 69

20

Upon a child that dyed
Here she lies, a pretty bud,
Hesperides 310 Martin 123

21

Upon a child
Here a pretty Baby lies
Hesperides 642 Martin 224

Reprinted in L. C. Martin (ed.), *The Poetical Works of Robert Herrick* (Oxford: Clarendon Press, 1956). Page numbers in Martin are given. First published in *Hesperides: or, The Works both Humane & Divine* (London: Printed for John Williams, and Francis Eglesfield, to be sold by Thomas Hunt, bookseller in Exeter, 1648). Herrick was vicar of Dean Prior, Devon, from the 1620s to the 1640s and then for a short period after the Restoration of 1660. He remained unmarried and is not known to have fathered any children.

22

Thomas Jordan (1612?–85?)
An Elegie on the Death of a Male-child Drown'd in Ice
Blest *Infant* to thy *Marble* I am sent
From Thomas Jordan, *Love's Dialect, or Poeticall Varieties; Digested into a Miscelanie of various Fancies* (London: Printed by Authority for the use of the Author, 1646), pp. 48–49.

23

Gertrude Thimelby (*c.*1615–*c.*1670)
Mrs Thimelby, on the Death of Her Only Child
Deare Infant, 'twas thy mother's fault
From Huntington Library, San Marino, California, Manuscript HM 904, reprinted in Jane Stevenson and Peter Davidson (eds), *Early Modern Women Poets: An Anthology* (Oxford: Oxford University Press, 2001), p. 255. Gertrude Aston married Henry Thimelby in the late 1630s or early 1640s. Both only child and husband died young. After their deaths, Mrs Thimelby retired to a convent in Louvain, Flanders. The Astons were a devout Catholic family from Tixall, Staffordshire.

24

Thomas Philipott (*c.*1616–82)
On a Gentlewoman dying in Child-bed of an abortive Daughter
What neare alliance was between the grave

25

On a Farmer, who having buried five of his Children of the Plague, planted on each of their Graves an Apple-tree

You whose bold thoughts do prompt you on to glorie

From Thomas Philipott, *Poems* (London: Printed by R. A. for John Wilcox, 1646), pp. 2 and 9; reprinted in L. C. Martin (ed.), *Thomas Philipott: Poems (1646)* (Liverpool: Liverpool University Press, 1950). Philipott also published *Elegies* (1641) and *Aesop's Fables* (1687).

26

Lady Mary Carey (*fl.* 1643–80)

WRETTEN BY ME AT THE DEATH OF MY 4TH SON AND 5TH CHILD PERIGRENE PAYLER

I thought my all was given before

27

What birth is this: a poore despissed creature?

Poem **26** from Bodleian Library, Oxford, Rawlinson Manuscript D 1308, of a copy made in 1681; reprinted in Jane Stevenson and Peter Davidson (eds), *Early Modern Women Poets: An Anthology* (Oxford: Oxford University Press, 2001), p. 310. Poem **27** reprinted in Germaine Greer *et al.* (eds), *Kissing the Rod* (London: Virago, 1988), pp. 157–58.

Lady Mary Carey's fifth child, Peregrine Payler, was buried on 14 May 1652, while **27** is linked with a miscarriage or the birth of a stillborn child on 31 December 1657 and is dated 12 January 1658.

28

Elizabeth Egerton, Countess of Bridgewater (1626–63)

ON MY BOY HENRY

Here lyes a Boy the finest child from me

Reprinted in Germaine Greer *et al.* (eds), *Kissing the Rod* (London: Virago, 1988), p. 117. From British Library, Egerton MS 607, f.119. Lord Henry Egerton died in 1655 aged only a few days. Elizabeth Egerton's death in childbirth is recounted by her sister in poem **29**.

29

Jane Cheyne, Vicountess Newhaven (1621–69)

ON THE DEATH OF MY DEARE SISTER THE COUNTESSE OF BRIDGEWATER DYING IN CHILDBED, DELIVERED OF A DEAD INFANT A SON, THE 14TH DAY OF JUNE 1663

O God thy Judgments unto sinfull eye

Reprinted in Germaine Greer *et al.* (eds), *Kissing the Rod* (London: Virago, 1988), p. 118. From Huntington Library, Ellesmere MS 8353. Jane Cheyne, Vicountess Newhaven, was present at the death of her sister Elizabeth Egerton, the author of poem **28**, on 14 June 1663.

30

Katherine Philips (1632–64)

EPITAPH. ON HER SON *H.P.* AT ST. SYTH'S CHURCH WHERE HER BODY ALSO LIES INTERRED

What on Earth deserves out Trust?

Reprinted in Patrick Thomas (ed.), *The Collected Works of Katherine Philips, The Matchless Orinda. Volume I: The Poems* (Stump Cross, Essex: Stump Cross Books, 1990), p. 205, and Robert Cummings (ed.), *Seventeenth-Century Poetry: An Annotated Anthology* (Oxford: Basil Blackwell, 2000), pp. 518–19. First published in *Poems* (London: Printed by John Macock for Henry Herringham, at the sign of the Blew Anchor in the Lower Walk of the New Exchange, 1667), p. 134. Katherine Philips's first child, Hector, was born on 23 April

1655 and died on 2 May (or June) of the same year. Her collection also includes 'Orinda upon little Hector Philips' (pp. 148–49) which is reprinted here on p. 181.

31

Matthew Stevenson (*fl.* 1654–85)

UPON A LADY AT YORK DYING IN CHILD-BIRTH

And, but Her fate was such, think ye that she

From Matthew Stevenson, *Poems* (London: Printed by R. Davenport for Lodowick Lloyd, 1665), pp. 112–13.

32

Anne Bradstreet (1613?–72)

ON MY DEAR GRANDCHILD SIMON BRADSTREET, WHO DIED ON 16 NOVEMBER, 1669, BEING BUT A MONTH, AND ONE DAY OLD

No sooner came, but gone, and fall'n asleep

Reprinted in Jeannine Hensley (ed.), *The Works of Anne Bradstreet* (Cambridge, MA: Harvard University Press, 1967), p. 237. Published in *Several Poems* (Boston: John Foster, 1678). Simon was the son of Samuel and Mercy Bradstreet. He died in infancy at Andover, Massachusetts, in 1669.

33

Aphra Behn (1640?–89)

EPITAPH ON THE TOMBSTONE OF A CHILD, THE LAST OF SEVEN THAT DIED BEFORE

This Little, Silent, Gloomy Monument,

Reprinted in Germaine Greer *et al.* (eds), *Kissing the Rod* (London: Virago, 1988), p. 258. Published in *Miscellany, Being a Collection of Poems by several Hands. Together with Reflections on Morality or Seneca Unmasqued*, edited by A. Behn (London: J. Hindmarsh, 1685), pp. 257–58. This may be a commissioned epitaph or one relating to the child of friends.

34

Thomas Flatman (1635?–88)

CORIDON ON THE DEATH OF HIS DEAR ALEXIS, OB. JAN. 28 1683. PASTORAL SONG. SET BY DR. BLOW.

Alexis! dear Alexis! lovely boy!

35

EPITAPH ON HIS ELDEST SON, THOMAS, 1682

Whoe'er thou art, that look'st upon,

Reprinted in George Saintsbury (ed.), *Minor Poets of the Caroline Period, Volume III* (Oxford: Clarendon Press, 1921), pp. 375–76 and 414–15. The coridon was originally published in *Poems and Songs* (London: Printed for Benjamin Tooke at the Ship in St Paul's Church-Yard, fourth edition 1686), pp. 199–200. The epitaph is from the inscription on Thomas's tomb in St Bride's church, Fleet Street, London. It is transcribed in John Strype's edition of John Stow, *A Survey of the Cities of London and Westminster. Now Corrected, and Brought Down to the Present Time* (London, 1720), Book III, p. 266. The subject of both **34** and **35** is Thomas Flatman, the eldest son of Thomas and Hannah, who died on 28 December 1682 aged 9 years. A coridon (or corydon) is a pastoral poem, one relating to the spiritual care of a flock (or of souls) (*OED*).

36
Alexander Pope (1688–1744)
ON MRS. CORBET WHO DIED OF A CANCER IN HER BREAST
Here rests a Woman, good without pretence,
Reprinted in Herbert Davis (ed.), *Pope: Poetical Works* (London: Oxford University Press, 1966), pp. 647–48. Appears in a collection of *Epitaphs* published in 1730. This is believed to be a commissioned epitaph for a person whom Pope had never met. Elizabeth Corbett died on 1 March 1725.

37
Mehetabel (Hetty) Wright (1697–1750)
TO AN INFANT EXPIRING THE SECOND DAY OF ITS BIRTH
Tender softness, infant mild
Reprinted in Roger Lonsdale (ed.), *Eighteenth-Century Women Poets: An Oxford Anthology* (Oxford: Oxford University Press, 1989), p. 115. First published in the *Gentleman's Magazine* (October 1733). Hetty Wright lost a number of prematurely born infants in the late 1720s. This poem probably relates to that experience.

38
Elizabeth Boyd (*fl.* 1730–44)
ON THE DEATH OF AN INFANT OF FIVE DAYS OLD, BEING A BEAUTIFUL BUT ABORTIVE BIRTH
How frail is human life! How fleet our breath
Reprinted in Roger Lonsdale (ed.), *Eighteenth-Century Women Poets: An Oxford Anthology* (Oxford: Oxford University Press, 1989), p. 135. First published in *The Humorous Miscellany* (London, 1733). *The Humorous Miscellany* also contains a poem entitled 'On an infant's lying some days unburied, for want of money'. Poem **38** probably refers to Elizabeth Boyd's own experience of bearing a stillborn child at some time in the 1720s.

39
Jane Colman Turell (1708–35)
PHOEBUS HAS THRICE HIS YEARLY CIRCUIT RUN
Phoebus has thrice his yearly circuit run
From *Memoirs of the Life and Death of the Pious and Ingenious Mrs Jane Turell* (Boston, 1735). Jane Turell died aged 27 at Medford, Massachusetts, on 26 March 1735. Her father, Rev Benjamin Colman, collected these *Memoirs*.

40
Anonymous
EPITAPH ON A CHILD KILLED BY PROCURED ABORTION
O thou, whose eyes were closed in death's pale night
Reprinted in Roger Lonsdale (ed.), *The New Oxford Book of Eighteenth-Century Verse* (Oxford: Oxford University Press, 1984), p. 335. First published in the *Gentleman's Magazine* (January 1740).

41
Samuel Bowden (*fl.* 1732–61)
ON THE DEATH OF AN ONLY CHILD, OF VERY PREGNANT PARTS
Ungentle Death with fatal dart
From Samuel Bowden, *Poems on Various Subjects* (London: Printed by T. Boddely, for the
Author, 1754), p. 76. This poem is said to be a translation. *Poems on Various Subjects* also
contains 'A parent's lamentation, On the death of an only promising child' (pp. 206–07),
which is reprinted here on p. 186; and 'To a young lady at Holt, on her recovery from the
small-pox, by inoculation' (pp. 49–53), as well as 'A Treatise on Health'. Bowden was a
physician from Frome in Somerset.

42
Thomas Gray (1716–71)
EPITAPH ON A CHILD
Here, freed from pain, secure from misery, lies
Reprinted in Roger Lonsdale (ed.), *The Poems of Thomas Gray, William Collins, Oliver
Goldsmith* (London: Longman, 1969), pp. 209–10. The child is believed to be Robert (Robin)
Wharton, the son of Dr Thomas Wharton, an old Cambridge friend of Gray's. Robin was
born in 1753 and died in April 1758.

43
Jane Cave (*c.*1754–1813)
WRITTEN A FEW HOURS BEFORE THE BIRTH OF A CHILD
My God, prepare me for the hour
Reprinted in Roger Lonsdale (ed.), *Eighteenth-Century Women Poets: An Oxford Anthology*
(Oxford: Oxford University Press, 1989), pp. 376–77. First published in *Poems on Various
Subjects, Entertaining, Elegiac, and Religious* (Bristol: Printed for the Author [By subscrip-
tion], 1786). These are the prenatal anxieties of Jane Cave, probably written in the early 1780s.
The second edition of her collection (Shrewsbury: Printed for the Author by T. Wood, 1789)
also contains 'Written about a month after the birth of my son' (pp. 182–87), which relates
to her son, Thomas.

44
Helen Leigh (*fl.* 1780–95)
THE NATURAL CHILD
Let not the title of my verse offend
Reprinted in Roger Lonsdale (ed.), *Eighteenth-Century Women Poets: An Oxford Anthology*
(Oxford: Oxford University Press, 1989), pp. 421–22. First published in *Miscellaneous Poems*
(Manchester: Printed by C. Wheeler and sold by Messers. Clarkes, 1788), pp. 10–12. The
cruel fate of the natural child related by a Cheshire curate's wife, Helen Leigh of Middlewich,
as it was observed in the 1780s.

45
Robert Burns (1759–96)
ON THE BIRTH OF A POSTHUMOUS CHILD, BORN IN PECULIAR CIRCUMSTANCES OF
FAMILY-DISTRESS
Sweet flow'ret, pledge o'meikle love
Reprinted in Andrew Noble and Patrick Scott Hogg (eds), *The Canongate Burns: The*

Complete Poems and Songs of Robert Burns (Edinburgh: Canongate Press, 2001), pp. 285–86. First printed in the Edinburgh edition of 1793. The first child of Susan Henri (daughter of Mrs Dunlop and sister of Sir Thomas Wallace) was born in November 1790. His father had died in June of that year. Mrs Dunlop and her daughter were family friends of Burns.

46
William Blake (1757–1827)
THE CHIMNEY-SWEEPER *Songs of Innocence*
When my mother died I was very young
47
THE CHIMNEY-SWEEPER *Songs of Experience*
A little black thing among the snow
Reprinted in Sir Geoffrey Keynes (ed.), *William Blake's Illuminated Book* Songs of Innocence and of Experience (Oxford: Oxford University Press, 1970). First published, respectively, in *Songs of Innocence*, 1789, and *Songs of Experience*, 1793. Published as a single volume in 1794. William Blake was married, but childless. His affection for children and their plight is obvious in these *Songs*.

48
Sir Brooke Boothby (1743–1824)
Sonnet I
Life's summer flown, the wint'ry tempest rude
From Sir Brooke Boothby, *Sorrows Sacred to the Memory of Penelope* (London: Printed by W. Bulmer and Co. and sold by Messers. Cadell and Davies, Strand; Edwards, Pall-Mall; and Johnson, St. Paul's Church-Yard, 1796), p. 7. A book of 24 sonnets, plus other miscellaneous poetry, dedicated to the memory of Penelope Boothby (1785–91) with engravings of the portrait of Penelope by Joshua Reynolds (1788) and her tomb monument by Thomas Banks (1793) in Ashbourne church, Derbyshire (**M** and **N** in Chapter 4).

49
Samuel Taylor Coleridge (1772–1834)
ON AN INFANT, WHO DIED BEFORE ITS CHRISTENING
Be rather than be *call'd* a Child of God!
From Ernest Hartley Coleridge (ed.), *Letters of Samuel Taylor Coleridge, Volume I* (London: Heinemann, 1895), p. 287. First published in 1834. It appeared in a letter from Coleridge to his wife, Sara, dated Göttingen, 8 April 1799. Berkeley, the Coleridges' second child, was born on 15 May 1798 and died on 10 February 1799.

50
William Wordsworth (1770–1850)
CHARACTERISTICS OF A CHILD THREE YEARS OLD
Loving she is, and tractable, though wild
51
Miscellaneous Sonnets XXVII SURPRIZED BY JOY – IMPATIENT AS THE WIND
Surprized by joy – impatient as the Wind
Reprinted in Stephen Logan (ed.), *William Wordsworth* (London: Everyman, J. M. Dent, 1998), pp. 91–92. First published in *Collected Shorter Poems* (London, 1815). Poems **50** and **51**

have been linked with the Wordsworths' fourth child, Catharine, who died in June 1812 aged 3 years. Their third child, Thomas, also died in December 1812 aged 6.

52 and 53
Percy Bysshe Shelley (1792–1822)
TO WILLIAM SHELLEY II
My lost William, thou in whom
Reprinted in Neville Rogers (ed.), *The Complete Poetical Works of Percy Bysshe Shelley* (Oxford: Clarendon Press, 1975). 'To William Shelley II' was originally published in *Posthumous Works* (1824), and III (**53**) appeared in *Posthumous Works* (1839). Both were written in 1819. 'To William Shelley I' was written in 1817 (Rogers, *Complete Poetical Works, Volume II* (1975), pp. 309–10). William Shelley died at Rome in June 1819 aged 3 years.

54
Amelia Alderson Opie (1769–1853)
ON THE DEATH OF A CHILD
And he is gone! that winning child
From Amelia Opie, *Lays for the Dead* (London: Longman, 1834), pp. 80–81. Opie was the daughter of a Norwich dissenting minister. She subsequently became a Quaker.

55
Mary Ann Browne (1812–44)
'MY BABY! MY BABY! THEY'VE TOLD ME HE IS DEAD'
My baby my baby! They've told me he is dead
Reprinted in Isobel Armstrong *et al.* (eds), *Nineteenth-Century Women Poets: An Oxford Anthology* (Oxford: Clarendon Press, 1996), pp. 340–41. First published in *The Birth-day Gift* (1834). Poem **55** probably captures Mary Ann Browne's own experience of infant loss in the 1830s.

56
Walter Savage Landor (1775–1864)
ON THE DEAD
Thou in this wide cold church art laid
Reprinted in Stephen Wheeler (ed.), *The Complete Works of Walter Savage Landor, Volume XV, Poems III* (London: Chapman and Hall, 1935), pp. 277–78. It was first published in *The Examiner* (8 January 1842); reprinted 1846. Dorothy Lyttleton, the probable subject of **56**, was buried in Studley church, Warwickshire, in 1811.
Note * In cursu vitae mors nobis instat.
[L. In 1846 the foot-note is: S. Franciscae Verchild, Nat. xv. Julii 1774.
The tablet in St Mary's church, Warwick, adds: ob. xix Aug. 1780.]

57
John Clare (1793–1864)
GRAVES OF INFANTS
Infants' graves are steps of angels, where
Reprinted in Geoffrey Grigson (ed.), *Poems of John Clare's Madness* (London: Routledge & Kegan Paul, 1949), 42, p. 120. Dated June 1844 from 'Poems written in Northampton General Lunatic Asylum, 1842–63'. Although Clare fathered at least seven children, there is no evidence that any of them died in childhood.

58
Louisa A. Horsfield (1830–65?)
To My Departed Baby
The flowers will bud and bloom again
Reprinted in Isobel Armstrong *et al.* (eds), *Nineteenth-Century Women Poets: An Oxford Anthology* (Oxford: Clarendon Press, 1996), p. 517. First published in *The Cottage Lyre: Being Miscellaneous Poetry* (London: W. Kent, 1861; London: Richard Davies, 1862). This poem probably dates from the late 1850s and reflects both Louisa Horsfield's experience and her Primitive Methodism.

59
Alexander Anderson (1845–1909)
The Dead Child
There is an angel sleeping in this room
From Alexander Anderson, *A Song of Labour, and other Poems* (Dundee: Printed at the Advertiser Office, 1873), pp. 17–18.

60
Edward Dowden (1843–1913)
To a Child Dead as soon as Born
A little wrath was on thy forehead, Boy
From Edward Dowden, *Poems* (London: Henry S. King, 1877). Dowden was a distinguished Shakespeare scholar.

61
Robert Bridges (1844–1930)
On a Dead Child
Perfect little body, without fault or stain on thee
From *Poetical Works of Robert Bridges* (London: Oxford University Press, 1912), pp. 268–69. Originally published in 1880, and in *Shorter Poems*, Books I–IV (Oxford: Clarendon Press, 1890), Book III, No. 4. In the late 1870s Robert Bridges was a physician at Great Ormond Street Hospital for Sick Children, London.

62
Thomas Hardy (1840–1928)
The Voice
Woman much missed, how you call to me, call to me
Reprinted in Samuel Hynes (ed.), *Thomas Hardy, Selected Poetry* (Oxford: Oxford University Press, 1996), p. 87. Dated December 1912. First published in 'Poems of 1912–13' in *Satires of Circumstance* (London: Macmillan, 1914), p. 109. Hardy's estranged first wife, Emma Gifford, died on 27 November 1912.

63
Dylan Thomas (1914–53)
A Refusal to Mourn the Death, by Fire, of a Child in London
Never until the mankind making
From Dylan Thomas, *Deaths and Entrances* (London: J. M. Dent and Sons, 1946), p. 8. Dated March 1945. Poem **63** comes from the closing months of the Second World War.

64
D. J. Enright (1920–2002)
ON THE DEATH OF A CHILD
The greatest griefs shall find themselves
From D. J. Enright, *The Laughing Hyena and Other Poems* (London: Routledge & Kegan Paul, 1953), p. 73.

65
Elizabeth Jennings (1926–2001)
FOR A CHILD BORN DEAD
What ceremony can we fit
From Elizabeth Jennings, *A Way of Looking: Poems* (London: Andre Deutsch, 1955), p. 46.

66
Sylvia Plath (1932–63)
STILLBORN
These poems do not live: it's a sad diagnosis
From Ted Hughes (ed.), *Sylvia Plath: Collected Poems* (London: Faber & Faber, 1981), number 124, p. 142. Originally published in Sylvia Plath, *Crossing the Water*, edited by Ted Hughes (London and New York: Faber & Faber and Harper & Row, 1971), p. 20. Poem **66** probably dates from mid-1960 after the birth of Plath's daughter in April.

67
Seamus Heaney (1939–)
ELEGY FOR A STILL-BORN CHILD
Your mother walks light as an empty creel
From Seamus Heaney, *Door into the Dark* (London: Faber & Faber, 1969), pp. 31–32.

68
Paula Meehan (1955–)
CHILD BURIAL
Your coffin looked unreal
From Paula Meehan, *The Man Who Was Marked by Winter* (Oldcastle, County Meath: Gallery Books, 1991), pp. 29–30.

69
Nina Bogin (1952–)
THE STILLBORN
The stillborn have no claim
From Nina Bogin, *The Winter Orchards* (London: Anvil Press, 2001), p. 19.

Notes

1 Introduction: 'the lines of life'

1 The chapter's sub-title comes from Shakespeare's Sonnet 16 (line 9). Rom Harré (ed.), *The Social Construction of Emotions* (Oxford: Basil Blackwell, 1986) provides an accessible introduction arguing from the 'social construction of emotions' perspective. Among historians, Keith Hopkins, *Death and Renewal, Sociological Studies in Roman History, Volume 2* (Cambridge: Cambridge University Press, 1983), pp. 221–26, gives a short and extremely lucid introduction to the problems of studying grief and mourning in the past. For the present day, the anthropologist Nancy Scheper-Hughes has written a challenging account based on her medical fieldwork: *Death Without Weeping: The Violence of Everyday Life in Brazil* (Berkeley: University of California Press, 1992). Here she argues that 'Mother love is anything *other* than natural and instead represents a matrix of images, meanings, sentiments, and practices that are everywhere socially and culturally produced' (p. 341). See also Nancy Scheper-Hughes, 'The cultural politics of child survival', in Nancy Scheper-Hughes (ed.), *Child Survival: Anthropological Perspectives on the Treatment and Maltreatment of Children* (Dordrecht: D. Reidel Publishing, 1987), pp. 1–29. The contributors to Margaret S. Stroebe, Wolfgang Stroebe and Robert O. Hansson (eds), *Handbook of Bereavement: Theory, Research, and Intervention* (Cambridge: Cambridge University Press, 1993) survey the specialist field, although they take little or no notice of historical changes.

2 Peter Laslett, 'The wrong way through the telescope: a note on literary evidence in sociology and in historical sociology', *British Journal of Sociology* 27 (1976), pp. 317–42.

3 Laslett, 'Telescope' (1976), pp. 324–25.

4 Laslett, 'Telescope' (1976), p. 337.

5 J. H. Plumb, 'The new world of children in eighteenth-century England', *Past and Present* 67 (1975), pp. 64–95. The paper is devoted mainly to the provision of education among the upper and middle classes in eighteenth-century England.

6 Plumb, 'New world' (1975), p. 70.

7 Plumb, 'New world' (1975), p. 90.

8 Plumb, 'New world' (1975), p. 67.

9 Steven Ozment, *Ancestors: The Loving Family in Old Europe* (Cambridge, MA: Harvard University Press, 2001). Arthur E. Imhof, *Lost Worlds: How Our European Ancestors Coped with Everyday Life and Why Life Is So Hard Today* (Charlottesville, VA: University of Virginia Press, 1996); Egle Becchi and Dominique Julia (eds), *Histoire de l'enfance en Occident. Tome 1: De l'Antiquité au XVIIe siècle. Tome 2: Du XVIIIe siècle à nos jours* (Paris: Éditions du Seuil, 1998), especially their introduction to volume 1, 'Histoire de l'enfance, histoire sans paroles?', pp. 7–39; David I. Kertzer and Marizio Barbagli (eds), *Family Life in Early Modern Times, 1500–1789* (New Haven, CT: Yale University Press, 2001), particularly chapter 7 by Linda A. Pollock, 'Parent–child relations', pp. 191–220; and Raffaella Sarti, *Europe at Home: Family and Material Culture, 1500–1800* (New Haven, CT: Yale University Press, 2002), especially pp. 224–40; also Albrecht Classen, 'Philippe

Ariès and the consequences: history of childhood, family relations, and personal emotions: where do we stand today?', in Albrecht Classen (ed.), *Childhood in the Middle Ages and the Renaissance: The Results of a Paradigm Shift in the History of Mentality* (Berlin: Walter de Gruyter, 2005), pp. 1–66, are also important references.

10   Ozment, *Ancestors* (2001), pp. 3–4. The old model is due to, among others, Philippe Ariès, Edward Shorter, Jean-Louis Flandrin and Lawrence Stone. Rudolf Dekker, *Childhood, Memory and Autobiography in Holland: From the Golden Age to Romanticism* (London: Macmillan, 2000), p. 4, makes a useful distinction between what he terms the 'black legend' (old model) in which parents are at some early historical stage indifferent to their children and the 'white legend' in which parents have always been caring and have mourned their children's deaths (Pollock, Ozment etc.). While the former is too bleak, the latter does not allow for changes and variations especially in death rites and the expression of grief. This point bears on Imhof's discussion in *Lost Worlds* (1996), pp. 81–87 and 126–27, of regional variations in what he calls a 'deeper reverence for life'. He finds evidence for this in northern (Lutheran) Germany compared with the Catholic south where the 'black legend' appears more appropriate.

11   Ozment, *Ancestors* (2001), p. 7.

12   Ozment, *Ancestors* (2001), pp. 58 and 60. Ozment's sources for these observations are: Klaus Arnold, *Kind und Gesellschaft in Mittelalter und Renaissance: Beiträge und Texte zur Geschichte der Kindheit* (Munich: Martin Lurz, 1980), p. 86; Heide Wunder, *He is the Sun, She is the Moon: Women in Early Modern Germany* (Cambridge, MA: Harvard University Press, 1998); and Steven Ozment, *Flesh and Spirit: Private Life in Early Modern Germany* (New York: Viking, 1999), p. 70. The statement on stillbirths is supported by a single example drawn from one family living in Nuremberg in the 1520s. See also Steven Ozment, 'The family in Reformation Germany: The bearing and rearing of children', *Journal of Family History* 8 (1983), pp. 159–76.

2 *Après la mort des enfants*

13   Patrick H. Hutton, *Philippe Ariès and the Politics of French Cultural History* (Amherst, MA: University of Massachusetts Press, 2004) provides an intellectual biography of Ariès. See also Patrick H. Hutton, 'Of death and destiny: the Ariès–Vovelle debate about the history of mourning', in Peter Homans (ed.), *Symbolic Loss: The Ambiguity of Mourning and Memory at Century's End* (Charlottesville, VA: University of Virginia Press, 2000), pp. 147–70, which discusses the debate between Ariès and Vovelle that took place between 1974 and 1982.

14   Philippe Ariès, *Centuries of Childhood* (London: Penguin, 1973). Ariès's principal publications are listed in table 2.1. Sheila Ryan Johansson, 'Centuries of childhood/centuries of parenting: Philippe Ariès and the modernization of privileged infancy', *Journal of Family History* 12 (1987), pp. 343–65, offers a twenty-fifth anniversary re-evaluation, and Egle Becchi and Dominique Julia, 'Histoire de l'enfance, histoire sans paroles?', in Egle Becchi and Dominique Julia (eds), *Histoire de l'enfance en Occident. Tome 1: De l'Antiquité au XVIIe siècle* (Paris: Éditions du Seuil, 1998), pp. 7–39, discusses Ariès's contribution at some length.

15   Johansson, 'Centuries of childhood' (1987) focuses on the eighteenth-century family limitation aspects of Ariès's arguments.

16   Philippe Ariès, 'The reversal of death: changes in attitudes toward death in Western societies', in David E. Stannard (ed.), *Death in America* (Philadelphia, PA: University of Pennsylvania Press, 1975), pp. 134–58, quoted from p. 146. See John McManners, 'Death and the French historians', in Joachim Whaley (ed.), *Mirrors of Mortality: Studies in the Social History of Death* (London: Europa Publications, 1981), pp. 106–30, for a critical commentary.

17   Ariès, 'The reversal of death' (1975), pp. 157 and 158.

18   Philippe Ariès, *Images of Man and Death* (Cambridge, MA: Harvard University Press, 1985), pp.

247 and 252.

19 We shall return to the matter of how to conceptualise time, particularly *la longue durée*, and of sentiments, feelings, attitudes (*les mentalités*) later in Chapter 2.

20 Philippe Ariès, *The Hour of Our Death* (New York: Alfred A. Knopf, 1981), p. xvii.

21 Pierre Chaunu, *Histoire, science sociale: La durée, l'espace et l'homme à l'époque moderne* (Paris: SEDES, 1974), pp. 53–77, contains a discussion of *l'histoire sérielle* as does Chaunu's collection of papers, *Histoire quantitative, histoire sérielle* (Paris: Librairie Armand Colin, 1978). Some of these issues were also introduced in Philippe Ariès, *Le temps de l'histoire* (Monaco: Èditions du Rocher, 1954).

22 Peter Burke, *The French Historical Revolution: The* Annales *School, 1929–89* (Cambridge: Polity Press, 1990), pp. 67–69, places Ariès's work in its French intellectual context. Roger Chartier's introduction to Ariès, *Le temps* (1986) also offers an outline of his work, as does Hutton, *Philippe Ariès* (2004).

23 Philippe Ariès, *L'enfant et la vie familiale sous l'Ancien Régime* (Paris: Libraire Plon, 1960), p. i. In the title of his memoirs Ariès also describes himself as *Un historien du dimanche* (Paris: Éditions du Seuil, 1980). Although Ariès was trained as an historian at the Sorbonne he spent most of his career working in an agricultural research institute and only in 1978 was he elected to the position of director of studies at L'Ecole des Hautes Études en Sciences Sociales, Paris.

24 Philippe Ariès, *Histoire des populations françaises et de leurs attitudes devant la vie depuis le XVIIIe siècle* (Paris: Éditions Self, 1948), pp. 471–93, and 'Attitudes devant la vie et devant la mort du XVIIe au XIXe siècle: quelques aspects de leurs variations', *Population* 4 (1949), pp. 463–70. At this time Ariès also published 'Sur les origines de la contraception en France', *Population* 8 (1953), pp. 465–72, and 'Deux contributions à l'histoire des pratiques contraceptives: Chaucer et Madame de Sévigné', *Population* 9 (1954), pp. 692–98, which began his discussion of the origins of family limitation in late eighteenth-century France, an issue that came to be closely connected in his argument with the reversal of parental indifference. Ariès's use of Montaigne's *Essays* is discussed at greater length in Robert Woods, 'Did Montaigne love his children? Demography and the hypothesis of parental indifference', *Journal of Interdisciplinary History* 33 (2003), pp. 421–42.

25 Edgar Morin, *L'homme et la mort dans l'histoire* (Paris: Éditions Corrêa, 1951). Most of Morin's book is an anthropological account of differences in human consciousness of death and dying.

26 Johan Huizinga, *The Waning of the Middle Ages: A Study of the Forms of Life, Thought and Art in France and the Netherlands in the XIVth and XVth Centuries* (London: Edward Arnold, 1924). Two further studies should be mentioned: Edmond Pilon, *La vie de famille au XVIIIe siècle* (Paris: Henri Jonquières, 1928) uses family group portraits and domestic accounts from the eighteenth century; and, Alberto Tenenti, *La vie et la mort à travels l'art du XVe siècle* (Paris: Librairie Armand Colin, 1952). Published the year after *L'enfant*, Roger Mercier, *L'enfant dans la société du XVIIIe siècle (avant l'Émile)*, Université de Dakar, Faculté des Lettres et Sciences Humaines, Publications de la Section de Langues et Littératures No. 6 (Dakar, 1961) also discusses parental indifference, demography and the use of wet-nurses, but it has been overshadowed by Ariès's work.

27 Lawrence Stone, *The Family, Sex and Marriage in England, 1500–1800* (London: Weidenfeld and Nicolson, 1977). Note 40 to p. 105 gives *Centuries of Childhood*, p. 39, as the source for the Montaigne quotation.

28 The quotation 'restraint ... scene' is taken from p. 58 of John Walzer, 'Comment', *History of Childhood Quarterly* 1 (1973), pp. 57–61.

29 Stone, *The Family* (1977), p. 81. Even here there is confusion: which is the dependent variable, mortality or affection? Curiously, Ariès's name appears only once in the text (p. 247) although Montaigne is referred to on several subsequent occasions. For two critical reviews, see Christopher Hill, 'Sex, marriage, and the family in England', *Economic History Review* 31 (1978), pp. 450–63, and, especially, Alan Macfarlane, 'Review of *The Family, Sex and Marriage in England, 1500–*

1800. By Lawrence Stone', *History and Theory* 18 (1979), pp. 103–26. Ariès's own, highly complimentary review appears in *American Historical Review* 83 (1978), pp. 1221–24. By 1981 Stone had become more sceptical concerning Ariès's argument that childhood developed as a separate concept only from the seventeenth century. See Lawrence Stone, 'Family history in the 1980s: past achievement and future trends', *Journal of Interdisciplinary History* 12 (1981), pp. 51–87, especially p. 68, and his review of Alan Macfarlane, *Marriage and Love in England, 1300–1840* (Oxford: Basil Blackwell, 1986) as 'Illusions of a changeless family', *Times Literary Supplement* (16 May 1986), pp. 525–26. Macfarlane is dismissive of 'parental indifference'. He observes 'The joy at the birth of children was clearly related to a widespread and deep affection felt towards them. This has been amply documented from English diaries over the sixteenth to nineteenth centuries [referring to Pollock, *Forgotten Children* (1983)], and so we need not labour the point' (p. 52).

30 Antonia Fraser, *The Weaker Vessel: Woman's Lot in Seventeenth-Century England* (London: Heinemann, 1984), p. 87. Fortunately, Fraser is not convinced. She rejects maternal indifference among both literate and inarticulate women (p. 88).

31 Clare Gittings, *Death, Burial and the Individual in Early Modern England* (London: Croom Helm, 1984), p. 81.

32 Viviana A. Zelizer, *Pricing the Priceless Child: The Changing Social Value of Children* (New York: Basic Books, 1985), p. 10. Zelizer gives the sources for quotations as (a) Stone, *Family, Sex and Marriage*, p. 105, and Ariès, *Centuries of Childhood*, and (b) Peter Uhlenberg, 'Death and the family', in Michael Gordon (ed.), *The American Family* (New York: St Martin's Press, 1978), p. 170.

33 Mark Poster, *Cultural History and Postmodernity* (New York: Columbia University Press, 1997), pp. 26 and 27. The essay dates from 1990. If 50 per cent of live births did not survive to age 20 this would imply that around 45 per cent would not reach age 10. It is perhaps ironic that while Poster is especially critical of Stone's 'utilitarian model of psychology' he also remarks that 'Lawrence Stone's considerable accomplishment was to correct for the demographic reductionism of *The World We Have Lost* [by Peter Laslett] by addressing the issue of the family's role in the creation of the self' in terms of the way he focused on emotional patterns, symbolic structures, hierarchical relations 'that distinguish in sharp discontinuity the early modern from the modern family.'

34 Nicholas Orme, *Medieval Children* (New Haven, CT: Yale University Press, 2001), pp. 5 and 113. Orme uses as his source table 7.19, p. 249, from E. A. Wrigley and R. S. Schofield, *The Population History of England, 1541–1871: A Reconstruction* (London: Edward Arnold, 1981), which provides estimates of the average probability of dying during the first year of life, ages 1–4 and 5–9 in a sample of 12 English parishes for the period 1550–90. But he does not read the data correctly. A range of 21 to 28 per cent would seem appropriate based on the best available evidence. See Chapter 3, especially table 3.2.

35 For example, Adrian Wilson, 'The infancy of the history of childhood: an appraisal of Philippe Ariès', *History and Theory* 19 (1980), pp. 132–53, outlines four levels of criticism (pp. 135–36): (1) use of printed sources only, (2) no explanations for developments, (3) 'pervasive chronological vagueness', (4) use of 'a present-minded point of view'. While justified, they are not completely destructive. Peter Laslett, 'Philippe Ariès and "La famille"', *Encounter* 46(3) (March 1976), pp. 80–83, reacting to Philippe Ariès, 'La famille', *Encounter* 45(2) (August 1975), pp. 7–12, but also to *Centuries of Childhood* in general, describes Ariès as a 'creative innovator' whose work is 'Original, imaginative, unexpected: novel in its sources, subtle and intriguing in its conclusions, always interesting to read' yet belonging to an 'intuitive/exploratory stage' (p. 80). Johansson, 'Centuries of childhood' (1987) finds much to praise in Ariès's 'cultural determinism'. Jean-Louis Flandrin, 'Enfance et société', *Annales: ESC* 19 (1964), pp. 322–29, provides one of the early French reviews. Steven Ozment, *Ancestors: The Loving Family in Old Europe* (Cambridge, MA: Harvard University Press, 2001) singles out Ariès as the originator of an old orthodoxy which his 'loving family' is

meant to replace. See Chapter 1.

36 John Palmer, *Molière: His Life and Works* (London: G. Bell and Sons, 1930), pp. 208–09.

37 Michel de Montaigne, *Essais*, edited in two volumes by Jean Plattard (Paris: Éditions Fernand Roches, 1931), I.14, p. 80. This edition, along with the significant English translations, distinguishes between passages that appeared in: A, the first 1580 edition; B, the 1588 edition; C, the handwritten additions to the 1588 edition which Montaigne inserted in his own copy. The three books of essays are referred to by Roman numerals, thus I.14 and II.8.

38 *Le petit Robert* (Paris, 2002), p. 1020, and Edmond Huguet (ed.), *Dictionnaire de la langue française du seizième siècle, Tome IV* (Paris: Librairie M. Didier, 1950), p. 43.

39 See Chapters 5 and 7.

40 Woods, 'Did Montaigne' (2003), pp. 421–41. It is curious to note examples of the use of Montaigne in some recent bereavement literature. Colin Murray Parkes, *Bereavement: Studies of Grief in Adult Life* (London: Penguin, new edition 1998), p. 122, has the following passage.

> It is only in the present century that loss of a child has become a rare event, and what evidence there is suggests that during earlier days, when most parents would expect to lose up to half of their children in infancy or early childhood, they accepted their losses more readily than we do today. Hence Montaigne can write: 'I have lost two or three children in their infancy, not without regret, but without great sorrow'.

Parkes is a distinguished clinical psychiatrist specialising in bereavement.

41 Ariès, *The Hour of Our Death* (1981), pp. 432–46.

42 Ariès, *The Hour of Our Death* (1981), pp. 434–35. Charlotte Brontë, *Jane Eyre*, edited by Margaret Smith with an introduction and notes by Sally Shuttleworth (Oxford: Oxford University Press, 2000), pp. 81–82, volume 1, chapter 9 in the original.

43 Ariès, *The Hour of Our Death* (1981), p. 436.

44 Ariès, *The Hour of Our Death* (1981), p. 442.

45 Ariès, *The Hour of Our Death* (1981), p. 443.

46 Ariès, *The Hour of Our Death* (1981), p. 433.

47 'Appendix II Lowood School, and the Rev. Mr. Brocklehurst', in Jane Jack and Margaret Smith (eds) *Jane Eyre* (Oxford: Clarendon Press, 1969), pp. 614–21, gives the historical background to the story.

48 Ian Jack, 'Introduction', in *Wuthering Heights* (Oxford: Oxford University Press, 1981), p. vii.

49 Peter Coveney, *Poor Monkey: The Child in Literature* (London: Rockliff, 1957), re-published in a revised edition as *The Images of Childhood: The Individual and Society, A Study of the Theme in English Literature* (London: Penguin, 1967). Quoted from the 1957 edition, p. ix.

50 The examples Coveney uses are drawn particularly from Blake's *Songs of Innocence and of Experience* (1794) (poems **46** and **47** in Chapter 6); Wordsworth's 'Ode on intimations of immortality' (1802–06); Dickens's novels *Oliver Twist* (1838) and *Dombey and Son* (1848); and *Jane Eyre* and *Wuthering Heights* (both 1847).

51 Philippe Ariès, 'At the point of origin', *Yale French Studies* 43 (1969), pp. 15–23, stresses the importance of Charles Perrault's *Contes du temps passé* (1697) and asserts again that 'There is a great difference in attitudes toward children between the end of the seventeenth century and the reigns of Henry IV and Louis XIII. Elsewhere [*L'enfant* (1960)] I have given examples of how little attention and respect was given to children and their lives at the time of Montaigne and during the youth of Louis XIII. This remains true still longer among the people' (p. 19). This also echoes his essay on 'Games, fashions and society', in Philippe Ariès *et al., The World of Children* (London: Paul Hamlyn, 1966), pp. 10–09, where Ariès asserts the following (p. 101).

> In our Western civilization, down to the eighteenth century at least, the words 'games' and 'play' did not suggest anything childish. They formed part of the vocabulary of adults and the activities they described were common to both adults and children, partly because both groups

shared in the same ceremonies, partly because the notion of children as a separate group to be worried about and treated differently from adults did not exist.

However, it must also be recognised that children's literature was used for moral correction, for consolation, but also to celebrate the deaths of children whose piety was exemplary. James Janeway's little book, *A Token for Children: Being an Exact Account of the Conversion, Holy and Exemplary Lives, and Joyful Deaths of several young Children* (London: Printed for Dorman Newman, 1676), dating from the 1670s and reprinted many times, was especially popular. It contained the 'examples' of thirteen children (aged from 2 to 12) who found God and experienced 'triumphant' or 'joyful' deaths.

52 David Herlihy, 'Medieval children', in Bede Karl Lackner and Kenneth Roy Philip (eds), *Essays on Medieval Civilization: The Walter Prescott Webb Memorial Lectures* (Austin, TX: University of Austin Press, 1978), pp. 109–41. Neglected by, for instance, Orme in his book of the same title (2001). See also Albrecht Classen, 'Philippe Ariès and the consequences: history of childhood, family relations, and personal emotions: where do we stand today?', in Albrecht Classen (ed.), *Childhood in the Middle Ages and the Renaissance: The Results of a Paradigm Shift in the History of Mentality* (Berlin: Walter de Gruyter, 2005), pp. 1–66.

53 Herlihy, 'Medieval children' (1978), p. 124. One index used by Herlihy is the development of a new system of foundling hospitals to care for abandoned infants. The record of these hospitals is still under discussion; it might even be argued that their presence encouraged parental neglect. Mark Golden, 'Did the ancients care when their children died?', *Greece and Rome* 35 (1988), pp. 152–63, offers some interesting perspectives in relation to Greek and Roman societies, especially the way in which the discussion of child abandonment (effectively infanticide) has been influenced by Ariès and Stone.

54 Herlihy, 'Medieval children' (1978), p. 112.

55 Fernand Braudel, *On History*, translated by Sarah Matthews (London: Weidenfeld and Nicolson, 1980), a set of papers and essays originally published in a collected form as *Écrits sur l'histoire* (Paris: Flammarion, 1969).

56 Braudel, *On History* (1980), p. 51.

57 Marx was rather unclear about his theory of society, but see Terrell Carver, *Marx's Social Theory* (Oxford: Oxford University Press, 1982), pp. 38–39.

58 Michel Vovelle, 'Sur la mort', in *Idéologies et mentalités* (Paris: Libraire François Maspero, 1982), pp. 92–119 (Paris: Gallimard, 1992), pp. 109–27. 'On death', in Michel Vovelle, *Ideologies and Mentalities*, translated by Eamon O'Flaherty (Cambridge: Polity Press, 1990), pp. 64–80. The essay was originally presented at seminars in 1978–79. *Mourir autrefois: attitudes collectives devant la mort aux XVIIe et XVIIIe siècles* (Paris: Gallimard, 1974), pp. 9–11, contains the first brief outline of the three-levels model. Vovelle's other books on the history of death are: *La mort et l'Occident de 1300 à nos jours* (Paris: Gallimard, 1983), mainly on the image of death; *La ville des morts: essai sur l'imaginaire contemporain d'après les cimetières provençaux* (with Régis Bertrand) (Paris: CNRS, 1983), on the archaeology of southern French cemeteries; *L'heur du grand passage: chronique de la mort* (Paris: Gallimard, 1993), an interesting book of pictures; *Les âmes du purgatoire ou le travail du deuil* (Paris: Gallimard, 1996), an essay on images of purgatory and the way they have changed since the middle ages. See also Malcolm Crook (ed.), 'The work of Michel Vovelle', *French History* 19 (2005), pp. 143–88, for a celebration of his work, and especially Vovelle's 'Respnse', pp. 177–88, which focuses on the history of death.

59 Vovelle, 'On death' (1990), p. 66.

60 Vovelle's 'three-levels model' has generally been ignored by English scholars. One exception is to be found in Nigel Llewellyn, *Funeral Monuments in Post-Reformation England* (Cambridge: Cambridge University Press, 2000), p. 36. Llewellyn's approach is considered in Chapter 4.

61 Vovelle, 'On death' (1990), p. 78.

62 Jacques Le Goff, 'Mentalities: a history of ambiguities', in Jacques Le Goff and Pierre Nora (eds), *Constructing the Past: Essays in Historical Methodology* (Cambridge: Cambridge University Press, 1985), pp. 166–80, quoted from p. 173. Originally published in *Faire de l'histoire* (Paris: Gallimard, 1974).

63 Philippe Ariès, 'L'histoire des mentalités', in Jacques Le Goff, Roger Chartier and Jacques Revel (eds), *La nouvelle histoire* (Paris: Retz-CEPL, 1978), pp. 402–23.

64 Michel Vovelle, 'Ideologies and mentalities', in Raphael Samuel and Gareth Stedman Jones (eds), *Culture, Ideology and Politics* (London: Routledge & Kegan Paul, 1982), pp. 2–11, quoted from pp. 10–11. See also Michel Vovelle, 'L'histoire et la longue durée', in Jacques Le Goff, Roger Chartier and Jacques Revel (eds), *La nouvelle histoire* (Paris: Retz-CEPL, 1978), pp. 316–43.

65 Peter Burke, *History and Social Theory* (Cambridge: Polity Press, 1992), pp. 91–96, discusses the differences at greater length as well as linking the notions back to Marx and Durkheim.

66 Peter Burke, 'Strengths and weaknesses of the history of mentalities', *History of European Ideas* 7 (1986), pp. 439–51, quoted from p. 439. Stuart Clark, 'French historians and early modern popular culture', *Past and Present* 100 (1983), pp. 62–99, also makes some telling points about 'emotionalism' and the ways in which the forms taken by human emotions are likely to have been linked to 'shared experiences which changed through time', but he gives several warnings against employing today's categories and concepts in order to describe the past.

67 Burke is not daunted by these problems, rather he suggests that a greater concern for interests (in whose interest?), categories (what is associated, or contrasted, with what in whose thought?), and metaphors and symbols (how do modes of linguistic expression, oral or literate, influence modes of thought?) will help to revitalise the historical study of mentalities. See Burke, 'Strengths and weaknesses' (1986), and *History and Social Theory* (1992). His call appears to have fallen on deaf ears among historians.

68 We shall return to this distinction on several occasions in, for example, Chapter 5 ('grief work' and 'mourning work', and figure 5.1) and in Chapter 7 when we consider the language of grief (table 7.2, for example).

69 Michel Vovelle, *Piété baroque et déchristianisation en Provence au XVIIIe siècle* (Paris: Éditions Plon, 1973; Éditions du Seuil, 1978; Éditions du CTHS, 1997), figure 16, p. 124, in the 1997 edition. This figure has been widely reproduced, often with some minor modification, but it has also been pointed out that the time-series also reflects the rising mood of anti-clericalism in France during the eighteenth century and not just loss of religious belief. Michel Vovelle, 'A century and one-half of American epitaphs (1660–1813): toward the study of collective attitudes about death', *Comparative Studies in Society and History* 22 (1980), pp. 534–47, also illustrates Vovelle's thinking about mentalities and collective attitudes, and how their change may be measured. See Chapter 4, p. 94.

70 Vovelle, *Ideologies and Mentalities* (1990), pp. 177–203.

71 Emmanuel Le Roy Ladurie, 'Chaunu, Lebrun, Vovelle: the new history of death', in *The Territory of the Historian*, translated by Ben and Sian Reynolds (Hassocks, Sussex: Harvester Press, 1979), pp. 273–84, offers some interesting remarks on Vovelle's approach, especially his emphasis on how rather than why attitudes change.

72 Pierre Chaunu, *La mort à Paris, XVIe, XVIIe et XVIIIe siècles* (Paris: Fayard, 1978). See also Pierre Chaunu, 'Mourir à Paris (XVIe-XVIIIe siècles)', *Annales: ESC* 31 (1976), pp. 29–50.

73 Chaunu, 'Mourir à Paris' (1976), p. 30. As an economic historian of imports, exports, wages and prices Chaunu was undoubtedly one of the most enthusiastic advocates of quantitative methods among other French historians in the 1970s. See Pierre Chaunu, 'Un nouveau champ pour l'histoire sérielle: le quantitatif au troisième niveau', in *Histoire quantitative, histoire sérielle* (Paris: Librairie Armand Colin, 1978), pp. 216–30, originally published in 1973.

74 Vovelle, *Ideologies and Mentalities* (1990), pp. 24–35.

75 For example, Vovelle also indicates the importance of 'silences', what does not appear in literature, the 'habitually not-said'. Ariès's attempts to use *Jane Eyre* and *Wuthering Heights* should also be recalled at this point (pp. 19-21). Other ways of approaching level 3 have been considered in Gaby Vovelle and Michel Vovelle, *Vision de la mort et de l'au-delà en Provence d'après les autels des âmes du purgatoire XVe-XXe siècles* (Paris: Librairie Armand Colin, 1970) which focuses on the artistic representation of purgatory, a theme now popular among French historians. See also Vovelle, 'Response' (2005), pp. 185-88, where he reflects again on death as a forgotten theme.

76 Daniel Roche, '"La mémoire de la mort" Recherche sur la place des arts de mourir dans la Librairie et la lecture en France aux XVIIe et XVIIIe siècles', *Annales: ESC* 31 (1976), pp. 76-119.

3 Mortality, Childcare and Mourning

77 Simon Schama, *The Embarrassment of Riches: An Interpretation of Dutch Culture in the Golden Age* (London: Collins, 1987), p. 652, note 63. The footnote is to p. 531 on which Schama discusses the work of the Dutch midwife Catharina Schrader who between 1693 and 1745 kept a detailed account of her professional activities.

78 Jacques Dupâquier *et al.* (eds), *Histoire de la population française: 2, De la Renaissance à 1789* (Paris: Presses Universitaires de France, 1988), pp. 9-50, discusses the availability and quality of French demographic sources. See also: Jacques Dupâquier *et al.* (eds), *Histoire de la population française: 3, De 1789 à 1914* (Paris: Presses Universitaires de France, 1988); Jacques Dupâquier, *La population française aux XVIIe et XVIIIe siècles* (Paris: Presses Universitaires de France, third edition, 1995, first edition, 1979); Agnès Fine and Jean-Claude Sangoli, *La population française au XIXe siècle* (Paris: Presses Universitaires de France, 1991). Noël Bonneuil, *Transformation of the French Demographic Landscape, 1806-1906* (Oxford: Clarendon Press, 1997) assesses the quality of French demographic data in the nineteenth century, and the contributors to Catherine Le Grand-Sébille, Marie-France Morel and Françoise Zonabend (eds), *Le foetus, le nourrisson et la mort* (Paris: L'Harmattan, 1998) consider reactions to early-age deaths in France.

79 Louis Henry, *Techniques d'analyse en démographie historique* (Paris: INED, 1980) outlines the various methods developed by Henry and others to analyse French sources of historical data.

80 Family reconstitution involves the linking of named individuals from register to register: baptism to burial; baptism to marriage to baptism of offspring to marriage of offspring to burial, for example. It is particularly effective where the population is immobile; where there are distinctive family names; where the parish clerk or priest is very conscientious; where baptism occurs immediately after live birth; where stillbirths are not disguised as live births to enable baptism to take place; where all residents of the parish are involved in every ecclesiastical event which can then be used as proxies for vital events (baptism for live birth, burial for death); and where it is possible to derive the 'at risk' population, those at risk of dying by age and sex, of marrying, of giving birth.

81 René Berthieu, 'Les nourrissons à Cormeilles-en-Parisis (1640-1789)', *Annales de Démographie Historique* (1975), pp. 259-89; Alain Bideau, 'L'envoi des jeunes enfants en nourrice. L'example d'une petite ville: Thoissey-en-Dombes (1740-1840)', in *Hommage à Marcel Reinhard. Sur la population française au XVIIIe et au XIXe siècles* (Paris: Société de Démographie Historique, 1973), pp. 49-58; and Jean Ganiage, 'Nourrissons parisiens en Beauvaisis', also in *Hommage à Marcel Reinhard* (1973), pp. 271-90, provide important examples of attempts to analyse the demographic and social significance of *la mise en nourrice*. For detailed surveys of the French experience see: François Lebrun, *La vie conjugale sous l'Ancien Régime* (Paris: Armand Colin, 1975), pp. 111-39, and especially Pierre Goubert and Daniel Roche, *Le français et l'Ancien Régime. 2. Culture et société* (Paris: Armand Colin, third edition, 2000), pp. 100-77.

82 Dupâquier *et al.*, *Histoire de la population française: 2* (1988), table 10, p. 230. Jean-Louis Flandrin, *Families in Former Times: Kinship, Household and Sexuality* (Cambridge: Cambridge University

Press, 1979), originally published as *Familles: parenté, maison, sexualité* (Paris: Librairie Hachette, 1976), pp. 198–209, emphasises the links between marital fertility, infant mortality and the effects of wet-nursing in seventeenth- and eighteenth-century France.

83 Etienne van de Walle and Samuel H. Preston, 'Mortalité de l'enfance au XIXe siècle à Paris et dans le département de la Seine', *Population* 29 (1974), pp. 89–107, table A.1, p. 103.

84 Figure 3.6 has been redrawn from data given in Dupâquier *et al.*, *Histoire de la population française: 3* (1988), p. 281. It should be remembered that France was at war during these years, and that urban and rural mortality are not separated. Goubert and Roche, *Le français et l'Ancien Régime. 2* (2000), p. 122, give an infant mortality rate in the range 200–400 for the beginning of the eighteenth century and suggest that regional variations were associated with the following: a naturally unhealthy environment (e.g. marshes of the Sologne region); wealth distribution; the effects of urbanisation; and the presence of infants put out to wet-nurse.

85 Dupâquier *et al.*, *Histoire de la population française: 2* (1988), p. 225. These estimates are based on the substantial collection of village studies undertaken by Louis Henry and his colleagues at the Institut National d'Études Démographiques in Paris during the 1950s and 1960s. It should also be noted that there appear to have been significant regional variations in the extent of infant deaths registration during the seventeenth and eighteenth centuries; the northeast and northwest were better provided for than the southwest and southeast.

86 Lebrun, *La vie conjugale* (1975), pp. 118–20. See also Elisabeth Badinter, *Mother Love: Myth and Reality of Motherhood in Modern History* (New York: Macmillan, 1981) translated from *L'amour en plus: Histoire de l'amour maternal, XVIIe-XXe siècle* (Paris: Flammarion, 1980).

87 Gautier and Henry, *Crulai* (1958), p. 170. Henry, *Techniques* (1980), p. 79, thinks that *les ondoyés décédés* may represent 3 per cent of births although he acknowledges that this proportion could be substantially higher in some cases. Alain Bideau, 'Accouchement 'naturel' et accouchement à 'haut risqué'', *Annales de Démographie Historique* (1981), pp. 49–66, comes to roughly the same conclusion using the example of a single village, but he also stresses the importance of high-risk subgroups within the general population. Catherine Rollet, 'Lorsque la mort devint mortalité', in Catherine Le Grand-Sébille *et al.* (eds), *Le foetus, le nourrisson et la mort* (Paris: L'Harmattan, 1998), pp. 105–26, illustrates the importance of cultural, especially religious, values and registration practices in relation to stillbirths. She shows (p. 117) a map of France for 1907–10 giving the proportion of all stillborn (*les mort-nés*) who were said to have breathed (14.8 per cent in France as a whole); these were *les faux mort-nés*. The regions with the highest proportions (over 18 per cent) were Brittany, parts of the Massif Central and Savoy, all areas with a high religious affiliation. Jacques Gélis, 'Miracle et médecine aux siècles classiques: le corps medical et le retour temporaire à la vie des morts-nés', *Historical Reflections* 9 (1982), pp. 85–101, has found examples of how 'signs of life' might be recognised in a 'dead-born' infant just so that it could be baptised. Arthur E. Imhof, *Lost Worlds: How Our European Ancestors Coped with Everyday Life and Why Life Is So Hard Today* (Charlottesville, VA: University of Virginia Press, 1996), p. 132, also describes these *Kinderzeichnen* as they were used in southern Germany.

88 Dupâquier, *La population française* (1995), p. 100. He proposes a $q(0-9)$ of 393 per 1000 and an $e(20)$ of 32 years for the rural parts of the Paris Basin during the reign of Louis XIV (p. 64). This suggests a lower level of mortality than most of those estimates shown in table 3.1 with an $e(0)$ of 30–32 years (closer to Crulai).

89 The post-1837 civil registration based estimates apply to England and Wales while the parish register based estimates for periods prior to 1837 are either for specific parishes, usually villages, or they represent attempts to combine data from a number of parish studies in order to approximate conditions in England. High-quality family reconstitution studies have not been possible in Wales where the range of family names is limited. Baptisms, burials and marriages continued to be recorded in parish registers after 1837, but the civil registration of births, deaths and marriages

should be far superior for demographic purposes. See E. A. Wrigley, R. S. Davies, J. E. Oeppen and R. S. Schofield, *English Population History from Family Reconstitution, 1580–1837* (Cambridge: Cambridge University Press, 1997), and Robert Woods, *The Demography of Victorian England and Wales* (Cambridge: Cambridge University Press, 2000) for discussions of the varying quality of these sources.

90   Chapter 2, pp. 14–17.

91   This brief description hardly does justice to the highly sophisticated analysis summarised in Wrigley *et al.*, *English Population History* (1997), and E. A. Wrigley and R. S. Schofield, *The Population History of England, 1541–1871: A Reconstruction* (London: Edward Arnold, 1981). The latter describes the back projection model devised to estimate $e(0)$, along with a number of other demographic measures including total population size and the level of fertility.

92   These problems are all well known and have been rehearsed many times. What is less obvious, however, is exactly what effects there are likely to have been on specific components of the mortality pattern. Chris Galley, Naomi Williams and Robert Woods, 'Detection without correction: problems in assessing the quality of English ecclesiastical and civil registration', *Annales de Démographie Historique* (1995), pp. 161–83, focuses on the early-age mortality series.

93   Roger Schofield, 'Did the mothers really die? Three centuries of maternal mortality in "The World We Have Lost"', in Lloyd Bonfield, Richard M. Smith and Keith Wrightson (eds), *The World We Have Gained: Histories of Population and Social Structure* (Oxford: Basil Blackwell, 1986), pp. 131–60. Maternal mortality is especially difficult to estimate in the absence of accurate cause of death data which can be used to identify the particular reasons for deaths during or as a direct consequence of pregnancy. During the parish register period rates must relate to those females who died (were buried) within a specified period after producing a live born (baptised) infant. The specified period is usually taken as sixty days, but thirty would do nearly as well. Schofield shows how it is also important to adjust for (1) normal background mortality which is likely to affect females in the reproductive age group; (2) cases where the mother dies after producing a stillborn child; and (3) those cases where there is no record of a child being born, live or still. In the case of sources [2] and [4] in table 3.3, the same correction procedure has been applied. What differs is the number of family reconstitution studies involved (13 in [2] and 26 in [4]) and thus the basic MMR related to live births.

94   Schofield, 'Did the mothers really die?' (1986), table 9.7, p. 248. However, Schofield rather plays down the matter of heightened risk arguing that people in the past are unlikely to have 'thought in terms of probabilities cumulated over a span of years' (p. 259), and that 'the risk of dying in childbed was no greater than the risk she ran every year of dying from infectious disease and a whole variety of other causes' (p. 260). Edward Shorter, *A History of Women's Bodies* (New York: Basic Books, 1982), pp. 69–102, argues that 6 to 10 per cent of women died in or after childbirth, and that from 1 up to 2 per cent of all births ended in the mother's death. But Shorter relies on cases from the records of lying-in hospitals rather than the more general demographic accounts. Similarly, Audrey Eccles, *Obstetrics and Gynaecology in Tudor and Stuart England* (London: Croom Helm, 1982), p. 125, suggests that the maternal mortality rate for England in the sixteenth and seventeenth centuries was obviously high and may have been 250 per 10,000 birth events, that is five or six times higher than in the nineteenth century. She appears to have been especially influenced by the case notes prepared by certain men-midwives. Bideau, 'Accouchement' (1981) also presents high estimates for maternal mortality in one French village (Mogneneins, 1660–1814): 98 maternal deaths can be linked to 4153 deliveries, or 236 per 10,000 birth events.

95   Robert Woods, 'The measurement of historical trends in fetal mortality in England and Wales', *Population Studies* 59 (2005), pp. 147–62, discusses the derivation of these SBR estimates in detail.

96   Jacques Dupâquier, 'Pour une histoire de la prématurité', *Annales de Démographie Historique*

(1994), pp. 187–202, and Etienne van de Walle, 'Pour une histoire démographique de l'avortement', *Population* 53 (1998), pp. 273–90, offer some interesting views on prematurity, perinatal mortality and abortion, but they are not able to provide a quantitative perspective on fetal mortality prior to the nineteenth century. This point is reflected by table 3.1.

97   Philippe Ariès, 'Attitudes devant la vie et devant la mort du XVIIe au XIXe siècle', *Population* 4 (1949), pp. 463–70; 'Sur les origines de la contraception en France', *Population* 8 (1953), pp. 465–72; 'Deux contributions à l'histoire des practiques contraceptives: Chaucer et Mme de Sévigné', *Population* 9 (1954), pp. 692–98. Jean-Pierre Bardet and Jacques Dupâquier, 'Contraception: les Français les premiers, mais porquoi?', *Communications* 44 (1986), pp. 3–33, reviews the principal issues, as well as returning to Ariès's use of Montaigne (p. 14).

98   For example, Etienne van de Walle and Francine van de Walle, 'Allaitement, stérilité et contraception: les opinions jusqu'au XIXe siècle', *Population* 27 (1972), pp. 685–701, on the effects of breast-feeding and Etienne van de Walle, '"Marvellous secrets": Birth control in European short fiction, 1150–1650', *Population Studies* 54 (2000), pp. 321–30, on literary evidence for birth control.

99   This brief outline does not do justice to the full, long and complicated story. See Dupâquier *et al.* (eds), *Histoire de la population française: 2* (1988), pp. 349–411, and E. A. Wrigley, 'The fall of marital fertility in nineteenth-century France: exemplar or exception?', in *People, Cities and Wealth* (Oxford: Basil Blackwell, 1987), pp. 270–321. It also gives too much attention to France and England. Imhof, *Lost Worlds* (1996), pp. 81–87, compares the experiences of two German villages for the period 1780–1899, although he regards them as 'patterns of long duration'. Hesel (East Frisia, Lutheran, northern Germany) had an IMR of 130 while Gabelbach (Swabia, Roman Catholic, southern Germany) had one of 340. In Hesel there were 794 maternal deaths within forty-one days of childbirth per 10,000 mothers, while in Gabelbach here were 1068 deaths. 'The villagers from Hesel developed a greater respect for the lives of wives and mothers, or, seen from the point of view of mothers, a greater fear of death from childbirth' (p. 82). Would it be too simple to substitute England for Hesel and France for Gabelbach?

100 Keith Thomas, 'Children in early modern England', in Gillian Avery and Julia Briggs (eds), *Children and their Books: A Celebration of the Work of Iona and Peter Opie* (Oxford: Clarendon Press, 1989), pp. 45–77, makes the useful distinction between the history of children and the history of adult attitudes to children. It also describes children, like women, as a 'muted group' whose history has to be excavated, and, for this reason, it acknowledges that such a history is extremely difficult to construct tending as it does to focus on the visible and material (toys, games, education) rather than the emotional. Here we persist with the traditional approach by emphasising the views of adults.

101 Jay Mechling, 'Advice to historians on advice to mothers', *Journal of Social History* 9 (1975), pp. 44–63, makes some very critical and telling points about the use by historians of childrearing advice manuals as evidence of childrearing behaviour. The importance of learning parenting from one's parents is stressed in particular. Alice Judson Ryerson, 'Medical advice on child rearing, 1550–1900', *Harvard Educational Review* 31 (1961), pp. 302–23, avoids this problem by dealing simply with advice. She shows some very interesting time-series for certain medical recommendations, such as swaddling, breastfeeding, age at weaning, all of which tend to change substantially in the mid-eighteenth century. Adrian Wilson, 'Participant or patient? Seventeenth century childbirth from the mother's point of view', in Roy Porter (ed.), *Patients and Practitioners: Lay Perceptions of Medicine in Pre-industrial Society* (Cambridge: Cambridge University Press, 1985), pp. 129–44, also has good advice for historians: try to adopt the mother's perspective and not the professional's.

102 The literature in this field has grown considerably in recent years; the following offer some guidance. Ralph Houlbrooke, *The English Family, 1450–1700* (London: Longman, 1984), especially chapter 6, 'Parents and children: infancy and childhood'; Mary Prior (ed.), *Women in English*

Society, 1500–1800 (London: Methuen, 1985); Valerie Fildes (ed.), *Women as Mothers in Pre-Indus-trial England* (London: Routledge, 1990); Laura Gowing, *Common Bodies: Women, Touch and Power in Seventeenth-Century England* (New Haven, CT: Yale University Press, 2003); Jacques Gélis, Mireille Laget and Marie-France Morel, *Entrer dans la vie: naissances et enfances dans la France traditionelle* (Paris: Éditions Gallimard, 1978); Mireille Laget, *Naissances: L'accouchement avant l'age de la clinique* (Paris: Éditions du Seuil, 1982); Jacques Gélis, *History of Childbirth: Fertility, Pregnancy and Birth in Early Modern Europe* (London: Polity Press, 1991) originally published as *L'arbre et le fruit* (Paris: Libraire Arthème Fayard, 1984), and especially his *La sage-femme ou le médecin: une nouvelle conception de la vie* (Paris: Fayard, 1988).

103   This is, perhaps, a rather pessimistic conclusion, but it is difficult to read the textbooks and case notes prepared by women- and men-midwives during the early modern period, or Jacques Gélis's detailed survey, particularly for France (*History of Childbirth* (1991), especially pp. 157–254), without being sceptical about what was understood and what positive measures could be taken to assist the pregnant woman and the fetus. Linda A. Pollock, 'Embarking on a rough passage: the experience of pregnancy in early-modern society', in Valerie Fildes (ed.), *Women as Mothers in Pre-Industrial England* (London: Routledge, 1990), pp. 39–67, describes a similar picture. The midwives' question is an especially interesting one which recent research has helped to outline in terms of knowledge, institutional organisation etc., but has done little to illustrate in terms of suc-cess rate and contribution to survival chances. See Hilary Marland (ed.), *The Art of Midwifery: Early Modern Midwives in Europe* (London: Routledge, 1993); Adrian Wilson, *The Making of Man-Midwifery: Childbirth in England, 1660–1770* (London: UCL Press, 1995); and Lisa Forman Cody, 'Living and dying in Georgian London's lying-in hospitals', *Bulletin of the History of Medi-cine* 78 (2004), pp. 309–48; also Hilary Marland (ed.), *Mother and Child were Saved* (Amster-dam: Rodopi, 1987) which edits and translates the memoirs (1693–1740) of the Dutch midwife Catharina Schrader (1656–1746) mentioned by Simon Schama, see note 77. The French experi-ence is summarised in Lebrun, *La vie conjugale* (1975), pp. 111–39; and Goubert and Roche, *Le français et l'Ancien Régime. 2* (2000), pp. 100–77; while Mireille Laget, 'La naissance aux siècles classiques. Pratique des accouchements et attitudes collectives en France aux XVIIe et XVIIIe siècles', *Annales: ESC* 32 (1977), pp. 958–92, provides a particularly good example of how fruitful the combination of textual, social and demographic analysis can be in this area.. Research on the wives of British peers by Judith Schneid Lewis, 'Maternal health in the English aristocracy: myths and realities, 1790–1840', *Journal of Social History* 17(1) (1983), pp. 97–114, and her *In the Family Way: Childbearing in the British Aristocracy, 1760–1860* (New Brunswick, NJ: Rutgers University Press, 1986), focuses on 50 well-documented cases in which both early-age and maternal mortality were low (50 women produced 393 live births, had 32 miscarriages and 6 stillbirths; there were 39 infant deaths and 2 maternal deaths). It cannot be assumed that induced abortion and infanticide were insignificant in the past, yet questions concerning their exact levels still pose more problems for demographers than social or literary historians who are content to cite instances and elaborate cultural significances. See Peter C. Hoffer and N. E. H. Hull, *Murdering Mothers: Infanticide in England and New England, 1558–1803* (New York: New York University Press, 1984), and the introduction to Josephine McDonagh, *Child Murder and British Culture, 1720–1900* (Cambridge: Cambridge University Press, 2003).

104   See, especially, Patricia Crawford, '"The sucking child": Adult attitudes to child care in the first year of life in seventeenth-century England', *Continuity and Change* 1 (1986), pp. 23–51, and her *Blood, Bodies and Families in Early Modern England* (London: Pearson Longman, 2004). Rudolf Dekker, *Childhood, Memory and Autobiography in Holland: From the Golden Age to Romanticism* (London: Macmillan, 2000), p. 99, makes the entirely reasonable point that to hire a wet-nurse could be construed as a 'gesture of care' in those circumstances where the mother could not breast-feed. The alternative was to give the baby some form of pap. He also provides examples of cases in

which the wet-nurse and the child developed a lasting emotional attachment.

105 Linda Pollock, '"Teach her to live under obedience": The making of women in the upper ranks of early modern England', *Continuity and Change* 4 (1989), pp. 231–58; Sara Mendelson and Patricia Crawford, *Women in Early Modern England, 1550–1720* (Oxford: Clarendon Press, 1998), and Crawford, *Blood, Bodies and Families* (2004) survey these complicated issues. On the question of literacy, see Adam Fox, *Oral and Literate Culture in England, 1500–1700* (Oxford: Oxford University Press, 2000), especially pp. 14–19. His estimates suggest that, around 1600, 30 per cent of men and 10 per cent of women may have had 'basic reading skills' with the differential declining as literacy levels improved during the following centuries.

106 Ralph Houlbrooke, *Death, Religion, and the Family in England, 1480–1750* (Oxford: Clarendon Press, 1998), pp. 234–37; the first paragraph is quoted in full while the following six sentences are the first in the six subsequent paragraphs. The specific point about diaries is considered in Chapter 5 (p. 104).

107 The contributors to Peter C. Jupp and Clare Gittings (eds), *Death in England: An Illustrated History* (Manchester: Manchester University Press, 1999) make very little of the deaths of children before the nineteenth century, see pp. 210–15 and 237–42. Julian Litten, *The English Way of Death: The Common Funeral since 1450* (London: Robert Hale, 1991), pp. 61–65, uses brasses and carved effigies to illustrate the various ways in which infants were prepared for burial, but his chapter on 'The common funeral' (pp. 143–71) does not mention the funerals of children, although it does chart the various practices co-ordinated by clergy, undertakers and the 'Order for the Burial of the Dead' in the *Book of Common Prayer*.

108 Will Coster, 'Tokens of innocence: infant baptism, death and burial in early modern England', in Bruce Gordon and Peter Marshall (eds), *The Place of the Dead: Death and Remembrance in Late Medieval and Early Modern Europe* (Cambridge: Cambridge University Press, 2000), pp. 266–87, discusses the way in which the term 'chrisom infant' appears to have changed its meaning in sixteenth- and seventeenth-century England from one relating to infants who died before their mothers had undergone the churching ceremony of purification at about a month after giving birth, to an unbaptised infant, to the even more general sense of a child under a month old. See also Will Coster, *Baptism and Spiritual Kinship in Early Modern England* (London: Ashgate, 2002).

109 Coster, 'Tokens of innocence' (2000) attempts to chart these changes in seventeenth-century England. See also, Anne Laurence, 'Godly grief: individual responses to death in seventeenth-century Britain', in Ralph Houlbrooke (ed.), *Death, Ritual, and Bereavement* (London: Routledge, 1989), pp. 62–76; Clare Gittings, *Death, Burial and the Individual in Early Modern England* (London: Croom Helm, 1984); Gillian Avery and Kimberley Reynolds (eds), *Representations of Childhood Death* (London: Macmillan, 2000).

110 David E. Stannard, *The Puritan Way of Death: A Study in Religion, Culture, and Social Change* (New York: Oxford University Press, 1977) especially chapter 3, 'Death and childhood', pp. 58–59. However, it is important to note the differences between the New England communities identified by Philip Greven, *The Protestant Temperament: Patterns of Child-Rearing, Religious Experience, and the Self in Early America* (New York: Alfred A. Knopf, 1977). He singles out the 'evangelical', the 'moderate' and the 'genteel' ministers–congregations each of which had a rather different approach to sin and the infant (p. 12). In these matters the evangelical Puritans were the most extreme and the least compromising, while for the moderates: 'They welcomed their children into the world with pleasure, affection and happy anticipation of the years to come, during which their children would grow to maturity and become responsible and virtuous members of the community' (p. 156). It is also worth noting in passing that colonial New England is believed to have experienced 'a relatively benign demographic regime' in which life expectancy at birth could have been as high as 50 years even in the late seventeenth century. Infant mortality rates of

112–115 have been derived for small towns such as Andover, Massachusetts, but these may not allow for the under-registration of infant deaths, and they appear to have worsened to 150 in the eighteenth century. It is very unlikely that infant mortality was so low in the larger towns, Boston included. See Philip J. Greven, *Four Generations: Population, Land, and Family in Colonial Andover, Massachusetts* (Ithaca, NY: Cornell University Press, 1970); Robert V. Wells, 'The population of England's colonies in America: old English or new Americans?', *Population Studies* 46 (1992), pp. 85–102, especially table 3, pp. 94–95, which compares life expectancies for England and the American colonies; Daniel Scott Smith and J. David Hacker, 'Cultural demography: New England deaths and puritan perception of risk', *Journal of Interdisciplinary History* 26 (1996), pp. 367–92; and Robert V. Wells, *Facing the "King of Terrors": Death and Society in an American Community, 1750–1990* (Cambridge: Cambridge University Press, 2000). Nancy Schrom Dye and Daniel Blake Smith, 'Mother love and infant death, 1750–1920', *Journal of American History* 73 (1986), pp. 329–53, focus attention on demographic and attitudinal changes in the twentieth century.

111 Philippe Ariès, 'Two successive motivations for the declining birth rate in the West', *Population and Development Review* 6 (1980), pp. 645–50, quoted from p. 645.

112 For example, Laurence, 'Godly grief' (1989), p. 65, 'The incidence of death inevitably affects the experience of death and thus of grief'; and Goubert and Roche, *Le français et l'Ancien Régime. 2* (2000), p. 123, quote the saying 'Petits enfants, petits deuils'.

113 Two recent studies have challenged conventional assumptions by focusing explicitly on grief and mourning in nineteenth-century England: Pat Jalland, *Death in the Victorian Family* (Oxford: Oxford University Press, 1996), especially pp. 119–42, and Julie-Marie Strange, *Death, Grief and Poverty in Britain, 1870–1914* (Cambridge: Cambridge University Press, 2005), especially pp. 230–62. Both take a short-term perspective; both are 'class driven' in their interpretations; and neither one is demographically sensitive. Jalland is mainly concerned with the middle classes and the role of religion. She observes that 'The grief of Victorian parents for adult children may have exceeded that for very young children, because such deaths were not expected beyond the age of 10, and the emotional investment was far greater' (p. 277). Strange is highly critical of Jalland's approach, her neglect of the working classes and her particular use of diaries (p. 9); she is sceptical about Ariès's theories and speculations (pp. 18–19); and she regards the Victorian culture of death as a 'myth of our making' (p. 20). On the more substantive side, Strange makes some important points about Victorian burial practices, especially in relation to the disposal of stillbirths (pp. 240–43) and the cost of funerals and interments in general. Her conclusion is particularly perceptive (p. 262).

> High infant mortality rates did not annul the hope that one's children would live. Indeed, it is worth remembering that whilst infant death was common, a great many children survived, even in the cities with the worst infant mortality rates, to reach adulthood. The language of resignation was part of a common vocabulary in which people aimed to make sense of life and death; the fatalism commonly associated with bereavement could express many things, not least a sense of exhaustion and weariness. Material circumstances were not irrelevant to responses to death.

As we shall see, these remarks could be extended to cover several centuries rather than merely late Victorian and Edwardian Britain.

4 Children in Pictures and Monuments

114 Francis Haskell, *History and its Images: Art and the Interpretation of the Past* (New Haven, CT: Yale University Press, 1993), pp. 9–10. This survey offers an important account of the uses of art by historians. Peter Burke, *Eyewitnessing: The Uses of Images as Historical Evidence* (London: Reak-

tion, 2001) also provides a balanced, yet generally positive summary, and Shearer West, *Portraiture*, Oxford History of Art (Oxford: Oxford University Press, 2004) gives an extremely readable account of the history of portrait painting. As far as the portrayal of children is concerned, there have been several book-length treatments: Margaret Boyd Carpenter, *The Child in Art* (London: Methuen, 1906); Anita Schorsch, *Images of Childhood: An Illustrated Social History* (New York: Mayflower Books, 1979); Sara Holdsworth and Joan Crossley (eds), *Innocence and Experience: Images of Children in British Art from 1600 to the Present* (Manchester: Manchester City Art Galleries, 1992); Jan Baptist Bedaux and Rudi Ekkart (eds), *Pride and Joy: Children's Portraits in the Netherlands, 1500–1700* (New York: Harry N. Abrams, 2001); Marie-Christine Autin Graz, *Children in Painting* (Milan: Skira Editore, 2002); Marilyn R. Brown (ed.), *Picturing Children: Constructions of Childhood between Rousseau and Freud* (London: Ashgate, 2002). Over-zealous extraction of meaning is often associated with Erwin Panofsky, *Meaning in the Visual Arts* (New York: Doubleday, 1955; London: Penguin, 1970) and especially his essay 'Iconography and iconology' originally published in 1939. Here Panofsky distinguishes between three strata of meaning: (1) simple description, primary, natural, factual; (2) iconography which requires knowledge of the conventions being used by the artist, the 'disguised symbolism' for instance; (3) iconology, that is, the intrinsic meaning or content, which may involve interpretation of the basic, probably unconscious, attitudes, feelings and emotions of the artist. This chapter is content to remain at levels 1 and 2, although 3 is attempted on occasions.

115 Andor Pigler, 'Portraying the dead: painting – graphic art', *Acta Historiae Artium Academiae Scientarium Hungaricae* 4 (1957), pp. 1–74. Frederick Parkes Weber, *Aspects of Death and Correlated Aspects of Life in Art, Epigram, and Poetry. Contributions Towards an Anthology and an Iconography of the Subject*. (London: T. Fisher Unwin, 1922; first edition, 1910) provides a collection of articles which, despite the title, deal mainly with the iconography of death in medals and coins. However, there is also an interesting discussion of death in medieval and renaissance art, especially 'the dance of death' motifs, death's heads and artistic skeletons. Bert C. Sliggers (ed.), *Naar het lijk: Het Nederlandse doodsportret 1500-heden* (Zutphen: Teylers Museum, 1998) contains many important discussions of Dutch attitudes to death, especially those reflected in art, including Jan Baptist Bedaux, 'Funeraire kinder-portretten uit de 17de eeaw', pp. 86–115. Karl S. Guthke, *The Gender of Death: A Cultural History in Art and Literature* (Cambridge: Cambridge University Press, 1999) makes an important contribution partly by combining artistic and literary evidence, but it focuses on gender rather than age categories. Although Elizabeth Klaver (ed.), *Images of the Corpse: From the Renaissance to Cyberspace* (Madison, WI: University of Wisconsin Press, 2004) gives many interesting examples of ways in which corpses have been represented, its contributors neglect paintings of dead bodies in general, preferring to concentrate on the autopsy and literary accounts. Pigler goes unmentioned.

116 Pigler, 'Portraying the dead' (1957), pp. 2 and 69.

117 Pigler, 'Portraying the dead' (1957), p. 43. Three examples are provided, pp. 50, 51 and 66 (Hungarian example, baby in swaddling clothes). Ann Sumner (ed.), *Death, Passion and Politics: Van Dyck's Portraits of Venetia Stanley and George Digby* (London: Dulwich Picture Gallery, 1995), p. 119, provides two additional Dutch examples from the same period. Also in this collection, Clare Gittings, 'Venetia's death and Kenelm's mourning', pp. 54–68, has a highly revealing analysis of Sir Kenelm Digby grieving for his wife who died suddenly in 1633 (11 in table 4.1).

118 Philippe Ariès, *Images of Man and Death* (Cambridge, MA: Harvard University Press, 1985), pp. 247 and 252. Ariès gives two examples (p. 207) of the representation of dead children before the eighteenth century: one a Dutch painting of the seventeenth century and a second of an infant in swaddling bands on a tombstone. However, several illustrations are shown for the nineteenth century in his chapter on 'The death of others' (pp. 241–65), especially cemetery effigies of children. In his 1951 essay 'L'attitude devant l'histoire: le XVIIe siècle', reprinted in *Le temps de*

l'histoire (Monaco: Editions du Rocher, 1954), pp. 155–256, Ariès discusses the history of picture and antiquity collections, *les galeries historiques* and *les musées iconographiques* of the kings and nobles which were used to display family connections and continuities (pp. 195–214). Jean-Pierre Néraudau, *Être enfant á Rome* (Paris: Societé d'Éditions Les Belles Lettres, 1984) has taken up this challenge in the case of ancient Rome, especially in the chapter on 'La mort de l'enfant' (pp. 373–92), by using pictorial in combination with literary evidence.

119 Louis Hautecoeur, *Les peintres de la vie familiale: évolution d'un thème* (Paris: Éditions de la Galerie Charpentier, 1945) provides a catalogue of French paintings held in Paris in 1944 as well as a detailed commentary on many other largely French family paintings, especially from the seventeenth to the nineteenth centuries. Artists such as Le Nain (father and brothers), de la Tour, Nocret, Watteau, Chardin, Greuze, Fragonard, David, Millet, Manet, Monet, Renoir, Berthe Morisot, Degas, Seurat, Bonnard and many others are illustrated. Jeaurat's *Le départ de la nourrice* and Mallet's *Visite à la nourrice* are also illustrated. This was a particularly useful source for, or confirmation of, Ariès's ideas on the family and iconography. Very few historical demographers have explored the possibility of using family portraits, but a notable exception is Arthur E. Imhof, *Lost Worlds: How Our European Ancestors Coped with Everyday Life and Why Life Is So Hard Today* (Charlottesville, VA: University of Virginia Press, 1996), pp. 59–64. Imhof uses paintings by Jan Steen, Gonzales Coques and Frans Hals to consider the effects of religion on family size in the seventeenth-century Netherlands. He has no clear answer to his own question, however.

120 Burke, *Eyewitnessing* (2001), pp. 104–08, discusses images of children and Ariès's contribution to popularising their analysis as a source of historical evidence. See also the illustrations to Linda A. Pollock, 'Parent–child relations', in David I. Kertzer and Marizio Barbagli (eds), *Family Life in Early Modern Times, 1500–1789* (New Haven, CT: Yale University Press, 2001), pp. 191–220.

121 Philippe Ariès, *Centuries of Childhood* (London: Penguin, 1973), p. 341.

122 Ariès, *Centuries of Childhood* (1973), p. 338.

123 Jonathan Goldberg, 'Fatherly authority: the politics of Stuart family images', in Margaret W. Ferguson, Maureen Quilligan and Nancy J. Vickers (eds), *Rewriting the Renaissance: The Discourses of Sexual Difference in Early Modern Europe* (Chicago: University of Chicago Press, 1986), pp. 3–32, for example, remarks that 'Readings of the family in such political matrices are only possible thanks to the ongoing revaluation of the idea of the family that owes its impetus to the pioneering work of Philippe Ariès, whose *Centuries of Childhood* first studied the family not as a natural unit but as a social institution with a history' (p. 6). Goldberg's argument that family images were 'ideological constructs' is a particularly powerful one to which we shall return. As he says, 'Reproduction as trope is not reproduction in fact' (p. 8).

124 Ilene H. Forsyth, 'Children in early medieval art: ninth through twelfth centuries', *Journal of Psychohistory* 4 (1976), pp. 31–70, quoted from p. 33.

125 Nicholas Orme, *Medieval Children* (New Haven, CT: Yale University Press, 2001), p. 9. See also p. 17 above and David Herlihy, 'Medieval children', in Bede Karl Lackner and Kenneth Roy Philip (eds), *Essays on Medieval Civilization: The Walter Prescott Webb Memorial Lectures* (Austin, TX: University of Austin Press, 1978), pp. 109–41. Pierre Riché and Danièle Alexandre-Bidon, *L'enfance au Moyen Age* (Paris: Seuil, Bibliothèque Nationale de France, 1994) has the most comprehensive assessment of children and childhood as represented in medieval art. Most of the examples are taken from Italian and French illustrated manuscripts, but they do show infants and children in many different roles: being born, learning to walk (with a walking frame), at school, at play, at work, with their mothers or fathers, growing up. However, the first examples provided of children as the subjects of portrait paintings are (p. 65), *Portrait of the Dauphin Charles Orlant, son of Charles VIII, aged 26 months*, 1494 (Louvre, Paris) by Jean Hey, Maître de Moulins (the dauphin died in 1495); and (p. 92) two father and son portraits from late fifteenth-century Italy including *Portrait of an old man and his grandson*, c.1490 (Louvre, Paris) by Domenico Ghir-

landaio (1449–94). Although their identity is not know (the old man's nose is disfigured by a skin disease), it is clear that the viewer is intended to see a close bond between the two.

126 James Christen Steward, *The New Child: British Art and the Origins of Modern Childhood, 1730–1830* (Berkeley, CA: University Art Museum and Pacific Film Archive, University of California, Berkeley, 1995), p. 19. The 'new child' in eighteenth-century British art is still a popular theme, and one usually treated in an uncritical way. See, for example, Hannah Neale, 'The changing face of childhood in British portraiture of the 18th century', in *Pictures of Innocence: Children in 18th-century Portraiture, A Guide to the Exhibition at Abbot Hall Art Gallery, Kendal, 12 July to 8 October 2005* (Kendal: Lakeland Arts Trust, 2005), pp. 5–9.

127 Steward, *The New Child* (1995), p. 82. It is also worth noting that Steward provides a substantial amount of critical comment on the Ariès interpretation in general although it may be significant that he does not refer to the original illustrated edition of *L'enfant* (1960), but the 1973 abridged and unillustrated French reprint. Anne Higonnet, *Pictures of Innocence: The History and Crisis of Ideal Childhood* (London: Thames and Hudson, 1998), p. 25, has also been critical of Ariès and made the same mistake about *L'enfant*.

128 Karin Calvert, 'Children in American family portraiture, 1670 to 1810', *William and Mary Quarterly* 39 (1982), pp. 87–113. Of the 476 children identified in this particular study (334 family portraits), 103 appear in paintings from the 1670–1750 period and the remainder come from the decades 1750–1809. See also Stephen Brobeck, 'Images of the family: portrait paintings as indices of American family culture, structure and behavior, 1730–1860', *Journal of Psychohistory* 5 (1977), pp. 81–106.

129 Calvert, 'Children in American family portraiture' (1982), p. 97. Karin Calvert, *Children in the House: The Material Culture of Early Childhood, 1600–1900* (Boston: Northeastern University Press, 1992), pp. 51–52, takes the argument even further by claiming that modern childhood as we know it did not exist in the seventeenth and early eighteenth century.

130 Mary Frances Durantini, *The Child in Seventeenth-Century Dutch Painting* (Ann Arbor, MI: UMI Research Press, 1983), p. 297. The Appendix (pp. 299–311) has a particularly interesting discussion of 'The newborn child and his reception into the family', including Jan Steen's much reproduced *The christening feast* (1664).

131 Simon Schama, *The Embarrassment of Riches: An Interpretation of Dutch Culture in the Golden Age* (London: Collins, 1987), p. 495. There are also several interesting observations on Ariès and Stone (pp. 496 and 517–18), and in the case of the Dutch Republic at least, Schama is sceptical that culture was conditioned by morbidity (p. 521). See also Chapter 3 above, pp. 55–57. Schama's argument that the Netherlands was a special case in the way children were presented in portraits has come under attack in Jeroen J. H. Dekker and Leendert F. Groenendijk, 'The Republic of God or the Republic of Children? Childhood and child-rearing after the Reformation: an appraisal of Simon Schama's thesis about the uniqueness of the Dutch case', *Oxford Review of Education* 17 (1991), pp. 317–35. Jeroen J. H. Dekker, 'A Republic of Educators: educational messages in seventeenth-century Dutch painting', *History of Education Quarterly* 36 (1996), pp. 155–82, argues that 'the Dutch portrayal of children was less a celebration of childhood as a unique stage of life than an attempt to show adults how children could be moulded and shaped through a variety of educative processes' (p. 155) and that 'painters were less concerned with portraying childhood than with instructing parents in the proper upbringing of their children' (p. 172). However, many of the portraits of children illustrated in Bedaux and Ekkart, *Pride and Joy* (2001), indicate that children were also painted as individuals, in their own right; so that their parents could remember them.

132 Simon Schama's, *Rembrandt's Eyes* (London: Allen Lane, The Penguin Press, 1999), pp. 414–15, has some examples of Rembrandt's drawings of children from the late 1630s which could be used to suggest that the artist was himself besotted. B. Remmo Hamel, 'The image of the child: Dutch

and Flemish paintings', *Journal of Psychohistory* 24 (1996), pp. 72–89, describes a larger survey of Dutch and Flemish paintings (799 examples with children) from the fifteenth to the nineteenth centuries. The eighteenth century contributes only 25, and most of these are small votive paintings commissioned by parents as an act of gratitude for the child's survival, compared with 463 from the seventeenth century. Were the Dutch not besotted to the same extent after their Golden Age?

133　The analysis and interpretation of family photographs has become both highly sophisticated and explicitly theoretical in recent years. Here are three contrasting examples. Julia Hirsch, *Family Photographs: Content, Meaning, and Effect* (New York: Oxford University Press, 1981) discusses form and content, especially the distinction between 'formal' or posed and 'candid' photographs, but also makes reference to paintings by William Dobson (**H**) and Arthur Devis (19), among others. Marianne Hirsch, *Family Frames: Photography, Narrative and Postmemory* (Cambridge, MA: Harvard University Press, 1997) is concerned with the way family 'photographs offer a prism through which to study the postmodern space of cultural memory' (p. 13). Robert Pols, *Family Photographs, 1860–1945* (London: Public Record Office, 2002), especially pp. 110–11, discusses the 'sentimental idealization of children' in late Victorian photographs and high child mortality.

134　See Bedaux and Ekkart, *Pride and Joy* (2001), p. 90.

135　Karen Hearn (ed.), *Dynasties: Painting in Tudor and Jacobean England, 1630–1630* (London: Tate Publishing, 1995), p. 99. Roy Strong, *The English Icon: Elizabethan and Jacobean Portraiture* (London: Paul Mellon Foundation for British Art in association with Routledge and Kegan Paul, 1969) provides an invaluable reference too for this period.

136　Karen Hearn, *Marcus Gheeraerts II: Elizabethan Artist* (London: Tate Publishing, 2002), p. 35.

137　Hearn, *Gheeraerts* (2002), pp. 41–51. It is particularly unusual to find the subject of a portrait smiling, especially one who is close to giving birth. Such a combination goes against the tradition that the risks of maternity were especially high in the past. These risks were described in table 3.3 and figure 3.8 (pp. 50 and 52).

138　'To Penshurst' was probably written in the summer of 1612 and first published in 1616 as the second poem in *The Forest*, part of Jonson's epigrams. J. C. A. Rathmell, 'Jonson, Lord Lisle, and Penshurst', *English Literary Renaissance* 1 (1971), pp. 250–60, and Don E. Wayne, *Penshurst: The Semiotics of Place and the Poetics of History* (London: Methuen, 1984), especially pp. 68–75, provide commentaries.

139　'To Penshurst', lines 76–98. George Parfitt (ed.), *Ben Jonson: The Complete Poems* (London: Penguin, 1975), pp. 97–98.

140　John T. Hopkins, '"Such a twin likeness there was in the pair." An investigation into the painting of the Cholmondeley sisters', *Transactions of the Historic Society of Lancashire and Cheshire* 141 (1991), pp. 1–37.

141　Jane Poultney married Sir Clipsby Crewe, a friend of Robert Herrick. She is commemorated in poems **11** and **12**. See Chapter 5, p. 121, and Chapter 7, p. 138.

142　Julian Treuherz, 'New light on John Souch of Chester', *Burlington Magazine* 139 (1130) (1997), pp. 300–07. John Hayes, *The Portrait in British Art* (London: National Portrait Gallery, 1991), 8, pp. 46–47, is clear that the two women are both Lady Aston. Souch's, *Unidentified marriage portrait*, 1640s, is also shown on p. 18.

143　George Ormerod, *The History of the County Palatine and City of Chester*, edited by Thomas Helsby (London: George Routledge and Son, 1882), volume I, p. 727, from an inscription in Aston chapel, Aston, Cheshire.

144　Malcolm Rogers, *William Dobson, 1611–46* (London: National Portrait Gallery, 1983), p. 67; also William Vaughan, *Endymion Porter & William Dobson* (London: Tate Gallery, 1970), pp. 14–21, which discusses Dobson's work in Oxford, 1642–45, most of which involved portraits of Royalist officers.

145 See www.worcesterart.org/Collection/Early_American/ for a detailed description and analysis of the painting, and Susan E. Stricker, 'Recent findings on the Freake portraits', *Worcester Art Museum Journal* 5 (1981–82), pp. 48–55. Jonathan L. Fairbanks, 'Portrait painting in seventeenth-century Boston', in Jonathan L. Fairbanks and Robert F. Trent (eds), *New England Begins: The Seventeenth Century, Volume 3: Style* (Boston: Museum of Fine Arts, 1982), pp. 413–79, has a detailed and well-illustrated account of the early American portraits.

146 Steward, *The New Child* (1995), plate 1, p. 29.

147 Steward, *The New Child* (1995), plate 9, p. 37.

148 Nicholas Penny (ed.), *Reynolds* (London: Weidenfeld and Nicolson, 1986), p. 319; Steward, *The New Child* (1995), plate 16, p. 44.

149 Nicholas Penny, *Church Monuments in Romantic England* (New Haven, CT: Yale University Press, 1977), p. 115.

150 Jan Hulsker, *Van Gogh. En Zijn Weg. Het Complete Werk* (Amsterdam: Meulenhoff, 1978), p. 377. The van Gogh Museum, Amsterdam has another version.

151 John Richardson, *A Life of Picasso. Volume I: 1881–1906* (London: Jonathan Cape, 1991), p. 215.

152 David Jaffé (ed.), *Titian* (London: National Gallery and Yale University Press, 2003), picture 24, pp. 134–35. See also Laurel Reed, 'Art, life, charm and Titian's *Portrait of Clarissa Strozzi*', in Albrecht Classen (ed.), *Childhood in the Middle Ages and the Renaissance: The Results of a Paradigm Shift in the History of Mentality* (Berlin: Walter de Gruyter, 2005), pp. 355–71. It is interesting to speculate that the first portraits of identifiable young children either on their own (**A**, 2) or in small groups (9) and not accompanied by adults were inspired by Italian artists and culture, and that this style was spread north to France and Flanders. Note 125 mentions a French example from 1494. Louis Haas, *The Renaissance Man and His Children: Childbirth and Early Childhood in Florence, 1300–1600* (London: Macmillan, 1998) contains many examples of the loving parent, some involving members of the Strozzi family.

153 Diane Owen Hughes, 'Representing the family: portraits and purposes in early modern Italy', *Journal of Interdisciplinary History* 17 (1986), pp. 7–38, also reminds us that 'the significance of familial representation may lie less in what it can tell us about a particular family or moment of decisive change in family configurations and more in the messages, ideas, and often outright lies that families passed on to future generations about the bonds, affections, and familial attitudes of their ancestors. For pictures surely supply, as we know family diaries sought to do, not only a history but also an ethos of the family, a controlling myth that shaped its later growth' (p. 38).

154 *pearl*, something especially precious, noble, or choice; the finest or best member or part; a fine or noble example or type (*OED*). The lady in **Cii** wears a particularly elaborate pearl-rope and many pearls are sewn on to her dress. *cherry-bob*, a plaything made from two cherry stalks (*OED*). Cherries also appear in Dutch child portraits of the same period. See Bedaux and Ekkart, *Pride and Joy* (2001), pp. 100, 107, 110 and 137.

155 The portrait of Barbara Gamage and her children has sometimes been compared with the marvellous painting known as *The Tasburgh family*, c.1615, unknown British artist (private collection). The latter also shows a mother lined up with her children, four daughters and two sons. Again, Lady Lettice Tasburgh touches her eldest son's shoulder while the youngest child holds a bunch of cherries. She also has a pair of gloves suspended on a tape round her neck; a touch of motherly care in what is otherwise a formal display. See Andrew Moore and Charlotte Crawley (eds), *Family and Friends: A Regional Survey of British Portraiture* (London: HMSO, 1992), pp. 18 and 83. Neither the Gamage or Tasburgh paintings fit easily with Goldberg's ('Fatherly authority' (1986)) claims that in Tudor and Stuart family portraits we can make the following connections: male–culture–head and female–nature–body. Both pictures are headless in this sense. Goldberg's selection includes **B**, **F**, **G**, **H** and 15, all of which have a strong paternal presence.

156 Hearn, *Dynasties* (1995), pp. 99–100.

157 Judith W. Hurtig, 'Death in childbirth: seventeenth-century English tombs and their place in contemporary thought', *Art Bulletin* 65 (1983), pp. 603–15, and Nigel Llewellyn, *Funeral Monuments in Post-Reformation England* (Cambridge: Cambridge University Press, 2000) give several examples.

158 Treuherz, 'John Souch' (1997), pp. 303–04, provides translations of the Latin inscriptions. The placing of texts, often, as here, biblical in origin, is discussed in Svetlana Alpers, *The Art of Describing: Dutch Art in the Seventeenth Century* (Chicago: University of Chicago Press, 1983), pp. 169–221. The practice had been abandoned by the mid-seventeenth century, although, as **B** also illustrates, it was popular before then.

159 Of these the most important are undoubtedly the three separate paintings of Robert Gibbs's children: *Margaret Gibbs, Robert Gibbs aged 4½ years* (both at Museum of Fine Arts, Boston) and *Henry Gibbs aged 1½ years* (Avampato Discovery Museum, Charleston, West Virginia); and *The Mason children: David, Joanna, and Abigail* (Fine Art Gallery and Museums of San Francisco). Each of these was painted in the early 1670s. The significance of these paintings is discussed by Fairbanks, 'Portrait painting' (1982), pp. 431–35, 443–44 and 458–61. The painting of the three Mason children (1670) is the first American group portrait.

160 As has already been noted, Calvert, 'Children in American family portraiture' (1982), points out that no portraits of the nuclear family exist for colonial America before 1730.

161 Mary Webster, 'An eighteenth-century family: Hogarth's portrait of the Graham children', *Apollo* 130(31) (1989), pp. 171–73, argues that the youngest Graham child, Thomas, had in fact already died before the painting was completed in 1742. The children are Henrietta Catherine (8 November 1733–1800), Richard Robert (8 January 1735–1816), Anna Maria (7 July 1738–after 1788) and Thomas (18 August 1740–buried 4 February 1742). However, Desmond Shawe-Taylor, *The Georgians: Eighteenth-Century Portraiture and Society* (London: Barrie and Jenkins, 1990), especially pp. 209–12, suggests the associations of boy–cat and girl–bird; that this is a moral tale on the dangers of sexual temptation, young ladies beware. Henrietta Catherine Graham became the mother of Thomas Robert Malthus, the advocate of 'moral restraint'. David Kunzle, 'William Hogarth: The ravaged child in the corrupt city', in Virginia Tufte and Barbara Myerhoff (eds), *Changing Images of the Family* (New Haven, CT: Yale University Press, 1979), pp. 99–140, stresses the importance of 'reason' rather than 'sentiment' or 'emotion' in Hogarth, although he finds *The Graham children* something of an exception well before the influence of Rousseau.

162 Hans Holbein, *Artist's wife and two of their older children*, c.1528 (Kunstmuseum, Basel) is an early example of a mother and children painting. Steward, *The New Child* (1995), p. 20, also makes much of the fact that **K** was probably painted some six years before the publication of Jean-Jacques Rousseau's *Émile, ou de l'éducation* in 1762 (first English translation, 1763). Rousseau (1712–78) is often credited with revolutionising thinking on the education of children who, he believed, were born innocent but corrupted by society: 'God makes all things good; man meddles with them and they become evil'. He was a strong advocate of maternal breastfeeding, although his own mother had died shortly after his birth, opposing wet-nursing and the practice of wrapping infants in swaddling bands. See Maurice Cranston, *The Noble Savage: Jean-Jacques Rousseau, 1754–1762* (London: Allen Lane, 1991), pp. 175–98.

163 Carpenter, *Child in Art* (1906), pp. 152–53, offers an Edwardian interpretation.
    Her portrait shows her to be the quaintest little lady in a huge cap, cross-over bodice, and long mittens. Behind her delightful little air of solemnity there lurks a suspicion of merriment, and her mouth is compressed like a tiny rosebud in the effort to repress the smile which threatens to break out. Though not so well-known as many others of his portraits, this is one of the most perfect child-faces from Sir Joshua's brush, and deserves to be classed among his masterpieces.

164 Higonnet, *Pictures of Innocence* (1998), pp. 29–31, takes up the theme of the 'romantic child' as inspired, apparently, by *Penelope Boothby*, but which reached its peak in Sir John Everett Millais's

Bubbles (1886) forever associated with the Pear's soap advertisement.

165 Peter Thornton and Helen Dorey, *Sir John Soane: The Architect as Collector, 1753–1837* (New York: Abrams, 1992), p. 61, discusses reactions to Banks's monument, a model of which is also kept in the Soane Museum, London.

166 Steward, *The New Child* (1995), p. 27.

167 John Barrell, *The Dark Side of the Landscape: The Rural Poor in English Painting, 1730–1840* (Cambridge: Cambridge University Press, 1980), pp. 89–129, discusses at greater length the popular, sentimental and comic aspects of Morland's work in general.

168 The modern British artist Richard Wathen gives the children in his paintings strikingly adult heads, slightly out of proportion with the body and sometimes with greying hair. The effect is similar to that of **O**. Schorsch, *Images of Childhood* (1979) has several other examples from early nineteenth-century America. The French artist Henri Rousseau (1844–1910) also created several pictures of children with adult-like heads. In his case it has been suggested that they may have represented his own four children who died from tuberculosis at an early age. *Boy on the rocks*, 1895–97 (Chester Dale Collection, National Gallery of Art, Washington DC), *To fête baby*, 1903 (Kunstmuseum, Winterthur), and *Portrait of a child*, 1905 (Jean Walter-Paul Guillaume Collection, Musée de l'Orangerie, Paris) are three excellent examples.

169 Lloyd Goodrich, *Thomas Eakins* (Cambridge, MA: Harvard University Press, 1983). Jules David Prown, *Art as Evidence* (New Haven, CT: Yale University Press, 2001), pp. 205–14, discusses the child's perspective employed by Eakins in his *Baby at play*.

170 Kathryn J. Zerbe, 'Mother and child: a psychobiographical portrait of Mary Cassatt', *Psychoanalytic Review* 74 (1987), pp. 45–61, raises the possibility that 'loss of several siblings during critical developmental sub-phases may have produced intense survival guilt in Mary, motivating her to "recreate" her siblings on canvas and to devote her life to care of survivors' (p. 59). However, the more standard lives of the artist, such as Nancy Mowll Mathews, *Mary Cassatt: A Life* (New Haven, CT: Yale University Press, 1994), avoid exposing their subject to psychoanalysis on this matter. Griselda Pollock, *Mary Cassatt: Painter of Modern Women* (London: Thames and Hudson, 1998) has a more theoretically informed approach. She notes that picture 33 was advised by Degas, and that it is 'one of the most radical images of childhood painted at this period' (p. 129) because of its boldness and the psychological tension it conveys. Pollock also stresses the importance of seeing Cassatt as a painter of children and of mothers, together and separately, as her first biographer's title suggests: Achille Segard, *Mary Cassatt: Un peintre des enfants et des mères* (Paris: Librarie Paul Ollendorff, 1913).

171 Greg M. Thomas, 'Impressionist dolls: on the commodification of girlhood in Impressionist painting', in Marilyn R. Brown (ed.), *Picturing Children* (London: Ashgate, 2002), pp. 103–25, takes a different perspective by linking the French doll-making industry which became prominent between 1860 and 1880, and some of the paintings of Renoir, Manet, Cassatt (33 included) and Berthe Morisot. **M** and 25 might provide counter examples to the French theme.

172 Paul Smith, *Seurat and the Avant-Garde* (New Haven, CT: Yale University Press, 1997) discusses late nineteenth-century colour theory, especially its influence on Seurat, including the publication of Ogden Rood's *Théorie scientifique des couleurs* in 1881. John Gage, *Colour and Meaning: Art, Science and Symbolism* (London: Thames and Hudson, 1999) deals with the complex issues relating to artists' use of colours in far more detail.

173 Llewellyn, *Funeral Monuments* (2000), p. 358.

174 Llewellyn, *Funeral Monuments* (2000), p. 258.

175 Hurtig, 'Death in childbirth' (1983), quoted from pp. 614–15.

176 Hurtig, 'Death in childbirth' (1983), illustration 14, p. 609; also Llewellyn, *Funeral Monuments* (2000), p. 109.

177 Ormerod, *History* (1882), volume III, p. 675, note b. Catherine Belsey, *Shakespeare and the Loss of*

Eden: The Construction of Family Values in Early Modern Culture (London: Palgrave, 2001), pp. 108–10, has some interesting observations, a modernised copy of the inscription and comparison with **E**. There are several versions of the inscription giving different dates in July 1603 for Lady Margaret's death. Sir Peter Legh had extensive estates at Lyme Park in Cheshire, but he was also a Member of Parliament with a house at Fulham where, presumably, Lady Margaret died.

178 Evelyn, Lady Newton, *The House of Lyme From its Foundation to the End of the Eighteenth Century* (London: Heinemann, 1917) describes and illustrates these paintings which used to be at Lyme Park. Lady Margaret's appearance (**Ri**) is described in particular detail (pp. 53–54).

She wears a yellow silk gown with green horizontal stripes, the dress standing out from her slight figure in the grotesque fashion of the period, with very high lace ruff, and large puffed sleeves, terminating in lace cuffs at the wrist. On her head is a curious kind of aigrette, almost like a crown, with two ornaments which fall from each side. Her dark hair is drawn very high above her lovely and pathetic face with its small delicate features and dark blue eyes. Round her neck is a double row of small pearls, below this another necklace in a design of points, also of pearls; hanging from her bodice is a necklace of four rows of large pearls. Over her whole dress there falls a sort of transparent material almost resembling chiffon, and from her shoulders and falling to the ground a cobweb-like cloak sewn with large pearls. In her right hand she holds a fan, hanging by a ribbon from her waist. Her left hand which rests on the front of her gown, shows no wedding-ring, but on the third finger is what appears to be a thin silken string, knotted and crossed over the back of the hand and disappearing into the cuff. The picture is inscribed: 'Sir Peter Legh's first Lady, Thomas Lord Gerard of Bromley, Master of the Rolls his daughter'.

A further remarkable painting in the Legh family collection shows Lady Margaret's eldest daughter, Anne, in the arms of her great-grandmother, Dame Margaret Legh, who in 1595 was in her nineties. It is also interesting to compare **Ri** with **Ci**, Barbara Gamage in **D**, and especially **Cii**. Only the unidentified lady finds anything to smile about in her pregnancy.

179 Belsey, *Shakespeare* (2001), pp. 110–11.

180 Nicholas Penny, 'English church monuments to women who died in childbed between 1780 and 1835', *Journal of the Warburg and Courtauld Institutes* 38 (1975), pp. 314–32, quoted from p. 315.

181 Penny, 'English church monuments to women' (1975), pp. 314 and 332.

182 James A. Hijiya, 'American gravestones and attitudes toward death: a brief history', *Proceedings of the American Philosophical Society* 127 (1983), pp. 339–63.

183 This point has been emphasised by Robert V. Wells, *Facing the "King of Terrors": Death and Society in an American Community, 1759–1990* (Cambridge: Cambridge University Press, 2000), p. 5. See also Sarah Tarlow, *Bereavement and Commemoration: An Archaeology of Mortality* (Oxford: Basil Blackwell, 1999) which has an interesting analysis of tombstones on Orkney since the sixteenth century. Unfortunately, Tarlow has little or nothing to say about mortality or age categories (especially children), and her perspective as an archaeologist encourages observations and claims which might appear uncontroversial to the historian. For example, 'The lack of fit between feeling and the expression of feeling causes some ambivalence about the usefulness of monuments in the creation of emotional histories', and 'The interpretation of memorial monuments offered here differs significantly from most others in that it considers these monuments primarily in terms of their involvement in the expression and the creation of emotional relationships' (p. 25). Armando Petrucci, *Writing the Dead: Death and Writing Strategies in the Western Tradition,* translated by Michael Sullivan (Stanford, CA: Stanford University Press, 1998) asks some interesting questions about what proportion of the dead had a right to a 'written death' in any period, place or culture. His evidence is derived from tombstone inscriptions but, unfortunately, he does not provide any systematic analysis, and thus answers to his own questions.

184 Michel Vovelle, 'A century and one-half of American epitaphs (1660–1813): toward the study of

collective attitudes about death', *Comparative Studies in Society and History* 22 (1980), pp. 534–47. This paper has largely been ignored (by Hijiya, for instance), yet it is another early example of how certain forms of text can be made to yield quantitative evidence in time-series form. Unfortunately, only 3 per cent of the sample of 750 epitaphs date from the seventeenth century and 71 per cent are from the period 1780–1813. Nonetheless, Vovelle finds an important turning point at about 1780 when 'the notion of slumber in expectation of resurrection' gave way to 'an active and wholly human survival in memory of those whom one had loved' (p. 546).

> Toward the middle of the eighteenth century, first, the world of the patriarchs gave way to one which included young adult men and began to make way for women. Then, around 1780, there appear children, increased numbers of young mothers and girls, as well as adolescent boys who died too young. The function of the epitaph itself had changed; from a perpetuation of honors, it became an expression of family grief, which felt as durable as stone. (p. 540)

As a postscript and gentle corrective to these efforts with funeral monuments and tombstones, Janet Huskinson's *Roman Children's Sarcophagi: Their Decoration ant its Social Significance* (Oxford: Clarendon Press, 1996) is especially helpful. She discusses the images used to represent premature death, especially the *ahoroi*, the 'untimely dead', infants and young children (the unmarried). Her conclusions are cautious. Images of children are said to be 'shifting' and 'unstable'; different interpretations can be simultaneously valid; but it is possible, nonetheless, to distinguish via images and symbols between responses to the deaths of children (*acerba*) and those of mature adults (*naturalis*).

5 Emotions and Literature

185 It is remarkable, but these questions still appear to be fashionable. Richard P. Wheeler, 'Deaths in the family: the loss of a son and the rise of Shakespearean comedy', *Shakespeare Quarterly* 51 (2000), pp. 127–53; Stephen Greenblatt, *Will in the World: How Shakespeare became Shakespeare* (London: Jonathan Cape, 2004), especially pp. 288–322, 'Speaking with the dead'; and James Shapiro, *1599: A Year in the Life of William Shakespeare* (London: Faber & Faber, 2005), p. 15, give them a fresh airing.

186 Peter Forbes (ed.), *Scanning the Century: The Penguin Book of the Twentieth Century in Poetry* (London: Penguin, 1999) offers an interesting parallel in which poems are used to tell a story, and Michael Donaghy (ed.), *101 Poems about Childhood* (London: Faber & Faber, 2005) has many good examples of poets speaking of children and childhood over the centuries. Of course, it might be objected that popular culture was and still is not expressed in literary terms, and that poetry is incapable of touching the emotions of the mass of the population. The skills of writing and reading are required and these were far from universal in the past. But this position is too restrictive; it rules out diaries, letters and wills, among other sources. See also note 246.

187 Ian Watt, *The Rise of the Novel: Studies in Defoe, Richardson and Fielding* (London: Chatto & Windus, 1957) discusses the rise of the novel in the eighteenth century and the new 'realism' that was entailed. Garrett Stewart, *Death Sentences: Styles of Dying in British Fiction* (Cambridge, MA.: Harvard University Press, 1984), Michael Wheeler, *Death and the Future Life in Victorian Literature and Theology* (Cambridge: Cambridge University Press, 1990), Wendy Simonds and Barbara Katz Rothman, *Centuries of Solace: Expressions of Maternal Grief in Popular Literature* (Philadelphia, PA: Temple University Press, 1992) and Laurence Lerner, *Angels and Absences: Child Deaths in the Nineteenth Century* (Nashville, TN: Vanderbilt University Press, 1997) all provide examples of the use of Victorian literature.

188 Peter Coveney, *Poor Monkey: The Child in Literature* (London: Rockliff, 1957), republished as *The Image of Childhood: The Individual and Society: A Study of the Theme in English Literature* (London: Penguin, 1967).

189 See Chapter 2, table 2.3, for Vovelle's three-levels model.

190 Charles Darwin, *The Expression of the Emotions in Man and Animals* (London: John Murray, 1872).

191 Darwin, *Expression of Emotions* (1872), p. 80. The 'excellent observer' was Margaret Oliphant (1828–97) in her novel *Miss Marjoribanks* (1866), p. 362. Between 1853 and 1859, when her husband died, Mrs Oliphant had six children, four of whom had died by 1864. Darwin was himself deeply affected by the death of his 10-year-old daughter, Annie, in 1851; he could not attend the funeral. See Randal Keynes, *Annie's Box: Charles Darwin, His Daughter and Human Evolution* (London: Fourth Estate, 2001). Annie's death is one of the cases considered by Pat Jalland, *Death in the Victorian Family* (Oxford: Oxford University Press, 1996), p. 345, alongside those of Thomas Huxley's son (aged 3, died 1860) and Joseph Hooker's daughter (aged 6, died 1863). Two of Darwin's other children also died young: Mary aged 3 weeks in 1842, and Charles aged 18 months in 1858. Neither were grieved over by their parents as much as Annie.

192 Sigmund Freud, 'Mourning and melancholia', *Collected Papers, Volume IV* (London: Hogarth Press, 1957), pp. 152–70. Freud defines grief in order to distinguish it from melancholia which involves self-reproach and culminates in 'a delusional expectation of punishment'. Warwick Middleton *et al.*, 'Pathological grief reactions', in Margaret S. Stroebe, Wolfgang Stroebe and Robert O. Hansson (eds), *Handbook of Bereavement: Theory, Research, and Intervention* (Cambridge: Cambridge University Press, 1993), pp. 44–61, review subsequent developments in this literature.

193 Paul C. Rosenblatt, *Bitter, Bitter Tears: Nineteenth-Century Diarists and Twentieth-Century Grief Theorists* (Minneapolis, MN: University of Minnesota Press, 1983).

194 In order: Nancy Kohner and Alix Henley, *When a Baby Dies: The Experience of Late Miscarriage, Stillbirth and Neonatal Death* (London: Routledge, 2001); Susan Borg and Judith Lasker, *When Pregnancy Fails: Coping With Miscarriage, Stillbirth and Infant Death* (London: Routledge & Kegan Paul, 1982); and Rosanne Cecil (ed.), *The Anthropology of Pregnancy Loss: Comparative Studies in Miscarriage, Stillbirth and Neonatal Death* (Oxford: Berg, 1996). Ann K. Finkbeiner, *After the Death of a Child: Living with Loss through the Years* (Baltimore, MD: Johns Hopkins University Press, 1998) discusses the continuing responses of parents to the deaths of children expressed in their own words.

195 Catherine A. Lutz and Lila Abu-Lughod (eds), *Language and the Politics of Emotions* (Cambridge: Cambridge University Press, 1990) provides a stimulating introduction from the anthropologists, while Anna Wierzbicka, *Understanding Cultures through Their Key Words* (Oxford: Oxford University Press, 1997) focuses on linguistics and psychology. Raymond Williams, *Keywords: A Vocabulary of Culture and Society* (London: Fontana Press, 1976) was probably the first study to encourage people to think along these lines.

196 Catherine A. Lutz, *Unnatural Emotions: Everyday Sentiments on a Micronesian Atoll and Their Challenge to Western Theory* (Chicago: University of Chicago Press, 1988).

197 Anna Wierzbicka, *Emotions Across Languages and Cultures: Diversity and Universals* (Cambridge: Cambridge University Press, 1999). John Leavitt, 'Meaning and feeling in the anthropology of emotions', *American Ethnologist* 23 (1996), pp. 514–39, has a sensible discussion of the body/mind, biology/culture, universal/locally constructed dichotomies. He favours the notion of emotions as 'feeling-thoughts'.

198 This is a rather troublesome point. See, for example, Amélie Oksenberg Rorty, 'From passions to emotions and sentiments', *Philosophy* 57 (1982), pp. 159–72, and Thomas Dixon, *From Passions to Emotions: The Creation of a Secular Psychological Category* (Cambridge: Cambridge University Press, 2003). The six passions are: wonder, joy and grief, love and hate, and desire. In English the change from 'passions' to 'emotions' occurred by about 1850, according to Dixon.

199 Peter N. Stearns, 'Historical analysis in the study of emotion', *Motivation and Emotion* 10 (1986),

pp. 185–93, quoted from p. 187.

200 William M. Reddy, *The Navigation of Feeling: Framework for the History of Emotions* (Cambridge: Cambridge University Press, 2001), and Peter N. Stearns and Jan Lewis (eds), *An Emotional History of the United States* (New York: New York University Press, 1998).

201 Antony Easthope, *Poetry as Discourse* (London: Methuen, 1983) provides an introduction, as does David Lodge (ed.), *Modern Criticism and Theory: A Reader* (London: Longman, 1988).

202 Kiernan Ryan (ed.), *New Historicism and Cultural Materialism: A Reader* (London: Arnold, 1996).

203 A. C. Bradley, *Shakespearean Tragedy: Lectures on* Hamlet, Othello, King Lear, Macbeth (London: Macmillan, 1904), pp. 486–92, and L. C. Knights, *How Many Children Had Lady Macbeth? An Essay in the Theory and Practice of Shakespeare Criticism* (Cambridge: Minority Press, 1933), pp. 9–10. This is still a strangely intriguing question. At 1.7.54 Lady Macbeth attempts to strengthen her husband's resolve to kill the king with the following:

>   I have given suck, and know
> How tender 'tis to love the babe that milks me;
> I would, while it was smiling in my face,
> Have plucked my nipple from his boneless gums
> And dashed the brains out, had I so sworn
> As you have done to this.

Among other disturbing items the witches throw into their cauldron there is (4.1.30):

> Finger of birth-strangled babe
> Ditch-delivered by a drab:

and at 4.1.91, the second apparition that appears to Macbeth is a 'bloody child'. When (4.3.215) Macduff is told that his entire household, wife and children included, has been murdered on Macbeth's orders he cries out:

> He has no children. All my pretty ones?
> Did you say all? O hell-kite! All?
> What, all my pretty chickens and their dam
> At one fell swoop?

The murdered king's son uses this 'deadly grief' to encourage 'great revenge' and it is indeed Macduff, who proves to have been 'from his mother's womb | Untimely ripped' (5.7.45), who kills Macbeth. Untimely death provides one of the play's most powerful themes. Harriet Walter, *Macbeth* (London: Faber & Faber, 2002), pp. 27–37, has an interesting insight from the perspective of an actress playing Lady Macbeth. She emphasises the importance of the maternity question and suggests that Lady Macbeth may have had a child from an earlier marriage, but that Macbeth was infertile and knew it. Not surprisingly perhaps, Mary Beth Rose, 'Where are the mothers in Shakespeare? Options for gender representation in the English Renaissance', *Shakespeare Quarterly* 42(3) (1991), pp. 291–314, hardly mentions Lady Macbeth except to note her 'infanticidal longings'.

204 Virginia Mason Vaughan, *Othello: A Contextual History* (Cambridge: Cambridge University Press, 1994), and Catherine Belsey, *Shakespeare and the Loss of Eden: The Construction of Family Values in Early Modern Culture* (London: Macmillan, 1999). Belsey's chapter on parenthood is also interesting because it combines literary discourse with illustration from paintings and funeral monuments, taking its cue from Hermione's statue in *The Winter's Tale*.

205 Jonathan Goldberg, *James I and the Politics of Literature: Jonson, Shakespeare, Donne, and their Contemporaries* (Baltimore, MD: Johns Hopkins University Press, 1983) gives many other examples as well as using some of the pictures discussed in Chapter 4.

206 Lauro Martines, *Society and History in English Renaissance Verse* (Oxford: Basil Blackwell, 1985), and Cleanth Brooks, *Historical Evidence and the Reading of Seventeenth-Century Poetry* (Colum-

bia, MO: University of Missouri Press, 1991), p. 156. There are, of course, many more examples of the uses of history or literature across the disciplinary divide. Love, marriage and match-making have proved an especially popular area: Ann Jennalie Cook, *Making a Match: Courtship in Shakespeare and His Society* (Princeton, NJ: Princeton University Press, 1991); Bruce W. Young, 'Haste, consent, and age at marriage: some implications of social history for Romeo and Juliet', *Iowa Journal of Research* 62 (1988), pp. 459–74; Mary Prior, 'Conjugal love and the flight from marriage: poetry as a source for the history of women and the family', in Valerie Fildes (ed.), *Women as Mothers in Pre-Industrial England* (London: Routledge, 1990), pp. 179–203. Levin L. Schücking, *The Puritan Family: A Social Study from Literary Sources* (London: Routledge & Kegan Paul, 1969), originally published as *Die Puritanische Familie* (Leipzig, 1929), was one of the very first attempts to use literature (mainly Milton, Bunyan and Defoe, but with some reference to Shakespeare, Richardson and Austen) as a source of evidence for the writing of social history. However, it must be acknowledged that the 'new historicism' has proved most successful in the analysis of 'public poetry' and its use in the political ideology of the sixteenth and seventeenth centuries. See David Norbrook, *Poetry and Politics in the English Renaissance* (Oxford: Oxford University Press, revised edition 2002), especially pp. 270–316.

207 Linda A. Pollock, *Forgotten Children: Parent–Child Relations from 1500 to 1900* (Cambridge: Cambridge University Press, 1983). See Linda Pollock (ed.), *A Lasting Relationship: Parents and Children Over Three Centuries* (London: Fourth Estate, 1987), but also Irina Stickland (ed.), *The Voices of Children, 1700–1914* (Oxford: Basil Blackwell, 1973).

208 In fact Stephen Greenblatt, *Renaissance Self-Fashioning: From More to Shakespeare* (Chicago: University of Chicago Press, 1980) had already begun to develop these ideas in the 1970s, but they were not taken up by historians until much later. Rudolf Dekker, *Childhood, Memory and Autobiography in Holland: From the Golden Age to Romanticism* (London: Macmillan, 2000), p. 12, also criticises Pollock for ignoring the 'development of the diary as a genre over more than two centuries'. He uses the term 'egodocuments' which focuses attention on the importance of self, as well as covering a number of different forms of documentary material. See Rudolf Dekker (ed.), *Egodocuments and History: Autobiographical Writing in its Social Context since the Middle Ages* (Hillversum: Verloren, 2002).

209 Brigitte Glaser, *The Creation of the Self in Autobiographical Forms of Writing in Seventeenth-Century England: Subjectivity and Self-Fashioning in Memoirs, Diaries, and Letters* (Heidelberg: Universitätverlag C. Winter, 2001), p. 5. This argument follows a line developed in literary theory by Roy Pascal, *Design and Truth in Autobiography* (London: Routledge and Kegan Paul, 1960) and Paul John Eakin, *Fictions in Autobiography* (Princeton, NJ: Princeton University Press, 1985), and illustrated in cultural history by Mariel C. McClenden, Joseph P. Ward and Michael MacDonald (eds), *Protestant Identities: Religion, Society, and Self-Fashioning in Post-Reformation England* (Stanford, CA: Stanford University Press, 1999). Robert A. Fothergill, *Private Chronicles: A Study of English Diaries* (London: Oxford University Press, 1974) gives an early and challenging account of the literary evolution of diaries as a 'manifestation of the history of "sensibility" – the reflection, at the level of the individual consciousness, of the succession of social and cultural epochs' (p. 11).

210 Linda A. Pollock, 'Parent–child relations', in David I. Kertzer and Marzio Barbagli (eds), *Family Life in Early Modern Times, 1500–1789* (New Haven, CT: Yale University Press, 2001), pp. 192-–220, reflects her more recent concern for the ways in which grief was expressed, the language used to convey multiple emotions (grief and resignation, grief and anger, for example) and whether that mixture of feelings changed even though grief in some form was always present. Chapters 7 and 8 take up this point; see also Dekker, *Childhood* (2000), pp. 127–38.

211 Paul S. Seaver, *Wallington's World: A Puritan Artisan in Seventeenth-Century London* (London: Methuen, 1985), especially note 89, p. 229, and pp. 73–74, 85–90.

212 Alan Macfarlane, *The Family Life of Ralph Josselin, A Seventeenth-Century Clergyman* (Cambridge: Cambridge University Press, 1970), especially pp. 81–91 and 199–204.

213 Page numbers refer to Alan Macfarlane (ed.), *The Diary of Ralph Josselin, 1616–1683* (Oxford: Oxford University Press for the British Academy, 1976).

214 Mary, in particular, was mentioned on six occasions after May 1650.

215 A study on the 'uses of Josselin' would offer a valuable account of how historians have found what they sought in the diary.

216 In Chapter 2 we have already considered a third form, the fictional autobiography, in the case of Ariès's use of *Jane Eyre* and other writings by the Brontë sisters (p. 19).

217 See Chapter 4, pp. 110–12. The Haringtons may have been married in 1583 or later in 1587; they had nine or eleven children, and two sons died in infancy. Ian Grimble, *The Harington Family* (London: Jonathan Cape, 1957).

218 Taken from Norman Egbert McClure (ed.), *The Letters and Epigrams of Sir John Harington together with* The Prayse of Private Life (Philadelphia, PA: University of Pennsylvania Press, 1930) with some modernisation of spellings. The numbering is McClure's.

219 Jason Scott-Warren, *Sir John Harington and the Book as Gift* (Oxford: Oxford University Press, 2001), especially pp. 102–03 and 110–13, provides a more detailed reading of the epigrams as cultural history.

220 A. L. Rowse, *Shakespeare's Sonnets: The Problems Solved* (London: Macmillan, first edition 1964, second edition 1973, third edition 1984), p. ix. This needs to be read in conjunction with John Dover Wilson (ed.), *The Sonnets* (Cambridge: Cambridge University Press, 1966), especially the 'Preface' and 'Introduction' to gain some measure of the dispute over the identity of 'Mr W. H.', the person to whom *Shakespeare's Sonnets* (1609) is dedicated; the fair friend; the rival poet; and the Dark Lady. The dispute eventually became personal and rather silly with the 'Cornish privateer' remarking that 'Dover Wilson had bright insights, but was enthusiastic and notoriously erratic' (Rowse, *Sonnets* (1984)), p. x. Rowse is now much out of fashion. He is ignored by Greenblatt, *Will in the World* (2004), who, nonetheless, makes similar 'suggestions' about autobiographical details.

221 Rowse, *Sonnets* (1973), p. x.

222 Sir Arthur Quiller-Couch and John Dover Wilson (eds), *As You Like It* (Cambridge: Cambridge University Press, 1926) use the reference to date the play closer to 1593 than is usually believed, arguing that such an allusion would go unrecognised in, say, 1599 (pp. 104–05). But Agnes Latham (ed.), *As You Like It*, Arden Shakespeare, Second Series (London: Methuen, 1975), pp. xxxiiii–xxxiv on 'The death of Marlowe', is far more sceptical; she prefers 1599. Rowse, *Sonnets* (1973), pp. 176–78, is convinced that Shakespeare's Sonnet 86 also contains reference to Marlowe's death and that it too was written in 1593. See also Katherine Duncan-Jones (ed.), *Shakespeare's Sonnets*, Arden Shakespeare, Third Series (London: Thomas Nelson, 1997), pp. 282–83. Shapiro, *1599* (2005), pp. 243–44, suggests a longer struggle on Shakespeare's part to come to terms with his rival, Marlowe, a struggle that surfaces in several plays of the 1590s, including *As You Like It*.

223 William A. Ringler Jr. (ed.), *The Poems of Sir Philip Sidney* (Oxford: Clarendon Press, 1962), p. 439. It is generally agreed that Astrophil is Sidney himself and that Stella is Penelope Devereux, daughter of the Earl of Essex, who was obliged to marry the young and wealthy Lord Rich in November 1581. Sonnet 37 uses the word 'Rich' four times and concludes rather unambiguously with the words 'Rich she is'. Philip and Penelope's names had been linked as potential marriage partners in 1576, but the match was not contracted. See also Katherine Duncan-Jones, 'Sidney, Stella, and Lady Rich', in Jan van Dorsten, Dominic Baker-Smith and Arthur F. Kinney (eds), *Sir Philip Sidney: 1586 and the Creation of a Legend* (Leiden: E. J. Brill, 1986), pp. 170–92. Clark Hulse, 'Stella's wit: Penelope Rich as reader of Sidney's sonnets', in Margaret W. Ferguson, Maureen Quilligan and Nancy J. Vickers (eds) *Rewriting the Renaissance: The Discourses of Sexual*

Difference in Early Modern Europe (Chicago: University of Chicago Press, 1986), pp. 272–86, has an interesting argument about the struggle between Sidney as writer and Rich–Stella as reader. Penelope Rich's fame and beauty have even inspired a CD collection of songs: *My Lady Rich, Her Teares and* Joy (Avie Records and Heartsease Productions, 2005).

224 Edgar I. Fripp, *Shakespeare: Man and Artist, Volume I* (London: Oxford University Press, 1938), p. 435. Fripp has an entire section entitled 'Death of Hamnet Shakespeare' (pp. 434–37) in which he traces the various references to children and childhood in Shakespeare's plays. More recently, Katherine Duncan-Jones, *Ungentle Shakespeare: Scenes from His Life*, Arden Shakespeare (London: Thomson, 2001), pp. 90–91, and especially Greenblatt, *Will in the World* (2004), p. 233, which refers to the 'madly fluttering biographical speculations' that have been encouraged by the 'painful intimacy' of the Sonnets.

225 Duncan-Jones, *Sonnets* (1997), p. 265.

226 Compare Dover Wilson, *Sonnets* (1966), pp. 181–82; Rowse, *Sonnets* (1973), p. 157; Duncan-Jones, *Sonnets* (1997), pp. 264–65.

227 Park Honan, *Shakespeare: A Life* (Oxford: Oxford University Press, 1998), p. 235, quoting lines 2–4. Honan claims that the death of Hamnet in 1596 significantly changed Shakespeare's approach, that he developed a more complicated, intelligent view of suffering in his later work. Michael Wood, *In Search of Shakespeare* (London: BBC Books, 2003), pp. 184–85, favours Sonnet 33 with its reference to 'he was but one hour mine'.

228 Duncan-Jones, *Sonnets* (1997), p. 185.

229 For example, Stephen Booth, *An Essay on Shakespeare's Sonnets* (New Haven, CT: Yale University Press, 1969), pp. 10 and 112–14, discusses Sonnet 37 as though it is an expression of the poet's shame.

230 Duncan-Jones, *Sonnets* (1997), p. 129.

231 Dover Wilson, *Sonnets* (1966), p. xcix. The friend's mother, the Countess of Pembroke, was also Sir Philip Sidney's sister, Mary. Of course Rowse, *Sonnets* (1973) tells a very different story: the sonnets were written earlier in the 1590s; the friend is Henry Wriothesley, Earl of Southampton, who was certainly one of Shakespeare's patrons during that period; the rival poet is Christopher Marlowe; and the Dark Lady of Sonnets 127 to 152 is Emilia Lanier, a former mistress of the Lord Chamberlain, comptroller of theatres and players. Aemilia Lanyer (1569–1645) became a significant poet in her own right, but, as Susanne Woods, *Lanyer: A Renaissance Woman Poet* (New York: Oxford University Press, 1999), pp. 72–98, points out, there is still no conclusive evidence to link her with Shakespeare. At least one recent editor has despaired of those who wish 'to decode the sequence into a personal narrative', preferring to emphasise the poetry above the suppressed autobiography: see G. Blakemore Evans (ed.), *The Sonnets* (Cambridge: Cambridge University Press, 1996), p. 15, but the desire to decode the Sonnets has a long and honourable history reaching back at least to the early nineteenth century. For example, Charles Armitage Brown, *Shakespeare's Autobiographical Poems. Being His Sonnets Clearly Developed: With His Character Drawn Chiefly from His Works* (London: James Bohn, 1838), p. 44, has W. H. as Master William Herbert, nephew of Sir Philip Sidney and after 1601, Earl of Pembroke. Brown (pp. 46–47 and 50–99) also makes the following interesting analysis of *Shakespeare's Sonnets*:

First Poem: Stanzas 1–26 To his friend, persuading him to marry.

Second Poem: Stanzas 27–55 To his friend, who had robbed the poet of his mistress, forgiving him.

Third Poem: Stanzas 56–77 To his friend, complaining of his coldness and warning of life's decay.

Fourth Poem: Stanzas 78–101 To his friend, explaining that he prefers another poet's praises, and reproving him for faults that may injure his character.

Fifth Poem: Stanzas 102–26 To his friend, excusing himself for having been some time silent, and disclaiming the charge of inconstancy.

Sixth Poem: Stanzas 127–52 To his mistress, on her infidelity.

232 Paul Edmondson and Stanley Wells, *Shakespeare's Sonnets* (Oxford: Oxford University Press, 2004) offers some very sensible judgements on the 'autobiography' issue. For example, they regard the Sonnets as an 'emotional autobiography', as a journey of literary self-examination, as a gallery of 154 exhibits which may be viewed as well as read, and as Shakespeare's sketchbook.

233 Sir Sidney Lee, *Elizabethan and Other Essays* (Oxford: Clarendon Press, 1929), pp. 85–115, quoted from p. 115. Here Lee is emphasising the concern originally expressed by Samuel Taylor Coleridge regarding the need for 'aloofness' in relation to feelings in private life and those of which the artist or analyst is the interpreter.

234 Lee, *Elizabethan Essays* (1929), p. 113.

235 Morton Luce (ed.), *The Tempest*, Arden Shakespeare, First Series (London: Methuen, first edition 1902, fourth edition 1938). After considering dating and sources, Luce's 'Introduction' turns to 'Characteristics of the Play: As a work of art; As a criticism of life; As an autobiography'. One of his examples of the autobiographical comes from 5.1.307–11 in which Prospero hopes to see everyone happy and settled, his daughter married, his dukedom restored, 'And thence retire me to Milan, where | Every third thought shall be my grave.' to which Luce remarks 'Surely these, if any, are the final resolve and the parting words of the greatest poet and philosopher who ever lived' (p. lxiii).

236 Luce, *Tempest* (1902), pp. xlix–l.

237 Luce, *Tempest* (1902), p. l.

238 Sir Sidney Lee, *A Life of William Shakespeare* (London: Smith, Elder & Co., first edition 1898; John Murray, second edition 1922). See 'Fanciful interpretations of "The Tempest" in which Lee (1922), pp. 436–37, scorns as without much reason the 'philosophical pronouncements' of critics.

239 John Dover Wilson, *The Essential Shakespeare: A Biographical Adventure* (Cambridge: Cambridge University Press, 1932), p. 42. This is, of course, a moot point, for Wordsworth and Dickens were of a very different age, one in which it was assumed that literature should offer 'emotional self-revelation' and be in touch with nature. Shakespeare was far more subtle.

240 Frank Kermode (ed.), *The Tempest*, Arden Shakespeare, Second Series (London: Methuen, 1954), p. lxxxii. Virginia Mason Vaughan and Alden T. Vaughan (eds), *The Tempest*, Arden Shakespeare, Third Series (London: Thomas Nelson, 1999) ignores the autobiographical possibilities, preferring to emphasise the 'brave new world' theme.

241 Harold Bloom, *Shakespeare: The Invention of the Human* (London: Fourth Estate, 1999), p. 662.

242 Kate Chedgzoy, *Shakespeare's Queer Children: Sexual Politics and Contemporary Culture* (Manchester: Manchester University Press, 1995) and Ann Thompson, '"Miranda, where's your sister?": reading Shakespeare's *The Tempest*', in Susan Sellers (ed.), *Feminist Criticism: Theory and Practice* (Hemel Hempstead: Open University Press, 1991), pp. 45–55.

243 Edward Bond, *Bingo: Scenes of Money and Death* (London: Eyre Methuen, 1974) and William Black, *Judith Shakespeare: A Romance* (London: Sampson Low, Marston & Co., 1893).

244 A. L. Rowse, *William Shakespeare: A Biography* (London: Macmillan, 1963), p. 242, repeated in *Shakespeare: The Man* (London: Macmillan, 1973), p. 152. See also Fripp, *Shakespeare* (1938), pp. 334–37.

245 John Dover Wilson (ed.), *King John* (Cambridge: Cambridge University Press, 1936), p. vii. Greenblatt, *Will in the World* (2004), p. 290, and Wheeler, 'Deaths in the family' (2000), p. 141, both use Constance's speech and link it with Hamnet's death, although they recognise that the link is not secure. They also tie *Hamlet* to Hamnet, and the 'recovery of the lost twin boy' in *Twelfth Night* etc.

246 Adam Fox, *Oral and Literate Culture in England, 1500–1700* (Oxford: Oxford University Press, 2000) argues that 'by 1700 at least half of the adult population could read print' (p. 19), that in London and the major towns literacy was substantially higher, and that the 'gentle and professional

classes' were 'universally literate' by that time. He also makes some important points about the mutually supporting roles of oral and literate cultures that also have a bearing on the reception of poetry as it was heard and read. Far less attention has been given to 'popular numeracy', but Keith Thomas, 'Numeracy in early modern England', *Transactions of the Royal Historical Society, Fifth Series* 37 (1987), pp. 103–32, argues that ages, for example, 'were reported with precision for people under twenty' yet much more vaguely thereafter since among adults the accurate measurement of age had less social significance than among the young (p. 128). Inscriptions on funeral monuments, tombstones and some portraits could be used to support the view that at least among the social elite of early modern England there was a high degree of numeracy, as well as literacy, and a sensitivity to gradations of age.

247 Jane Stevenson and Peter Davidson (eds), *Early Modern Women Poets (1520–1700): An Anthology* (Oxford: Oxford University Press, 2001), pp. 44–45. Nigel Llewellyn, *Funeral Monuments in Post-Reformation England* (Cambridge: Cambridge University Press, 2000), p. 81, illustration 54, shows Sir Thomas Hoby's monument.

248 F. P. Wilson, *The Plague in Shakespeare's London* (Oxford: Clarendon Press, 1927), pp. 112–13.

249 The marriage does not appear to have been a happy one. Anne is referred to as 'a shrew, but honest'. Rosalind Miles, *Ben Jonson: His Life and Work* (London: Routledge & Kegan Paul, 1986) and David Riggs, *Ben Jonson: A Life* (Cambridge, MA.: Harvard University Press, 1989) tell what little can be told of Jonson's life. Riggs has Jonson converting to Roman Catholicism in 1598 and Mary born in 1601 as the third child (after Benjamin and Joseph), but then he also has the Jonsons practising *coitus interruptus* between 1596 and 1598 (p. 54).

250 G. H. Bentley, *Times Literary Supplement* (30 May 1942), p. 276; Riggs, *Jonson* (1989), pp. 91–92.

251 Most recently in Robert Cummings (ed.), *Seventeenth-Century Poetry: An Annotated Anthology* (Oxford: Basil Blackwell, 2000), pp. 80–81 and 83–84.

252 Ann Donne's life was commemorated by a small tablet composed in Latin by her husband and erected at his expense in the Church of St Clement Danes, London. The tablet is now lost, but there remains a copy of the text mentioning the seven surviving children; see R. C. Bald, *John Donne: A Life* (Oxford: Clarendon Press, 1970), p. 325.

253 Stevenson and Davidson, *Early Modern Women Poets* (2001), pp. 222–23.

254 William Riley Parker, *Milton: A Biography* (Oxford: Clarendon Press, 1968), p. 738, gives one account of the subject of poem **8**, but this is challenged by John Carey and Alastair Fowler (eds), *The Poems of John Milton* (London: Longmans, 1968), p. 14. According to Parker, the infant is Anne Phillips (12 January 1626–22 January 1628) and the date of composition is therefore 1628. Milton's 'An epitaph on the Marchioness of Winchester' is reminiscent of **8** in its classical allusions, as well as length, and some lack of subtlety and feeling. It was written sometime before 1645 to commemorate the early death at the age of 23 of Jane Paulet. She died of an infection after giving birth to a stillborn infant on 15 April 1631. See Chapter 7, p. 184.

> But whether by mischance or blame
> Atropos for Lucina came;
> And with remorseless cruelty,
> Spoiled at once both fruit and tree:
> The hapless babe before his birth
> Had burial, yet not laid in earth,
> And the languished mother's womb
> Was not long a living tomb.

255 Henry King's 'An Exequy To his Matchlesse never to be forgotten Friend' is a farewell poem to his wife, Anne, who was buried at St Gregory by St Paul's, London, on 5 January 1624. Margaret Crum (ed.), *The Poems of Henry King* (Oxford: Clarendon Press, 1965), p. 10, argues that no pair of King's children could have been buried together, but the serious tone of this and all the other

poems suggests otherwise. 'The witty poetry of deadly seriousness' as Ronald Berman, *Henry King and the Seventeenth Century* (London: Chatto & Windus, 1964), p. 118, terms it. Lawrence Mason (ed.), *The English Poems of Henry King* (New Haven, CT: Yale University Press, 1914), p. 173, ascribes to Henry King the poem 'Upon ye untimely death of J. K. first born of H. K.', but Crum, *Henry King* (p. 249) believes it to be the work of John King (1595–1639), Henry's brother.

256 F. W. Moorman, *Robert Herrick: A Biographical and Critical Study* (London: The Bodley Head, 1910), p. 118. *Hesperides* has proved a valuable source-book for seventeenth-century social historians; see, for example, the numerous references in David Cressy, *Birth, Marriage and Death: Ritual, Religion, and the Life-Cycle in Tudor and Stuart England* (Oxford: Oxford University Press, 1997).

257 L. C. Martin (ed.), *The Poetical Works of Robert Herrick* (Oxford: Clarendon Press, 1956) (poems hereafter cited by Martin page number). First published in *Hesperides* (London, 1648).

258 Clipsby Crewe (1599–1648) was knighted in 1620. On the occasion of his marriage to Jane Poulteney (the sister of Lady Aston in painting **F**) on 7 July 1625 Herrick wrote 'A nuptiall song, or epithalamie, on Sir Clipseby Crew and his Lady' (*Hesperides* 283; Martin 112–16). Lady Jane died in childbirth on 2 December 1639 aged 29. There is a monument to her in Westminster Abbey; see Llewellyn, *Funeral Monuments* (2000), pp. 51 and 53. She could have been little more than 16 in 1625, and is believed to have had four children; Frances died aged 5 in February 1636. See Cummings, *Seventeenth-Century Poetry* (2000), pp. 153–58.

259 There is still some scholarly debate about Herrick's intentions in *Hesperides*, the extent to which the poems have been arranged and whether they are all autobiographical. For example, John L. Kimmey, 'Robert Herrick's persona', *Studies in Philology* 67 (1970), pp. 221–36, points out the many 'satirical epigrams that attack the local inhabitants for their lack of manners and normal hygiene' (p. 230), best exemplified here by **d**. Ann Baynes Coiro, *Robert Herrick's* Hesperides *and the Epigram Book Tradition* (Baltimore, MD: Johns Hopkins University Press, 1988) places *Hesperides* in a wider literary genre. There may also be some unease as to the way in which Herrick makes light of suffering, and even the deaths of children. Dekker, *Childhood* (2000), p. 128, also mentions the position of dead children in Dutch humour of the seventeenth century.

260 Stevenson and Davidson, *Early Modern Women Poets* (2001), pp. 254–55.

261 Germaine Greer, Susan Hastings, Jeslyn Medoff and Melinda Sansone (eds), *Kissing the Rod: An Anthology of Seventeenth-Century Women's Verse* (London: Virago, 1988), pp. 155–62.

262 Llewellyn, *Funeral Monuments* (2000), p. 23. Linda Levy Peck, *Consuming Splendor: Society and Culture in Seventeenth-Century England* (Cambridge: Cambridge University Press, 2005), especially pp. 277–310, discusses the construction, symbolism and significance of Lady Jane Cheyne's funeral monument in All Saints church, Chelsea, London, as well as comparing it with that of her sister, Elizabeth, Countess of Bridgewater, in Little Gaddesden church, Hertfordshire. The former has a very elaborate, life-sized reclining statue of Lady Jane while the latter is all simplicity, inscription and heraldry.

263 See 'Biographical note' in Patrick Thomas (ed.), *The Collected Works of Katherine Philips, The Matchless Orinda. Volume I: The Poems* (Stump Cross, Essex: Stump Cross Books, 1990), pp. 1–39.

264 Elizabeth Wade White, *Anne Bradstreet: "The Tenth Muse"* (New York: Oxford University Press, 1971). Philip Greven, *The Protestant Temperament: Patterns of Child-Rearing, Religious Experience, and the Self in Early America* (New York: Alfred A. Knopf, 1977), pp. 29–30, has noted Anne Bradstreet's evangelical views of infants and childrearing 'portraying infancy and early childhood in the sombre imagery of innate depravity'. Life in colonial Andover, including the financial activities of the Bradstreet family, is described in Philip J. Greven, *Four Generations: Population, Land, and Family in Colonial Andover, Massachusetts* (Ithaca, NY: Cornell University Press, 1970).

265 Janet Todd, *The Secret Life of Aphra Behn* (London: Andre Deutsch, 1996), pp. 328–29.

266 Maynard Mack, *Alexander Pope: A Life* (New Haven, CT: Yale University Press, 1985) provides a

detailed account of Pope's life and times. Pope's mother gave birth to her first and only child aged 44 in 1688; she died in 1733. The family was Roman Catholic, but it seems that Alexander, while not renouncing the old religion, was not active in its pursuit. As far as Mrs Corbett's epitaph is concerned, Maynard Mack, *Collected by Himself* (Newark, DE: University of Delaware Press, 1982), p. 329, speculates that Pope may never have met the lady.

267 Kenneth A. Requa (ed.), *Poems of Jane Turell and Martha Brewster* (Delmar, NY: Scholars' Facsimiles & Reprints, 1979), pp. 103–04. The original was first published in Boston in 1735.

268 None of William Blake's siblings had children either. Catherine acted as Blake's helpmate in what biographers portray as a long and loving marriage. See especially Peter Ackroyd, *Blake* (London: Sinclair-Stevenson, 1995), pp. 77, 80 and 122–26; also, Zachary Leader, *Reading Blake's* Songs (London: Routledge and Kegan Paul, 1981). Unfortunately, Leader is much influenced by the Stone thesis that parents were obliged to limit their psychological involvement with their infant children because in London in the 1760s, for instance, 60 per cent of all children died before they reached age 5. Stanley Gardner, *Blake's* Innocence *and* Experience *Retraced* (London: Athlone Press, 1986), p. 66, speculates that Tom Dacre is a 4-year-old foundling and that Blake borrowed the name from that of Lady Dacre's Almshouse between James Street and Buckingham Road, London. The position of young chimney sweeps in the general use of child labour and the rise of 'a romantic concept of the child' are outlined by Hugh Cunningham, *The Children of the Poor: Representations of Childhood since the Seventeenth Century* (Oxford: Basil Blackwell, 1991), pp. 50–64.

269 Stephen Gill, *William Wordsworth: A Life* (Oxford: Clarendon Press, 1989).

270 Walter Edwin Peck, *Shelley: His Life and Work* (London: Ernest Benn, 1927) and Richard Holmes, *Shelley: The Pursuit* (London: Weidenfeld and Nicolson, 1974) provide the details of Shelley's complicated sexual relations with at least three women. Of the seven children known to have been fathered by Shelley, five died in infancy or childhood (ages 0, 1, 2, 3, 12). Between the births of William and Clara, Mary Shelley also wrote *Frankenstein*. See Miranda Seymour, *Mary Shelley* (London: John Murray, 2000).

271 Beth Darlington (ed.), *The Love Letters of William and Mary Wordsworth* (London: Chatto & Windus, 1982), Paula R. Feldman and Diana Scott-Kilvert (eds), *The Journals of Mary Shelley, 1814–1844. Volume I: 1814–1822* (Oxford: Clarendon Press, 1987).

272 R. H. Super, *Walter Savage Landor: A Biography* (London: John Calder, 1957), p. 29. Charles Dickens is supposed to have conceived the character of Little Nell (*The Old Curiosity Shop*, 1841) while visiting Landor at his house in Bath.

273 J. W. Tibble and Anne Tibble, *John Clare: A Life* (London: Cobden-Sanderson, 1932) provides the biographical details. Roy Porter, '"All madness for writing": John Clare and the asylum', in Hugh Haughton, Adam Phillips and Geoffrey Summerfield (eds), *John Clare in Context* (Cambridge: Cambridge University Press, 1994), pp. 259–78, deals with Clare's illness in a sensitive way. J. L. Cherry, *The Life and Remains of John Clare* (London: Frederick Warne and Co., 1872), p. 139, and Eric Robinson and David Powell (eds), *The Later Poems of John Clare, 1837–64* (two volumes) (Oxford: Clarendon Press, 1984) also cover the period in Northampton Asylum.

274 Edward Dowden, *Shakspere: A Critical Study of His Mind and Art* (London: Henry S. King, 1876), and Dowden (ed.), *The Sonnets of William Shakspere* (London: Kegan Paul, Trench & Co., 1889). In his introduction to the latter (p. lx) he summarised what we may learn from the Sonnets: 'that Shakspere was capable of measureless personal devotion; that he was tenderly sensitive, sensitive above all to every diminution or alteration of that love his heart so eagerly craved; and that, when wronged, although he suffered anguish, he transcended his private injury and learned to forgive'. Dowden has been placed in the sentimental camp, a forerunner of the New Historicism now associated with Stephen Greenblatt.

275 John Ackerman, *Dylan Thomas: His Life and Work* (London: Oxford University Press, 1964), p.

118, explains that the reason the poet does not mourn is because 'Thomas wishes to accept the natural and inevitable process of life. He is the religious artist who celebrates life.'

276 Erica Wagner, *Ariel's Gift: A Commentary on* Birthday Letters *by Ted Hughes* (London: Faber & Faber, 2000). Plath's journal entries for March 1959 suggest that she may have been trying to conceive for some time with no success. Karen V. Kukil (ed.), *The Journals of Sylvia Plath, 1950–1962* (London: Faber & Faber, 2000), p. 474.

7 The Vocabulary of Grief

277 The most important studies are: G. W. Pigman III, *Grief and English Renaissance Elegy* (Cambridge: Cambridge University Press, 1985); Peter M. Sacks, *The English Elegy: Studies in the Genre from Spenser to Yeats* (Baltimore, MD: Johns Hopkins University Press, 1985); Joshua Scodel, *The English Poetic Epitaph: Commemoration and Conflict from Jonson to Wordsworth* (Ithaca, NY: Cornell University Press, 1991); W. David Shaw, *Elegy & Paradox: Testing the Conventions* (Baltimore, MD: Johns Hopkins University Press, 1994); and Jeffrey A. Hammond, *The American Puritan Elegy: A Literary and Cultural Study* (Cambridge: Cambridge University Press, 2000). Karl S. Guthke, *Epitaph Culture in the West: Variations on a Theme in Cultural History* (Lampeter, Dyfed: Edwin Mellen Press, 2003) reviews the changing cultural significance of epitaphs.

278 For example, W. David Shaw, 'Elegy and theory: is historical and critical knowledge possible?', *Modern Language Quarterly* 55 (1994), pp. 1–16.

279 Linda A. Pollock, 'Parent–child relations', in David I. Kertzer and Marzio Barbagli (eds), *Family Life in Early Modern Times, 1500–1789* (New Haven, CT: Yale University Press, 2001), pp. 192–220, has argued for the need to consider the ways in which grief was expressed, particularly the language used to convey multiple emotions (grief and resignation, grief and anger, for example) and whether that mixture of feelings changed even though grief in some form was always present. Readers may wish to refresh their memories by referring back to Vovelle's three-levels model (table 2.3, p. 25), the 'grief work' models (figure 5.1, p. 98) and the model of reception theory (figure 5.2c, p. 102).

280 See Chapter 5, pp. 99–101, for a discussion of 'Grief and other emotions', especially the contrasting approaches of psychologists, anthropologists and historians to the understanding of emotions as 'socially and culturally constructed' or 'biologically determined'. The use of keywords by comparative linguists is also outlined. Joel R. Davitz, *The Language of Emotion* (New York: Academic Press, 1969) looks at the definition and use of emotion words, including 'grief' (p. 60), but he does not emphasise the way their uses have changed.

281 The titles of the four poems are: 'In memory of my dear grandchild Elizabeth Bradstreet, who deceased August, 1665, being a year and half old', 'In memory of my dear grandchild Anne Bradstreet who deceased June 20, 1669, being three years and seven months old', 'On my dear grandchild Simon Bradstreet, who died on 16 November, 1669, being but a month, and one day old' (**32**, p. 146), and 'To the memory of my dear daughter-in-law, Mrs. Mercy Bradstreet, who deceased Sept. 6, 1669 [*sic* 1670], in the 28 year of her age'. Jeannine Hensley (ed.), *The Works of Anne Bradstreet* (Cambridge, MA: Harvard University Press, 1967), pp. 235–39, uses Anne Bradstreet, *Several Poems* (Boston: John Foster, second edition 1678) as her copy text.

282 Elizabeth Wade White, *Anne Bradstreet: 'The Tenth Muse'* (New York: Oxford University Press, 1971), pp. 350 and 356, discusses the circumstances in which the poems to Elizabeth and Mercy were written. Hammond, *American Puritan Elegy* (2000) provides a full account of the development and use of elegy in early American poetry. For example, Hammond (p. 198) argues that 'Elegy concentrated and intensified the three great Puritan lessons regarding life in the world', namely the importance of 'a lifelong preparation for death', 'the convincing power of sorrow in exposing the vast gulf between human wishes and divine will', and 'the related disparity between

earth and heaven'. Bradstreet's calm assurance and her acceptance that God has reasons but that they are beyond human understanding follow these lessons. See also poem **39** and table 4.2, p. 74.

283 While it is reasonably easy to allocate every poem to its decade of composition (see table 5.4, p. 128), giving each a single year so it can be placed in order for visual display can only be done in a very *ad hoc* fashion. However, it may be thought that the modernisation of spellings does more violence to the original texts by moving them further from their creators' own language. See Stanley Wells, *Modernising Shakespeare's Spelling* (Oxford: Clarendon Press, 1979) for a discussion of the pros and cons by a moderniser.

284 Mary E. Fissell, *Vernacular Bodies: The Politics of Reproduction in Early Modern England* (Oxford: Oxford University Press, 2004), pp. 53–89, has a chapter entitled 'The womb goes bad' in which she argues that from 1603 onwards the womb took on darker significance as the source of female maladies rather than the site of natural reproduction. The tomb–womb association may bear an interesting link with this idea.

285 As well as using 'untimely' for 'prematurely, too soon before due time', Shakespeare also uses the expression 'timely-parted' for 'naturally departed, one who has died a natural death'. See David Crystal and Ben Crystal (eds), *Shakespeare's Words: A Glossary and Language Companion* (London: Penguin, 2002), pp. 453 and 474.

286 The paintings of children discussed in Chapter 4 do not reflect this culture of death, but it is revealed in photographs and by Victorian cemeteries. See, for example, Pat Jalland, 'Victorian death and its decline: 1850–1918', in Peter C. Jupp and Clare Gittings (eds), *Death in England: An Illustrated History* (Manchester: Manchester University Press, 1999), pp. 230–55.

287 'Elegy for a child' in Paula Meehan, *The Man Who Was Marked by Winter* (Oldcastle, County Meath: Gallery Press, 1991), p. 27, has these closing lines.

> It is not that I was your mother,
> nor the rooted deep down loss,
> that has brought me this moment
> to sit by the window and weep.
>
> You were but a small bird balanced
> within me
> ready for flight.

288 The Oxford English Dictionary (second edition) gives 'abortive' the sense of 'born prematurely', 'fruitless', and 'coming to naught', as well as miscarriage. It also provides examples of its use in this way from the seventeenth and early eighteenth centuries. This is consistent with the use of 'abortive' in certain seventeenth-century parish registers. See, for example, the case of Hawkshead discussed by Roger Schofield, 'Perinatal mortality in Hawkshead, Lancashire, 1581–1710', *Local Population Studies* 4 (1970), pp. 11–16.

289 Parental responses to late-fetal and neonatal deaths were discussed in Chapter 5, p. 99.

290 Wilbur Sanders, *John Donne's Poetry* (Cambridge: Cambridge University Press, 1971), p. 136.

291 Table 7.6 shows that Katherine Woodcock was Milton's second wife, that she died in February 1658 and in the following month her 5-month-old daughter also died. E. A. J. Honigmann, *Milton's Sonnets* (London: Macmillan, 1966), pp. 190–94, has a detailed examination of biographical associations and the language of the poem. E. M. W. Tillyard, *The Metaphysicals and Milton* (London: Chatto & Windus, 1956), pp. 2–11, uses the two sonnets (**6** and **9**) as a way of introducing and comparing Milton with the metaphysical poets, Donne being chief among them. His principal point is that while Milton is deliberately and consistently concerned with his dead wife, Donne's self-absorption is to the fore.

292 See Chapter 5, p. 119.

293 From Ben Jonson, *The Underwood*, Epigram 35. First published in a folio edition of 1640. Eliza-

beth, the daughter of Sir George Chute, died 18 May 1627 aged 3½. The epitaph appears on her funeral monument in Sonning church, Berkshire. Ian Donaldson (ed.), *Ben Jonson*, Oxford Authors (Oxford: Oxford University Press, 1985), p. 355.

294 On 'father Ben' see L. A. Beaurline, 'The selective principle in Jonson's shorter poems', *Criticism* 8 (1966), pp. 64–74, W. David Kay, 'The Christian wisdom of Ben Jonson's "On my first sonne"', *Studies in English Literature, 1500–1900* 11 (1971), pp. 125–36; J. Z. Kronenfeld, 'The father found: consolation achieved through love in Ben Jonson's "On my first sonne"', *Studies in Philology* 75 (1978), pp. 64–83; on 'anal Ben', E. Pearlman, 'Ben Jonson: an anatomy', *English Literary Renaissance* 9 (1979), pp. 364–94; on his ego and classical allusions, Wesley Trimpi, '"BEN. IONSON his best piece of *poetrie*"', *Classical Antiquity* 2 (1983), pp. 145–55.

295 Wesley Trimpi, *Ben Jonson's Poems: A Study of the Plain Style* (Stanford, CA: Stanford University Press, 1962), p. 236.

296 Trimpi, *Ben Jonson's Poems* (1962), pp. 180–83. Trimpi also calculates that Jonson wrote about 15 epitaphs in his three volumes of epigrams noting that 'they are beautifully executed and perfectly realise the virtues' of the plain style, and that they are 'the most perfect realisation in English of a traditional classical form'.

297 Pearlman, 'Ben Jonson' (1979) discusses both the story that Jonson had a premonition of Benjamin's death from plague in a dream (p. 372), and Jonson's relationship with women (p. 376). Biographers have found it very difficult to recount the facts of Jonson's life, including those of his marriage and the births of his children. Literary historians have been inclined either to give him unique social significance or to suggest that his work is unrepresentative of its time. For example, Kay, 'Christian wisdom' (1971), p. 136, claims that 'No other English poet in the period opened himself so fully in his verse to the grief and sorrow which his children's deaths may have caused him', while Pigman, *Grief* (1985), p. 1, says that Jonson's 'attitude towards mourning is a throwback to the 1550s'.

298 Scodel, *English Poetic Epitaph* (1991), p. 193. Clearly Scodel has not noticed Jonson's epitaph to Elizabeth Chute.

299 A. Leigh DeNeef, *"This Poetick Liturgie" Robert Herrick's Ceremonial Mode* (Durham, NC: Duke University Press, 1974) offers a detailed analysis of 'ceremonial' in Herrick's work, including the funereal, and John L. Kimmey, 'Robert Herrick's persona', *Studies in Philology* 67 (1970), pp. 221–36, discusses the poet's multiple personalities: classical scholar, ageing lover, autobiographer and story teller.

300 Jack Goody, *The Culture of Flowers* (Cambridge: Cambridge University Press, 1993), p. 201, makes several telling points about Herrick's use of flowers, their pagan cum classical associations, and their symbolism in the seventeenth century when Puritans attempted to prohibit their use in church (including celebrations in which flowers had an especially important role, such as the maypole). See also figure 7.1i (p. 178) and the frequency of references to group 9 (flower) words.

301 See Chapter 2, p. 13, and Peter Coveney, *Poor Monkey: The Child in Literature* (London: Rockliff, 1957), republished in a revised edition as *The Images of Childhood: The Individual and Society, A Study of the Theme in English Literature* (London: Penguin, 1967).

302 The three anthologies are: Jerome J. McGann (ed.), *The New Oxford Book of Romantic Period Verse* (Oxford: Oxford University Press, 1993), Duncan Wu (ed.), *Romanticism: An Anthology* (Oxford: Blackwell, second edition 1998), and Jonathan Wordsworth and Jessica Wordsworth (eds), *The New Penguin Book of Romantic Poetry* (London: Penguin, 2001). McGann excludes the 'Chimney-sweeper' poems.

303 See Janet Todd, *Sensibility: An Introduction* (London: Methuen, 1986).

304 Martin K. Nurmi, 'Fact and symbol in "The chimney sweeper" of Blake's *Songs of Innocence*', *Bulletin of the New York Public Library* 68 (1964), pp. 249–56, and Heather Glen, *Vision and Disenchantment: Blake's* Songs *and Wordsworth's* Lyrical Ballads (Cambridge: Cambridge University

Press, 1983), pp. 95–109, draw out these interesting contrasts.

305 Leo Tolstoy, *Anna Karenina*, translated by Louise and Aylmer Maude (Oxford: Oxford University Press, 1995), part VI, chapter XVI, p. 603, originally published in 1877. Countess Tolstoy had 13 children and Tolstoy is believed to have had at least 12 others by peasant women on his estates. Perhaps this passage is intended to draw a sharp distinction between the attitudes of the aristocracy and the peasantry concerning their children. See Orlando Figes, *Natasha's Dance: A Cultural History of Russia* (London: Allen Lane, The Penguin Press, 2002), p. 119.

306 Mark Twain, *The Adventures of Huckleberry Finn* (London: Penguin, 1966), pp. 161–62.

307 Twain, *Huckleberry Finn* (1966), p. 162.

308 William Harmon (ed.), *The Oxford Book of American Light Verse* (New York: Oxford University Press, 1979), pp. 141–42 and 187–88. Julia A. Moore's collections include *The Sentimental Songbook* (Cleveland, OH: J. F. Ryder, 1877), and *The Sweet Singer of Michigan* (Grand Rapids, MI: Eaton, Lyon & Co., 1878). Hilaire Belloc's *Cautionary Tales for Children* (1907) also contains humorous poems in which children suffer fatal accidents. But see also Samuel Pickering Jr., '"The grave leads but to paths of glory." Deathbed scenes in American children's books, 1800–1860', *Dalhousie Review* 59 (1979), pp. 452–62, which discusses the older tradition, in New England at least, of using child deaths to encourage piety. Twain and Moore were, in their different ways, reacting to this tradition.

309 Sigmund Freud, 'Mourning and melancholia', *Collected Papers, Volume IV* (London: Hogarth Press, 1957), pp. 152–70. Paper first published in 1917. See Chapter 5, pp. 96–99, and especially figure 5.1.

310 Freud, 'Mourning and melancholia' (1957), p. 153. Peter Gay, *Freud: A Life for Our Time* (London: J. M. Dent and Sons, 1988), pp. 372–73, discusses the pivotal position of 'Mourning and melancholia' in Freud's work, especially in the ways it treats aggression towards the self and its possible culmination in suicide as a potential extreme consequence of melancholia.

311 For example, Helene Deutsch, 'Absence of grief', *Psychoanalytic Quarterly* 6 (1937), pp. 12–22, considers the possibility that young children who lose a parent may be insufficiently developed emotionally to complete effective mourning; and Erich Lindemann, 'Symptomatology and management of acute grief', *American Journal of Psychiatry* 101 (1944), pp. 141–48, compares the syndrome of acute morbid grief with that of normal grief, suggesting that the former often involves delayed or postponed reaction which may give the initial appearance of grief being unfelt; while James R. Averill, 'Grief: its nature and significance', *Psychological Bulletin* 70 (1968), pp. 721–48, provides a benchmark review. The literature on parental bereavement is growing rapidly, especially on the counselling aspects. The introduction to Nancy Kohner and Alix Henley, *When a Baby Dies: The Experience of Late Miscarriage, Stillbirth and Neonatal Death* (London: Routledge, 2001), p. 1, makes a common assertion about the grief that is felt, but ignored by others: 'The significance of a baby's death has not been recognised in the past and bereaved parents often struggled alone with a grief which others have neither understood nor acknowledged.' The highly original and very important study by Nancy Scheper-Hughes, *Death Without Weeping: The Violence of Everyday Life in Brazil* (Berkeley, CA: University of California Press, 1992) has a chapter entitled 'Two feet under and a cardboard coffin: The social production of indifference to child death' (pp. 268–339). In this area of northeast Brazil during the 1960s child death had become 'routinized', part of the 'average expectable environment'.

312 The standard biography is R. C. Bald, *John Donne: A Life* (Oxford: Clarendon Press, 1970). John Carey, *John Donne: Life, Mind and Art* (London: Faber & Faber, 1981) is an absorbing literary-historical account. Izaak Walton wrote the first *Life of John Donne* (1640). It contains many anecdotes, some of which may be true.

313 George Parfitt, *John Donne: A Literary Life* (London: Macmillan, 1989), p. 62.

314 Bald, *John Donne* (1970), pp. 139, 242, 252 and 324, on being 'undone', and various incidents of

family crisis in Donne's life, including Ann's death in 1617.

315 Jane Josselin produced 10 live births in twenty years (table 5.2, p. 107) and Lady Margaret Legh was married at 16 and died at 33 in childbirth (table 4.3, p. 90).

316 C. A. Patrides (ed.), *John Donne: The Complete English Poems* (London: Everyman, J. M. Dent, second edition 1994), p. 74. In Greek mythology, Niobe was turned to stone after her seven sons and seven daughters were killed by Apollo and Artemis.

317 R. C. Bald, *Donne and the Drurys* (Cambridge: Cambridge University Press, 1959) tells the story of the relationship. Bald reproduces a painting of Elizabeth Drury (plate II) in which she lies full-length on a couch, her head propped by an elbow. Elizabeth strikes the same attitude on her funeral monument in Hawstead church, Suffolk. Again, the monument follows an earlier portrait as in the case of **R**.

318 John Carey (ed.), *John Donne: Selected Poetry* (Oxford: Oxford University Press, 1996), pp. 147–83, 'Poems about deaths'.

319 Bald, *John Donne* (1970), p. 242.

320 Carey, *John Donne* (1981), pp. 118 and 156.

321 Carey, *John Donne* (1981), pp. 59, 71, 35, 82 and 44.

322 The contributors to M. Thomas Hester (ed.), *John Donne's "desire of more": The Subject of Anne More Donne in His Poetry* (Newark, DE: University of Delaware Press, 1996) tell a different story. They find references to Ann, although not by name, in several poems and insist that 'A nocturnal upon St Lucy's Day' relates to her death. However, apart from Lucy, no other children are mentioned. Pages 20–21 reprint the Latin text, with English translation, of the epitaph to Ann composed by Donne for her funeral tablet in St Clement Danes church, London. The epitaph describes Ann as a dear and chaste spouse, a loving mother. It says that she was carried off by a great fever seven days after her twelfth parturition , and that her husband is most wretched, beyond grief.

323 Patrides (ed.), *John Donne* (1994), p. 61.

324 Carey, *John Donne* (1981), pp. 87, 155 and 173, remarks that the 'Anniversaries' lavishly gratify Donne's appetite for excess (p. 87), and argues that Elizabeth is reduced to an imaginary woman in the first 'Anniversary' and has vanished altogether by the second.

325 J. B. Leishman, *The Monarch of Wit: An Analytical and Comparative Study of the Poetry of John Donne* (London: Hutchinson, 1951), p. 44, puts the attractively simple proposition that much of Donne's wit was merely an attempt to escape from the melancholy and depression of his everyday family life.

326 There are 98,996 lines in the 36 plays. The word 'death' occurs 850 times (8.6 per 1000 lines) and 'grief' 251 times (2.5). John Bartlett, *A Complete Concordance of Shakespeare* (London: Macmillan, 1962) provides the word counts, and Caroline F. E. Spurgeon, *Shakespeare's Imagery and What it Tells Us* (Cambridge: Cambridge University Press, 1935), p. 361, the number of lines.

327 Charles R. Forker (ed.), *King Richard II,* Arden Shakespeare, Third Series (London: Thompson, 2002), pp. 82–83, suggests the importance for the play of these motifs and the *memento mori* symbolism in general.

328 Jill L. Levenson (ed.), *Romeo and Juliet*, Oxford Shakespeare (Oxford: Oxford University Press, 2000), pp. 16–42, discusses the interlinked themes of love and death, including 'death as Juliet's bridegroom'.

329 Stephen Orgel (ed.), *The Winter's Tale*, Oxford Shakespeare (Oxford: Oxford University Press, 1996), pp. 32–36, discusses the two deaths.

8 Parallel Histories: Experience and Expression

330 See tables 3.1 and 3.2 (pp. 40 and 46) and the accompanying figures.

331 Two of the most important examples of diary-based studies, both from 1983, are: Linda A. Pollock, *Forgotten Children: Parent–Child Relations from 1500 to 1900* (Cambridge: Cambridge University Press, 1983), and Paul C. Rosenblatt, *Bitter, Bitter Tears: Nineteenth-Century Diarists and Twentieth-Century Grief Theorists* (Minneapolis, MN: University of Minnesota Press, 1983). They were discussed on pp. 104 and 97. See also Linda A. Pollock, 'Parent–child relations', in David I. Kertzer and Marizio Barbagli (eds), *Family Life in Early Modern Times, 1500–1789* (New Haven, CT: Yale University Press, 2001), pp. 191–220.

332 Pollock, *Forgotten Children* (1983), pp. 141–42; see also Chapter 5, p. 97.

333 This is a point emphasised by Sheila Ryan Johansson, 'Centuries of childhood / Centuries of parenting: Philippe Ariès and the modernization of privileged infancy', *Journal of Family History* 12 (1987), pp. 343–65, in reacting to Pollock's (*Forgotten Children* (1983)) 'explicitly socio-biological treatment of parental behaviour'. More recently Pollock, 'Parent-child relations' (2001), p. 219, suggests that 'Rather than search for the existence of absence of love in the past, for example, we should investigate what love meant in a given culture and era, and how it was expressed'. An excellent example of this form of approach is provided by Rudolf Dekker, *Childhood, Memory and Autobiography in Holland: From the Golden Age to Romanticism* (London: Macmillan, 2000). His concluding paragraph is worth quoting in full (p. 138).

> Over the course of three centuries [1500–1800 in the Netherlands] the manner in which parents reacted to the death of their children has changed in egodocuments. Only after 1750 are there more lengthy expressions of grief. This turning point was initially caused by a change in the character of diaries and autobiographies which later became an outlet for expressing personal feelings. Before that time personal feelings were depicted in poetry. Secondly, there was a change in the way people mourned the dead. Initially, parents were expected to adopt a Christian-stoic attitude when their child died, but after the middle of the eighteenth century people could give vent to their feelings, and were expected to surrender to grief. The social conventions in regard to emotions have changed. So have the literary conventions in which they were expressed.

Dekker's principal source of egodocuments is diaries and autobiographies from six families (59 children, 19 infant deaths, infant mortality rate of 322). He is sceptical of both the black and white legends of parental response (Chapter 1, note 10), as well as the uncritical use of egodocuments. Like other scholars, he is appalled by the suggestion of parental indifference, but dismayed by the prospect of having to accept ahistorical psychological continuity over the long term. His final position seems closer to Ariès than might have been anticipated; it is decidedly dark grey. Dekker's conclusions bear interesting comparison with those of Julie-Marie Strange, *Death, Grief and Poverty in Britain, 1870–1914* (Cambridge: Cambridge University Press, 2005), pp. 261–62 (see Chapter 3, note 113), as well as the insistence by Arthur E. Imhof, *Lost Worlds: How Our European Ancestors Coped with Everyday Life and Why Life Is So Hard Today* (Charlottesville, VA: University of Virginia Press, 1996), pp. 81–87, that it is important to consider geographical variations in the 'reverence for life' which is likely to affect attitudes to women and children especially.

334 The literature on this issue is now substantial. See Keith Hopkins, *Death and Renewal, Sociological Studies in Roman History, Volume 2* (Cambridge: Cambridge University Press, 1983); Mark Golden, 'Did the ancients care when their children died?', *Greece and Rome* 35 (1988), pp. 152–63; Beryl Rawson, *Children and Childhood in Roman Italy* (Oxford: Oxford University Press, 2003); and James Z. Lee and Wang Feng, *One Quarter of Humanity: Malthusian Mythology and Chinese Realities* (Cambridge, MA: Harvard University Press, 1999). However, it is not always clear what should be counted as infanticide, or even abandonment. Nancy Scheper-Hughes, *Death Without Weeping: The Violence of Everyday Life in Brazil* (Berkeley, CA: University of California Press,

1992) found that some of the women she interviewed made a distinction among their children between 'thrivers' and 'keepers', on the one hand, and those thought of 'as born "already wanting to die"' (p. 342), on the other.

335 London did have an important foundling hospital which was established in the eighteenth century. See Alysa Levene, 'The measurement of mortality at the London Foundling Hospital, 1741–99', *Population Studies* 59 (2005), pp. 87–97. However, there was a sharp difference of opinion in Europe as to the way in which bastard children and unmarried mothers should be treated. Catholic societies, France included, tended to take a harsher line. See Jean-Louis Flandrin, *Families in Former Times: Kinship, Household and Sexuality* (Cambridge: Cambridge University Press, 1979) and, especially for Italy, John Eastburn Boswell, 'Espositio and oblation: The abandonment of children and the ancient and medieval family', *American Historical Review* 89 (1984), pp. 10–33, and David I. Kertzer, *Sacrificed for Honor: Italian Infant Abandonment and the Politics of Reproductive Control* (Boston: Beacon Press, 1993). Kertzer (p. 13) estimates that for France, 1828–33, 34,160 babies were abandoned annually (5238 in Paris, 1893 in Lyon).

336 Robert Woods, *The Demography of Victorian England and Wales* (Cambridge: Cambridge University Press, 2000), p. 3.

Select Bibliography

Ariès, Philippe, *Histoire des populations françaises et de leurs attitudes devant la vie depuis le XVIIIe siècle* (Paris: Éditions Self, 1948)

Ariès, Philippe, *L'enfant et la vie familiale sous l'Ancien Régime* (Paris: Libraire Plon, 1960; Éditions du Seuil, 1973 [published in an abridged form, without illustrations, but with a new preface by Ariès]), translated by Robert Baldick as *Centuries of Childhood* [abridged edition without illustrations and footnotes] (New York: Vintage Books, 1962; London: Jonathan Cape, 1962; Penguin, 1973, 1979; Pimlico, 1996)

Ariès, Philippe, 'La mort inversée. Le changement des attitudes devant la mort dans les sociétés occidentales', *Archives Européennes Sociologie* 8 (1967), pp. 169–95, translated and reprinted as 'The reversal of death: changes in attitudes toward death in Western societies', *American Quarterly* 26 (1974), pp. 536–60, and in David E. Stannard (ed.), *Death in America* (Philadelphia, PA: University of Pennsylvania Press, 1975), pp. 134–58

Ariès, Philippe, *Centuries of Childhood* (London: Penguin, 1973)

Ariès, Philippe, 'The reversal of death: changes in attitudes toward death in Western societies', in David E. Stannard (ed.), *Death in America* (Philadelphia, PA: University of Pennsylvania Press, 1975), pp. 134–58

Ariès, Philippe, 'L'histoire des mentalités', in Jacques Le Goff, Roger Chartier and Jacques Revel (eds), *La nouvelle histoire* (Paris: Retz–CEPL, 1978), pp. 402–23

Ariès, Philippe, *The Hour of Our Death* (New York: Alfred A. Knopf, 1981)

Ariès, Philippe, *Images of Man and Death* (Cambridge, MA: Harvard University Press, 1985)

Averill, James R., 'Grief: its nature and significance', *Psychological Bulletin* 70 (1968), pp. 721–48

Avery, Gillian and Kimberley Reynolds (eds), *Representations of Childhood Death* (London: Macmillan, 2000)

Badinter, Elisabeth, *Mother Love: Myth and Reality of Motherhood in Modern History* (New York: Macmillan, 1981), translated from *L'amour en plus: Histoire de l'amour maternal, XVIIe–XXe siècle* (Paris: Flammarion, 1980)

Becchi, Egle and Dominique Julia, 'Histoire de l'enfance, histoire sans paroles?', in Egle Becchi and Dominique Julia (eds), *Histoire de l'enfance en Occident. Tome 1: De l'Antiquité au XVIIe siècle* (Paris: Éditions du Seuil, 1998), pp. 7–39

Becchi, Egle and Dominique Julia (eds), *Histoire de l'enfance en Occident. Tome 1: De l'Antiquité au XVIIe siècle. Tome 2: Du XVIIIe siècle à nos jours* (Paris: Éditions du Seuil, 1998)

Bedaux, Jan Baptist, 'Funeraire kinder-portretten uit de 17de eeaw', in Bert C. Sliggers (ed.), *Naar het lijk: Het Nederlandse doodsportret 1500-heden* (Zutphen: Teylers Museum, 1998), pp. 86–115

Bedaux, Jan Baptist and Rudi Ekkart (eds), *Pride and Joy: Children's Portraits in the Netherlands, 1500–1700* (New York: Harry N. Abrams, 2001)

Belsey, Catherine, *Shakespeare and the Loss of Eden: The Construction of Family Values in Early Modern Culture* (London: Macmillan, 1999)

Bideau, Alain, 'Accouchement 'natural' et accouchement à 'haut risqué'', *Annales de Démographie Historique* (1981), pp. 49–66

Bideau, Alain, Bertrand Desjardins and Héctor Pérez Brignoli (eds), *Infant and Child Mortality in the Past* (Oxford: Clarendon Press, 1997)

Borg, Susan and Judith Lasker, *When Pregnancy Fails: Coping With Miscarriage, Stillbirth and Infant Death* (London: Routledge & Kegan Paul, 1982)

Brown, Marilyn R. (ed.), *Picturing Children: Constructions of Childhood between Rousseau and Freud* (London: Ashgate, 2002)

Burke, Peter, 'Strengths and weaknesses of the history of mentalities', *History of European Ideas* 7 (1986), pp. 439–51

Burke, Peter, *The French Historical Revolution: The* Annales *School, 1929–89* (Cambridge: Polity Press, 1990)

Burke, Peter, *History and Social Theory* (Cambridge: Polity Press, 1992)

Burke, Peter, *Eyewitnessing: The Uses of Images as Historical Evidence* (London: Reaktion, 2001)

Calvert, Karin, 'Children in American family portraiture, 1670 to 1810', *William and Mary Quarterly* 39 (1982), pp. 87–113

Calvert, Karin, *Children in the House: The Material Culture of Early Childhood, 1600–1900* (Boston: Northeastern University Press, 1992)

Carpenter, Margaret Boyd, *The Child in Art* (London: Methuen, 1906)

Cecil, Rosanne (ed.), *The Anthropology of Pregnancy Loss: Comparative Studies in Miscarriage, Stillbirth and Neonatal Death* (Oxford: Berg, 1996)

Chaunu, Pierre, *Histoire, science sociale: La durée, l'espace et l'homme à l'époque moderne* (Paris: SEDES, 1974)

Chaunu, Pierre, 'Mourir à Paris (XVIe–XVIIIe siècles)', *Annales: ESC* 31 (1976), pp. 29–50

Chaunu, Pierre, *La mort à Paris, XVIe, XVIIe et XVIIIe siècles* (Paris: Fayard, 1978)

Chaunu, Pierre, *Histoire quantitative, histoire sérielle* (Paris: Librairie Armand Colin, 1978)

Classen, Albrecht (ed.), *Childhood in the Middle Ages and the Renaissance: The Results of a Paradigm Shift in the History of Mentality* (Berlin: Walter de Gruyter, 2005)

Cody, Lisa Forman, 'Living and dying in Georgian London's lying-in hospitals', *Bulletin of the History of Medicine* 78 (2004), pp. 309–48

Coster, Will, 'Tokens of innocence: infant baptism, death and burial in early modern England', in Bruce Gordon and Peter Marshall (eds), *The Place of the Dead: Death and Remembrance in Late Medieval and Early Modern Europe* (Cambridge: Cambridge University Press, 2000), pp. 266–87

Coster, Will, *Baptism and Spiritual Kinship in Early Modern England* (London: Ashgate, 2002)

Coveney, Peter, *Poor Monkey: The Child in Literature* (London: Rockliff, 1957) republished as *The Image of Childhood: The Individual and Society: A Study of the Theme in English Literature* (London: Penguin, 1967)

Crawford, Patricia, '"The sucking child': Adult attitudes to child care in the first year of life in seventeenth-century England', *Continuity and Change* 1 (1986), pp. 23–51

Crawford, Patricia, *Blood, Bodies and Families in Early Modern England* (London: Pearson Longman, 2004)

Cressey, David, *Birth, Marriage and Death: Ritual, Religion, and the Life-Cycle in Tudor and Stuart England* (Oxford: Oxford University Press, 1997)

Dekker, Jeroen J. H., 'A Republic of Educators: educational messages in seventeenth-century Dutch painting', *History of Education Quarterly* 36 (1996), pp. 155–82

Dekker, Jeroen J. H. and Leendert F. Groenendijk, 'The Republic of God or the Republic of Children? Childhood and child-rearing after the Reformation: an appraisal of Simon Schama's thesis about the uniqueness of the Dutch case', *Oxford Review of Education* 17 (1991), pp. 317–35

Dekker, Rudolf, *Childhood, Memory and Autobiography in Holland: From the Golden Age to Romanticism* (London: Macmillan, 2000)

Dekker, Rudolf (ed.), *Egodocuments and History: Autobiographical Writing in its Social Context since the Middle Ages* (Hillversum: Verloren, 2002)

Deutsch, Helene, 'Absence of grief', *Psychoanalytic Quarterly* 6 (1937), pp. 12–22

Dupâquier, Jacques *et al.* (eds.), *Histoire de la population française: 2, De la Renaissance à 1789* (Paris: Presses Universitaires de France, 1988)

Dupâquier, Jacques *et al.* (eds), *Histoire de la population française: 3, De 1789 à 1914* (Paris: Presses Universitaires de France, 1988)

Dupâquier, Jacques, 'Pour une histoire de la prématurité', *Annales de Démographie Historique* (1994), pp. 187–202

Dupâquier, Jacques, *La population française aux XVIIe et XVIIIe siècles* (Paris: Presses Universitaires de France, third edition, 1995, first edition, 1979)

Durantini, Mary Frances, *The Child in Seventeenth-Century Dutch Painting* (Ann Arbor, MI: UMI Research Press, 1983)

Easthope, Antony, *Poetry as Discourse* (London: Methuen, 1983)

Edmondson, Paul and Stanley Wells, *Shakespeare's Sonnets* (Oxford: Oxford University Press, 2004)

Fildes, Valerie (ed.), *Women as Mothers in Pre-Industrial England* (London: Routledge, 1990)

Fine, Agnès and Jean-Claude Sangoï, *La population française au XIXe siècle* (Paris: Presses Universitaires de France, 1991)

Finkbiner, Ann K., *After the Death of a Child: Living with Loss through the Years* (Baltimore, MD: Johns Hopkins University Press, 1998)

Flandrin, Jean-Louis, 'Enfance et société', *Annales: ESC* 19 (1964), pp. 322–29

Flandrin, Jean-Louis, *Families in Former Times: Kinship, Household and Sexuality* (Cambridge: Cambridge University Press, 1979)

Forsyth, Ilene H., 'Children in early medieval art: ninth through twelfth centuries', *Journal of Psychohistory* 4 (1976), pp. 31–70

Fox, Adam, *Oral and Literate Culture in England, 1500–1700* (Oxford: Oxford University Press, 2000)

Freud, Sigmund, 'Mourning and melancholia', *Collected Papers, Volume IV* (London: Hogarth Press, 1957), pp. 152–70

Galley, Chris, *The Demography of Early Modern Towns: York in the Sixteenth and Seventeenth Centuries* (Liverpool: Liverpool University Press, 1998)

Galley, Chris, Naomi Williams and Robert Woods, 'Detection without correction: problems in assessing the quality of English ecclesiastical and civil registration', *Annales de Démographie Historique* (1995), pp. 161–83

Gélis, Jacques, *History of Childbirth: Fertility, Pregnancy and Birth in Early Modern Europe*

(London: Polity Press, 1991), originally published as *L'arbre et le fruit* (Paris: Libraire Arthème Fayard, 1984)

Gélis, Jacques, *La sage-femme ou le médicin: Une nouvelle conception de la vie* (Paris: Fayard, 1988)

Gélis, Jacques, Mireille Laget and Marie-France Morel, *Entrer dans la vie: naissances et enfances dans la France traditionelle* (Paris: Éditions Gallimard, 1978)

Gittings, Clare, *Death, Burial and the Individual in Early Modern England* (London: Croom Helm, 1984)

Glaser, Brigitte, *The Creation of the Self in Autobiographical Forms of Writing in Seventeenth-Century England: Subjectivity and Self-Fashioning in Memoirs, Diaries, and Letters* (Heidelberg: Universitätverlag C. Winter, 2001)

Goldberg, Jonathan, *James I and the Politics of Literature: Jonson, Shakespeare, Donne, and their Contemporaries* (Baltimore, MD: Johns Hopkins University Press, 1983)

Goldberg, Jonathan, 'Fatherly authority: the politics of Stuart family images', in Margaret W. Ferguson, Maureen Quilligan and Nancy J. Vickers (eds), *Rewriting The Renaissance: The Discourses of Sexual Difference in Early Modern Europe* (Chicago: University of Chicago Press, 1986), pp. 3–32

Golden, Mark, 'Did the ancients care when their children died?', *Greece and Rome* 35 (1988), pp. 152–63

Gordon, Bruce and Peter Marshall (eds), *The Place of the Dead: Death and Remembrance in Late Medieval and Early Modern Europe* (Cambridge: Cambridge University Press, 2000)

Goubert, Pierre and Daniel Roche, *Le français et l'Ancien Régime. 2. Culture et société* (Paris: Armand Colin, third edition, 2000)

Gowing, Laura, *Common Bodies: Women, Touch and Power in Seventeenth-Century England* (New Haven, CT: Yale University Press, 2003)

Graz, Marie-Christine Autin, *Children in Painting* (Milan: Skira Editore, 2002)

Greenblatt, Stephen, *Renaissance Self-Fashioning: From More to Shakespeare* (Chicago: University of Chicago Press, 1980)

Greenblatt, Stephen, *Will in the World: How Shakespeare became Shakespeare* (London: Jonathan Cape, 2004)

Greer, Germaine, Susan Hastings, Jeslyn Medoff and Melinda Sansone (eds), *Kissing the Rod: An Anthology of Seventeenth-Century Women's Verse* (London: Virago, 1988)

Greven, Philip J., *Four Generations: Population, Land, and Family in Colonial Andover, Massachusetts* (Ithaca, NY: Cornell University Press, 1970)

Greven, Philip J., *The Protestant Temperament: Patterns of Child-Rearing, Religious Experience, and the Self in Early America* (New York: Alfred A. Knopf, 1977)

Guthke, Karl S., *The Gender of Death: A Cultural History in Art and Literature* (Cambridge: Cambridge University Press, 1999)

Guthke, Karl S., *Epitaph Culture in the West: Variations on a Theme in Cultural History* (Lampeter, Dyfed: Edwin Mellen Press, 2003)

Hamel, B. Remmo, 'The image of the child: Dutch and Flemish paintings', *Journal of Psychohistory* 24 (1996), pp. 72–89

Hammond, Jeffrey A., *The American Puritan Elegy: A Literary and Cultural Study* (Cambridge: Cambridge University Press, 2000)

Harré, Rom (ed.), *The Social Construction of Emotions* (Oxford: Basil Blackwell, 1986)

Haskell, Francis, *History and its Images: Art and the Interpretation of the Past* (New Haven, CT: Yale University Press, 1993)

Hautecoeur, Louis, *Les peintres de la vie familiale: évolution d'un thème* (Paris: Éditions de la Galerie Charpentier, 1945)

Hearn, Karen (ed.), *Dynasties: Painting in Tudor and Jacobean England, 1630–1630* (London: Tate Publishing, 1995)

Hearn, Karen, *Marcus Gheeraerts II: Elizabethan Artist* (London: Tate Publishing, 2002)

Herlihy, David, 'Medieval children', in Bede Karl Lackner and Kenneth Roy Philip (eds), *Essays on Medieval Civilization: The Walter Prescott Webb Memorial Lectures* (Austin, TX: University of Austin Press, 1978), pp. 109–41

Higonnet, Anne, *Pictures of Innocence: The History and Crisis of Ideal Childhood* (London: Thames & Hudson, 1998)

Hijiya, James A., 'American gravestones and attitudes toward death: a brief history', *Proceedings of the American Philosophical Society* 127 (1983), pp. 339–63

Hill, Christopher, 'Sex, marriage, and the family in England', *Economic History Review* 31 (1978), pp. 450–63

Hirsch, Julia, *Family Photographs: Content, Meaning, and Effect* (New York: Oxford University Press, 1981)

Hirsch, Marianne, *Family Frames: Photography, Narrative and Postmemory* (Cambridge, MA: Harvard University Press, 1997)

Holdsworth, Sara and Joan Crossley (eds), *Innocence and Experience: Images of Children in British Art from 1600 to the Present* (Manchester: Manchester City Art Galleries, 1992)

Hopkins, John T., '"Such a twin likeness there was in the pair." An investigation into the painting of the Cholmondeley sisters', *Transactions of the Historic Society of Lancashire and Cheshire* 141 (1991), pp. 1–37

Hopkins, Keith, *Death and Renewal, Sociological Studies in Roman History, Volume 2* (Cambridge: Cambridge University Press, 1983)

Houlbrooke, Ralph A., *The English Family, 1450–1700* (London: Longman, 1984)

Houlbrooke, Ralph A. (ed.), *Death, Ritual, and Bereavement* (London: Routledge, 1989)

Houlbrooke, Ralph A., *Death, Religion, and the Family in England, 1480–1750* (Oxford: Clarendon Press, 1998)

Hughes, Diane Owen, 'Representing the family: Portraits and purposes in early modern Italy', *Journal of Interdisciplinary History* 17 (1986), pp. 7–38

Huizinga, Johan, *The Waning of the Middle Ages: A Study of the Forms of Life, Thought and Art in France and the Netherlands in the XIVth and XVth Centuries* (London: Edward Arnold, 1924)

Hurtig, Judith W., 'Death in childbirth: seventeenth-century English tombs and their place in contemporary thought', *Art Bulletin* 65 (1983), pp. 603–15

Hutton, Patrick H., 'Of death and destiny: the Ariès–Vovelle debate about the history of mourning', in Peter Homans (ed.), *Symbolic Loss: The Ambiguity of Mourning and Memory at Century's End* (Charlottesville, VA: University of Virginia Press, 2000), pp. 147–70

Hutton, Patrick H., *Philippe Ariès and the Politics of French Cultural History* (Amherst, MA: University of Massachusetts Press, 2004)

Imhof, Arthur E., *Lost Worlds: How Our European Ancestors Coped With Everyday Life and Why Life Is So Hard Today* (Charlottesville, VA: University of Virginia Press, 1996), translated by Thomas Robisheaux, originally published as *Die verlorenen Welten* (Munich: Beck, 1984)

Jalland, Pat, *Death in the Victorian Family* (Oxford: Oxford University Press, 1996)

Jalland, Pat, 'Victorian death and its decline: 1850–1918', in Peter C. Jupp and Clare Gittings (eds), *Death in England: An Illustrated History* (Manchester: Manchester University Press, 1999), pp. 230–55

Johansson, Sheila Ryan, 'Centuries of childhood/centuries of parenting: Philippe Ariès and the modernization of privileged infancy', *Journal of Family History* 12 (1987), pp. 343–65

Jupp, Peter C. and Clare Gittings (eds), *Death in England: An Illustrated History* (Manchester: Manchester University Press, 1999)

Kertzer, David I. and Marizio Barbagli (eds), *Family Life in Early Modern Times, 1500–1789* (New Haven, CT: Yale University Press, 2001)

Kohner, Nancy and Alix Henley, *When a Baby Dies: The Experience of Late Miscarriage, Stillbirth and Neonatal Death* (London: Routledge, 2001)

Landers, John, *Death and the Metropolis: Studies in the Demographic History of London, 1670–1830* (Cambridge: Cambridge University Press, 1993)

Laget, Mireille, 'La naissance aux siècles classiques. Pratique des accouchements et attitudes collectives en France aux XVIIe et XVIIIe siècles', *Annales: ESC* 32 (1977), pp. 958–92

Laget, Mireille, *Naissances: L'accouchement avant l'age de la clinique* (Paris: Éditions du Seuil, 1982)

Laslett, Peter, 'The wrong way through the telescope: a note on literary evidence in sociology and in historical sociology', *British Journal of Sociology* 27 (1976), pp. 317–42

Laslett, Peter, 'Philippe Ariès and "La famille"', *Encounter* 46(3) (March 1976), pp. 80–83

Laurence, Anne, 'Godly grief: individual responses to death in seventeenth-century Britain', in Ralph Houlbrooke (ed.), *Death, Ritual, and Bereavement* (London: Routledge, 1989), pp. 62–76

Le Goff, Jacques, 'Mentalities: a history of ambiguities', in Jacques Le Goff and Pierre Nora (eds), *Constructing the Past: Essays in Historical Methodology* (Cambridge: Cambridge University Press, 1985), pp. 166–80

Le Grand-Sébille, Catherine, Marie-France Morel and Françoise Zonabend (eds), *Le foetus, le nourrisson et la mort* (Paris: L'Harmattan, 1998)

Le Roy Ladurie, Emmanuel, 'Chaunu, Lebrun, Vovelle: the new history of death', in *The Territory of the Historian*, translated by Ben and Sian Reynolds (Hassocks, Sussex: Harvester Press, 1979), pp. 273–84

Leavitt, John, 'Meaning and feeling in the anthropology of emotions', *American Ethnologist* 23 (1996), pp. 514–39

Lebrun, François, *La vie conjugale sous l'Ancien Régime* (Paris: Armand Colin, 1975), pp. 111–39

Lerner, Laurence, *Angels and Absences: Child Deaths in the Nineteenth Century* (Nashville, TN: Vanderbilt University Press, 1997)

Lewis, Judith Schneid, 'Maternal health in the English aristocracy: myths and realities, 1790–1840', *Journal of Social History* 17(1) (1983), pp. 97–114

Lewis, Judith Schneid, *In the Family Way: Childbearing in the British Aristocracy, 1760–1860* (New Brunswick, NJ: Rutgers University Press, 1986)

Lindemann, Erich, 'Symptomatology and management of acute grief', *American Journal of Psychiatry* 101 (1944), pp. 141–48

Litten, Julian, *The English Way of Death: The Common Funeral since 1450* (London: Robert Hale, 1991)

Llewellyn, Nigel, *Funeral Monuments in Post-Reformation England* (Cambridge: Cambridge University Press, 2000)

Loudon, Irvine, *Death in Childbirth: An International Study of Maternal Care and Maternal Mortality, 1800–1950* (Oxford: Clarendon Press, 1992)

Lutz, Catherine A., *Unnatural Emotions: Everyday Sentiments on a Micronesian Atoll and Their Challenge to Western Theory* (Chicago: University of Chicago Press, 1988)

Lutz, Catherine A. and Lila Abu-Lughod (eds), *Language and the Politics of Emotions* (Cambridge: Cambridge University Press, 1990)

Macfarlane, Alan, *The Family Life of Ralph Josselin, A Seventeenth-Century Clergyman* (Cambridge: Cambridge University Press, 1970)

Macfarlane, Alan (ed.), *The Diary of Ralph Josselin, 1616–1683* (Oxford: Oxford University Press for the British Academy, 1976)

Macfarlane, Alan, 'Review of *The Family, Sex and Marriage in England, 1500–1800*. By Lawrence Stone', *History and Theory* 18 (1979), pp. 103–26

Marland, Hilary (ed.), *Mother and Child were Saved* (Amsterdam: Rodopi, 1987)

Marland, Hilary (ed.), *The Art of Midwifery: Early Modern Midwives in Europe* (London: Routledge, 1993)

Martines, Lauro, *Society and History in English Renaissance Verse* (Oxford: Basil Blackwell, 1985)

McClenden, Mariel C., Joseph P. Ward and Michael MacDonald (eds), *Protestant Identities: Religion, Society, and Self-Fashioning in Post-Reformation England* (Stanford, CA: Stanford University Press, 1999)

McDonagh, Josephine, *Child Murder and British Culture, 1720–1900* (Cambridge: Cambridge University Press, 2003)

McManners, John, 'Death and the French historians', in Joachim Whaley (ed.), *Mirrors of Mortality: Studies in the Social History of Death* (London: Europa Publications, 1981), pp. 106–30

Mechling, Jay, 'Advice to historians on advice to mothers', *Journal of Social History* 9 (1975), pp. 44–63

Mendelson, Sara and Patricia Crawford, *Women in Early Modern England, 1550–1720* (Oxford: Clarendon Press, 1998)

Mercier, Roger, *L'enfant dans la société du XVIIIe siècle (avant l'Émile)*, Université de Dakar, Faculté des Lettres et Sciences Humaines, Publications de la Section de Langues et Littératures No. 6 (Dakar, 1961)

Morin, Edgar, *L'homme et la mort dans l'histoire* (Paris: Éditions Corrêa, 1951)

Orme, Nicholas, *Medieval Children* (New Haven, CT: Yale University Press, 2001)

Ozment, Steven, *Flesh and Spirit: Private Life in Early Modern Germany* (New York: Viking, 1999)

Ozment, Steven, *Ancestors: The Loving Family in Old Europe* (Cambridge, MA: Harvard University Press, 2001)

Panofsky, Erwin, *Meaning in the Visual Arts* (New York: Doubleday, 1955; London: Penguin, 1970)

Penny, Nicholas, 'English church monuments to women who died in childbed between 1780 and 1835', *Journal of the Warburg and Caurtauld Institutes* 38 (1975), pp. 314–32

Penny, Nicholas, *Church Monuments in Romantic England* (New Haven, CT: Yale University Press, 1977)

Petrucci, Armando, *Writing the Dead: Death and Writing Strategies in the Western Tradition*, translated by Michael Sullivan (Stanford, CA: Stanford University Press, 1998)

Pigler, Andor, 'Portraying the dead: painting—graphic art', *Acta Historiae Artium Academiae Scientarium Hungaricae* 4 (1957), pp. 1–74

Pigman III, G. W., *Grief and English Renaissance Elegy* (Cambridge: Cambridge University Press, 1985)

Plumb, J. H., 'The new world of children in eighteenth-century England', *Past and Present* 67 (1975), pp. 64–95

Pollock, Linda A., *Forgotten Children: Parent–Child Relations from 1500 to 1900* (Cambridge: Cambridge University Press, 1983)

Pollock, Linda A. (ed.), *A Lasting Relationship: Parents and Children Over Three Centuries* (London: Fourth Estate, 1987)

Pollock, Linda A., '"Teach her to live under obedience": The making of women in the upper ranks of early modern England', *Continuity and Change* 4 (1989), pp. 231–58

Pollock, Linda A., 'Embarking on a rough passage: the experience of pregnancy in early-modern society', in Valerie Fildes (ed.), *Women as Mothers in Pre-Industrial England* (London: Routledge, 1990), pp. 39–67

Pollock, Linda A., 'Parent–child relations', in David I. Kertzer and Marizio Barbagli (eds), *Family Life in Early Modern Times, 1500–1789* (New Haven, CT: Yale University Press, 2001), pp. 191–220

Pols, Robert, *Family Photographs, 1860–1945* (London: Public Record Office, 2002)

Preston, Samuel H. and Etienne van de Walle, 'Urban French mortality in the nineteenth century', *Population Studies* 32 (1978), pp. 275–97

Prior, Mary (ed.), *Women in English Society, 1500–1800* (London: Methuen, 1985)

Prior, Mary, 'Conjugal love and the flight from marriage: poetry as a source for the history of women and the family', in Valerie Fildes (ed.), *Women as Mothers in Pre-Industrial England* (London: Routledge, 1990), pp. 179–203

Prown, Jules David, *Art as Evidence* (New Haven, CT: Yale University Press, 2001)

Rawson, Beryl, *Children and Childhood in Roman Italy* (Oxford: Oxford University Press, 2003)

Reddy, William M., *The Navigation of Feeling: Framework for the History of Emotions* (Cambridge: Cambridge University Press, 2001)

Riché, Pierre and Danièle Alexandre-Bidon, *L'enfance au Moyen Age* (Paris: Seuil, Bibliothèque Nationale de France, 1994)

Roche, Daniel, '"La mémoire de la mort" Recherche sur la place des arts de mourir dans la Librairie et la lecture en France aux XVIIe et XVIIIe siècles', *Annales: ESC* 31 (1976), pp. 76–119

Rollet, Catherine, 'Lorsque la mort devint mortalité', in Catherine Le Grand-Sébille *et al.* (eds), *Le foetus, le nourrisson et la mort* (Paris: L'Harmattan, 1998), pp. 105–26

Rosenblatt, Paul C., *Bitter, Bitter Tears: Nineteenth-Century Diarists and Twentieth-Century Grief Theorists* (Minneapolis, MN: University of Minnesota Press, 1983)

Ryerson, Alice Judson, 'Medical advice on child rearing, 1550–1900', *Harvard Educational Review* 31 (1961), pp. 302–23

Sacks, Peter M., *The English Elegy: Studies in the Genre from Spenser to Yeats* (Baltimore, MD: Johns Hopkins University Press, 1985)

Sarti, Raffaella, *Europe at Home: Family and Material Culture, 1500–1800* (New Haven, CT: Yale University Press, 2002)

Schama, Simon, *The Embarrassment of Riches: An Interpretation of Dutch Culture in the Golden Age* (London: Collins, 1987)

Scheper-Hughes, Nancy (ed.), *Child Survival: Anthropological Perspectives on the Treatment and Maltreatment of Children* (Dordrecht: D. Reidel Publishing, 1987)

Scheper-Hughes, Nancy, *Death Without Weeping: The Violence of Everyday Life in Brazil* (Berkeley, CA: University of California Press, 1992)

Schofield, Roger, 'Perinatal mortality in Hawkshead, Lancashire, 1581–1710', *Local Population Studies* 4 (1970), pp. 11–16

Schofield, Roger, 'Did the mothers really die? Three centuries of maternal mortality in "The World We Have Lost"', in Lloyd Bonfield, Richard M. Smith and Keith Wrightson (eds), *The World We Have Gained: Histories of Population and Social Structure* (Oxford: Basil Blackwell, 1986), pp. 131–60

Schofield, Roger, David Reher and Alain Bideau (eds), *The Decline of Mortality in Europe* (Oxford: Clarendon Press, 1991)

Schofield, Roger and E. A. Wrigley, 'Infant and child mortality in England in the late Tudor and early Stuart period', in Charles Webster (ed.), *Health, Medicine and Mortality in the Sixteenth Century* (Cambridge: Cambridge University Press, 1979), pp. 61–95

Schorsch, Anita, *Images of Childhood: An Illustrated Social History* (New York: Mayflower Books, 1979)

Schücking, Levin L., *The Puritan Family: A Social Study from Literary Sources* (London: Routledge & Kegan Paul, 1969), originally published as *Die Puritanische Familie* (Leipzig, 1929)

Scodel, Joshua, *The English Poetic Epitaph: Commemoration and Conflict from Jonson to Wordsworth* (Ithaca, NY: Cornell University Press, 1991)

Seaver, Paul S., *Wallington's World: A Puritan Artisan in Seventeenth-Century London* (London: Methuen, 1985)

Shaw, W. David, 'Elegy and theory: is historical and critical knowledge possible?', *Modern Language Quarterly* 55 (1994), pp. 1–16

Shaw, W. David, *Elegy & Paradox: Testing the Conventions* (Baltimore, MD: Johns Hopkins University Press, 1994)

Shorter, Edward, *A History of Women's Bodies* (New York: Basic Books, 1982)

Simonds, Wendy and Barbara Katz Rothman, *Centuries of Solace: Expressions of Maternal Grief in Popular Literature* (Philadelphia, PA: Temple University Press, 1992)

Smith, Daniel Scott and J. David Hacker, 'Cultural demography: New England deaths and puritan perception of risk', *Journal of Interdisciplinary History* 26 (1996), pp. 367–92

Stannard, David E., *The Puritan Way of Death: A Study in Religion, Culture, and Social Change* (New York: Oxford University Press, 1977)

Stearns, Peter N., 'Historical analysis in the study of emotion', *Motivation and Emotion* 10 (1986), pp. 185–93

Stevenson, Jane and Peter Davidson (eds), *Early Modern Women Poets (1520–1700): An Anthology* (Oxford: Oxford University Press, 2001)

Steward, James Christen, *The New Child: British Art and the Origins of Modern Childhood, 1730–1830* (Berkeley, CA: University Art Museum and Pacific Film Archive, University of California, Berkeley, 1995)

Stewart, Garrett, *Death Sentences: Styles of Dying in British Fiction* (Cambridge, MA: Harvard University Press, 1984)

Stickland, Irina (ed.), *The Voices of Children, 1700–1914* (Oxford: Basil Blackwell, 1973)

Stone, Lawrence, *The Family, Sex and Marriage in England, 1500–1800* (London: Weidenfeld and Nicolson, 1977)

Stone, Lawrence, 'Family history in the 1980s: past achievement and future trends', *Journal of Interdisciplinary History* 12 (1981), pp. 51–87

Strange, Julie-Marie, *Death, Grief and Poverty in Britain, 1870–1914* (Cambridge: Cambridge University Press, 2005)

Stroebe, Margaret S., Wolfgang Stroebe and Robert O. Hansson (eds), *Handbook of Bereavement: Theory, Research, and Interventi*on (Cambridge: Cambridge University Press, 1993)

Tarlow, Sarah, *Bereavement and Commemoration: An Archaeology of Mortality* (Oxford: Basil Blackwell, 1999)

Tenenti, Alberto, *La vie et la mort à travels l'art du XVe siècle* (Paris: Librairie Armand Colin, 1952)

Thomas, Keith, 'Children in early modern England', in Gillian Avery and Julia Briggs (eds), *Children and their Books: A Celebration of the Work of Iona and Peter Opie* (Oxford: Clarendon Press, 1989), pp. 45–77

Todd, Janet, *Sensibility: An Introduction* (London: Methuen, 1986)

van de Walle, Etienne, 'Pour une histoire démographique de l'avortement', *Population* 53 (1998), pp. 273–90

van de Walle, Etienne, "Marvellous secrets': Birth control in European short fiction, 1150–1650', *Population Studies* 54 (2000), pp. 321–30

van de Walle, Etienne and Samuel H. Preston, 'Mortalité de l'enfance au XIXe siècle à Paris et dans le département de la Seine', *Population* 29 (1974), pp. 89–107

van de Walle, Etienne and Francine van de Walle, 'Allaitement, stérilité et contraception: les opinions jusqu'au XIXe siècle', *Population* 27 (1972), pp. 685–701

Vovelle, Gaby and Michel Vovelle, *Vision de la mort et de l'au-delà en Provence d'après les autels des âmes du purgatoire XVe–XXe siècles* (Paris: Librairie Armand Colin, 1970)

Vovelle, Michel, *Piété baroque et déchristianisation en Provence au XVIIIe siècle* (Paris: Éditions Plon, 1973; Éditions du Seuil, 1978; Éditions du CTHS, 1997)

Vovelle, Michel, *Mourir autrefois: attitudes collectives devant la mort aux XVIIe et XVIIIe siècles* (Paris: Éditions Gallimard, 1974)

Vovelle, Michel, 'L'histoire et la longue durée', in Jacques Le Goff, Roger Chartier and Jacques Revel (eds), *La nouvelle histoire* (Paris: Retz–CEPL, 1978), pp. 316–43

Vovelle, Michel, 'A century and one-half of American epitaphs (1660–1813): toward the study of collective attitudes about death', *Comparative Studies in Society and History* 22 (1980), pp. 534–47

Vovelle, Michel, 'Ideologies and mentalities', in Raphael Samuel and Gareth Stedman Jones (eds), *Culture, Ideology and Politics* (London: Routledge & Kegan Paul, 1982), pp. 2–11

Vovelle, Michel, 'Sur la mort', in *Idéologies et mentalités* (Paris: Libraire François Maspero, 1982), pp. 92–119 (Paris: Éditions Gallimard, 1992), pp. 109–27; and 'On death', in Michel Vovelle, *Ideologies and Mentalities*, translated by Eamon O'Flaherty (Cambridge: Polity Press, 1990), pp. 64–80

Vovelle, Michel, *La mort et l'Occident de 1300 à nos jours* (Paris: Éditions Gallimard, 1983)

Vovelle, Michel and Régis Bertrand, *La ville des morts: essai sur l'imaginaire urbain contemporain d'après les cimetières provençaux* (Paris: CNRS, 1983)

Vovelle, Michel, *L'heur du grand passage: chronique de la mort* (Paris: Éditions Gallimard, 1993)

Vovelle, Michel, *Les âmes du purgatoire ou le travail du deuil* (Paris: Éditions Gallimard, 1996)

Vovelle, Michel, 'Response', in Malcolm Crook (ed.), 'The work of Michel Vovelle', *French History* 19 (2005), pp. 177–88.

Weber, Frederick Parkes, *Aspects of Death and Correlated Aspects of Life in Art, Epigram, and Poetry. Contributions Towards an Anthology and an Iconography of the Subject.* (London: T. Fisher Unwin, 1922; first edition, 1910)

Wells, Robert V., *Facing the "King of Terrors": Death and Society in an American Community, 1750–1990* (Cambridge: Cambridge University Press, 2000)

West, Shearer, *Portraiture*, Oxford History of Art (Oxford: Oxford University Press, 2004)

Whaley, Joachim (ed.), *Mirrors of Mortality: Studies in the Social History of Death* (London: Europa Publications, 1981)

Wheeler, Michael, *Death and the Future Life in Victorian Literature and Theology* (Cambridge: Cambridge University Press, 1990)

Wheeler, Richard P., 'Deaths in the family: the loss of a son and the rise of Shakespearean comedy', *Shakespeare Quarterly* 51 (2000), pp. 127–53

Wierzbicka, Anna, *Understanding Cultures through Their Key Words* (Oxford: Oxford University Press, 1997)

Wierzbicka, Anna, *Emotions Across Languages and Cultures: Diversity and Universals* (Cambridge: Cambridge University Press, 1999)

Williams, Raymond, *Keywords: A Vocabulary of Culture and Society* (London: Fontana Press, 1976)

Wilson, Adrian, 'The infancy of the history of childhood: an appraisal of Philippe Ariès', *History and Theory* 19 (1980), pp. 132–53

Wilson, Adrian, 'Participant or patient? Seventeenth century childbirth from the mother's point of view', in Roy Porter (ed.), *Patients and Practitioners: Lay Perceptions of Medicine in Pre-industrial Society* (Cambridge: Cambridge University Press, 1985), pp. 129–44

Woods, Robert, *The Demography of Victorian England and Wales* (Cambridge: Cambridge University Press, 2000)

Woods, Robert, 'Did Montaigne love his children? Demography and the hypothesis of parental indifference', *Journal of Interdisciplinary History* 33 (2003), pp. 421–42

Woods, Robert, 'Urban–rural mortality differentials: an unresolved debate', *Population and Development Review* 29 (2003), pp. 29–46

Woods, Robert, 'The measurement of historical trends in fetal mortality in England and Wales', *Population Studies* 59 (2005), pp. 147–62

Wrigley, E. A., 'The fall of marital fertility in nineteenth-century France: exemplar or exception?', in *People, Cities and Wealth* (Oxford: Basil Blackwell, 1987), pp. 270–321

Wrigley, E. A. and R. S. Schofield, *The Population History of England, 1541–1871: A Reconstruction* (London: Edward Arnold, 1981)

Wrigley, E. A., R. S. Davies, J. E. Oeppen and R. S. Schofield, *English Population History from Family Reconstitution, 1580–1837* (Cambridge: Cambridge University Press, 1997)

Index

Numbers in italics refer to notes.

Abu-Lughod, Lila *195*
Ackerman, John *275*
Ackroyd, Peter *268*
Alexandre-Bidon, Daniéle *125*
Alpers, Svetlana *158*
Anderson, Alexander 126, 161, 193, 229
Anna Karenina 200
Ariès, Philippe 1, 5, 7–24, 26–32, 39, 53, 57,
    59–60, 62–63, 78, 94, 196, 211–12, *9–10,*
    13–14, 16–18, 20–24, 26, 29, 32, 35, 41–46,
    51–53, 63, 75, 97, 111, 113, 118–19, 121–23,
    127, 131, 216
Arles 78, 85
Arnold, Klaus *12*
Ashbourne, Derbys. 71, 77, 83, 125
Aston, Lady Magdalene 75–76, 81, 211
Aston, Sir Thomas 69, 75–76, 80–81
Austen, Jane 126
Averill, James R. *311*
Avery, Gillian *109*

Badinter, Elizabeth *86*
Bald, R. C. 203, *252, 312, 314, 317, 319*
Banks, Thomas 71, 77, 83, 125
Barbagli, Marizio *9*
Bardet, Jean-Pierre *97*
Barker, Juliet 22
Barrell, John *167*
Bartlett, John *326*
Beaurline, L. A. *294*
Becchi, Egle *9, 14*
Bedaux, Jan Baptist *114–15, 131, 134, 154*
Behn, Aphra 123, 146, 185, 224
Belloc, Hilaire *308*
Belsey, Catherine 93, 103, *177, 179, 204*

Bentley, G. H. *250*
Berman, Ronald *255*
Berthieu, René *81*
Bertillon, Jacques 41
Bideau, Alain 50, *81, 87, 94*
Bisham, Berks. 113
Black, William 171, *243*
Blake, William 21, 125, 154, 196, 198, 227, *50*
Blayo, Yves 40
Bloom, Harold 117, *241*
Bogin, Nina 127, 168, 189, 230
Bond, Edward *243*
Bond, William 117
Bonneuil, Noël *78*
Booth, Stephen *229*
Boothby, Penelope 70–71, 76, 83, 125, 198, 200,
    211
Boothby, Sir Brooke 77, 83, 125, 155, 196, 198,
    200, 227
Borg, Susan *194*
Boswell, John Eastburn *335*
Bowden, Samuel 124, 151, 185–86
Boyd, Elizabeth 124, 149, 189, 225
Bradley, A. C. 103, *203*
Bradstreet, Anne 123, 146, 171–72, 174, 177, 182,
    224, *281*
Braudel, Fernand 24, *55–56*
breastfeeding 40–42, 53, 55–56, 84
Bridges, Robert 126, 162, 187, 229
Brobeck, Stephen *128*
Brontë family 18–21, 210
Brontë, Charlotte 19–20, *42, 216*
Brontë, Emily 19–20
Brooks, Cleanth 104, *206*
Brown, Charles Armitage *231*

Brown, Marilyn R. *114*
Browne, Mary Ann 126, 158, 183, 186, 228
Budd family 71, 78, 84
Burke, Peter 27, *22, 65–67, 114, 120*
Burns, Robert 2, 125, 153, 196, 226
Byron, Lord 196

Calvert, Karin 65, *128, 129, 160*
Cambridge 3, 120–21, 124
Canning, Mehetabel 70, 83
Canterbury, Kent 123
Carey, John *254, 312, 318, 320–21, 324*
Carey, Lady Mary 122–23, 143, 181, 223
Carpenter, Margaret Boyd *114, 163*
Carver, Terrell *57*
Cassatt, Mary 71, 85, 87
Cave, Jane 124, 151, 226
Cecil, Rosanne *194*
Champaigne, Philippe de 63
Chartier, Roger *22*
Chaunu, Pierre 1, 14, 29, 31, *21, 72–73*
Chedgzoy, Kate *242*
cherries 79–80, 82, 87
Cherry, J. L. *273*
Cheshire 75, 92, 121, 124, 192
Cheyne, Jane (Vicountess Newhaven) 123, 188, 223
Chichester, Sussex 120
China 8, 18, 212, *334*
Cholmondeley ladies 68, 75, 79, 81
Chute, Elizabeth 194, *293, 298*
Clare, John 126, 160, 187, 228
Clark, Stuart *66*
Classen, Albrecht *9, 52*
Coale, Ansley J. 34
Cobham, Lord (William Brooke) 68, 72, 79–80
Cody, Lisa Forman *103*
Coiro, Ann Baynes *259*
Coleridge, Samuel Taylor 125, 155, 195–96, 200, 227
Colmworth, Beds. 120
content analysis 171, 175
Cook, Ann Jennalie *206,*
Corbett, Elizabeth 124, 148, 190, 192
Cornwall 126
Coster, Will *108–9*
Coveney, Peter 21, *49–50, 188, 301*
Cranston, Maurice *162*
Crawford, Patricia *104–105*

Crawley, Charlotte *155*
Cressy, David *256*
Crewe, Lady Jane 75, 81, 121, 138, 190, 192, 195, 211
Crewe, Sir Clipsby 121, *141, 258*
Crossley, Joan *114*
Crulai, Normandy 39–40, 43
Crum, Margaret *255*
Crystal, Ben *285*
Crystal, David *285*
Cummings, Robert *251, 258*
Cunningham, Hugh *268*

Dacre, Tom 125, 154, 196, *268*
Darlington, Beth *271*
Darwin, Charles 96–97, *190–91*
Davidson, Peter *247, 253, 260*
Davies, R. S. 47, 50, *89*
Davitz, Joel R. *280*
Dean Prior, Devon 222
Degas, Edgar 85
Dekker, Jeroen J. H. *131*
Dekker, Rudolf *10, 104, 208, 210, 259, 333*
Demeny, Paul 34
DeNeef, A. Leigh *299*
Denmark 53–54, 72
Des Granges, David 69, 76, 81
Deutsch, Helene *310*
Devis, Arthur 69–70, 76–77, 82, *133*
Devon 45–46, 120, 193, 195, 222
diaries 2, 54, 104–6, 210, *29*
Dickens, Charles 21, 117, *50, 271–72*
Dixon, Thomas *198*
Dobson, William 69, 76, 80, *133*
Donaghy, Michael *186*
Donaldson, Ian *293*
Donne, Ann 119–20, 190, 202–5, 210, 220, *252, 322*
Donne, John 119–20, 133, 190, 194, 202–5, 208, 210, 220
Dorey, Helen *165*
Dover Wilson, John 115, 117–18, *220, 222, 226, 231, 239, 245*
Dowden, Edward 126, 162, 183, 229, *274*
Drury, Elizabeth 204–5
Dublin 126–27
Duncan-Jones, Katherine 222–226, 228, 230
Dupâquier, Jacques 40–41, 43, *78, 82, 84–85, 88, 96–97, 99*

Durantini, Mary Frances 65, *130*
Durkheim, Emile *65*
Dye, Nancy Schrom *110*
Dyer, Lady Katherine 120, 134, 192, 220
Dyer, Sir William 120, 134, 190, 192, 220

Eakin, Paul John *209*
Eakins, Thomas 71, 85
Earls Colne, Essex 105
Easthope, Antony *201*
Eccles, Audrey *94*
Edmondson, Paul *232*
Egerton, Elizabeth (Countess of Bridgewater) 123, 143, 181, 190, 223
Ekkart, Rudi *114, 131, 134, 154*
elegies 169–208, 214
Elizabeth I 72, 89, 119, 220
England 2, 5, 18, 36, 43–56, 88, 209, 212
Enright, D. J. 126–27, 164, 184, 230
Evans, G. Blakemore *231*

Fairbanks, Jonathan L. *145, 159*
family history 4–5, 7
Farr, William 47
Feldman, Paula R. *270*
fertility 53–55, 59, *24, 97, 103*
Figes, Orlando *305*
Fildes, Valerie *102*
Fine, Agnés *78*
Finkbeiner, Ann K. *194*
Finlay, Roger 47
Fissell, Mary E. *284*
Flanders 72, 122
Flandrin, Jean-Louis *10, 35, 82, 335*
Flatman, Thomas 123, 147, 182, 224
Floris, Frans 63
Forbes, Peter *186*
Forker, Charles R. *327*
Forsyth, Ilene H. 64, *124*
Fothergill, Robert A. *209*
foundlings *335*
Fowler, Alastair *254*
Fox, Adam *105, 246*
France 2, 5, 10, 18, 29–32, 36–44, 50–56, 59, 87, 209, 212, *99, 335*
Fraser, Antonia 16, *30*
Freake, Elizabeth Clarke 69, 76, 81–82
Freake-Gibbs limner 81
French historians 1, 5, 7, 27, 29, 32, *66, 73*

Freud, Sigmund 6, 97, 194, 201–2, *192, 309–10*
Fripp, Edgar I. 113, *224*
Fulham, Middlesex 88–89, 91
Fuseli, Henry 77

Gage, John *172*
Gainsborough, Lincs. 45–46
Gainsborough, Thomas 64, 70, 77, 83, 87
Galley, Chris 47, 51, *92*
Galliano, Paul 41
Gamage, Barbara (Lady Sidney) 68, 73–75, 79, 210–11, *155, 178*
Ganiage, Jean 41, *81*
Gardner, Stanley *268*
Gatierrez, Hector 50
Gautier, Alain *87*
Gautier, Etienne 40
Gay, Peter *310*
Gélis, Jacques *102, 103*
Germany *10, 12, 99*
Gheeraerts the Younger, Marcus 68, 72–73, 89, 91
Gibbs children 82
Gifford, Emma 126, 190, 192, 229
Gill, Stephen 197, *268*
Gittings, Clare 16, *31, 107, 109, 117*
Glaser, Brigitte 105, *209*
Glen, Heather *304*
Goldberg, Jonathan 103, *123, 205*
Golden, Mark *53, 334*
Goodrich, Lloyd *169*
Goody, Jack *300*
Goubert, Pierre *81, 84, 103, 113*
Gowing, Laura *102*
Graham children 69, 82
gravestones 92–93, *118, 182–84*
Gray, Thomas 124, 151, 185–86, 226
Graz, Marie-Christine Autin *114*
Greece 212, *334*
Greenblatt, Stephen *185, 208, 220, 224, 274*
Greer, Germaine *261*
Greven, Philip H. *110, 264*
grief work 97–99, 201–2, 214, 216
Grimble, Ian *217*
Groenendijk, Leendert F. *131*
Grossaert, Jan 68, 72
Grylls, R. Glynn 199
Guthke, Karl S. *115, 277*

Haas, Louis *152*
Hacker, J. David *110*
Hamel, B. Remmo *132*
Hammond, Jeffrey A. *277, 282*
Hansson, Robert O. *1*
Hardy, Thomas 126, 163, 190, 192, 229
Harington, Sir John 72–73, 110–12
Harmon, William *308*
Harré, Rom *1*
Hartland, Devon 45–46
Haskell, Francis 61, *114*
Hautecoeur, Louis *119*
Hay, Millicent V. 74
Heaney, 127, 166, 190, 230
Hearn, Karen *135–137, 156*
Henley, Alix *194, 311*
Henry, Louis 39, 40, 55, *79, 87*
Hensley, Jeannine *281*
Herlihy, David 23, *52–54, 125*
Herrick, Robert 120–22, 138, 179, 188, 192–95,
    214, 221, *141*
Hester, M. Thomas *322*
Highmore, Joseph 69, 82
Higonnet, Anne *127, 164*
Hijiya, James A. 92–93, *182*
Hill, Christopher *29*
Hirsch, Julia *133*
Hirsch, Marianne *133*
historicism 103–4, *274*
Hoby, Lady Elizabeth 119, 131, 179, 219
Hoffer, Peter C. *103*
Hogarth, William 69, 82
Holbein, Hans 62, *162*
Holdsworth, Sara *114*
Holmes, Richard 199, *270*
Honan, Park 114, *227*
Honigmann, E. A. J. *291*
Hopkins, John T. *139*
Hopkins, Keith *1, 334*
Horsfield, Louisa 126, 160, 183, 229
Houdaille, Jacques 40, 50
Houlbrooke, Ralph 58, *102, 106*
Hughes, Diane Owen *153*
Hughes, Ted 127, *276*
Huguet, Edmond *38*
Huizinga, Johan 15, *26*
Hull, N. E. H. *103*
Hulse, Clark *223*
Hulsker, Jan *150*

Hurtig, Judith W. *157, 175–176*
Huskinson, Janet *184*
Hutton, Patrick H. *13, 22*

iconography 13, 63, 79, *114*
Imhof, Arthur E. *9–10, 99, 119, 333*
infanticide 212, *103, 334*
Italy 18, 23, 28, 72

Jack, Ian *48*
Jaffé, David *152*
Jakobson, Roman 101
Jalland, Pat *113, 191, 286*
James family 70, 76, 82
James I 79, 88
Jane Eyre 19–20, 105, *42, 50, 75, 216*
Janeway, James *51*
Japan 212
Jenner, Edward 8
Jennings, Elizabeth 127, 165, 190, 230
Johansson, Sheila Ryan *14–15, 35, 333*
Johnson, Dr Samuel 171–73
Jonson, Ben 73, 79, *103*, 119–20, 132, 179, 190,
    193–95, 204, 214, 219, *138, 293*
Jordan, Thomas 122, 141, 185, 222
Josselin, Jane 107–8, 210, *315*
Josselin, Ralph 105, 107–10, 210
Julia, Dominique *9, 14*
Jupp, Peter C. *107*

Kay, W. David *294, 297*
Keats, John 196
Kent 73–74, 76, 123, 211
Kermode, Frank 117, *240*
Kertzer, David I. *9, 335*
Keynes, Randal *191*
keywords 100, 173, 175, 214
Kimmey, John L. *259, 296*
King, Henry 120, 137, 179, 221, *255*
Klaver, Elizabeth *115*
Knights, L. C. 103, *203*
Kohner, Nancy *194, 311*
Kronenfeld, J. Z. *294*
Kukil, Karen V. *276*
Kunzle, David *161*

Lachiver, Marcel 41
Laget, Mirielle *102, 103*
Landers, John 47

Landor, Walter Savage 126, 159, 186, 228
Lasker, Judith *194*
Laslett, Peter 1–4, *2–4, 33, 35*
Latham, Agnes *222*
Laurence, Anne *109, 113*
Le Goff, Jacques 27, *62*
Le Grand-Sébille, Catherine *78*
Le Nain, Antoine 63
Le Play, Frederic 15
Le Roy Ladurie, Emmanuel *71*
Leader, Zachery *268*
Leavitt , John *197*
Lebrun, François *81, 86, 103*
Lee, James Z. *334*
Lee, Sir Sidney 115, *233–34, 238*
Legh, Lady Margaret 68, 88–91, 93, 210–11,
    177–78, 315
Leigh, Helen 124, 152, *192–93,* 226
Leishman, J. B. *324*
Lerner, Laurence *187*
letters 2, 10
Levene, Alysa *335*
Levenson, Jill L. *328*
Lewis, Jan *200*
Lewis, Judith Schneid *103*
Lindemann, Erich *311*
literacy 31, 57, *105, 186, 246*
Litten, Julian *107*
Liverpool 21, 45, 46
Llewellyn, Nigel 88, *60, 157, 173–174, 176, 247,
    257, 261*
Locke, John 3
Lodge, David *201*
London 44–47, 89, 123–26, 187, 194, 214
Loudon, Irvine 50
Louis XIII *51*
Louis XIV 39
Luce, Morton 115, 117, *235–37*
Lutz, Catherine A. 100, *195–96*
Lyon 40, *335*

Macbeth, Lady 103, *203*
MacDonald, Michael *209*
Macfarlane, Alan 107, *29, 212–13*
Mack, Maynard *266*
Malthus, Thomas Robert *161*
Manchester 45–46
Marland, Hilary *103*
Marlowe, Christopher 113

Marseilles 31, 40
Marshall, John 47
Martial 193–94
Martin, L. C. 121, 222, *257*
Martines, Lauro 103, *206*
Marx, Karl 24, *57, 65*
Mason children 82
Mason, Lawrence *255*
Massachusetts 76, 123–24
Mathews, Mowll *170*
McClenden, Mariel C. *209*
McClure, Norman Egbert *218*
McDonagh, Josephine *103*
McGann, Jerome J. *302*
McManners, John *16*
Mechling, Jay *101*
medieval era 11, 13, 17, 23, 64
Meehan, Paula 127, 167, 184, 230, *287*
Mendelson, Sara *105*
Mercier, Roger *26*
Meslé, France 36
Meulan 39–40
Middleton, Warwick *192*
midwives 43, 55–56, 108
Miles, Rosalind *249*
Millais, Sir John Everett *164*
Milton, John 120, 135, 184, 190–92, 210, 220
Milton, Katherine 190–92
Molière 8, 10, 18–19, *36*
Montaigne, Michel de 8, 10, 15, 18–19, *24, 27, 29,
    37, 40, 51, 97*
Moore, Andrew *155*
Moore, Julia A. 201, *308*
Moorman, F. W. *256*
Morel, Marie-France *97, 102*
Morin, Edgar 15, *25*
Morland, George 64, 77, 83–84
mortality, child 33–60, 93, 108, 119, 215
    fetal (*see* stillbirths) 35, 37, 43, 49, 51, 53, 56, 58–
        60, 99, 108, 179, 183, 188–90, 215, *87, 95*
    infant 17, 33–60, 93, 99, 108, 194, 213, 215
    maternal 49–52, 56, 60, 76, 80–81, 83, 88, 93,
        119, 179, 188, *93–94, 103*
mourning 57–60, 96–101, 214
mourning curve 10–13, 28–29, 57–59, 213

Neale, Hannah *126*
Néraudau, Jean-Pierre *118*
Netherlands 50–52, 62–66, 73, 83, *115, 118,*

131–32, 259, 333
New England 18, 59, 65, 82, 123, 183, *110*
Newton, Evelyn, Lady 90. *178*
Nocret, Jean 63
Norbrook, David *206*
Normandy 42–43
Northampton 126
Northumberland 123
Norway 53–54
Norwich 125
numeracy *246*
Nurmi, Martin K. *304*
Oeppen, J. E. 47, 51, *89*
Oliphant, Margaret *191*
Opie, Amelia Alderson 125, 157, 186–87, 228
Orgel, Stephen *329*
Orme, Nicholas 17, 64, *34, 52, 125*
Ormerod, George *143, 177*
Oxford 124
Oxfordshire 76
Ozment, Steven 4–5, *9–12, 35*

Palmer, John *36*
Pamela 2
Panofsky, Erwin *114*
Parfitt, George *139, 313*
Paris 29, 31–32, 40–42, 55, 78, 85–86, *335*
parish registers 36, 39, 43, 48–49, 51, *89*
Parker, William Riley 191, *254*
Parkes, Colin Murray *40*
Parsons, Tomasin 120, 122, 195
Pascal, Roy *209*
Patrides, C. A. *316, 323*
Pavy, Salomon 119, 133, 193–94, 220
Pearlman, E. *294, 297*
pearls 79, 89, *154*
Peck, Linda Levy *262*
Peck, Walter Edwin *270*
Pembroke, Countess of 115
Penny, Nicholas 78, 93, *148–49, 180–81*
Penshurst Place, Kent 73–74, 211
Petrucci, Armando *183*
Philipott, Thomas 122, 142, 185, 188, 222
Philips, Katherine 123, 144, 181, 223
photography 87, *133*
Picasso, Pablo 71, 78, 85–86
Pickering Jr, Samuel *308*
Pigler, Andor 61–62, 88, *115–17*
Pigman III, G. W. *277, 297*

Pilon, Edmond *26*
plague 23, 45, 119, 142
Plath, Sylvia 127, 165, 190, 230
Plumb, J. H. 3–4, *5–8*
Pollock, Griselda *170*
Pollock, Linda A. 104–5, 211, *9–10, 29, 103, 105,*
　　120, 207, 210, 279, 331–33
Pols, Robert *133*
Pope, Alexander 124, 148, 192, 225
Porter, Roy *273*
Poster, Mark 17, *33*
Poultney, Jane *141*
Powell, David *273*
Preston, Samuel H. 41, *83*
Prior, Mary *102, 206*
Provence 29–31, 42, 104
Prown, Jules David *169*
psychohistory 101

Quiller-Couch, Arthur *222*

Rathmell, J. C. A. *138*
Rawson, Beryl *334*
reception theory 96, 101–4, 216
Reddy, William N. *200*
Reed, Layrel *152*
Rembrandt *132*
Renoir, Auguste 71, 85, 87
Requa, Kenneth A. *267*
Restoration comedy 2
Reynolds, Kimberley *109*
Reynolds, Sir Joshua 64, 67, 70, 77, 83
Richardson, John *151*
Richardson, Samuel 2
Riché, Pierre *125*
rickets 56
Riggs, David *249–250*
Ringler, William A. 113, *223*
Robinson, Eric *273*
Roche, Daniel 1, 31–32, *76, 81, 84, 103, 113*
Rogers, Mary (Lady Harington) 68, 72–73,
　　110–12
Rogers, William *144*
Roget, Dr Peter Mark 171–72
Rollet, Catherine *87*
Romantic era 11, 15, 21, 96, 177, 179, 195–200, 211
Rome 8, 18, 125, 199, 212, *1, 184, 334*
Romney, George 10, 83
Rood, Ogden *172*

Rorty, Amélie Oksenberg *198*
Rose, Mary Beth *203*
Rosenblatt, Paul C. 97, *193, 331*
Rothman, Barbara Katz *187*
Roulin daughter 71, 78, 85
Rousseau, Henri *168*
Rousseau, Jean-Jacques 15–16, 77, 83, 93, *161–62*
Rowse, A. L. 112, 114, 118, *220–221, 226, 231, 244*
rubella 56
Rubens, Sir Peter Paul 69
Russell children 68
Ryan, Kiernan *202*
Ryerson, Alice Judson *101*

Sacks, Peter M. *277*
Saltonstall family 69, 76, 80–81
Sanders, Wilbur *290*
Sangolï, Jean-Claude *78*
Sarti, Raffaella *9*
Saussure, Ferdinand de 101
Schama, Simon 33, 64–65, *77, 103, 131–32*
Scheper-Hughes, Nancy *1, 311, 334*
Schofield, Roger S. 47, 49–51, *34, 89, 91, 93–94, 288*
Schorsch, Anita *114, 168*
Schrader, Catharina *77, 103*
Schücking, Levin L. *206*
Scodel, Joshua *277, 299*
Scotland 36
Scott, Sir Walter 126
Scott-Kilvert, Diana *271*
Scott-Warren, Jason *219*
Seaver, Paul S. 106, 108, *211*
Segard, Achille *170*
Seymour, Miranda *270*
Shakespeare, Anne 113, 116, 210
Shakespeare, Hamnet 95, 113, 115, 117–18, 208, 219
Shakespeare, William 95, 112–19, 126, 131, 182, 194, 205–8, 210, 219, *1*
   plays 103, 112–13, 115, 117–19, 131, 182, 202, 205–7, 219
   sonnets 112–18
Shapiro, James *185, 222*
Shaw, W. David *277–78*
Shawe-Taylor, Desmond *161*
Shelley, Mary 125, *270*
Shelley, Percy Bysshe 125–26, 157, 196, 199–200, 210, 228

Shorter, Edward *10, 94*
Sidney family 73–75, 79, 113, 210–11
Sidney, Sir Philip 113, 118
Simonds, Wendy *187*
Sliggers, Bert C. *115*
smallpox 56
Smith, Daniel Blake *110*
Smith, Daniel Scott *110*
Smith, Paul *172*
Somerset 72, 110, 124
Souch, John 69, 81
Spain 18
Spurgeon, Caroline F. E. *326*
Staffordshire 122
Stanley, Lady Venetia 69, 81, *117*
Stannard, David E. *16, 110*
Stearns, Peter N. *199–200*
Steen, Jan 63–64, *130*
Stevenson, Jane *247, 253, 260*
Stevenson, Matthew 123, 145, 188, 224
Steward, James Christen 64, 82–83, *126–27, 146–48, 162, 166*
Stewart, Garrett *187*
Stickland, Irina *207*
Stillbirths (*see* mortality, fetal) 5, 40–41, 43, 46–47, 49, 51–54, 57–58, 99, 119, 183, 188–90, 202, 215, *12, 87*
Stone, Lawrence 13, 15–17, 211–12, *10, 27, 29, 32, 33, 53, 131, 268*
Strange, Julie-Marie *113, 333*
Stratford-upon-Avon, Warwks. 113
Streatfield family 69, 76, 80
Stricker, Susan E. *145*
Stroebe, Margaret S. *1*
Stroebe, Wolfgang *1*
Strong, Roy 72–73, *135*
Strozzi, Clarice 68, 78
Studley, Warwks. 126
Sumner, Ann *117*
Super, R. H. *272*
Surrey 46
swaddling 56, 68, 88–89
Sweden 49, 53–54

Tarlow, Sarah *183*
Tasburgh family *155*
Tenenti, Alberto *26*
Thimelby, Gertrude 122, 141, 181, 222
Thomas, Dylan 126, 164, 198, 229

Thomas, Greg M. *171*
Thomas, Keith *100, 246*
Thompson, Ann *242*
Thornton, Peter *165*
Tibble, Anne *273*
Tibble, J. W. *273*
Tillyard, E. M. W. *291*
Titian 68, 78
Todd, Janet *265, 302*
Tolstoy, Leo *305*
tombstones 92–93, *118, 182–84*
Treuherz, Julian *142, 158*
Trimpi, Wesley 194, *294–96*
tuberculosis 36
Turell, Jane Colman 124, 149, 182–83, 189, 225
Twain, Mark 200–1, *306–7*

Uhlenberg, Peter *32*
United States 18, 84, 92–93, 101

Vallin, Jacques 36
Van Dyck, Sir Anthony 69
van de Walle, Etienne 41, *83, 96, 98*
van de Walle, Francine *98*
van Gogh, Vincent 67, 71, 78, 85, 87
Vaughan, Alden T. *240*
Vaughan, Virginia Mason 103, *204, 240*
Vaughan, William *144*
Venice 68, 78, 199, 125
Vos, Martin de 63
Vovelle, Gaby *75*
Vovelle, Michel 1, 5–7, 14, 24, 57, 62, 94, 96, 104, 213
'three-levels model' 1, 5, 25–29, 60, 96, 213, *13, 58–61, 64, 69–71, 74–75, 184, 189, 279*

Wagner, Erica *276*
Wales 36, 44, 46–47
Wallington, Grace 105–6, 108, 210
Wallington, Nehemiah 105–6, 108, 110, 210
Walter, Harriet *203*
Walton, Izaak *312*
Walzer, John *28*
Wang Feng *334*
Ward, Joseph P. *209*

Wathen, Richard *168*
Watt, Ian *187*
Wayne, Don E. *138*
Weber, Frederick Parkes *115*
Webster, Mary *161*
Wells, Robert V. *110, 183, 283*
Wells, Stanley *232*
West, Shearer *114*
Westminster Abbey 88, 124, *258*
wet nursing 39, 41, 53, 56, 84, 106, *84, 104*
Whaley, Joachim *16*
Wheeler, Michael *187*
Wheeler, Richard P. *185*
White, Elizabeth Wade *264, 282*
Wierzbicka, Anna 100, *195, 197*
Williams, Naomi 51, *92*
Williams, Raymond *195*
Willoughby, Juliana 70, 83
wills 14, 18, 29–31, 104
Wilson, Adrian *35, 101, 103*
Wilson, F. P. *248*
Windsor, Lord 68, 80
Wood, Michael *227*
Woods, Robert 51, 54, *24, 40, 92, 95, 336*
Woods, Suzanne *231*
Wordsworth, Jessica *302*
Wordsworth, Jonathan *301*
Wordsworth, Mary 125, 197
Wordsworth, William 21, 117, 125, 156, 186, 195–99, 210, 227, *50*
Wright of Derby, Joseph 71, 77
Wright, Mehetabel 124, 148, 182, 225
Wrigley, E. A. 47, 51, *34, 89, 91, 99*
Wu, Duncan *302*
Wunder, Heide *12*
Wuthering Heights 20–21, *48, 50, 75*

York 45, 47, 123, 188
Yorkshire 123
Young, Bruce W. *206*

Zelizer, Viviana A. 16, *32*
Zerbe, Kathryn J. *170*
Zonabend, Françoise *78*